VIETNAM ABOVE THE TREETOPS

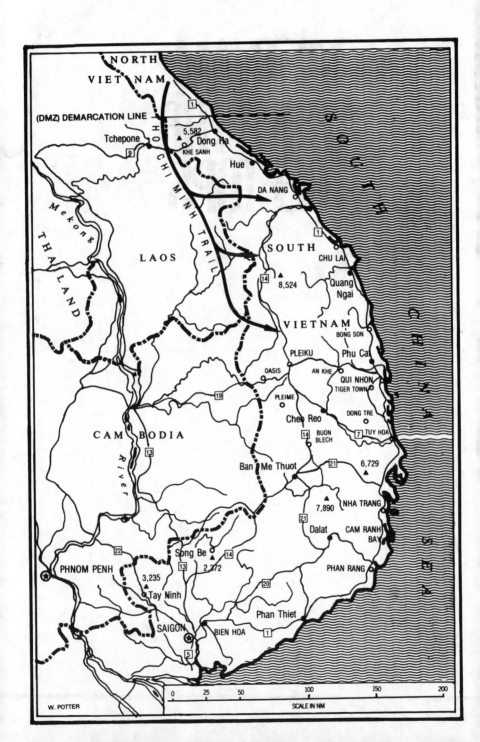

VIETNAM ABOVE THE TREETOPS

A FORWARD AIR CONTROLLER REPORTS

JOHN F. FLANAGAN

PRAEGER

New York
Westport, Connecticut
London

Copyright © 1992 by John F. Flanagan

All rights reserved. No portion of this book may be reproduced, by any process or technique, without the express written consent of the publisher.

First published in 1992

Praeger Publishers, One Madison Avenue, New York, NY 10010
An imprint of Greenwood Publishing Group, Inc.

Printed in the United States of America

ISBN 0-275-93738-0

To Russ and Willie—I tried my best

Contents

Photographs follow page 128.

Acknowledgments

Books like this come painfully—prodded by conscience and friends—simultaneously exorcising the burdens of tragic memories while capturing an essential part of military history. My high school compatriot and lifelong friend, Bart Fleming, encouraged and supported the personal catharsis that was essential to the successful completion of this book. Dennis Keegan, a public relations professional and reserve colonel, drew the first chapters from me in August 1988 while sequestered in the Adirondack Mountains. Valerie Wilenchik, the wife of an Air Force sergeant, transcribed those first chapters while I leaped ahead recognizing that the ultimate tale of lost warriors and compromised values lurked in the monsoon-swept and enemy-infested jungle surrounding Khe Sanh. Norm Doney was tireless with his help, reading manuscripts and adding details of the reconnaissance jungle patrols from his personal experience and extensive network of contacts to the former members of Project Delta. When the pain was at its worst, Mal Wakin, professor of philosophy and ethics at the Air Force Academy, and Dr. Richard Kohn, chief of Air Force history, convinced me of the value of finishing the manuscript and motivated me past the final threshold.

Dr. Joyce Harrington, who vicariously shared many of the Vietnam experiences, transcribed my letters of 1966 as primary source material. Reuel Dorman, a fellow FAC and business associate, lent me his maps of Vietnam which he had retained. Ed Webber, a fellow Zoomie, helped me recall the specifics of the honor code of the early 1960s. Larry Lanier, stockbroker and fellow Vietnam veteran, scrupulously applied his Latin studies and penchant for crosswords to the manuscript. Chip Maxwell, another vet and print shop owner, patiently stored, copied, and bound successive manuscripts. My greatest thanks go to Janet Gaines, the daughter of a deceased three-war veteran fighter pilot, who, between her international trips as a flight attendant, relentlessly reviewed and input necessary changes to the computerized manuscript.

Finally, thanks to Dan Eades, my editor, whose subtle input turned a manuscript into a contribution to recorded warfare and a deeper understanding of values.

Introduction

Khe Sanh, South Vietnam, December 2, 1966.

"Sergeant Doney," I said, "I don't like it at all." Doney was a Green Beret in charge of the long-range reconnaissance teams for Project Delta. "They can't find the recon team, the choppers are running low on fuel, and there are no fighters available. The monsoons are so bad I'm not even sure I could get the O–1 airborne, let alone get it back to Khe Sanh."

As I outlined the situation to Doney, the bitter taste of bile crept into my mouth and the tightness in my throat kept me from swallowing. I realized why the North Vietnamese troops didn't shoot at me yesterday. It was a trap and the team was the bait. I walked behind the communications van and threw up what little I had in my stomach.

A plaintive call came over the command net, "We can't locate the team. Can you send the FAC to help?" The decision was all mine. It was my eleventh month in Vietnam; I was short. I picked up my carbine and map and, shrugging, ducked out from under the tarp, walked into the driving rain, and headed to the airplane. I hadn't gone more than a dozen steps through the water and mud when one of the ever-present Green Beret troopers was at my side, ready to fly. He had his full complement of web gear, extra grenades, and M–16 rifle. I stopped and turned to him.

"Sarge, I'm going alone on this flight. I don't like this one. I'm not sure I'm coming back." We had lost a FAC and his Green Beret observer to ground fire three weeks earlier in the same area.

He responded, "FAC, no matter how bad it's been, no matter what kind of trouble we've gotten in, you've never let us down. If you get shot down, it's my job to take care of you on the ground." I noticed that Doney and the other recon sergeants were watching us from the operations tent. They had that grim look on their faces; the look they have when they are going on a mission. OK, they win. I'd rather take on the entire North Vietnamese Army than the guys from Project Delta.

★   ★   ★   ★   ★

In 1966, I was a first lieutenant in the Air Force serving as a forward air controller (FAC) flying single-engine spotter planes, the link between fighter-bomber pilots and ground combat forces. I worked with American, Korean, and Vietnamese forces and fought with airmobile forces, para-troopers, conventional infantry, and the Special Forces. Twenty-three years later, I agreed to record my experiences, observations, and reflections of that year. I had repressed many of the events from that time, yet I would relive them in my dreams, nightmares, unconscious perceptions, and re-flexive actions.

I initially wrote to exorcise the nightmares and explain the actions. I then turned to research: reading the letters, examining the maps, deciphering the pocket diaries, interviewing old comrades, recalling command decisions—both my own and those of senior officers, Army and Air Force. I reviewed these events through the perspective of history, the perspective of the en-suing 23 years. Although conscience obscures fact and recollection, time adds objectivity and purpose. Linked to the war-fighting story, patterns and messages emerged, of warrior values and their role for individuals and institutions. I could see a portrait of bravery, of physical and moral courage, a portrait of honesty and integrity. I could also see these values compromised and prostituted. With that realization came a renewed determination to capture these historical perceptions before they disappeared in the haze of unrecorded history.

I did not know that 1966 would be a pivotal year, a turning point in history. But in that year the war in Southeast Asia ceased to be a Vietnamese war and became an American war fought in Vietnam. Popular support for the war was eroding, eventually polarizing the country.

The FAC came into his own in Vietnam. With rudimentary technology, we FACs perfected close air support and the hunting of trucks and bicycles on the jungle trails. The FAC, as I knew him, has been made obsolete by weapons technology, but his bravery will never be obsolete.

For eight months, I was assigned to Project Delta, Detachment B–52, 5th Special Forces Group, to support the six-man—two Americans and four Vietnamese—hunter-killer teams from recon. I was with Delta longer than any other FAC. This book chronicles many of Delta's hazardous missions: it is a tale of spectacular air strikes, of teams rescued, of teams lost, and of thwarted attempts to save fellow warriors. After Vietnam, Delta became the core of the counter-terrorist Delta Force.

This book is also an account of the important role the Koreans played in

Vietnam. Very little has been written about the bravery and success of the Korean forces that served in Vietnam; their performance belied their reputation from the Korean conflict. I fought with them and had an extraordinary opportunity to contrast the Asiatic and Western cultures, and to compare their command structure, tactics, and values with the U.S. 101st Airborne Brigade, the 1st Cavalry Division, and the 25th Infantry Division.

This book will appeal to many different people. It may be read by families and friends of Vietnam veterans who seek understanding of the people behind the events. It may be read by students at the military academies, seeking to understand their chosen role as military practitioners. It may be read by historians and political scientists, or by students seeking a new perspective. It can also be read, and enjoyed, by the vicarious adventurer who is welcome to climb into the backseat with me, fasten his goggles, knot his scarf, and prowl the jungles at treetop level.

When I started to capture the values and histories, many of my fellow Vietnam veterans came to me and asked, "John, are you going to tell it all? Are you going to tell the truth?" Yes, I am, I have, and I will. The air strikes are historically accurate: the dates, call signs, bomb loads, results, and target coordinates. If you flew a fighter-bomber in 1966 with the call sign Ramrod, Yellowbird or Redbird, Hobo, Sabre, Sharkbait, Boxer, Surf, Kilo, Silver, Demon, Tiger, Buzzard, Whiskey, Dice, or Spooky, we worked together.

I've tried to bring context to the events. I've tried to show how the junior officers and non-commissioned officers carried the brunt of the war, inexorably trapped between the convoluted politico-military command structure and the welfare of the warriors who were fighting an unpopular war.

Who was I? From January through mid-April 1966, my call sign was "Ragged Scooper 74." After that, it changed with each operation—Airedale, Snake, Typhoon—as Project Delta roamed through I, II, and III Corps, raising havoc with the VC and NVA. I wore tiger suit fatigues with no rank or insignia and I smelled like rotten fish from my Vietnamese diet.

This book is written for us—the Americans, Koreans, and Vietnamese; the infantry, the helicopter pilots, the Special Forces, both Green Beret and the Vietnamese LLDB, and my fellow FACs and fighter pilots who did more than they thought they could. And it is written to uphold the values we fought and lived by.

1
Setting the Values

My hometown of White Plains, in the affluent suburbs of Westchester County, situated between the Hudson River and Long Island Sound, was the breeding ground of bankers and lawyers, advertising executives and doctors, and commercial traders who thrived on the shipping and air transport activities of the port of New York. The only labor-intensive occupation that was acceptable in my culture was, possibly, the lucrative position of airline pilot. The time was the 1950s; Korea was behind us, President Eisenhower was warning the nation against the incestuous relationship of the military-industrial complex, and rock and roll was being born. Houses sold for under $25,000. People were beginning to use the phrase *civil rights*. The Soviets were stirring up trouble in Hungary and Czechoslovakia. The Chinese hordes had faded after the Korean War. Japan was insignificant. Europe was a cheap place for a summer vacation.

My younger sister and I were raised in a church-going family. We went to mass on Sundays, holy days of obligation, and first Fridays. I was president of the altar boys. I loved the smell of incense and I remember the sticky sweetness of the altar wine. As an adolescent, I was independent. I collected bottles to earn pocket money before I got my first job—a paper route. In high school, I held several jobs at one time—stock clerk, gas attendant, caddy, and nurseryman—and earned letters in interscholastic football and track.

I was educated from the fourth grade through high school in the Catholic school system. I was taught by nuns in grammar school, and then by priests and brothers at Archbishop Stepinac High School in White Plains. My education was regimented and disciplined, stressing values and encouraging responsibility. Those Catholic institutions prepared me for college and the challenges of the Air Force Academy.

There was a spiritual side to my education. The Church taught the life hereafter and that the good Christian did not fear death. Years later, when I was thrust into extremely dangerous combat situations, I could have withdrawn without dishonor. Yet I pressed on. I was afraid, but I was not afraid to die; I drew a contrast between the emotion of fear and the spirituality of death.

★ ★ ★ ★ ★

The reconnaissance team was surrounded by NVA troops, and the rescue helicopter had already been shot down. Due to the low clouds, I was flying at only 300 feet, but I needed more airspeed. I pushed the nose over and crammed the throttle full open. I told my Green Beret sergeant, in the backseat, to look to the left and check out the downed chopper for survivors while I looked to the right to locate the ambushed team and toss some smoke grenades out the window for screening. I leveled off at 50 feet above the elephant grass, the Bird Dog going as fast as it could. I knifed between the team and the burning chopper. Unseen bullets snapped past the window. Out with the smokes.

"*Look out FAC, on the left!*" screamed Tommy from the backseat. I looked up to see a hail of tracer fire converging on us. I yanked back on the stick so hard I thought the wings would come off. We hurtled straight up, disappearing into the dense monsoon clouds. The tracers fell behind us. Now I had a problem. The attitude gyro had tumbled, the airspeed was bleeding off, and I had no references by which to control the aircraft. I was going to die in a crash.

★ ★ ★ ★ ★

I always had an interest in flying. As a boy I built and flew model airplanes, and I read every aviation book I could find. I would ride my bicycle to the local airports to hear the roar of the engines and watch the planes. Occasionally, one of the pilots would invite me to sit in the cockpit, where he would patiently explain to me the functions of the switches and controls. To this day I never deny an earnest youngster the opportunity to learn more about flying.

I was looking for a career, and the military had great appeal. I was close to West Point and went there with my parents to watch parades. The pageantry of patriotism appealed to me. This was in the mid-1950s: our president was a West Point graduate, and the movies we saw on Saturday afternoons featured John Wayne and Gary Cooper in acts of courage and valor. It was a powerful combination: a strong sense of patriotism and the Catholic commitment of Crusaders.

The newly founded Air Force Academy offered an excellent education, a chance to fly, and the opportunity to begin a career. It was located in a temporary facility at Lowry Air Force Base, near Denver, while the permanent complex north of Colorado Springs was being constructed. I had read about the Academy, and the deputy director of athletics from the Academy had visited my high school. He cautioned that the first year, particularly the training summer, was very demanding; strict discipline, marching, long days, constant hazing, both physical and mental, by the upperclassmen. They would try to break you. He was honest.

I applied through my congressman, Edwin B. Dooley, from the New York Twentieth Congressional District. After a week of physical, mental, and medical testing, I qualified. I didn't make the cut for one of the 314 primary appointments, but I did receive an alternate appointment. I had other choices: a Regents Scholarship for anywhere in New York, a scholarship to the University of Pennsylvania, and various offers from schools in the Midwest. I selected Penn, but halfway through my freshman year, the Academy contacted me to reapply. This time I received one of the primary 465 appointments (the Academy was expanding) and I elected to start over at the academy. My college courses would not transfer for credit and it would now take five, not four, years to attain a college degree. However, my courses at Penn would enable me to enter accelerated courses and to add enrichment courses in mathematics, economics, international relations, and philosophy.

When I arrived at the Academy, I knew I would graduate and become an officer. It was my ambition to continue on to pilot training, but I was not absolutely committed to a lifetime in the military. I had a five-year active-duty obligation after graduation, which was as far as I was able to project.

I was not surprised by the Academy. As promised, there was the initial emphasis on physical conditioning, marching, military history and heritage, riflery, bayonet drills, and hand-to-hand combat. I was comfortable with guns, had played football in high school and college, and had my share of fistfights. When I was a freshman at Penn, I pledged a fraternity, Phi Gamma Delta. I went through the pledge season, hell night, and hazing, which prepared me for the psychological harassment that upperclassmen heaped upon the "Doolies," the basic cadets. The upperclassmen were unmerciful during summer training at Lowry. I had two roommates, one who seemed to be breaking down from the pressure, and the other who cried himself to sleep at night. One of them ultimately dropped out and the other persevered to become a fine officer. This was about average; 64 percent of the entrants in my class finished the four grueling years.

During my four years at the Academy, my basic value structure was reinforced. Chapel attendance was mandatory; it was nice to know that at least God loved fourth classmen, since it was the job of every upperclassman to remind us that we were the very lowest form of existence. In our last two years we could go off-base to chapel, which was a treat; I was beginning to think that the only God I knew was a colonel.

One important element of Academy life was the honor code: *I will not lie, cheat, or steal, or tolerate anyone who does.* The honor code worked. I had good friends who had committed honor violations, turned themselves in, and were subsequently dismissed from the Academy. I respected them for it. Certainly for me, the Academy reinforced my own values.

I was disappointed when, near the end of my senior year, the second chance for honor code violations was introduced. If a cadet committed an honor violation within his first year, he would be sent to his squadron honor rep, counseled, and receive a second chance. That bothered me, because I thought it was diluting the honor code. I had lost classmates who, under the revised rules, would still be cadets. Perhaps there should have been a probationary period or a stronger instructional program to ensure that the new cadets understood how the code worked.

One of the important aspects of the honor code was the term *All Right*. In the evenings, cadets were required to be in their rooms studying, at the library, or in several other authorized places. Visiting from room to room was prohibited except for academic tutoring. In order to enforce this regulation, an upperclassman would periodically pass through the halls and, instead of opening each door and physically looking in, would knock and inquire, "All right?" The occupants of the room would respond, "All right, sir," thereby indicating that the occupants of the room were either properly present or on an authorized absence. Failure to respond to the inquiry would require a physical inspection of the room. The All Right had a very specific purpose and it worked.

When it came to rules and regulations, I didn't follow them to the letter. We had little tricks, like hiding clean clothes with your dirty laundry to avoid refolding them. One night I slipped out after taps and, armed with leaflets and bags of flour from the dining hall, led a pre–football game foray to the University of Colorado campus, returning just before reveille. We skirted regulations, challenged the system, and tempted the consequences.

By regulation, we could not have liquor in our rooms, and, periodically there were liquor inspections. In my senior year, my classmates would render a verbal "All Right for liquor" to the room inspectors to avoid having their room torn up in a search. They were stating on their honor that they didn't have liquor in their room. This bothered me. The honor code was being used to enforce a regulation. Inability to render an All Right implied that you had liquor in your room. If a cadet had concealed liquor in the shared storage space over the door, he could not permit his roommate to give an All Right. This would be an honor violation, and at the same time the cadet was incriminating himself for a violation of regulations. This compromised the integrity and purpose of the honor code. The code was beautiful, as long as it was used for what it was intended—to mold an honorable warrior.

★　★　★　★　★

I stood in front of the supply sergeant in a warehouse at Nha Trang Air Base, Vietnam, to have some personal flying equipment replaced.

"Sir," explained the sergeant, "we've pulled your records and they show you've been issued this equipment back at Tan Son Nhut in January. You will have to account for it before we can reissue any of it. We thought you were new to the base."

"Oh, sorry Sarge, I thought you knew. My plane was shot down. Another FAC was flying it. All my flight gear was on board and we never recovered it. The plane burned." I could tell by the look on his face that he didn't believe me.

"Lieutenant, you'll have to clear this with the Supply Squadron administration."

"May I please borrow your telephone to get this cleared up?" I asked. I rang the Supply Squadron orderly room, reached the admin officer, and told him that I needed someone to please tell the good, conscientious, sergeant that I wasn't trying to "rip off" the government and that yes, my equipment was lost in the crash, and would he please authorize replacements.

"Well, Lieutenant, that is highly irregular," said the voice on the other end. "You'll have to come over here and complete a report of survey, and then we will name an investigating officer to confirm your alleged loss, and if everything is in order we should have your new equipment in a week or two."

A lot of good living under the honor code at the Academy for four years was doing me now. One of my fellow officers would not believe me. All I wanted was some new equipment so I could resume waging war, and these desk warriors with their typewriters and regulation books were trying everything in their power to stop me.

★　★　★　★　★

Part of the curriculum of the Academy was military history and professional military studies. We studied the history of wars and examined the classical land and sea battles. We watched World War II bombing films of the Ploesti oil fields and the Schweinfurt ball-bearing plants where entire squadrons of B–17s and B–24s were blown out of the sky, and gun camera films from Korea of close air support and dogfights between the MIGs and the F–86s. It was realistic, but distant, more like a Hollywood movie than people dying.

I studied extra courses in political science and economics to understand the formulation and application of national goals and international power. Why does a country resort to war? How does war come about? War, I learned, is the last tool of international power; countries should exhaust all means of power and influence before resorting to war. The world of the late 1950s and early 1960s was forging swords into plowshares. Conflicts, notwithstanding the Cold War confrontations of Berlin and Cuba, would be resolved peacefully. There was always the threat of nuclear war, but that was the unthinkable—it was mutual destruction.

There was a senior elective course that focused on the use of military power to attain political objectives. I selected three books that examined the power and politics in the emerging Third World nations: one book was by Che Guevara, Castro's tactician in Cuba; the other two were about the post–World War II insurgent wars fought by the British and French in the jungles of Malaysia and Indo-China. Fate was guiding me to combat in Southeast Asia.

In spite of my military studies at the Academy, I didn't really expect to see combat. But I felt that I would be prepared for it. Summer training focused primarily on military skills, leadership, survival training, weaponry, flight physiology, touring military bases, temporary assignments to Air Force units, and training new cadets. We were prepared psychologically, academically, physically, and ethically to be followers initially, and then leaders—but always warriors.

June Week at a service academy is the highlight of the year. The lowly fourth classmen are recognized by the upperclassmen and become members of the cadet wing. The third classmen move up in responsibility, the second classmen receive their class rings and prepare to assume command of the cadet wing. Finally graduation day arrives, everyone moves up, and the former first classmen become the newest second lieutenants in the Air Force. Some say that it is the only demotion in your career, but we were anxious to join the "real" Air Force. The Academy had left its mark on us, although we didn't know it yet. I was headed for a 13-month pilot training course in Oklahoma.

There were two significant events that occurred in pilot training that had a lifelong impact. The first was personal. In the earliest stage of pilot training, I was having problems landing the twin-engine training jet, the T–37. I could get it on the ground, but my technique didn't meet the demanding standards of my instructor. After several marginal flights, I was scheduled for the most dreaded of all flights, the elimination flight. If I didn't perform satisfactorily on that flight, I would be washed out of pilot training. Sink or swim.

Finally, on that elim ride, I saw what it took. I consistently handled the aircraft in a series of touch-and-go landings to the satisfaction of the check pilot. I passed. If my instructor hadn't recognized that I had made progress, my life would have been markedly different.

Whereas the first event was personal, the second was institutional. Our training class of 30 officers was half Academy graduates. During the final phase of training, the flying instructors, all senior to us, decided we weren't diligently applying ourselves to the text-book portion of flying. They directed us to report to the flight line for close order drill, on a Sunday afternoon, in Class A uniforms with coats. The temperature on the concrete ramp was near 100 degrees. The logic of achieving academic excellence through a forced drill absolutely escaped me. I was utterly amazed—neither cadets nor enlisted troops, let alone officers, should be subject to this demeaning treatment which was a potential violation of military justice. This was a different leadership philosophy and apparently a carryover from the days of aviation cadets. When the Academy grads realized what was planned, they saw the punishment as a violation of the military code. They made a query to the Academy's Law Department. The department advised us to obey orders and wait. The drill took place. Early Monday morning, a call was made to the Academy, confirming the incident. Shortly thereafter, the responsible commander was relieved of his duties, his career in jeopardy. We recognized a wrong, stood behind our convictions, and made it right.

I earned my pilot's wings in August 1963 and went directly to survival school. Each flight crew member had to attend at some point in his career. The commandant of the school was a B–47 navigator who had been forced down by the Soviets in an incident near Siberia. He had been a prisoner of the Cold War who was eventually released through diplomatic channels. The school taught us the essential skills of surviving if we had to bail out of a crippled airplane or were shot down in enemy territory. We learned how to live off the land, to set traps and snares, to navigate and trek over the ground, to avoid capture, to kill with our hands—personal war skills— in a near-combat environment. We were also introduced to a prisoner-of-war environment and the structure of a covert escape organization. We were interrogated by skilled professionals and subjected to various mild forms of torture, including solitary confinement and sleep deprivation. For the first time, we discussed war as a real possibility, but in retrospect, no one ever imagined the torture and hardship of the Vietnamese prisons, the infamous "Hanoi Hilton" of the North and the tiger cages of the South.

After survival school I reported to Otis Air Force Base on Cape Cod. My first operational duty assignment was flying the Lockheed Constellation, which was equipped with airborne radar and intercept systems. It was the predecessor of the sophisticated AWACS aircraft that can be deployed worldwide to provide radar tracking of hostile aircraft and control of friendly interceptors.

We had non-commissioned officers as flight engineers on the four-engine

Connies. I remember flying over the North Atlantic, missions of 12 to 14 hours, and talking with the flight engineers. Some of them flew combat in World War II on B–17s, B–24s, and B–29s as flight mechanics, gunners, and engineers. They trained as crews in the United States and were deployed to combat as a cohesive fighting unit, a flight crew. They often ferried their own aircraft to the war zone. They told me hair-raising stories about combat, stories about an entire crew being shot up. One engineer told me how, on one mission over Germany, he had to drag the dead copilot, whose head had been blown off, out of the seat. The pilot, immobilized but conscious, instructed the flight engineer how to crash-land the crippled bomber on an emergency airstrip in England, saving the lives of the remaining crew. These men were twice my age, and I respected them. Military protocol dictated a separation between officers and enlisted men, but I enjoyed their company and learned by listening to them, particularly their expectations—of fairness and integrity—of officers.

Now I was gaining operational experience, flying over the North Atlantic in thunderstorms, ice, and fog. I learned how to work with a highly trained crew of 19 men and observed them work magic with radar scopes, directing fighters against unseen targets far out over the Atlantic. I watched St. Elmo's fire dance on the wings and propellers, and the blue balls of static electricity roll down the aisle and puff into nothingness. On clear days we could observe the Soviet fishing trawlers with their numerous antennae monitoring our radios and radars. On clear nights their lights mingled with those of the fishing fleets from New Bedford, Provincetown, Boston, and Gloucester.

I had a very favorable perception of the Air Force and a high opinion of the officers. As a cadet, I had toured bases, and during one of our summers we served as "third lieutenants" on active Air Force bases, performing operational tasks. I came into contact with some excellent officers, particularly the military training officers and the academic instructors at the Academy. They were all handpicked—the best of the best. I was surprised to learn that one of my English professors, an articulate and sensitive man, was a highly decorated combat pilot from the Korean War. Now I too was an officer, flying with a combat crew. I was a line pilot, my primary job was to fly, and nothing else took precedence. There was no better job in the Air Force. I was comfortable with myself. I was able to apply the education, the training, and the values that were imbued in me at the Academy.

While at Otis, a group of us decided to work on our master's degrees. Boston College had an MBA program that offered courses at night. There were three or four of us, depending upon the semester, who drove two nights a week from Cape Cod to Boston, 190 miles round-trip. We enrolled in the same classes. Some of us were flight crew members, juggling flight schedules to avoid missing a class. One was a maintenance officer and could make every class; he would take notes for the rest of us. The professors were understanding when we missed classes.

Eventually, I had enough credits to attend classes full-time for two semesters and complete my degree. However, my flying squadron was short of pilots because of early Vietnam transfers. I had made a commitment to stay combat-ready, so I reversed my commute by moving my family to Boston and driving to Otis. Halfway through pilot training I had married, and our first child was ten months old when we moved to Boston. Her sister was born just prior to final exams in January 1965.

Graduate school meant I was studying during the day, attending class at night, and flying missions on weekends. It was a hectic schedule, but it allowed me to enjoy my children's first years. I welcomed the revelry of the Boston College–Air Force football game. To my chagrin, but to the delight of my fellow students, the Eagles triumphed over the Falcons.

Upon finishing graduate school, we returned to Cape Cod. Instead of living on the base, we bought a house close to Otis. Vietnam service was inevitable and I needed a place for my family to live while I was overseas.

War and death were creeping into my life. Vietnam was heating up. The Air Commandos' participation was increasing. World War II–vintage light bombers, B–26s, were being stripped down to the basic airframe and rebuilt for combat missions. Gradually, American pilots were now becoming combatants, no longer just military advisors.

During pilot training one of the instructors received an assignment to the Vietnamese Air Force. He accepted his duty willingly. Another instructor pilot received similar orders. He was disturbed about his assignment and reluctant to go. His reluctance bothered me. During my assignment to Otis, there were two other pilots who received orders to Vietnam. One of them had his orders rescinded by securing the intervention of his congressman; the other one suddenly could not handle survival school, and was discharged from the Air Force. He didn't have "what it took." I was critical of these shirkers; I felt they were escaping the duties, commitments, and responsibilities of military service. Yet at the same time, I learned of the tragic death of my former Academy roommate and football teammate, George Toffel, who was killed in a bomber crash. Death was getting close.

Three years after the Academy, at age 25, I had completed pilot training, married, fathered two children, accumulated over 1,500 hours of flying time, earned an MBA, bought a house—and now had to make a big decision to repay some of the debt I owed my country. I was going to volunteer for Vietnam.

2
Prelude to Combat: Creating a Warrior

Vietnam was inevitable; it was only a matter of when my turn would come. I had probably delayed my Vietnam tour by attending grad school. Two of my pilot friends at Otis received their orders while I was in school. One was a classmate from the Academy and in the same pilot training class. He had his orders to Vietnam to fly cargo aircraft, the C–123 Provider. I didn't want to fly cargo; I had been flying with a crew of 19 for the last two years, and I wanted to do something on my own. Besides the B–26s and C–123s, they were flying A–1 attack airplanes, and the venerable C–47, the Gooney Bird. All were reciprocating-engine aircraft. Forward air controllers, flying small spotter aircraft, were just being introduced. Pilots who had recip-engine experience were needed and the major sources in the Air Force were McClellan Air Force Base in California and Otis. Both bases received a disproportionate number of Vietnam assignments and most of them were assigned to multi-engine cargo transports.

I met two pilots who had recently returned from Vietnam; one spent his year's tour as a forward air controller, and the other spent half of his tour as a FAC and then transferred into the A–1 Skyraider fighter-bombers. They told me about their missions and experiences. It was true combat, no longer "advising."

I wanted combat, either in A–1s as a Skyraider fighter-bomber pilot or in O–1s, the Cessna Bird Dog, as a forward air controller. If I were going to war, I wanted to be in combat and not in support. I considered myself a warrior. I was looking for excitement and risk, to measure myself. The role of the Skyraider pilots and FACs strongly appealed to me.

I discussed the situation with my wife and told her I intended to volunteer for a combat mission. She didn't try to dissuade me. We had met at a student conference at the Academy; she knew and understood the strength of my commitment to my profession; the commitment to duty, honor, and country was as important to her as it was to me. This was 1965, and many of us, regardless of our personal political views, were still under the spell of the late President Kennedy's "Ask not what your country can do for you, ask what you can do for your country."

I went to the Base Personnel Office, Assignments Branch, to volunteer for Vietnam. The assignments officer was dumbfounded. I explained to him it was inevitable that I was going to Vietnam, and I wanted my choice of aircraft.

Four weeks after I had volunteered, I received my orders. I had a port call date in San Francisco on January 26, 1966, but first I was to report to Hurlburt Field, near Fort Walton Beach, Florida, on December 5, 1965 for training. Hurlburt was the home base of the Air Commandos and a major training base for Vietnam. I had received my second choice. I was to be a forward air controller.

Basically, the FAC's mission was to fly a small, unarmed, single-engine observation aircraft. At that time it was the O–1, or Bird Dog; the Army called it a Cessna L–19. The Air Force didn't have these planes, so they had to commandeer them from the Army. The FAC would search out targets through visual reconnaissance, or, working with ground troops, find the enemy, and then direct the fighter-bombers to them. They were developed in response to a jungle environment in which fighters, especially jets, were too fast to see through the jungle canopy to identify targets. It was the job of the FACs to become intimately familiar with a specific locale and to follow the deployment of forces. I looked forward to being a combat FAC.

The 1,500-mile drive south to Hurlburt Field with two small children was an experience in itself. After a half-day of searching, we found a three-room efficiency motel suite on the Gulf of Mexico. Shades of Cape Cod—it was only 75 yards from the back door to the water, and the children, now 2 years old and 11 months old, loved it.

Since Fort Walton was primarily a summer resort, many of the apartments and efficiencies were available during the off-season. The motel owners were pleased to rent to us and the rates were reasonable. The military did not authorize payments for our families, but almost everyone brought them. In my motel alone there were two A–1 pilots, two FACs, a FAC instructor pilot, a U–10 pilot, and a couple of C–47 pilots. I shared rides to work with the other FAC, Karl Worst. We partied through Christmas and New Year's and gorged on succulent Gulf shrimp. But there was the pall of Vietnam. Soon we would leave our families and go to war. Some of us would die there. Except the instructors; they had already been.

At Hurlburt, the training consisted of academic instruction and flying instruction. The academic instruction focused on the responsibilities of the air liaison officer/forward air controller (ALO/FAC) in the Southeast Asian

War as an advisor to the Army for the employment of tactical air support. The course was AGOS, Air-Ground Operations School. We learned the various techniques of the Viet Cong—how they hid, the way they operated—and about the structure of the South Vietnamese government, provinces, and military. We received technical information of various types of weapons' destructive capabilities, when to use napalm, the types of bomb fuses, and the capabilities of various fighter aircraft. We also learned about the capabilities of the enemy weapons that we were most likely to encounter.

We learned how to work with the Army in the Air Request Net. This network was used by a FAC, or an ALO, to request air support. It was absolutely essential to understand the command, control, and communications network because your life, and those of the troops you were supporting, depended on your knowledge. There would be no one looking over your shoulder in Vietnam. The bottom line was that you either lived or died, based on your training and expertise. We paid close attention to our training.

There were two types of requests for tactical air strikes by fighter-bombers. One was for a preplanned strike in which the Army, for various reasons, decided in advance they needed air support. In Vietnam, the request went from the user level, to be consolidated at the corps level at the Direct Air Support Center, the DASC, then forwarded to Saigon, to the Tactical Air Control Center, the TACC. There, the request was either approved or disapproved, according to the priorities and availability of aircraft throughout the country. If approved, mission details would pass down through both Air Force and Army channels, advising the Army they had fighter aircraft allocated to hit the requested target, while a fragmentation order went to the Air Force fighter base, matching the available fighters to the Army's request. The FAC then coordinated the details with the local Army unit and ultimately controlled the strike.

The other type of request was for an immediate request strike which was used to support troops in contact, to hit perishable targets, to break up an ambush, to defend an attacked camp, or to hit Viet Cong spotted on the move. Each operational location had a base station with a radio operator, equipped with a HF/SSB (high frequency/single side band) radio for immediate contact with the DASC. The DASC had the authority to contact the nearest fighter base and scramble the fighter-bombers. The fighters were on five-minute alert; when scrambled they were told where to rendezvous with the FAC. In critical situations, the DASC could directly contact the radar control combat reporting centers and divert airborne fighters that were on their way to a lower priority mission. We learned the concepts and worked the system. Only the combat environment was missing.

We were also introduced to the political aspects of the Vietnam War. The buzzword was "COIN", *counter insurgency* warfare. This had replaced the classic guerrilla warfare concept as the impact of the political motivation, and the underlying causes of low-intensity conflicts were better understood. As part of the background training, we flew to the Air University, where civilian and military experts delivered lectures on the concepts, strategies, and doctrine of our now-inherited Vietnam War. Representatives from the State Department linked the political aspects with the military threat and explained the underlying socio-economic factors of COIN warfare. We were taking on the dual roles of combatants and political emissaries. We would be working with Vietnamese government officials, the province chiefs, and the local military assistance group. We learned about the Army of the Republic of Vietnam (ARVN), and the local militia, the Regional Forces and Popular Forces. In theory, it was a joint politico-military structure with a balance between Saigon's central control and local autonomy. In reality, I discovered that the province chief was the ranking military official and a political hack of Saigon. The ARVN was used primarily to back the squabbling political factions, and the RFs and PFs were worthless combatants. But the Air Force gave us the latest government policy and a foundation in COIN warfare doctrine. I wondered how many bullets my new knowledge would stop.

The other major segment of the training program was the flying portion and the techniques of a FAC, marking targets and controlling air strikes. Ground school consisted of basic knowledge of the aircraft and its systems. It was a simple aircraft: no sophisticated performance instruments, no exotic electronics or flight control systems, no radar transponders, just basic navigational instruments, open window, seat-of-the-pants Piper Cub–style flying. We were all trained as "jet jockeys" but we were to fly a plane from an era 30 years past. There was no Air Force flight manual for the O–1s; just an Army field manual. We didn't bother to read it. But that's the way it was when flying an O–1; only one engine, one pilot, cruise speed 100 mph, 130 mph in a drive. At least it was made of metal, instead of canvas.

We flew out of a small auxiliary field, Holly Field, adjacent to Hurlburt. Mornings, we bounced along rutted dirt roads in a blue school bus and were greeted at a rustic gate with a sign: *Welcome to Holly Field—Home of the FACing Air Force.* There were no buildings; we were working out of tents, a harbinger of Vietnam. The training atmosphere was relaxed, but realistic. The instructors had all been FACs in Vietnam, sent to Florida on temporary duty to train us. Their combat was behind them; they were self-confident, and cavalier toward regulations and command. They wore uniforms only because it was convenient. Many of them preferred flying in jeans, which some of them did in Vietnam. They were biding their time for airline jobs.

The training was stimulating for future FACs because virtually everybody had been flying jet aircraft, a high performance fighter, a transport, a tanker, or even a B–52 bomber. Some, like myself, came from multi-engine reciprocating aircraft. The O–1 was a conventional gear aircraft, a taildragger, requiring a different technique to land. It was light and constantly bounced around in turbulence. We had fun.

★　★　★　★　★

It was a windy day at Qui Nhon airport along the South China Sea, Republic of South Vietnam. The winds were gusting up to 25 knots off the sea, from the southeast. The active runway at Qui Nhon was 18, requiring a crosswind takeoff. I leapt off for the five-minute flight over the mountains to Tiger Town, which had a narrow, 1,000-foot long, pierced-steel planking strip, cut out of the mountainside. The winds raced up the valley and slammed into the mountain. As I descended, the vicious turbulence grabbed the airplane and I cracked my head against the top of the cockpit. The runway was on a heading of 05–23, more as an accommodation to the pitched terrain than the prevailing winds. I now had a 90 degree crosswind. The god Aeolas was not smiling on me. These were the conditions where flying would have been canceled as unsafe during training at Holly. It took me three tries, finally using no flaps, to keep that recalcitrant bird on the runway. My pride suffered.

★　★　★　★　★

At Holly Field, we did about everything that you shouldn't do to an airplane. We'd ground loop it, stand it on its nose, and tip it on its wing. We bounced our landings and blew out tires. We ran fuel tanks dry and laughed about it. One of the guys started to make a touch-and-go landing and the engine just quit on him, right on the runway; he hadn't switched the fuel tanks. In a more structured flying training environment, the pilot would have been called before the squadron commander, been reprimanded, and grounded for a week. But here we just laughed about it and said, "What are you going to do about it? Send him to Vietnam?" It still cost the poor bastard a case of beer.

After we learned how to fly the airplane, we started precision map reading and navigation, and range missions with inert warhead rockets. At the range, we would fire at scattered targets: vehicle hulks, bunkers, gun emplacements, and scoring circles. There was no gun-sight on the aircraft; we used a grease-penciled crosshairs on the windshield for our aiming reference. The rockets were old; the stabilizing fins didn't always open, sending the rockets to God-only-knew-where in the Florida swamps.

In the next phase of training we started working with fighters. We would rendezvous with them on the gunnery ranges, go through the air-strike control procedures, mark the targets, and then direct them via the radio. Target marking was a joke; we had no smoke rockets for training, so we used rocket splashes in the dirt and smoke grenades hurled from the open window. The Skyraiders, usually in flights of four aircraft, dropped 25-pound practice bombs with a smoke charge that usually failed to go off. After each aircraft's bomb drop, we would give our corrections to the next fighter to get the subsequent bombs on the target. All this time we were trying to keep the target in view while avoiding the fighters and the falling bombs. We had our hands full, but the instructors warned us that it would be worse in Vietnam as helicopters, artillery fire, ground troops, and enemy fire were added to the confusion. Mastering the coordination role would only come with experience.

We also flew some night missions, an eye-watering experience. The C–47 flare ships would orbit over the gunnery range, dropping flares suspended from parachutes. We would follow the same procedures as daytime, except that it was virtually impossible to see. Flying into a burned-out flare would be a sure cause of an emergency landing. We couldn't see the fighters; they'd dive out of the darkness from an orbit above the flares. Invariably, the flares would burn out just as we would be in a diving rocket pass. We'd suddenly lose night vision and end up hurtling at the ground without visual references. The instruments were so primitive that most of the time the artificial horizon was worthless. It was the classic situation for vertigo and disorientation. To end the night's mission, we'd land without lights, a blackout landing, on a dirt strip outlined only by flickering flare pots. It was challenging, and it built confidence and proficiency. The Air Force did a particularly good job with that phase of training.

The training at Hurlburt lasted six weeks. Our veteran instructors gave us tips on how to survive (stay out of bars), what to avoid (the water), and how to search out the Viet Cong in the jungles (no problem, they were everywhere). They talked about the weather patterns, the monsoons, and the thunderstorms. They had come through it. By the time I finished training, I felt I was prepared for combat.

There was one problem, however. As is often the case in many training courses, the instruction did not reflect the future requirements. While we were learning COIN, the White House was escalating the conflict by committing conventional U.S. troops and the deployment of jet fighter-bomber wings. From the end of 1965 to the end of 1966, U.S. forces in Vietnam increased from 184,000 to 389,000 personnel. The 1st Cav Division, 101st Airborne Division, 25th Infantry Division, 1st Infantry Division, or elements thereof, were committed to Vietnam. While we were sitting in the classroom, Korean troops were on their way to Vietnam and the Australians were making preparations to send troops and airplanes. All these units would require ALOs and FACs, operating under a conventional command structure. Increased interdiction bombing along the Ho Chi Minh trail in Laos required more FACs to find the targets. We were falling behind the power curve.

At the completion of training we drove back to Cape Cod. It was now imminent, a matter of only a few days, before I was to leave. I was anxious to get Vietnam behind me.

I departed from Boston's Logan Airport to Denver's Stapleton Airport, stopping for a short visit at the Air Force Academy, before proceeding to San Francisco. I was in the "pipeline" for graduate school after Vietnam and a subsequent assignment to the Political Science faculty. I turned off the interstate highway and headed west to the academic complex. The morning sun was at my back. The Academy was absolutely majestic. The brilliant marble and aluminum buildings glistened against the dark ever-greens and towering cliffs of the Rockies' Rampart range. I reflected back to August 1958 when I was a basic cadet. We had completed our summer encampment and had unloaded from buses to march the remaining five miles to the cadet area. The scene before us was the first view of our home for the next four years. As tired as we were from the grueling training, we didn't mind the weight of our field packs and rifles. We had survived the summer and were looking forward to the academic year.

Now it was seven and a half years after that march, and I was on my way to war. I gazed at the 17 spires of the chapel reaching to the heavens. The chapel had been completed after I graduated. I drove past the giant portal that led from the parade ground to the cadet dorms—many times I had marched up that ramp in those four years with my M–1 rifle on my shoulder—and read the inscription over the portal: *Bring Me Men.*

During my stopover, I walked across the Terrazo, scanning the surrounding grounds and returning the salutes of the passing cadets. I recalled with new poignancy and meaning some of the knowledge that we had to recite as fourth classmen, especially MacArthur's quotation on athletics: "On the fields of friendly strife are sown the seeds, which on other days and other fields, will bear the fruits of victory." The "other days" were now, and I was on my way to those "other fields," and hopefully, to the fruits of victory. Little did I realize that, regardless of how hard we fought, we were to be denied those fruits.

I thought back to West Point, their enshrined heroes, and the untold number of graduates they had lost in many wars. The Air Force Academy was new; this was our first war and already we had lost a graduate, Lt. Val Bourque, class of 1960, KIA October 24, 1964. The instructors at Hurlburt had not told us about death in Vietnam; they told us about shot-up airplanes and forced landings, but nobody was killed in their stories. I was determined to come back—alive.

* * * * *

I chambered a round into my M–16 rifle, stepped off the road, and gingerly slid into the rice paddies. I was with a Korean Army patrol and we were headed into the heart of the Viet Cong controlled area. We climbed over the tops of the dikes and ploughed through the paddies, hiking to an observation post close to the targeted VC village. It suddenly dawned on me that, at six feet, three inches tall, I was a head taller than everybody else; the Viet Cong would be sure to pick out the American. The other mistake I made was that I had a radio; the VC usually shot the radio operator first. I was a double loser.

★   ★   ★   ★   ★

I boarded a military charter from Travis AFB, California, and after an 18-hour flight, with a refueling stop at Yokoda, Japan, I arrived at Clark Air Force Base, the Philippines. My orders read to report to Clark AFB, for further assignment. I deplaned in the middle of the night, uncomfortable from the oppressive heat and humidity, and entered the terminal. I located a processing counter labeled *Incoming Personnel* and approached a sergeant standing under a sign that read, *Personnel with Orders, Report Here*. Extending the sheaf of papers, I said, "Here are my orders. They say I'm to report here. I think it's for me to attend jungle survival school." This was one of the additional training programs that the Air Force mandated for air crews, to prepare them for Vietnam.

He scanned my orders, then reread them, noting the Air Force speciality code, 1441. He looked up and said, "You're a forward air controller, aren't you?"

"Yes, that's right," I replied.

"Well, sir, you are to get back on that airplane. It's going on to Saigon. Your training at Clark has been waived. We've been told not to hold any forward air controllers here." That didn't sound good to me. I reboarded, and the next thing I knew, I was looking down at the jungles of Vietnam and circling over Tan Son Nhut Airport in Saigon.

The war seemed detached, almost nonexistent as we flew over the lush countryside. As we descended for the approach to Tan Son Nhut, water-filled bomb craters and scorched jungle canopy became visible. The jetliner had to make three approaches before landing because of the priority given to bomb-laden fighters taking off. Taxiing to the terminal, I had never seen such an arsenal of military aircraft: helicopters, attack planes, light bombers, reconnaissance, utility, and cargo aircraft of every imaginable type. Closer to the terminal, I saw the civilian airliners: Pan American; Air France; Air Vietnam with their sleek Caravelle passenger jets. A military bus, with heavy wire mesh over the windows as a precaution against hand grenades, drove us to transient quarters in Saigon.

The city of Saigon was impressive to me. I could understand why it was referred to as the "Paris of the Orient," with its wide boulevards and palatial buildings. War didn't belong here. Even though business went on as usual, there were grim reminders of war: the rolls of barbed wire, machine-gun bunkers, the guards on the street corners and always the haunting, surreptitious, and insidious bombings by VC agents. Only the previous Saturday night, seven bars in Saigon were hit within a few hours of each other.

After two days in Saigon, the 504th Tactical Air Support Group processed my orders and assigned me to a field unit. Several of us were going up-country to the Qui Nhon area, half-way up the coast between Saigon and Da Nang, assigned to a Korean Army unit.

I didn't even know the Koreans were in Vietnam, but they had committed a full Army division. There were rumors that they were also bringing in the Korean Marines, to be followed by elements of yet another division. Working with third country forces had never been introduced in training at Hurlburt. I knew about the Vietnamese, their culture, their political system, and I had an English-Vietnamese dictionary. Now I was suddenly assigned to Koreans, and without a dictionary.

I remember the issuing of equipment at Tan Son Nhut. We drew jungle fatigues, boots, gas masks, survival radios, M–16 rifles, steel helmets, .38 caliber pistols, and ammunition. The reality of war crept in as I was given the tools of combat. I was prepared to be in an airplane, but loading a rifle and putting on a gunbelt was much different. There were no doubts now; I was going to war.

Near the equipment issue warehouse was the mortuary. I tried not to notice the stacks of aluminum coffins alongside the building. One of the supply sergeants remarked that he could tell when the fighting up-country was unusually fierce; the coffins spilled out into the street.

I packed my belongings into duffle bags and, with several other FACS, boarded a transport flight to Nha Trang. It was on the way to Qui Nhon.

We had to remain overnight at Nha Trang before we could continue; transport flights didn't operate at night. I met another transient Air Force officer in the barracks. He was wearing jungle fatigues, and carried a rucksack and a full complement of weapons. Fragmentation grenades, smoke grenades, ammo pouches, first aid kit, and a red-lens flashlight hung from his web gear. I looked at him: eyes sunken into the back of his head, physically exhausted, and a pallor to his skin. Cautiously, I engaged him in conversation.

"I'm a forward air controller," he said. "I've just humped from the South China Sea across the Central Highlands to the Cambodian border and back."

"You mean you weren't flying?" I asked.

"No, I was on the ground with the Army." His words shocked me—I was headed for the Korean Army. When I asked him why he was carrying frag grenades, he said that they are the best weapon to use in a close firefight; they don't give your position away. I learned something right there about ground combat. Now I was having grave reservations about my preparation for my assignment. I hadn't been trained for this. The thought was frightening, especially after he told me about ambushes and not being able to find the enemy.

Did he know about people dying? I was afraid to ask the question, probably because I didn't want the answer. You can sense by the face, the jaw, the tight lip, that there are certain questions you don't ask somebody. It was obvious to me that this young captain was overburdened, even haunted. I never asked the question.

I'll never forget looking into this FAC's eyes. I knew there was somebody behind those eyes, but they revealed nothing and he offered no further insights. It was scary, absolutely scary. I was face-to-face with the harsh reality of war.

For the first time in my life, I felt vulnerable, and I hadn't even seen combat. A chilling fear crept over me. I realized I would have to learn more by watching and listening to any combat veteran that I could meet. It was now basic survival: shoot or be shot, kill or be killed. Visions of the stacked coffins flashed through my mind.

I hardly slept that night in the open barracks of Nha Trang.

3
Orientation and Transition to Combat

After a troubled sleep under mosquito nets, my fellow FACs and I were up well before daylight to report to the Aerial Port Detachment at the passenger terminal. We wanted to continue our trip from Nha Trang up the coast to Qui Nhon. I packed my gear and tiptoed past the bunk of the veteran FAC that I had met the day before. He was sound asleep. I was still in shock from our brief conversation, probably more frightened by what he didn't tell me. I stepped out of the barracks and looked for the first light of day. No brilliant sunshine, only an eerie grey mist that hovered over the city to the east and the rice paddies to the west. An artillery battery was firing in the distance. I later learned that the VC in the area usually moved and resupplied at night. The artillery would fire randomly along the trails and at the caves, hoping to catch the VC before they reached their daytime hiding places or melted into the populace of the city.

At the terminal, I drank a cup of coffee and a GI gave me the pound cake from his C-rations. Our flight was delayed from Saigon. It was the coastal shuttle; a C–123 from Saigon to Nha Trang, Qui Nhon, and Da Nang. Some of my buddies from Otis were probably flying these missions. There were American and Vietnamese soldiers milling about, some in full battle gear, and civilians with screaming babies, chickens and ducks in cages, and pigs being led on ropes—it was chaos and cacophony everywhere. All of us were trapped under a too small tin-roofed building afraid to move away because we might miss some scribbled message on a blackboard. Only a week ago I was sipping a beer in San Francisco International Airport.

Qui Nhon, a coastal city on the South China Sea and a major supply depot, was an hour's flight from Nha Trang, terminal to terminal. As we turned onto final approach toward the runway, I could see out the back of the open cargo ramp. Army LARCs and BARCs—giant, floating, rubber-tired vehicles—were shuttling between the ships anchored in the harbor and the expanse of beaches. At least I thought they were beaches; every open area was covered with stacks of supplies.

Qui Nhon was the supply center for the American 1st Cavalry Division and the Koreans. The 1st Cav had established a base to the west in the Central Highlands at An Khe, half way to Pleiku. There were almost daily convoys that departed Qui Nhon for the 35-mile trips to An Khe. These convoys were very lucrative targets for the VC.

The Republic of Korea (ROK) Tiger Division was assigned the tactical area of responsibility (TAOR) of Qui Nhon and the surrounding Binh Dinh Province. Their mission was to secure the entire port area and the highways that extended to the north and to the west. The north-south road, Highway 1, paralleled the coast. Highway 19 extended west from the coast to An Khe and Pleiku. A strategic objective of the Military Assistance Command of Vietnam (MACV) was to prevent the Viet Cong from cutting South Vietnam in half across the Central Highlands. The Viet Cong were so entrenched in Binh Dinh that the French forces virtually left them alone in the Indo-China War. The Viet Cong had established a base complex for their troops in the Phu Cat mountains 10 miles north of Qui Nhon. They issued their own currency, maintained their own hospitals and had access to the sea for resupply by boat. Digging out the VC and pacifying the area would be a formidable task for the Korean forces.

At Qui Nhon airport six of us loaded onto jeeps and trailers for the five-mile drive to the Korean base camp, Tiger Town, named after the unit's tiger emblem. There were nine American FACs assigned to the ROK Tiger Division; I was one of them. I vividly remember that first day, convoying through the streets of the city, and riding exposed in the jeep trailer with my M–16 across my legs. I was alert and apprehensive, wondering if I would survive the trip. We transitioned from city streets to dirt roads and then through the jungle and rice paddies. The drivers had told us that nobody had been ambushed during the daytime. I hoped the VC understood that.

Tiger Town was a tent city, bulldozed and erected on the rolling knolls between the jungle-covered mountains and the flooded rice paddies. The area that was not cultivated was overgrown with ten-foot high elephant grass, scattered clumps of bamboo, and isolated trees. A wide riverbed meandered through the valley which, during the dry season, carried no more water than a brook. During the monsoon season, it swelled to a life-threatening torrent. This riverbed was to be our operating base and living quarters.

Stateside training had prepared us for the traditional role of FAC, either with a Vietnamese or American unit. Vietnamese sector FACs were based in cities and villages, lived in a villa with U.S. Army advisors, and operated from nearby airstrips. FACs assigned to U.S. Army units moved with the unit, had a separate chain of command, and an established logistical support system. We had the worst of both worlds; we lived in an isolated tent city and were dependent on a low priority supply system.

The Koreans were required to improvise their battle tactics. They didn't have helicopters or dedicated U.S. Army helicopter support. The Army organized their support helicopter battalions on a geographic basis. The Koreans, Vietnamese, and Special Forces in the region were supported by the same U.S. helicopters. It was an efficient use of resources but required close coordination to avoid simultaneous requests for the helicopters. The flight crews never got any rest from sunup to sundown, and then they were on night alert for flare missions and medical evacuations (medevacs). On the Air Force side, there were sector FACs available, but they were committed to the Vietnamese province chiefs. The Koreans were on the short end of the stick for direct air support until we showed up.

During the first few days we didn't do anything except sit in tents and grumble about the heat and the dust. We didn't even know if this was going to be our semi-permanent base within Tiger Town; we were in the "condominium development" but we didn't know which condo was ours. We slept on cots, but neglected to protect ourselves with mosquito netting. We located a combination laundry service and drink vendor in the hamlet outside the gate. We occupied our time by drinking beer and driving to the river for a bath.

It appeared that we would be operating as FACs, not only in the air but, as I was beginning to suspect, on the ground as well. Organization was weak and confusion reigned. Morale was low. Finally the wheels started turning. We were assigned to our respective units, half going into the cav regiment located to the west along Highway 19. There was an ALO assigned to the regiment and a FAC to each of the three regimental battalions. I was assigned to the 1st Regiment, which was similarly structured but was co-located with the division headquarters. The non-commissioned officers and enlisted airmen were divided proportionately. Now we had organization and staffing and were able to establish formal working arrangements with the Korean staff.

The Air Force basic work unit was a tactical air control party (TACP). It was comprised of a minimum of an officer, an ALO or FAC, and an enlisted ROMAD (radio operator, maintenance, and driver). At the division level there was a TACP with the radio call sign of "Ragged Scooper 70." First Regiment was "Ragged Scooper 71" and the three FACs were respectively 72, 73, and 74. The cavalry regiment was "Ragged Scooper 75" and the FACs were 76, 77, and 78. Within the Corps Area the FACs kept their own call sign and were readily recognized by ground troops and fighter pilots alike. Through this link, the FAC's war was personalized and he earned the gratitude of the forces he supported. Conversely, the FAC couldn't hide his mistakes with the anonymity of a daily mission call sign.

Knowing where I was going to work, I was finally able to move into my permanent tent home. Outside, we had a shower, a 55-gallon drum on stilts, with hot water on sunny days. No more going to the river for a bath. I wasn't comfortable with the river bath; the Viet Cong could have ambushed us since the bathing area was outside the secure perimeter.

Within a few days after my assignment to the 1st Regiment, I had my first exposure to the dangers of combat. I was working on maps in the double-size general purpose tent that served as our living quarters, day room, and operations center. It had a wooden floor, electric lights, a refrigerator—and holes in it. Several of the other FACs lounged about writing letters and recording tapes to send home. A few of the ROMADs were playing cards. They had taken the radio pallet off the back of one of the jeeps and rigged it in a small auxiliary tent that connected with the main tent. We could always monitor the radio traffic from the day room. I had four 1:50,000-scale map sheets spread out on the table and was trying to cut off the edges and piece them together to cover our entire tactical area. On the ground single map sheets were fine, but in the air they were too small. Invariably we'd fly off the edge of the map. Also, it was helpful to follow the fighters' flight path on the map, particularly when rendezvousing under low clouds and in poor visibility. To a fighter pilot, all trees and rivers looked the same.

The regimental ALO, my boss, came up to me. "John," he said, "the regiment is running a company-size sweep about 10 miles up the road. They expect to meet some heavy resistance and they're inquiring about air support." I looked around the tent. Everyone else had miraculously disappeared. He continued, "I said we would send someone to the forward command post." Talk about a setup. That's why they have lieutenants. If they survive, it can't be all that bad.

"Where's the command post?" I asked. He wasn't sure, but indicated that if I went to the regimental operations center I could get the details. I folded my newly constructed map sheets, tucked them under my arm, and walked the 30 meters to the regimental CP. The company was deployed north, up Highway 1. According to the map coordinates, the forward CP was located on a hilltop 300 to 400 meters off a side road. Fair enough. The Koreans gave me some radio frequencies and call signs to get into their command net in case I ran into any problems. I hoped that if I did have a problem, someone on the net would understand English. Back to our tent.

I walked up to the ALO and said, "It looks like the CP is on this hillside," as I pointed to the circled location on my map. I continued, "All I have to do is find it. I'm to give regiment a call when I leave. They'll pass the word up the line to watch for me. Do you have a ROMAD to go with me and which radio jeep do you want me to take?"

He called to one of the ROMAD sergeants. "I want you to go with Lieutenant Flanagan on a little trip up the highway. Take one of the jeeps outside. No need to take the trailer. You should be back by tonight." He turned to me,

"Anything else, Lieutenant?"

"No thanks, sir. I think I can handle it from here." I picked up my rifle, put on my web belt with pistol, knife, ammo pouch, first aid packet, and the all-important canteen. I walked to the jeep and climbed in. The sergeant was already in the driver's seat and had the engine running. I could hear the background noise on the FM radio. I gave a quick comm check as I keyed the mike,

"Ragged Scooper seven-one Base, this is seven-four. How copy?"

"Five by," was the response indicating that he heard me loud and clear. He should. He was only 50 feet away, but I wanted to make sure that the transceiver was functioning properly and the antenna tuned. I glanced at the gas gauge. Half full. I turned to the sergeant.

"I know we have Texaco gas stations in Vietnam, but I seem to have forgotten my credit card and I'm a little short on piastres. What do you think?" He looked at me sheepishly.

"Sorry sir," he replied. "I'll go to the POL pit and get some gas." I swung out of the jeep.

"Just a second," I called as I shook the jerry can on the back of the jeep. It was empty. "Fill up the can, please. I'm not too sure how long we might have to stay." If we were stuck at the command post, we would have to rely on the jeep engine with its heavy-duty generator to power the radios. Without the radios I was useless as a FAC. While the sergeant was refueling the jeep I scrounged around the tent to find some additional equipment; a couple of smoke grenades, a thermite grenade to destroy the jeep and radios in case we had to abandon it, and a couple of cartons of C-rations. The sergeant came back. There was no water can on the jeep. I grabbed a full one from outside the tent and slung it behind the passenger seat and in front of the radios. My compass and plotter were in my fatigue pockets in case I had to plot some artillery fire for target marking. I thought the compass might be useful for navigating. There weren't too many road signs around and I couldn't read Vietnamese.

As we swung out from the tent complex, I glanced over my shoulder and noticed that the other ROMADs were checking jerry cans and measuring gas tanks. Our preparations for the road trip made an impression on the senior NCO; he had the troops "preflighting" the jeeps. Things were looking up. I just might survive this mess.

We drove out the main gate, returned the sentry's salute, and headed through the hamlet just outside the gate. Little kids waved, hoping for their chewing gum and candy. Kids don't change, regardless of the era or war. I disappointed them as we sped past the beer and soda hut. My mind was on other things. This was my first excursion into "Indian country."

We raced up the road, teeth rattling, dust flying. One rut after another. The road was so bad that we couldn't shift into fourth gear. "Drive as fast as you can without losing control. It's much harder to hit a moving target," I shouted as we tore along an open section of road in the middle of the rice paddies. We were so open that any VC who was half a shot could have waxed us right then and there.

"Keep going, keep going," I urged, when we slowed slightly.

"What about land mines?" my ROMAD asked.

"No, the road's too heavily traveled. Don't worry about them," I replied. We swung around an ox cart only to be confronted by a mass of heavily laden bicycles coming right at us. The bicycles were being pushed along the road, obviously heading to the market in Qui Nhon.

My ROMAD expertly swung back in front of the ox cart as the lead bicycle pusher dove for the ditch. Sorry 'bout that. Up ahead I saw a patrol of Korean troops moving across the far rice paddies. That reminded me that I had forgotten to call the regimental command post when I left the base. I quickly switched frequencies on the FM radio and gave them a call. In heavily accented English, the Korean operator acknowledged my transmission.

I started to breathe a bit easier as we approached a series of hooches bordering the road. I saw jeeps parked along the side. It was a beer and soda stop for some Korean troops. We slowed down and waved as we passed.

We were approaching an intersection. I had been following our progress on the map spread out on my lap. I told the driver to take the left fork as we passed onto a road that was more dirt than paved surface. I picked up the mike and called back to the base,

"Ragged Scooper seven-one, this is seven-four on Fox Mike," indicating to him that I was calling on the FM radio and not one of the other three. I released the transmit key.

"Roger, this is seven-one Mike, go ahead." The suffix "Mike" indicated to me that I was talking to the ROMAD. I transmitted.

"We passed the village of An Nhon. Heading November Whiskey to the Charlie Papa. Our Echo Tango Alpha is about one-zero minutes." Northwest to the CP, 10 minutes to arrival.

"Roger, copy all. We'll forward to our friends." This confirmed that the Koreans would be advised of our impending arrival. As we swung around the next curve I saw four Vietnamese Army deuce-and-a-half trucks pulled off the right side of the road next to a cluster of hooches. There was barely room to squeeze by. The troops had climbed out of the trucks and were buying cold drinks and milling around. My ROMAD started to slow down as he shifted from third into second gear.

"No, keep going. Giv'em the horn," I told him as we barely scraped by the first truck. Our left wheels were sliding into the ditch. I wished we'd had the foresight to shift into four-wheel drive when we hit the dirt road.

BOOM! A loud explosion went off over my right shoulder.

Crack! Crack! Two shots rang out.

"Go! Go!" I shouted to my ROMAD. I threw my map on the floor, grabbed my M–16 and swung it out the side of the jeep. Oh shit—I'd forgotten to chamber a round! I pulled the charging handle back, released it, and a round slammed in. Safety off. Locked and loaded. Now what? My heart pounded as we accelerated past the lead vehicle in the convoy. "Keep going, keep going," I urged. The four-cylinder engine screamed, then settled down as the ROMAD went back to third gear.

I scanned the last hooch and quickly surveyed the dikes and paddies. All clear. Another 300 meters up the road I spotted a Korean sentry. I felt safer; we slowed down. A wide trail cut to the left, up a steep hill. We stopped at the sentry and inquired about the location of the CP. He didn't speak English, but he acted as if he were expecting us and directed us up the trail. My ROMAD shifted the jeep into four-wheel drive and we started up the hill. I was impressed by the Koreans. They were expecting us; their command channels worked.

The outpost overlooked the hamlet that we had just driven through and the valley to the north. I met the commander, a captain. His company had been running a series of small sweeps over the last couple of weeks. I watched the infantry, on line, move cautiously forward to the tree line. Their advance was being supported by an artillery barrage that kept hitting about 200 meters in front of them. This was far enough to prevent their being hit by shrapnel, but close enough to keep the Viet Cong pinned down until the Korean infantry was virtually on top of the trenches. I discussed the tactics and strategy with the commander and artillery forward observer. My job was to request and direct an air strike should the troops meet heavy resistance. The FO taught me some of the finer points of artillery fire as he allowed me to adjust the fire mission. This would be invaluable to me several months later. Although the troops had not met any heavy resistance, they were confiscating substantial rice and arms caches. They had disrupted the supply flow to the VC.

Our work finished, we sped back to Tiger Town, anxious to reach the base before the VC recaptured the night. The Koreans had given me the details of the hamlet incident: A Viet Cong agent had thrown a hand grenade—the explosion I heard as we were passing—which killed four Vietnamese, wounded fifteen. The agent was shot instantly, accounting for the two cracks I'd heard. The afternoon's grenade incident had shaken me. A mere three seconds had separated us from possible death or severe injury.

Previously, I had feared only ground fire while flying. Now there were additional threats, insidious but equally dangerous: a grenade tossed into a jeep; an ambush along the road; being shot by a lucky sniper; blown up in a restaurant; crushed by an overturned jeep; maimed by a mine or booby trap; and there was some I didn't even know about—yet. Glorious death; ignominious death. The results were the same.

It became readily apparent to me that the Air Force assignments to the ROK division were on a purely random basis without much selectivity as to background and capabilities. When our group had arrived in Saigon, the word had filtered through the system that there was an entire division in the country, the Korean division, that had no permanent forward air controllers. So that's why the nine of us were shipped there en masse, all within a day of each other. It was an expedient roll of the dice. The second- and third-ranking officers became regimental ALOs. The Air Force's way was to give command to the senior officer, not necessarily the most qualified.

I measured my fellow officers upon whom my life could depend at a time of common threat. They were older than I, but I wasn't sure that this necessarily gave them more experience. One of the officers had been stationed in Korea during that war, flying transports. No combat, but at least he was familiar with the culture. One of the ALOs was a captain passed over for promotion. The other ALO had come from Systems Command, running an engineering lab. Some of them were eligible for promotion and achieving higher rank was more important to them than the current job. The most qualified pilot had been an instructor in F–100 fighter-bombers and possessed a great deal of knowledge about the deployment of tactical air support. He spent six weeks successfully seeking an assignment to the Air Force headquarters in Saigon. He thought it would be better for his career. Others had five or six kids. Would they take combat risks? Should they? Another had been flying fighters, but was overweight and out of shape. They had expected to be living in a villa, a city, or on an Air Force base; not living in a tent in the dust, dirt, and mud, and spending time on the ground prowling through the jungles and paddies.

I was disappointed with the disgruntled attitude displayed, particularly by the officers. It would be difficult to motivate the enlisted troops when the officers were despondent. As the reality of the situation struck home, some of my fellow officers proved to be resourceful and courageous.

One guy, whom we called Mac, resembled a big bear; he grew a handlebar mustache and at the earliest opportunity he volunteered for I Corps with the ROK Marines and some of the heavy fighting. I ran into him again about eight months later. He mentioned that the administrative system never permanently transferred him to the Marines. He was there TDY and unknowingly earning extra pay all the time.

Another one of the guys, who was really smooth and unflappable, went to Bong Son to work with the 1st Cav for a couple of weeks. He lost all his cockpit lighting one night and made the 30-minute flight back to Qui Nhon holding a pen flashlight in his mouth. He flew with one hand and kept track of his position on the map with his other hand.

A transport pilot with six kids turned out to be a real tiger. While supporting a Korean unit in heavy pursuit of a Viet Cong unit, he took some ground fire hits through the engine of the O–1, blowing one of the cylinders off. The division ALO threatened to ground him if he took any more hits. He contracted malaria after eight months and, upon release from the hospital, finished his tour in the DASC in Nha Trang.

Even though the staffing shortage was solved, there were still shortages in supplies, equipment, and training. We had only one O–1 for the entire division. Supplies and munitions were scarce. The temporary FACs from the Philippines advised us that 750-pound high-explosive bombs necessary to smash the deep bunkers were extremely scarce. We lived in World War II tents that leaked like a sieve. Food was C-rations mixed with rice from the Korean mess. The Koreans were trying their best to support us, but they in turn were dependent on the U.S. Army. The acute shortage of FACs prompted the cancellation of survival training at Clark. We consequently missed valuable training. Again I reached into my past, recalling lessons from my Academy days.

★　★　★　★　★

It was the end of our first summer training period, our boot camp. We had moved from the barracks at Lowry AFB and had hiked into the wilds of Colorado. We were deployed near a reserve airfield and were going through our last phase of training before the academic year would begin. It was a forward airstrip encampment, FASE training. We were living in two-man pup tents and learning patrolling techniques, perimeter defense, and weapons deployment. We strung barbed wire, dug foxholes, and hung empty cans with pebbles as detection devices against infiltrators. We pulled night sentry duty, sliding into our shallow foxholes, camouflaged behind the sage brush of the plains. The last rays of the sun sank behind the Rocky Mountains and the chill of the Colorado night crept into our bones. A bright moon emerged and I could see the silhouette of my classmates deployed 30 yards to either side of me. A can rattled. I could see nothing; it must have been the wind. Time crept on ever so slowly; my eyes were heavy with sleep from the grueling day of training. Another rattle. A shadow moved. The moon went behind the clouds. The shadow disappeared.

"Pst, Erv, did you see anything?" I tried to whisper to the man on my flank. Suddenly, I realized my error as a hand-held parachute flare arched over our positions and the muzzle flashes of two rifles winked at me, followed by the crack of the blanks. I had given away my position. The upperclassmen in their hoods and blackened faces had penetrated the wire. The flare burned out and I could see nothing for I had lost my night vision. Now I knew why I had been told to close one eye when a flare went off. A concussion grenade detonated. An automatic weapon opened up. No flash. The upperclassmen must have been using flash suppressors. A smoke grenade was lobbed at my position. If this were combat, I would be dead.

★   ★   ★   ★   ★

I had learned my lesson as a cadet, but I didn't know what level of training, beside Hurlburt, the other eight officers had received. I envisioned the situation where we would be on the perimeter wire or in a trench, standing off attackers and sappers, or absorbing mortar rounds. I was an experienced marksman with the M–1, but we had M–16s. They were supposed to be an improvement.

I now recognized that I would have to develop the skills of an infantry soldier if I were to survive. The Koreans would be the key to my training. I located their mess tent and started eating with them. The food was typical Oriental fare, but once I started to eat kimchee, a spicy cabbage salad, the officers accepted me. It was a rite of passage. Many of them spoke English. Some had attended the U.S. Army Command and Staff College and were well versed in U.S. tactics and procedures. They became my willing tutors. I learned about their weapons and the location of their perimeters, outposts, and artillery batteries. They took me to their rifle range. I spent the major part of an afternoon sighting in my M–16. If I had to use it, I had a reasonable chance of hitting something. The other officers and enlisted men followed my example; it was also fun to select full-automatic and riddle beer cans with 20 rounds per magazine. Sometimes our weapons jammed.

But our marksmanship practice had a penalty. We were exhausting our ammo supply. The M–16 fired the .223 caliber round; the Koreans used mainly the M2 carbine, with a .30 caliber round. Same problem with our sidearms. The Air Force used the .38 revolver, the Koreans the .45 automatic. There was a shortage of ammunition for the .38s and only half the shells would fire. We didn't have compatible ammunition for our weapons. We would have to fight with what we carried, our "basic load."

The Koreans invited me on patrol with them. I never told my boss because I didn't know how he would react. It was important to me to take advantage of the opportunity. We went several hundred meters beyond the perimeter, looking for signs of the enemy approaching the barbed-wire defenses, setting up booby traps, or laying bamboo poles stuffed with explosives. Not much risk, yet I was acclimating to the jungle environment.

I also tried to adapt to the culture. There were numerous children at the hamlet near the main gate. One likeable Lilliputian became my language tutor. As the father of two infants, I immediately identified with her. Now

I understood my daughters' faltering when they were learning to talk. Simple Vietnamese nouns and common objects were awkward to pronounce. The meanings of the same word change with the tonal inflection. Korean appeared easier to learn than Vietnamese, but the Air Force didn't have any conversational guidebooks. Communication with our allies was very difficult.

I was finally scheduled to Pleiku for my in-country check-out in the O–1. Most of the other officers had completed this and finally it was my turn. I climbed on an Army Caribou transport plane at Tiger Town for the 70-mile flight to the Central Highlands city.

Once we were airborne, I unstrapped myself and stumbled up to the cockpit as the plane bounced through the rising air pockets. I stood between the pilots' seats and looked out the windshield. I put on an extra headset to listen to the radio chatter. From 8,000 feet, everything appeared so peaceful and serene. It was easy to trace Highway 19 as it departed the city, snaked across the paddies, through the jungle, and into the highlands. My lofty view expanded my perceptions of Vietnam.

★ ★ ★ ★ ★

The countryside is lush and pastoral; no wonder Vietnam is considered the rice bowl of the Orient. Children herd the water buffaloes to and from the rice paddies and grazing fields. It is utterly amazing to watch the small kids prodding these giant animals along with nothing more than bamboo switches. The villages and hamlets are extremely primitive. The people live in thatched huts with dirt floors and no sanitation facilities, but in the cities some of the structures are architecturally magnificent and functionally efficient. The people are friendly. Communication is difficult, but some of the people speak French, a carryover from French colonialism. There is a tremendous gap in the society between the urban tradesmen and bureaucrats, and the rural peasants, farmers, and fishermen. The transition from one social strata to another, from urban to rural living, from concrete to thatch buildings, all occur within a quarter-mile of leaving the city gates. It was surrealistic; foggy mornings transitioned into another world, a twilight zone, never revealing what would lie ahead. In a way that probably described my plight. I was in another world, the world of war, and danger could always lie ahead.

★ ★ ★ ★ ★

Peacock Center, the radar controllers at Pleiku, interrupted my reverie as they transmitted an artillery advisory for a fire mission. We altered our course, slipped under the trajectory of the shells, and turned onto a short final approach. Nice landing, and with prop reverse, we stopped in less than 600 feet. Impressive.

I spent a week in Pleiku accomplishing my in-country orientation. I flew a couple of visual reconnaissance missions, becoming disoriented on one of them. It reinforced the importance of map reading and topography. There were few man-made features. Roads and trails were unreliable. It was better to navigate by ridge lines, streams and dry stream beds, contours, and vegetation patterns. We were flying some of these training missions over Plei Me, a Special Forces camp that had been under siege and almost overrun several months before. The burned-out hulks from the ambushed relief column were strewn about the dirt road leading to the camp.

One day I was scheduled for an early morning mission. I was waiting, with several local pilots and mechanics, for the bus that would transport us from the high ground of the military compound, across the rolling hills, to the airfield. During the night, fog had shrouded the field and settled across the hillside. Visibility was less than 100 meters, which would curtail flying operations until the sun heated the air. A blue Air Force bus emerged from the mist—it didn't belong here, this wasn't Florida or Holly Field, training was over—then I saw bullet holes. It was Vietnam; it was OK.

We climbed on board. I took a seat behind the driver who was wearing his steel helmet. He stood up and made an announcement. "Once we leave the compound I want everyone to keep their heads down, below the window level. We could get some sniper fire." He got back in his seat and we lurched out the gate.

"How do you know, the sniper?" I inquired.

"Foggy morning," he replied. "Some sniper sits on the hill and takes pot shots."

"Why doesn't a patrol go out and get him?" I asked, my head well below the seat back.

"The gook's such a lousy shot that he only managed to hit the bus once in three months. If we nail him he might be replaced by someone who is a better shot." Not bad logic. I was beginning to understand this war.

While I was at Pleiku I met a couple of A–1 pilots who were at Hurlburt when I was there. We shared some stories from Hurlburt and longed for the delicious Gulf Coast shrimp. I met one of my former professors from the Academy who was also flying the A–1. I later learned he was killed on a mission in North Vietnam.

*   *   *   *   *

By Tatum had been a professor of political science when I was a cadet. He was a West Point graduate and held a Ph.D. from Syracuse University. Around the Air Commando squadron he naturally became known as "Goose." It was in March 1989 when I learned the details of By's shoot-down from one of his squadron mates. In September 1966, By and his wingman were scheduled for an armed recce mission in the Route Pack 1 area of North Vietnam which was the DMZ and the area immediately north of it. On the return from their mission, By took on some heavy antiaircraft guns which succeeded in shooting him down. He was last seen running from the pursuing North Vietnamese troops, some 10 miles north of the DMZ. But he never turned up on any POW list. It seemed that whenever there was any heavy action, by some quirk of fate, Goose would miss out. This time he took on a little more than he could handle.

★ ★ ★ ★ ★

I also met some pilots who were flying F-4 Phantoms out of Cam Ranh Bay. They were in Pleiku for a week flying missions with the FACs in order to see the war from the FAC's perspective. Great idea; someone's thinking. I had a similar opportunity to fly a mission in the A-1, compliments of 1st Air Commando Squadron.

I went to the operations officer, Buz Blaylock, and asked if I could fly with them. No problem. They were glad to have me along, but I was cancelled from my first scheduled sortie because the target was in Laos. In early 1966, the United States had political reservations about bombing targets in neutral countries, clouding the out-country missions in secrecy. I was rescheduled for the next day on an in-country mission.

I remember sitting in the briefing room with the intelligence officer, Bob Winger, who was later to become a three-star general, and the two mission pilots. We were a flight of two aircraft. I would be in the right seat of the number two or wingman's aircraft and we were fragged to be an aircap mission. The A-1 could remain airborne approximately four hours, close to the battle area and poised for instant response. We would fly from Pleiku northeast toward the South China Sea to the area of Bong Son and the An Loa Valley. This sector of Binh Dinh Province was 45 miles north of Tiger Town. We were to support the American 1st Cav on Operation Masher.

The three of us hitched a ride on the flight line truck to the airplanes. Fortunately they were parked close to each other for easy engine start and taxi coordination. I followed the pilot as he did his walk-around inspection. Fuel tanks full and caps secure; we were carrying an auxiliary 150-gallon center-line fuel tank for extra range and loiter time. Access panels tight. Dzus fasteners flush with the skin. We checked the ordnance, particularly the safety wires on the bomb fuses. We had six, three on each side, Mark 82, 500-pound high-explosive bombs and four, two each side, 260-pound fragmentation clusters. The bombs were bunker smashers, while the frag clusters were antipersonnel weapons. Four stations were empty due to spacing. The four wing-mounted 20mm cannons were fully loaded with 800 HEI rounds, high explosive incendiary shells, the best. I climbed up on the right wing, swung my legs into the cockpit and wrestled into the seat-pack parachute. As I buckled the parachute and fastened the shoulder harness and seat belt, I reviewed the bailout procedure: slide the canopy back, open the lap belt, crouch on the seat, and dive at the trailing edge of the wing. (Same procedure as in World War II; we hadn't made any progress by 1966.) Helmet on. Sweat poured down my face from the oppressive heat. Gloves on. Plug in the mike cord. Ground power cart hooked up. Battery switch on. Intercomm check. Five by. Start signal to the crew chief. The four-bladed prop swings through eight blades. Mag switch on, eight more blades, then primer, mixture up and release the primer as the engine catches. The big Wright 3350 radial coughs, sputters, and roars into life; 2,800 eager horsepower. Exhaust fumes blow into the open cockpit. Heady, but cooling. I recognized the smell, the roar. This was the same engine that powered the Constellations that I flew in the States. We looked at Lead, he signaled ready to go. Comm check on the company Fox Mike frequency. The A–1s have FM capability. Good to remember.

"Go Uniform, button one," Lead transmitted. We switched to ground frequency as briefed.

"Hobo two-seven," said Lead.

"Two-eight," we replied. The UHF radio worked.

"Pleiku tower, Hobo two-seven. Taxi with two?"

"Roger, Hobo two-seven flight. Taxi runway zero-nine," and the tower continued the transmission giving the winds and altimeter setting. Chocks out. We taxied to the arming area. After the engine run-up was complete, we held our hands over our head, indicating to the ground crew that all was safe in the cockpit. They approached the aircraft and pulled the safety pins from the bombs and charged the guns. We were "hot." We slid the canopy shut and locked the handle.

We took off at ten-second intervals, and climbed through the broken cloud decks. We reached the tops of the clouds at around 7,000 feet and were bathed in brilliant sunshine. It was also much cooler as we leveled off at 9,000 feet and headed toward Bong Son. There was a standing joke about the A–1: It was the only aircraft that took off at 140 knots, cruised at 140, and landed at 140. But it carried a big bomb load, could take the punishment, and would get you home—it was a flying dump truck!

In just over 20 minutes after takeoff, we made radio contact with a Ragged Scooper FAC. Lead gave him our line up.

"Ragged Scooper, this is Hobo two-seven, flight of two A–1s. We each have six Mark 82s, four frag clusters and guns. We're about ten minutes out."

"Roger Hobo. Nothing happening right now." He was a good FAC. The standard briefing format called for weather, winds, altimeter setting, terrain elevation, safe bailout, and recovery airfield. But before you started with all that bullshit, what the fighter pilot really wanted to know was what he was getting into. Were troops in heavy contact? Had aircraft been shot down? Was there a helilift going in? What was all that smoke? Or could he relax and go with the flow?

Ragged Scooper continued, "When you reach Bong Son, follow the river to the northwest. I'm about 10 klicks [6 miles] up the river and talking to some of the ground troops now." The Army measured distances in kilometers and meters, with accuracy routinely to 100 meters and sometimes as finite as 10 meters. Target coordinates were given in UTM, Universal Transverse Mercator, grid coordinates. The Air Force worked in nautical miles, and latitude and longitude. The Army worked on FM radios. The Air Force worked on UHF radios. The FAC was the conductor who orchestrated the strike.

"How long can you stay with me?" the FAC inquired.

"About two and a half, maybe three hours." The FAC now knew that if something didn't develop with the ground troops in that time he would have to seek an alternate target. Every good FAC had at least two or three targets up his sleeve. There was always some location that looked suspicious. A FAC was always trying to get even with some VC position that had shot at him in the past.

We passed Bong Son and, about three minutes later, spotted the little O–1 far below us, darting in and out of the clouds, floating across the jungle. I realized how difficult it was to see anything under the jungle canopy, particularly from 7,000 or 8,000 feet. He told us to hold in orbit and he'd give us a call if he needed us. We orbited for just over two and a half hours and were getting close to our bingo fuel. We called the FAC.

"Scooper, we've got another half-hour or so that we can stay with you, do you have any targets?"

"No," he said. "I don't have anything real hot but earlier the patrols had spotted a trail and stream crossing. There may be some supply caches by the stream."

We rendezvoused with the FAC at a new location. The O–1's silver wings stood out sharply against the green jungle. He put a smoke rocket on the target and cleared us in with our Mark 82s. We set up the switches to drop the bombs in singles. Down we dove, the altimeter unwinding, the airspeed increasing, looking for 2,500 feet and 270 knots. Pickle. The aircraft lurched as the bomb dropped free. We pulled out as the G-forces crammed us into our seats, the blood rushing from our heads. We had no G-suits and we grunted to keep from blacking out. We craned our necks to watch the bomb go off.

"Good hit," exclaimed the FAC as the jungle parted, the shock wave erupted, and trees went flying every which way. At the FAC's direction we dropped the bombs throughout the target area. We uncovered a trail that was hidden underneath the canopy and the FAC found a submerged bridge, hidden underneath the water. Gradually, with the bombs, we took it apart and destroyed it. We knocked out all the cover and potential ambush sites that might be along the trail leading to the stream. Our troops could now travel that way in search of the VC with less possibility of being ambushed. The pilots described it as a "splinter and monkey-killing" mission. But, if the 1st Cav troops made contact, the A–1s were immediately available. We were replaced by another flight of two A–1s and headed back to Pleiku. That was my first real combat mission.

On the way back to Pleiku, while I was getting some stick time, I had a deep sense of disappointment. I had really wanted the A–1 for my Vietnam assignment. When I landed, I sought out the squadron commander and asked if there was any possibility of my transferring into the A–1s. Previously there had been, but no longer. I resigned myself to being a FAC, but I also committed to being the best FAC.

As part of the in-country indoctrination training, we carefully reviewed the rules of engagement, the rules we Americans were to fight under. We needed the clearance of the ground commander to hit a target. If the strike was in an area assigned to the ARVN, we needed clearance from the province chief or his designated representative. We were to honor the international boundaries of all neutral countries and restrict our attacks to military targets. We signed our name to a statement, acknowledging we read and understood the rules. I didn't realize how I would be tested in combat on my adherence to those rules. I thought, "Why shouldn't the Viet Cong have rules of engagement, too?"

Rules of Engagement—National Liberation Front
As Envisioned by Lt. John Flanagan, USAF

- No blowing up bars and restaurants.
- No ambushing civilian buses to collect taxes.
- Don't murder hamlet chiefs.
- No mortar or rocket attacks against civilian villages or urban population centers.
- Don't steal crops from the Montagnards.
- Don't blackmail the coffee or rubber plantation owners.
- Don't conscript the plantation workers or levy crop taxes.
- No hiding in Cambodia, a neutral country.
- No building military supply roads and trails in Laos, a neutral country.
- Don't shoot at helicopters with the Red Cross insignia.

I was confused by the duality of the existing rules. We had one set, the Viet Cong another. The North Vietnamese exploited our rules; they intentionally placed gun positions in close proximity to nonmilitary targets. I didn't know what rules the Saigon government was using, if any. The Koreans apparently had their own. But as I recalled, COIN warfare, in the absence of political hegemony, fostered its own rules from expediency.

I finally completed my three-mission checkout in Pleiku. I had been in Vietnam 25 days. I was now a fully qualified FAC. Only 340 days to go.

I hopped on a C–130 Hercules, a four-engine turboprop workhorse, back to Qui Nhon. Somebody in the higher chain of command had erred. The knowledge of the Korean division's deployment to Vietnam must have been known for months. The Air Force planners should have identified earlier the requirements to support a combat division. The Army, as well as the Air Force, had ample experience working with the Koreans in the Korean War. In World War II, the Army Air Corps formed and trained bomber crews stateside, then sent them into combat as a cohesive unit. The Air Force could have done that with us. They could have provided ground combat training, language training, assigned a Korean liaison officer, and deployed us as an integral unit to Vietnam. But it didn't happen; we had lost our corporate memory. Somehow we muddled through.

At Qui Nhon, I contacted the airport liaison officer for a jeep ride to Tiger Town. We drove past the cathedral—missed mass again. At Tiger Town, the regimental ALO called us together and briefed us on the deployment of the three battalions along Highway 1 and in the vicinity of Phu Cat village and the Phu Cat mountains. They were ten miles north from where I had the grenade incident. The 1st Cav Division had a forward base there for Operation Masher, now called White Wing. The Cav needed a viable base security force. The Viet Cong were chopping up the local Vietnamese forces and probing the helicopter base and field hospital with night attacks. The 3rd Battalion was to secure the area, run patrols and sweeps, and keep the Viet Cong out. They needed a forward air controller. As the ALO looked around the tent, the other officers avoided his eyes. He was looking for a volunteer. There was only one aircraft in Tiger Town, nine pilots trying to fly it, and not much happening. I wanted out of there. I didn't hesitate. "Sir, I'll go," I said. Had I not volunteered, I probably would have been selected anyway. That's what lieutenants are for. A RO-MAD would accompany me. We were going to the forward–most outpost to spend an indeterminate period directing air support. It was an undesirable and dangerous assignment.

I had been in-country almost a month. I had processed through Saigon, slept in Nha Trang, jeeped through Qui Nhon, and settled into Tiger Town. I had zeroed my weapons and sharpened my skills. I had resigned myself to ground FACing. I had journeyed to outposts, hiked on patrols, and nearly been killed by a VC hand grenade. I'd wrangled a bombing mission in the Skyraider and completed my O–1 checkout as a FAC. I had signed, but not tested, the rules of engagement. I was ready to take the war up Highway 1 to Charlie's backyard.

4
Defending Highway 1: Phu Cat with the Koreans

I had preempted the decision process by volunteering for the Highway 1 assignment with the 3rd Battalion. Sergeant Gagnon was assigned as my ROMAD. He was in his early twenties, only a couple of years younger than I. He joined me and we packed the radio jeep and trailer. We hooked them together, crossing the safety chains under the hitch. He had driven with me before and knew that once we got rolling we wouldn't stop for anything. While we were gathering our gear, we had the chance to share some thoughts. There are two ways to fight a war; one is allow the war to come to you and the other is to find the war. We took it a step further. We decided that not only would we find the war, we would make the war. Gagnon was bored sitting around the regiment copying radio messages. I liked his attitude. We scrounged some extra ammo magazines for our M–16s. We were ready to go.

The regimental ALO walked up to our jeep. He said, "If you have the chance to get out of the field for a day, that would be fine. We'll send the O–1 up whenever the weather permits and we'll drop mail to you." We climbed into the jeep.

"Okay. That's fair, sir," I replied. I chambered a round into my rifle, turned to Gagnon, who had the engine running, and said, aside, "Let's get the hell outta here, Sarge."

"Roger that, sir." He slammed the jeep into gear, let out the clutch, and intentionally kicked up dust that blew into the tent. Somebody flipped us the finger. So what. We were headed for Charlie country and some real fighting.

It was 25 miles north from Tiger Town to the center of the Binh Dinh Province. The French never ventured far from the highway in their fight against the Viet Minh. Things hadn't changed much. Territory more than a half-mile on either side of the highway belonged to the Viet Cong. The time of useful life was probably about five minutes. That was during the daytime. No one traveled after dark. Until the Koreans came along.

We passed through the hamlet where the grenade incident occurred a couple of weeks before. No problem. The ROKs had pacified the area.

★   ★   ★   ★   ★

There were many tales circulated about the fighting prowess of the Korean forces. I never knew which ones to believe, and which were merely folklore. One of the more credible stories involved an ambush near a small hamlet located on one of the single-lane dirt roads about a mile from Tiger Town. The enterprising Vietnamese peasants, with minimum capital, opened a beer and soda stand in their hamlet. The mamasans would take in laundry. Several of the ROK officers made a habit of ending the day there, sipping some cool beers. One evening, around twilight, the officers were ambushed on their return to Tiger Town. The Koreans tracked down the VC agent, extracted the identities of the local ambushers, then pursued and, in turn, ambushed them. As a message, they left the bodies hanging by the roadside. The Koreans understood this war; they denied the VC the sanctuary of the jungle and the anonymity of the populace.

★   ★   ★   ★   ★

We continued on our journey to the battalion command post. Since arriving in Vietnam, I had logged more hours in a radio jeep than I had in an airplane. The MRC–108 radio jeep was the major tool of the TACP. It was a standard Army M–151 jeep chassis with a pallet, rack, and four radios mounted in the back. The radio pallet contained a HF/SSB (high frequency/ single side band) radio, which had a range of hundreds of miles depending upon the antenna. Its output was 400 watts. We referred to this radio as "hotel" and its primary purpose was to link with the corps level command structure. On some slow nights we would contact the Philippines, Okinawa, and some ROMADs claimed, the States. The jeep also had a UHF (ultra high frequency) radio, which we referred to as "uniform" and it was used primarily for communicating with the fighters. This radio was limited to line of sight. The jeep also had an FM radio, called "Fox Mike," which was used primarily to talk to the ground troops because that radio was compatible with the Army communication nets. I never fully understood the capability of this radio. Sometimes it would work through and around hills or through heavy jungle, but other times it would just die. The jeep also had a VHF (very high frequency) radio, referred to as "Victor." This radio was used primarily for talking to airborne FACs and to helicopters. We would pass ground-to-air targets and coordination traffic on it.

The radio jeep was an efficient piece of equipment with the exception of the "pain in the ass" trailer that contained the main generator for the radios. The trailer severely limited mobility, but we also crammed it with our cots, sleeping bags, tents, and other assorted equipment. We would drop the trailer off whenever possible. We could run the radios from the jeep engine, but this supposedly strained the alternator. A tech order limited its use to 30 minutes, though we ran it for hours and never burned out an alternator. We bent the regulations. Also, the radios were extremely heavy, resulting in a high center of gravity. The vehicle had independent suspension which helped on rough terrain, but exacerbated the instability on sharp curves, particularly at high speed. We managed to flip some over. Also, the antennae stuck out making it difficult to hide or camouflage. The HF antenna was 32 feet high, and even with one-half wave-length sections, it was still 16 feet. We would erect it alongside a tree or tall structure to hide it from the enemy. But in spite of its limitations, it did the job, keeping the FAC at the hub of the air-ground war as the key coordinator between ground and air forces. He was on the leading edge of the transformation to an information society that was to occur in the 1980s.

Driving north, we found the headquarters, one mile north of the village of Phu Cat. Highway 1 was a narrow, asphalt and dirt, chuck-holed road, located ten to twelve miles inland from, and parallel to, the coast. It was barely wide enough for two military trucks to pass, let alone ox carts, motor scooters, and bicycles.

The S–2, intelligence officer, briefed us. We were surrounded by Viet Cong. The 1st Cav's helicopter base invited mortar attacks. To the west, within three miles, were two battalions, approximately 1,000 troops, of Viet Cong, and four miles to the east were more VC of greater than one battalion strength. The Koreans were outnumbered three to one at best. The VC knew where we were, but we didn't know where they were. It was a precarious position, but I had confidence in the ROKs.

Sgt. Gagnon and I moved into a two-man umbrella tent that was more than ample for ourselves and our equipment. The Koreans had prepared it for us. The tent was well dug-in and sandbagged; the tops of our cots were three feet below ground level which protected us from everything but a direct hit from a mortar round. The walls were lined with dirt-filled artillery shell boxes which slowed any structural erosion. We positioned the jeep under a camouflage net alongside the tent and pushed the generator trailer into the bushes, caching the jerry cans separately at the fullest extent of the feeder hoses. As we unloaded our gear, we were befriended by a Korean sergeant, Sgt. Hung. He didn't speak English, but somehow we communicated. He was our self-appointed benefactor, looking after our personal needs and physical comforts. Our water cans were always full, our sandbags leveled and plumbed daily, tent guys adjusted after the frequent rains, and canteen cups of steaming rice arrived at our tent for every meal. When he was on patrol, he delegated the responsibilities to one of his men. He never seemed to sleep, even after being out all night on an "ambushy." He would accept no favors, but indicated that he coveted the portable radios that the American GIs had. We offered to buy him one at the PX in Qui Nhon at the first opportunity. He made our physical stay in Phu Cat not only tolerable, but actually pleasant. The proximity of the VC was another matter.

Gagnon checked into division headquarters by HF radio every hour. Several times a day, I went to the adjacent tent, which housed the TOC (tactical operations center), to be briefed on the operation and to lend advice for tactical air support. We could process immediate requests for air support, which took about 15 minutes for approval, or preplanned requests for the following day. Gagnon would transmit the information up channel to the DASC, located 115 miles to the south at Nha Trang. The system worked the way it was taught at Hurlburt.

Activity was at a lull during the first week. Then, the short-term battle plan called for the other regiment, the cav regiment, to launch a small sweep through a suspected VC staging area. One of our companies would act as a blocking force. I intended to drive the jeep, accompanying the commander, to an observation point. I would be the only FAC at the core of the battle. The battalion command element, myself included, departed well before daybreak, plowing through elephant grass over our heads, to the preselected observation post. At barely first light, the artillery barrage opened up, followed by air strikes and the helicopter-lift of the assault company. We were one mile from the air strikes and helicopter landing zone. The troops landed in two waves, six helicopters each. The assault was successful because the next day our blocking company made heavy contact with the VC.

The VC had fled the cav regiment attack and retreated to a village. Our company attacked the village and forced out the Cong. The VC then fled to yet another village. The battalion staff monitored the battle over the radios and on the maps in the TOC. I couldn't understand Korean, but I could follow the changing map plots. It was time to cut the VC off with an air strike. We initiated an immediate request through the HF net to the DASC. We would hit the VC in the village or in the paddies when they tried to flee once again. The division headquarters monitored our request and immediately launched a FAC from Tiger Town in the O–1. The request was approved and we had the first of seven fighters on the target within 20 minutes. There were two B–57 Canberras, a light bomber of British design, three A–4E Skyhawks from the Marines at Chu Lai, and two F–4C Phantoms from the Air Force at Cam Ranh Bay. In the meantime, the battalion S–3, Captain Lee, and I were each bouncing up Highway 1 in our respective jeeps to the battle.

When we pulled our jeep off the highway, Captain Lee was already standing on the hood of his jeep, scanning the village and paddies to the west through field glasses. Gagnon never shut the engine off; he had the half-section HF antenna up in less than a minute. A patrol of Korean troops virtually materialized out of nowhere. I watched them fan out through the rice paddies and set up defensive positions around us. Our small party was less than 1,000 meters from the battle and it never dawned on me that the VC would break from the village and come right at us.

We watched the bombs fall and felt their concussion as they hit the village. We gave corrections to the airborne FAC. He re-marked the targets with smoke rockets. I monitored the conversations between the O–1 and the fighters on the UHF radio. I would give corrections directly to the fighters when Capt. Lee or I saw the VC escaping across the paddies. We had them on the run! They couldn't even shoot at the fighters. I saw the B–57s rolling in. They were on target. After their first few passes, we could see the bombs separate from the aircraft but they didn't explode. Capt. Lee looked at me, befuddled. I didn't have any answers. I grabbed the Uniform handset,

"What's wrong, Bird? This is Scooper on the ground. We see your bombs but they're not going off."

"I think those were delays," replied a B–57 pilot. The B–57s had been diverted from a trail-seeding mission. Their ordnance load included delayed-fuse bombs. I told Capt. Lee the bombs were OK, but not to let the troops into the area.

"Well, that's good. How long a delay?" I asked Lead.

"We're not sure. We think maybe twelve or up to seventy-two hours."

"Thanks a bunch. I'm glad you let us know," I said sharply. But it was my fault. I had given the target clearance. I knew they had bombs, but I didn't ask about the fuses. Lesson learned.

The Marine A–4Es came through next. They were experts in close air support. The three Skyhawks pounded the hell out of the target. They were followed by two F–4Cs, the alert flight from Cam Ranh Bay, carrying bombs and napalm. The airborne FAC had the targets clearly identified. Capt. Lee and I watched the show. The Korean troops, our security force, gave a jubilant thumbs-up every time a bomb exploded or napalm erupted. The Phantoms were making their passes from the north to the south, parallel to the highway. As they pulled off the target, they spotted our jeeps on the road.

"Hey, FAC is that you along the road?" one of them inquired.

"Yes, it is." I flashed them a mirror.

"Rog, we got your mirror. Is that you, Flanagan?" Lead asked.

"Yes. Who's this?"

"It's Webber." It was Arnie Webber and his backseater whom I met at Pleiku when they had been flying with the FACs on orientation missions. They knew I was with Koreans and working on the ground.

"Arnie, those are some damn fine bombs," I said. I took control of the strike and cleared the F–4s for another pass, this time strafing with their 20mm Gatling guns. I could see the hooches virtually disintegrate as the HEI shells ripped through the village. They pulled off dry—Winchester—out of bullets. I asked, "How about a low pass?" He said, "Sure." Those two F–4s rejoined in close formation and flew wingtip to wingtip, south to north, up that highway at treetop level, just on the verge of supersonic. They barely missed the jeep's radio antenna. That F–4 is noisy, leaves a smoke trail, and is aerodynamically ugly, but it is the most awesome animal coming down the chute—a wild rhino hell-bent on destruction. Arnie and his wingman pummeled the Viet Cong in Binh Dinh Province on February 27, 1966.

The battle lasted from mid-morning through early afternoon. Captain Lee was ecstatic and the ROKs were duly impressed by the awesome destructive power of tactical air. Back at the battalion CP, the soldiers gave me a thumbs-up and shouted "Numba One," whenever they saw me. The results of the battle were 41 VC killed, one VC nurse captured, two rifles, a rocket launcher, documents, and uniforms confiscated. The results of the air strikes in the area of the delayed-fused bombs were unknown. The ground troops couldn't get in there. The Koreans suffered two wounded, one of them the company commander. Talk about leadership by example: He was out in front, leading his troops when he was hit. We called a medevac chopper to get him out.

That evening the battalion commander, a lieutenant colonel, invited me to dine with his staff. Our dinner was periodically interrupted by the sound of the delayed-fuse bombs exploding in the distance. Some of the outpost and base camp personnel were alarmed, but when Captain Lee explained the source of the explosions, their fears disappeared. The troops in our camp were watching a movie. Every time one of the bombs detonated, they gave a loud cheer. I regretted my earlier sharp words with the B–57 pilots. I hadn't anticipated the psychological lift those delayed explosions would have on the troops.

Those two days of action made the entire week's boredom worthwhile. U.S. technology and firepower had been exploited. I had earned the respect of the Koreans and was offered the seat of honor when dining with the staff. But the back of my neck was flaming red and painful from the tropical sun. Functional design had not been applied to fatigue caps.

While sitting outside the tent a few nights later, we saw a half-dozen flares go off down the road toward the village of Phu Cat. They were accompanied by the sound of small-arms fire, followed shortly by machine-gun fire about 300 yards away. Tracer rounds spun crazily through the air as they ricocheted from the abandoned French redoubts scattered about the paddies. The S–2 officer, Captain Kwong, came running from the TOC.

"John, can you get Phu Cat on the radio? The telephone lines are down." We couldn't raise them or anybody else. Finally, we contacted our division headquarters; they weren't much help. The shooting stopped but we still couldn't reach Phu Cat by radio or phone. There was a district advisory team, Americans, in Phu Cat. They were protected only by regional forces, which is like having no protection. We feared they had been overrun, but without communications, the Koreans would not send a relief force. In this crazy war, they could get into a firefight with the undisciplined and over-anxious Vietnamese RFs. When the shooting first started, I saw a shadowy figure in combat dress lurking in the bushes, 20 meters from our tent. It was Sgt. Hung; I knew I was safe. Fortunately, the next day proved that the VC were only probing the outer wire of the DAT compound. They disappeared into the jungle once the machine guns opened up.

The jeeps ran on mogas (motor gas), we ran on the ubiquitous C-rations. Some of the C-rations, chicken, beef with sauce, and turkey were actually good when mixed with rice. Tiring of this fare, however, I would occasionally dine out. The 1st Cavalry's forward base camp was a half-mile across the highway. I would walk to their officers' mess for some western-style cooking. I chatted with some of the officers from the Cav's 3rd Brigade. Apparently, there had been some heavy fighting 15 to 20 miles north, in the vicinity of Bong Son and the An Loa Valley. Operation White Wing had forced the VC from the coastal plains and into the heavy jungle of the valley. An elite Special Forces unit, Project Delta, had been shot up while running reconnaissance patrols for the 1st Cav. As I continued my lunch, I saw the helicopters bring in some wounded and two KIAs. The helicopters were the Dustoff medevacs with large International Red Cross insignia painted on them. One was full of bullet holes and another had the front canopy shot out. A medic had a freshly bloodied bandage on his arm, just under his Red Cross armband. So this is the way Charlie fights. I lost my appetite.

I was overwhelmed. Somehow, in my naivete, I thought that some semblance of universal rules, if not morality, would exist in this war. I was wrong. The rules were apparently for me and not for others. This made such an impression on me that I wrote in my letters, not knowing if they would ever be mailed, the following:

War is truly hell. I think that if some of the politicians, statesmen and political scientists could experience . . . more of the death and gruesomeness of war, their reasoning would be considerably more clairvoyant and their negotiating more expeditious.

The action slowed down for a few days. The 3rd Battalion's continuous patrols and ambushes kept the VC off balance. One night I was drinking with the staff—Crown Beer, imported from Korea. The Koreans were fun-loving and musical. We took turns singing as we consumed several beers. The Korean melody was soft and lilting; songs about love and separation from lovers, the sadness and loneliness of awaiting a lover's return. The missing of loved ones is a universal sadness.

Our patrols kept probing the area from where the attack on the DAT compound had come. Finally, I requested an air strike and we expended a flight of A–1Es on a cluster of hooches and trenches. We were hoping to hit the ammunition cache from where the VC staged their raid. No secondary explosions. They must have pulled everything out.

During the time period that we were working along Highway 1, there was a 48-hour cease-fire. Usually a cease-fire coincided with the lunar New Year, known as Tet. However, Tet had passed and this cease-fire was for the peaceful conduct of local elections. I don't recall ever receiving official notification of a cease-fire, but the Koreans advised me that we would be standing down for a couple of days. I checked with the MACV advisors, the DAT, in the village and they confirmed that there was to be a cease-fire. They invited me to their compound for the duration. I left the battalion command post and drove the mile to Phu Cat. I parked the jeep within the secure area of the compound, left my weapons behind, and accompanied by some of the advisors, walked through the village. It was a festive occasion, similar to a street fair in the United States. I bought a broad-brimmed Aussie hat from a street vendor.

I was not prepared for the large Viet Cong banner strung across the main thoroughfare and the promotional booths set up near the banner. The booths were manned by members of the National Liberation Front who were distributing flyers and discussing politics with the local populace. One of the American advisors was fluent in Vietnamese and engaged the cadre official in a spirited debate. I recognized the words *Trung-uy*—Lieutenant—and *FAC*. I began to feel nervous. Finally, the translator turned to me.

"He," referring to the VC political officer, "knows you are the FAC with the Koreans. He wants to know why you are here and why you brought his brothers, the Koreans, to fight against his cause of national liberation."

I was so astonished that I had no response. We walked slowly back to the compound. Not only did the VC know who I was but they had a propaganda line for me. My regulation fatigues with *U.S. AIR FORCE* and my name and pilot's wings stitched above the chest pockets made identification simple. The propaganda was another matter. I had met the enemy face-to-face and they were committed to their cause no less than I was. I could only be impressed. The key factor in their favor was that this was their native land; I was an alien, an invader.

In spite of the war, there were moments of pleasure, relaxation, and camaraderie. These moments are much more valuable when the threat of dying is constantly present. I recorded in my notes:

The nights during the dry season are magnificent to behold, truly big sky country. Calm or just a gentle breeze, about 70 to 75 degrees with a large, bright moon. I usually sit under the palm trees in the evening with the battalion staff. With the series of air strikes I earned my acceptance as a warrior and I have become quite friendly with several senior Korean officers. They have a very pure and simple sense of humor and will laugh at most anything amusing. We often joke about "ugly Americans" or "ugly Koreans" and this is "number one" or "number ten." Last night we had an American movie, shown of course outdoors, which I walked into about half-way through. After a few minutes I announced, "This is number ten American movie"—which it was—and I thought they would die laughing. . . . I was readily recognizable by officer and soldier alike, so I really don't know if the laughter was genuine or just patronizing. I would like to think the former.

On some evenings, under the palms, we would be serenaded by several Korean musicians playing violins and harmonicas. What contrasts would whirl through your days and evenings: air strikes and movies; ambushes and beer call; mortar attacks and classical music; C-rations and dirt and white tablecloths and china. I really liked it in the sticks. However, the artillery fire at night was a constant reminder that the VC were out there. In spite of the numerous sweeps and ambushes run by the ROKs, it was still thick VC country.

Gagnon and I were completing two straight weeks in the field. By this time the DASC had taken a liking to us because we were the only TACP in the area around Phu Cat. The next combat location was the 1st Cavalry Brigade 20 miles north by Bong Son. By our presence, the Air Force briefers at Nha Trang, the corps headquarters, could demonstrate to the Army that they had full coverage of the area. Every morning the DASC would call us for a weather and combat situation briefing. The Army reporting network was rather cumbersome, first going through Korean channels and then into the U.S. Army channels. Timeliness of information and streamlining communication channels were lessons that I later applied in my international business career. But it was time for a break, to come out of the field for a day.

On a Sunday, Gagnon and I drove south to Tiger Town. I took the opportunity to attend Mass and to fly a visual reconnaissance mission over the area where I had been on the ground. I never realized there were so many enemy trenches, spiderholes, and foxholes surrounding our area. Now I was really worried. The division ALO told me that DASC Alpha wanted more preplanned air strikes. It appeared that the pencilpushers were getting their act together and realized that the most efficient use of tactical bombers was a coordinated and prioritized attack plan with the Army;

something I had been doing right along with the 3rd Battalion. There were a couple of targets that Captains Kwong and Lee and I had been saving.

While I was praying, flying, and coordinating in Tiger Town, Gagnon was drinking, reveling, and debauching in Qui Nhon. While we had been in Phu Cat chasing VC, his compatriot ROMADs had been in Qui Nhon chasing bar girls. He tried to make up for two weeks lost time in one day. Who could blame him? Maybe I was envious. At least he remembered to buy the radio for Sgt. Hung. I poured him into the jeep and I drove at max speed to Phu Cat. Darkness was approaching and I didn't care to meet my VC friends again. The cease-fire had ended days ago.

I had the blackout headlamps on when I turned off Highway 1 at the entrance to the battalion area. Night security had been set. The sentries were in their sandbagged posts, the Browning automatic rifle draped across the top, the tripod hanging in mid-air. They recognized me—I was wearing my Aussie hat—and waved us through. That was lucky. I didn't even know the password, let alone how to pronounce it. I pulled up to our tent. Sgt. Hung was waiting for us. I suspected he knew that we had his radio. He was as pleased as a small child with his first Christmas toy. We tried to make a gift of it, but he insisted on paying. The price tag said 17 dollars; we charged him six. We told him that the 17 dollars as the price in MPC, military payment currency. He paid us in U.S. green.

On Monday morning, March 7, we submitted a preplanned request for two flights of four aircraft each of A–1Es at 1500 and 1700 hours for the next day. The target was a VC village, along with the booby traps and bunkers that were protecting the village. The VC had been using this village as a staging area to harass the ROKs and the 1st Cav base camp. We were out to get even.

The DASC approved and confirmed the requests on Tuesday morning. After transmitting the usual weather report, I asked over the HF net, "Ragged Scooper, this is Ragged Scooper seven-four, what do you have on my requests?"

"Ragged Scooper seven-four, we've got your mission information for you. Are you ready to copy?" Bet your sweet ass we were! This data usually came via an overnight telex message or a secure radio circuit, but the HF voice was all we had in the boondocks. Gagnon was ready, pencil poised.

"Go. Ready to copy," I replied.

"We've got several flights for you starting at 1530 hours through 1830 hours." The message was lengthy and we furiously scribbled down the information. They gave us the call sign, mission number, number and type aircraft, time on target, and strike frequency for each strike flight. The TACC in Saigon had allocated us three flights of two A–1Es each, to be followed by a flight of four Navy A–4Ds, and finally three Air Force F–4Cs.

"Roger, copy all. Confirm one-three sorties?" I asked. We had requested eight.

"That's a charley-charley," they replied, using the radio shorthand for "correct, correct."

I was absolutely elated and ran to the TOC to locate Captain Lee. He was in the corner reviewing a clipboard of messages. "Captain Lee," I said, "we've got a live one. We've got more than what we asked for. Thirteen sorties." I gave him the additional details. He summoned one of the other officers and we walked to the operations map mounted on an easel stand in the corner of the tent. He plotted the coordinates, pointed to a hill a klick west of the targeted village, and gave an order in Korean to the other officer. He turned to me, nodded his head and said simply, "Right, John."

Suddenly the TOC was abuzz with activity. The battalion staff went to work. Field phones whirred and rang, orders were barked. Radio traffic blared in a language I couldn't understand, except I recognized the occasional word *FAC*. Jeeps arrived outside the tent. Some of the toughest-looking junior officers and senior NCOs, all wearing full combat gear, assembled in the adjacent briefing tent. Capt. Lee stood in front of them and, referring to a map, presented the concept of operations. Not an eyeball waivered. Maps were marked; frequencies and call signs were scribbled in pocket notebooks. The briefing was dismissed as rapidly as it was convened. These guys had their act together.

Captain Lee said, "Okay, John, we're ready to move out in six-zero minutes." The strike force convoy was formed in the battalion area: a platoon of infantry loaded into deuce-and-a-halfs; a weapons squad with a mounted machine gun and a recoilless rifle piled into jeeps; the force commander's radio jeep; artillery forward observer's radio jeep; and my Air Force radio jeep. We convoyed at tactical spacing up Highway 1, six miles from the battalion HQ.

We dismounted and a squad set up a perimeter defense around the dispersed vehicles. Sgt. Gagnon put up the HF antenna, and I broke out a backpack radio, selecting the PRC–25 FM. I stuffed an extra radio battery in the canvas case. It was the best radio for me to talk to both the Korean command net and also to the airborne FAC, who would be overhead marking the targets with smoke rockets. I had my M–16 rifle, .38 revolver, ammo, canteens of water, fragmentation grenades, and a couple of smoke grenades. I chambered a round into my M–16 and set out across the rice paddies with the Korean soldiers, positioning myself in the middle of the patrol. We started across the tops of the dikes and through the paddies, hiking to an observation post close to the targeted VC village.

I remember watching the soldier's feet in front of me, stepping every place that he did to avoid booby traps. We went through the mud, trying to stay just below the top of the dike where the footing was firmer. At other times we'd get down and wade through the rice paddies. As we approached a hamlet, the platoon leader motioned for me to stay behind while the troops fanned out in a skirmish line and moved forward into the hamlet. The hamlet was tucked into a patch of jungle on the edge of the rice paddies. We didn't take any fire from the hamlet and the troops systematically went through the hooches and checked them out. They signaled for me to come in. It was a primitive hamlet with thatched hooches and a small corral. Various farm animals were in the corral, while chickens scurried around loose. Large pots were suspended over open cooking fires. I watched the ROKs carefully search for weapons caches, but they did not disturb any personal belongings or abuse the peasants. We moved through the hamlet and, a thousand meters on the other side, we started up a steep hill, which was to be our observation post for the air strikes. We reached the top of the hill and I was utterly exhausted. I thought I was in good physical condition, but lugging that radio plus a weapon and gear in that oppressive heat and beating sun had brought me to my knees. A humbling experience. At the top of the hill the Koreans fanned out, performing a quick sweep and security check. Fortunately, there weren't any VC around. I took out my map and compass and oriented myself. We were a half-mile from the targeted village, which was a series of hamlets interconnected by tree-covered paths. There was a river, about ten meters wide, on the northern edge of the hamlets. There were dense clumps of trees surrounding each hamlet and along the river. Rice paddies and heavy grasses filled the open spaces between the hamlets. It looked like a giant chessboard of hamlets and fields.

The platoon commander gave me a pair of binoculars and I carefully noted the visible and potential targets. The entire complex was interspersed with rows of sharpened stakes and 15-foot-long poles that had been driven upright in the open fields and paddies. They were just tall enough to prevent helicopters from landing, smashing the rotor blades as the chopper came to a hover. The VC would usually sow the field with booby traps, mines, and pungi stakes. This prevented the assault troops from jumping or rappeling from the helicopters. As I scanned the tree lines, I could see trenches, redoubts, fortified hooches, and spiderholes, but no movement of troops, peasants, or animals.

Gagnon, back on the road and monitoring the jeep's UHF radio, called me on Fox Mike. "The fighters have just checked in with Ragged Scooper seven-three. It's the Surf flight." I acknowledged his transmission. Let the battle begin!

Ragged Scooper 73 was the airborne FAC. Surf 31 was two American A–1Es. While I had been attending the briefings at the TOC, Gagnon had recontacted the DASC and copied the ordnance loads on a sheet of paper. I removed it from my fatigue shirt pocket. It was soaked in sweat, barely legible. The Surfs carried ten 260-pound fragmentation bombs, six Willie

Petes (WPs or white phosphorous bombs), six 250-pound cans of napalm, two 750-pound cans of napalm, and their 20 Mike Mike cannon. I flashed my mirror up at the O–1 to positively identify our position. He gave me a "Rog" on the radio.

"Okay, seven-three," I transmitted, "Start with the hamlet, first one due east of me about 700 meters or so, and let's see what happens. You've got the Surfs overhead and they're cleared hot." The O–1 dove and fired a smoke rocket into the tree line and the Surfs came diving down right behind it. They started with a couple of cans of napalm each and the entire tree line erupted. I could hear the small arms ammunition that was stored in the trenches and hooches cooking off. As they rolled in on their second pass, automatic weapons fire opened up from the tree line. Apparently we had caught the VC by surprise and hit their open ammo caches. Now they had gotten to their guns and were in the trenches firing at the fighters. Surf kept attacking into the face of the ground fire. They knocked out 23 structures with a 40 percent target coverage.

Right after that, Spad 65, which was a pair of Vietnamese A–1s, checked in on schedule and they had no problem finding the target. I could hear them because they were talking to each other on the Fox Mike radio, as well as to the FAC on the UHF radio. I overheard them say, "Look at all the goddam smoke. We must have a hot one," and "this one looks real." The lead pilot was an American advisor talking to his Vietnamese wingman. I called the Spads on Fox Mike.

"Spad, this is Ragged Scooper seven-four on the ground. Let me flash my mirror." I didn't want to mark my position with a smoke grenade for fear that the VC would pick it up and throw some fire at us.

"We got you," Lead confirmed.

"Okay, west of the burning hooches there is an open field and a tree line. Get in there and see what happens." The Spads had the same bomb load as the Surfs. This time they didn't even get a first bombing pass before all hell broke loose. I could tell from the sound of the automatic weapons that it was .30 caliber, no big guns.

"You're taking ground fire," I advised.

"Rog," replied Lead as he pulled off the target, "I think I took a couple of hits." As they started dropping frag bombs through the tree line and field, the entire ground erupted as the suspected booby traps exploded. There was no longer any element of surprise. The VC kept firing from the trenches under the tree line. By this time, Hobo 81 was circling overhead and eager to join the fray. These were the same Hobos that I flew with when I was in Pleiku.

Ragged Scooper 73, in the O–1, positioned himself in an orbit to the east of the target while I could observe the target from my hillside observation point to the west. We had the VC in a visual trap; no matter where they moved we could spot them and pursue them with the fighters. This was great sport! We had them by the balls—their hearts and minds were sure to follow.

We worked Hobo along the trench line, then the village, and finally along the river. As soon as they dove, the entire tree line opened up once again. I could sit there and watch the smoke from the ground fire drift up through the trees. I looked for the muzzle flashes and pinpointed the gun positions.

"Hobo, you're taking some heavy ground fire from the northern trench." I was close enough that I could hear the unmistakable chatter of the AK–47 assault rifles and the heavier firing of several machine guns. The bursts were getting shorter; we must have hit some of their ammo. Hobo pressed home with the attack. They silenced the ground fire, fragged the trench lines, destroyed three hooches, and set off two secondary explosions when they hit an ammo cache. With their ordnance expended, Hobo got out of there; a job well done. This was no splinter and monkey-killer mission. The wrench turners and metal benders would be busy back at Pleiku patching up those two aircraft.

Now the Navy wanted a piece of the action as Kilo 73 checked in with Scooper 73. They were a flight of four A–4D Skyhawks off a carrier and each one was carrying four 500-pound bombs. I remembered how the FAC at Bong Son had used the bombs to destroy the camouflage when I was in the A–1. Okay Charlie, no more hiding under the trees. We started knocking the trees down with the 500-pounders, exposing the bunkers and trenches. Then they bombed the bunkers and the entire target area was virtually engulfed in smoke and haze. Every time the fighters rolled in they were still getting ground fire from the village and trenches. This was the first time I had worked with the Navy and they did a fine job. My hat's off to the Navy, even though they beat us in football during my Academy days.

Right behind the A–4s we had Hammer 51, a flight of three F–4C Phantoms. They were carrying napalm, bombs, and 20 Mike Mike cannons. The airborne FAC was running low on gas.

"John, I can't stay here much longer," he advised. We still had only one FAC airplane for the entire division. I transmitted to him on my only radio, the FM.

"Alright, get the fighters overhead, let me see how I can work this." There's no way that I was going to turn those fighters back and let the VC off the hook. The Koreans had a small 60mm mortar with them and I asked the commander, while pointing to the mortar, "Do you have any smoke rounds for that mortar?" I then held up a smoke grenade. He got the message. He nodded his head, said something in Korean to his platoon sergeant and the next thing I knew I had a half-dozen smoke rounds lined up on the ground. I had never thought about bringing smoke rounds, but they did—great troops. While I was waiting for Hammer 51 to rendezvous with 73, I had the Koreans fire a couple of smoke rounds from the mortar into the village. Great, that's what I can use to mark the target, I don't need the airborne FAC.

Now I had a communication problem with the F–4s because unlike the A–1s and A–4s, they did not have FM radios, only UHF. I had to transmit on FM from the hillside to my ROMAD at the jeep on the highway, and then he would relay to the fighters on UHF my controlling instructions. As long as I anticipated the delay and gave the corrections fast enough, I thought I could make it work. There was something in our FAC procedures about maintaining direct radio contact with the fighters, but I considered this direct enough. Bend the rules.

The airborne FAC started the fighters to my location. They spotted the jeeps on the highway, Gagnon popped a smoke, and I flashed a mirror at them. They had us. Gagnon relayed my instructions, "The target is 1,000 meters east of the mirror, where some of the fires are still burning. We've been taking heavy ground fire. Your passes will be from south to north with a left break." The Viet Cong had fled the structures and buildings and were into the fortified gun emplacements, trenches, and tree lines. We were now into the third hour of constant air strikes and were all over Charlie. Every time he moved or fired, we hit him. This was open warfare. They had concentrated their forces and they were determined to get a fighter. They still didn't know where I was. I think the Koreans were hoping the VC would locate and attack us because they were looking for a fight. These guys loved the air strikes, but they were hard-core infantry who wanted to mix it up face-to-face.

As I cleared the fighters in, they kept requesting, through my ROMAD, to hit the buildings. The fighters had spent much of their time on boring, tree-busting missions. Now I had buildings and structures for them and they wanted to go after these targets. Some of these structures had red tile roofs. They stuck out through the trees and made a beautiful target in a gun sight. That wasn't where the Viet Cong were; we kept hitting the tree lines. As the ground fire abated, I had the Koreans mark with the mortar a couple of red-roofed structures where we saw the VC carrying weapons and personnel. Maybe some of the personnel were wounded—we couldn't tell from a distance. I thought about the shot-up medevac helicopters and the wounded medic at the base in Phu Cat. Charlie, I can play by your rules. I directed the Phantoms in with their 20mm multi-barreled cannons and watched the roofs disintegrate under the concentrated fire of the HEI rounds. One of the buildings blew apart. It was an ammo cache.

The F–4s knocked out eight structures, took out eight trench lines, damaged four more, and hit a couple of small arms caches and gun emplacements that blew sky-high. They got off the target at 1830 hours; I cleared them home and recognized them for a professional job well done.

We saddled up. The platoon leader came to me and said in halting English,

while pointing to my radio, *"Jung-wi*, we will carry your radio for you."
Eat your pride, Flanagan.

"Kam sa ham ni da—Thanks," I replied.

I was physically and emotionally drained and very grateful for the help.
The soldier picked up the radio was if it were a toy and slung it on his
back. We marched west into the sinking sun. Down the hillside, through
the hamlet and the rice paddies, back to the highway. I hoped that the VC
had not moved in behind us, waiting to ambush us on our way out. As
we slogged those last several hundred meters across the paddies, I saw the
deuce-and-a-halfs coming up the road to pick up the troops. I was happy
to reach the road, exhausted but unscathed.

When we returned to the battalion headquarters, Captain Lee and the
battalion commander were absolutely elated. The Koreans, through their
command net, had relayed the results and we had a big party that night. It
was a long hard day, with risk, but it was also a rewarding day. Sergeant
Gagnon performed admirably in controlling the fighters and I was truly
proud of him. I had a great deal of confidence in the war-fighting capabilities
of the Koreans. We had successfully planned and executed a combined arms
operation. We ended up with over three hours of precision air strikes on
the VC and crippled one of their major staging areas.

Besides the visual results of the air strikes, our district intelligence agents
confirmed that they knew of at least two VC that had been killed and seven
wounded in just one small hamlet of the village complex. They also confirmed we had severely damaged the other hamlets and had either blown
up, or caused the VC to expend, most of their ammo supply. We didn't
lose a single soldier or aircraft, although the sheet metal mechanics were
probably putting some new patches on the planes. I violated some rules,
improvised where necessary, and achieved results. I did my job to the very
best of my ability.

Early the next morning I woke up and started thinking about how I could
turn this tactical victory into a strategic advantage. I came up with the
answer—a psychological warfare broadcast. I remembered a briefing during
my training at Hurlburt on the use of psychological warfare; thus, phase II
of "winning the hearts and minds." First thing Wednesday morning I suggested this concept to the intelligence officer and the civic actions officer.
They concurred. There was nothing in the procedures about requesting a
speaker-equipped bird but I was willing to try. While they drafted the text
of the psy-warfare message, I contacted the DASC and submitted a request
for an immediate psy-warfare aircraft. It amused me because I was asking
for an immediate bombload of bullshit. In fact, we called the psy-warfare
birds "Bullshit Bombers."

Concurrently, I submitted a preplanned strike request to the DASC for
the next day and told them if I didn't get the "speaker" bird to cancel my
strike request. I got the "speaker" bird, a single engine U–10 Courier that

with its STOL capabilities could land on a small airstrip in Phu Cat. It arrived in the early afternoon and we made a tape to the effect that the Koreans were your Oriental brothers, they had successfully defeated the Communists in their country, and would not harm you if you surrendered. If you didn't surrender, we were coming back to rain havoc on you again. It was my intention to alternate between psy-warfare broadcasts and air strikes until we achieved at least one defector under the *Chu Oui* or safe passage program. For an hour, the U–10 broadcast the message, along with Vietnamese funeral music, above the village that we had pounded the day before. The air strike scheduled for the day following the broadcast never materialized because of rain and very low clouds. I resubmitted the request for the next day, trying to stay on the alternating schedule of bombs, bullshit, bombs, bullshit. I was promised the strike aircraft but there was a foul-up someplace in the chain of command and they never materialized. After the air strikes didn't materialize, thereby losing our psychological impact, it appeared that things were winding down for us in Phu Cat.

I took an afternoon off and went into the village of Phu Cat to the district advisory team compound. They were the U.S. Army advisors to the local Vietnamese forces and it was their compound which had been probed the week before. I described our activities, results, and discoveries about the Viet Cong. I also told them about our air strikes and psychological warfare. We had opened the door for them. If they wanted to run an operation, we had pretty well softened it up. I had an honest discussion with some of the senior sergeants and one of the lieutenants on the team. They openly stated they were having a tough time getting anything going. As advisors to the Vietnamese forces, they experienced a lack of discipline, complacency, and careless planning. They suspected the local politicians of venality and nepotism, but defended several junior officers. They described lack of personal hygiene and communal sanitation, leading to contaminated water supplies and foot-long intestinal worms. I shuddered. They had sent one of the villagers to Qui Nhon for surgery. Even though Qui Nhon was the provincial capital and only 20 miles away, the villager had no concept of the city's existence. The advisors were fighting disease and ignorance, as well as the VC.

The advisors thanked me for what we were doing and appreciated the intelligence. Realistically, I felt they were embarrassed by my being there. The Koreans were acceptable, but once a fellow American appeared on the scene, they felt threatened and exposed. They were doing the very best job that they could. On the other hand, they were unable to accomplish much with their Vietnamese military counterparts, whereas, we came into their territory and absolutely kicked ass.

That evening, after dinner, I sat in the sandbagged entrance to my tent and listened to the sounds of the jungle. I reflected on the operation over the last three weeks. Toward the end, the support in the field was marginal:

I had no "Tiger Codes," a form of cryptology, with which I could process requests and information over the radio without compromising security or disclosing information to the VC. I felt that my chain of command had lost interest. I hadn't been in personal touch with my immediate boss, the regiment ALO, or the division ALO, for a week. The last contact was the Sunday when I was at division headquarters and they asked for more pre-planned air strikes. I stole off and started waging my own war with the concurrence of the Korean battalion and the tacit approval of my regiment and division ALOs. I felt that my command structure were saying, "If you're doing a good job, go right ahead and keep at it, but don't bother us. And above all, don't ask us for a decision." My immediate commander had visited me only once in three weeks and that was when he accompanied the ROK regimental commander on a helicopter tour of the battalions.

I recognized that a closely knit unit, given the supporting firepower, could be an extremely effective force in combatting the VC. We did the job. We kept the highway and base camp secure for the First Cav. and launched offensive operations. After three weeks of living in a sandbagged tent and roaming Highway 1 by jeep and foot, it was time to return to Tiger Town. Sgt. Hung brought us our last cup of rice. We gave him some spare batteries. We packed our gear, loaded and hitched the trailer, and said our good-byes.

"*An-nyong hi*, John" from Capt. Kwong.

"*Kam-sa-ham-ni-da, Jung-Wi*" from Captain Lee.

"You're welcome. *Dai-Wi*. Goodbye." I shook their hands. The battalion commander walked over from his tent. I saluted him, he shook my hand, and wished me well. I was sorry to leave the palm trees, the clear nights, and the camaraderie with the Koreans.

The Viet Cong were probably glad to see Sgt. Gagnon and me leave. With the Koreans, we were an effective team. We had invaded Charlie's backyard, bloodied his nose, and knocked him down. We kept our promise. We not only found the war, we made the war. Battles had been won. I had seen the war from the view of the foot soldier and it made me a better FAC. I respected the Koreans as warriors and I felt that I had earned the same from them. I was eager for the next challenge.

5

Clearing the Valley: Koreans Launch Tiger V

My ROMAD skillfully maneuvered the radio jeep and generator trailer between the stanchions defining the entrance to Tiger Town. The Korean sentry snapped to attention, bringing his rifle to the position of "present arms." I returned the salute, jaunty in my broad-brimmed Aussie go-to-hell hat. I felt like a stranger. Tiger Town was our base, but in my six weeks in-country, I had barely spent a week there. I was still without a place I could call home, but the three weeks on Highway 1 with the 3rd Battalion had dispelled my apprehensions of living and working in the jungle and rice paddies.

We drove through the dirt streets of the tent city, stirring the inevitable cloud of dust. It was either dust or mud, nothing in between. The city's population was now composed of several thousand troops. We headed toward the airstrip and the location of our Air Force detachment. We passed groups of soldiers, stripped to the waist, bodies glistened by sweat from the heat and humidity, trenching and crowning the road. Others were erecting poles and stringing wire, while bulldozers and road graders pushed back chunks of elephant grass, bamboo thickets, and dense jungle to be instantly replaced with canvas tents and bamboo hooches. Several white cement structures stood out on the hillside overlooking the camp. They were the quarters of the commanding general, Major General Myung Shin Chae, and his staff. On more than one occasion I noticed lights burning all night. I learned to associate night activity with forthcoming major operations. I hoped the VC weren't equally as observant.

As we swung around the final curve to our area, I saw another group of Koreans practicing Tae Kwon Do, a form of karate. The troops, impervious to the heat, used free moments to perfect their martial arts. We FACs didn't fit. We were from a temperate climate transplanted to the tropics, Caucasians in an Oriental culture, Air Force in an Army environment, and worst of all, pilots stuck on the ground. I had mixed emotions as we pulled into the Air Force mini-compound. I would miss the independence of Phu Cat, but I wanted the excitement of flying. The missions were flown from Tiger Town. We still had only one airplane to support the entire division in spite of the availability of nine pilots. The situation brought to mind the words of President Calvin Coolidge who, when advised that the fledgling Army Signal Corps wished to purchase additional airplanes for the growing pilot corps, asked, "Can't they just take turns flying the one they have?" That's just what we did, Cal, but it was 1966 and war, not the 1920s and peace.

During my absence our tent complex had been improved and made more livable. The radios still extended into the tented annex but their constant squealing and blaring had been dampened. The two general-purpose medium tents, which formed the core of our complex, had been joined tightly together, the gap between them now covered with canvas. This gave the illusion of spaciousness, while empty artillery shell boxes had been stacked at strategic locations creating a series of dividers, some privacy, and much-needed storage space. Someone had confiscated a supply of Mickey Spillane and Richard Prather novels from the USO in Qui Nhon. They were welcome additions to the other assorted paperbacks from the 1950s. A picnic table and gasoline stove defined the kitchen-dining area, and canvas cots were wedged into any available space. Gear was crammed under the cots, while rifles and web gear hung from tent poles. The wood floor had been extended with some additional plywood and split bamboo. Generators supplied power to the radios, a string of lights, and the wonder of wonders, a new refrigerator. At any given time, maybe fourteen people lived here, officers and enlisted men alike. Several others were living in bunkers and tents, five miles west at the cav regiment headquarters. It was the classic "hot bunk" arrangement—bedspace was in such short supply that bunks rarely stayed empty for long.

No matter how comfortable you tried to make the physical accommodations, there was no escaping the heat. The olive drab tents were great heat sinks. We rolled up the sides to allow the heat to escape but this also provided giant entrance ways for the clouds of dust stirred up by passing vehicles and hovering helicopters. Rain always brought welcome relief from the heat and dust, but it also brought mud, floods, and humidity. You could see daylight through the holes in the World War II–vintage tents.

"Welcome home, John," said my boss, looking askance at my non-issue hat. It was illegal by Air Force standards, but provided effective protection against the unyielding tropical sun and the chilling torrential rains. "Grab yourself an empty bunk and stow your gear wherever you find some space. There's some mail for you on the bookcase." Bookcase? No way. They were artillery shell boxes no matter what you called them. My tent at Phu

Cat was lined with similar boxes, except that they were filled with dirt, not books. This was civilization.

"Thanks, sir. Any chance for some flying? I've seen enough of the countryside from the ground. I'd like to see where I've been."

"No problem. You're scheduled for the backseat tomorrow morning on a reconnaissance and FAC mission. Get yourself oriented." That's not what I had in mind, but something was better than nothing. He continued, "And by the way, that hat of yours—it's okay in Phu Cat, but not around here."

"Yes, sir." No sense arguing. He was right.

I flew as scheduled. We directed a flight of A–1 Skyraiders to destroy a cluster of buildings along a river. I couldn't spot any ground fire and we had no secondary explosions. I had doubts about the military value of the target. This wasn't like the targets near Phu Cat from which we took constant ground fire and where the hooches literally blew apart from secondary explosions when we hit them. We recovered at Tiger Town.

I walked to the regimental command post where I had received my initial deployment briefings. Several Korean officers recognized me and introduced me to additional staff. To them, I was 3rd Battalion's FAC and was identified with the Phu Cat operations. They explained to me the purpose of the morning air strike. The Koreans planned to wrest the breadbasket of Binh Dinh Province from the Viet Cong. It was a rice-rich valley and coastal plain of approximately 100 square miles. The southern border of the rice fields was barely five miles north of the city of Qui Nhon and extended for ten miles north to the foot of the Phu Cat mountains. The eastern edge of the valley abutted a bay of the South China Sea. The harvested rice was flowing north by sampan and cart into the mountains. It was the base camp of the VC, and, according to updated intelligence, the NVA operating in Binh Dinh Province. The air strikes were targeted for the hamlets and villages which provided shelter, a labor source, and supply bases for the enemy forces.

For the next ten days we systematically bombed every hamlet and village of any significance in the valley. I flew my first solo combat FAC mission controlling a flight of A–1s from Qui Nhon. In my excitement and nervousness I armed the wrong rocket switch. By the time I corrected my mistake, I not only missed the targeted building but the entire village. Much to my chagrin, the smoke rocket splashed harmlessly into the adjacent river. The fighter jocks immediately seized the opportunity for some fun.

"Roger, Scooper, we have your mark in the river. What were you trying to hit? Fish? Submarines?" said Lead mockingly.

"Try the red-roofed structure closest to my splash," I replied sheepishly.

"Rog," Lead responded, "I'm rolling in on the fish house."

Number Two, his wingman, pursued the opening as he transmitted on the base leg of his bombing run, "Two's in on the submarine pen." I didn't say a word. I was still too embarrassed. I gained confidence as the strike progressed. I tried another rocket, this one hitting much closer to the target, but even that drew their good-natured ribbing. For their bomb damage assessment, BDA, I confirmed 30 hooches destroyed and 15 damaged. Settling into the mission, my nervousness disappeared and I adopted the flavor of the radio chatter.

"Add to your BDA, one fish school dismissed and one submarine pen eradicated." They gave me a Bronx cheer.

We continued the missions, three or four air strikes each day, as we tore the valley apart. The Peoples Liberation Army admonished their soldiers to "be polite with the people and love the people," while I flew at least a mission a day, destroying the people and their homes. This was my in-doctrination to airborne FACing.

On another mission, same target area, two F–100 Super Sabres showed up from Bien Hoa. It was March 16, 1966, the day before St. Patrick's Day. The Buzzards, their call sign, were at maximum fuel range to reach our area. They advised me they were carrying a new weapon, white phosphorous cluster bomb units. I had no idea what they could do, but I now had enough confidence to improvise.

"Buzzard, tell me about these CBUs?" I inquired.

"We don't know. We've never dropped them before. If they're like the others, they're softball-sized and come out in strings, about a thousand meters long. We deliver them level from three-hundred feet." The target on the frag order was a concentrated cluster of buildings, more suitable for hard bombs. Most of the buildings, after I located them, were cement and sun-baked mud and straw. White phosphorous burns and starts fires. Cement and dirt don't burn. The TACC in Saigon had sent an area weapon for a soft target against a point target that wouldn't burn.

"Standby one, Buzzard." I wanted to contact my regimental command post for clearance to change to a more suitable target.

"We can't, FAC. We're already at bingo fuel." The fighters had reached the point where, according to regulations, they had to return home. They were willing to stretch the regulations. So was I. A specific target clearance was good for a radius of 1,000 meters.

In no time, I found a line of thatched hooches, a hamlet, beside a stream. The first hooch was barely within the 1,000-meter radius of the approved target. The Koreans intended to bomb everything in the valley. OK, here goes.

"Buzzard, south to north, right break to the water. One pass, get every-thing off. No friendlies to the north."

"Rog. We got you. We're on downwind. Go ahead and mark." I was already rolling in on the first hooch. I centered the target under the grease-penciled cross hairs on the windshield (still no gunsight for the O–1), and squeezed off a marking rocket. Fortunately, it was one of the big-headed white phosphorous rockets and not one of the puny smoke rockets that was barely visible. I hit the hooch square. The white smoke blossomed above the trees. The smoke cloud measured ten meters across, making a good distance reference. It looked like a mini atomic bomb explosion. The lead fighter rolled in with the untried ordnance.

It was Christmas and the Fourth of July combined. The CBU bomblets exploded like a thousand blinking Christmas tree lights, spreading a blanket of white smoke through the hamlet. It was an instantaneous snow storm; everything was white. Then Fourth of July started. Rockets stored in the open bunkers ignited and arched skyward while others slithered across the ground like a basket of snakes, unleashed. Ammunition caches in the trenches erupted with orange fireballs. Black smoke from burning petroleum mixed with the white phosphorous, hiding the village and turning the sky an ugly gray. The rice straw of the hooches burst into flame, providing a glowing visual reference from above. Number Two turned final on his low-level pass.

"Holy shit! I can't see anything," exclaimed Two, as he entered the billowing and blowing smoke. I saw Lead pull off the target, climb for altitude, and head for the sea.

"Lead's off, Two. Hold your heading and altitude and pickle when you see the fires. You're lined up on the target," I transmitted. He was bombing by instruments at 300 feet and 450 knots. Two disappeared. Finally he emerged, pulled up, and chased Lead to the sea.

"Lead, I'm hurting for gas," he advised. Lead was quick to assess the situation.

"FAC, where can we dump these pods?" asked Lead. The pods, empty of their contents, were excess weight, causing high drag and eating up precious fuel.

"Are you over the bay or the open sea?" The bay was VC territory and I didn't care if they hit some VC sampan. The open sea was Qui Nhon harbor with ocean freighters and lighters. I didn't want to explain CBU pods crashing onto a deck, particularly if a couple of bomblets were hung up in the pods. I'd already stretched the rules by unilaterally changing targets and clearing a fighter pass without visual target acquisition.

"The bay."

"Dump'em." I saw the sun flash off the pods as they tumbled into the bay. I continued the transmission, "Nice work. I'll give you eighteen hooches destroyed, a half-dozen secondary explosions. That was about half of them. I'll come back tomorrow and recount when I can see."

We continued the air strikes in the valley. The TACC, anxious to correct their previous targeting errors, pressed for inordinate descriptions of the hamlets. I described the hamlets, then added, "interspersed with thirty-story skyscrapers of steel and concrete, playgrounds, and subway tracks." I now appreciated the barbed comments from the experienced Vietnamers about the ignorant REMFs (rear-echelon mother f____).

The Buzzards came back on the nineteenth, this time as a flight of three aircraft; two loaded with Willie Pete CBUs, and the third, a photo ship. Buzzard 61 flight made it to Hollywood. These guys were making movies and probably handing out medals and letters of commendation all the way up the chain of command. All I wanted was a tent without holes.

There were light moments between missions and field deployments. We FACs shared the rent for the second floor of a villa in Qui Nhon and rotated between the olive drab canvas of Tiger Town and the white stucco of the villa. Since my French was passable, I became a communicator with the landlord who occupied the ground floor. He was a provincial bureaucrat trained in government administration by the French. He invited us to dinner with his family. They were Catholics and feared the Viet Cong. They knew that if the VC triumphed in the war of liberation, they would be double losers: their property confiscated, their lives taken. They were very hospitable to us. Our rent was a source of income and we represented their future, whether it held life or death.

For some reason, the bars and restaurants were temporarily off-limits, closed to military personnel. Only the military police, on inspection tours, and civilian employees were seen in the night clubs. It wasn't that onerous for us. Our villa was next door to a private brothel that catered to wealthy Vietnamese, French businessmen and officials, and an occasional American. The second floors of our respective villas were connected by a common rooftop and we visited back and forth. During breaks, the girls came over for an American cigarette and brought Vietnamese appetizers from their kitchen. Once they closed their doors to the public for the night, they would invite us to share a late supper with them. The female companionship was a welcome respite to the male world of combat flying. I doubt anyone became involved with our neighbors; they were like sisters to some of us, like daughters to others.

Dave Skartvedt, one of the F–4 fighter pilots from Cam Ranh Bay, spent a couple of weeks flying with us. This was part of the on-going exchange with the fighter jocks. He bounced around the dusty roads in the jeeps and toured the outposts and artillery positions. We treated him to rice, C-rations, and French cuisine. He found the living and social arrangements with our neighbors utterly amazing. I met Dave again in the 1970s when we flew together in the National Guard. I kidded him about how I'd taught him that you could pilot an airplane without wearing a parachute. He recalled how his fellow pilots at Cam Ranh wouldn't believe his tale that the Tiger Division FACs had a brothel next door to their villa. It was virtually every man's fantasy come true.

We had other interesting visitors. A researcher from the Rand Corporation, the Air Force think tank, flew some missions with us. His job was to determine why we were losing so many FACs. He would only admit it was in excess of 20 percent; the exact number was classified. I thought it would be useful to know what the odds were for my finishing my tour alive. He did disclose that some VC prisoners revealed there was a premium on FACs; we were not the best-liked people. Tell me something I didn't know. The VC knew all about me when I encountered them during the cease fire in Phu Cat village. For this information the Air Force was paying some civilian contractor big money.

A classmate from the Academy, Scott Fisher, skipped through Qui Nhon airport one day. I spotted him on the ramp while he was waiting for the C–130 Hercules transport he was flying to be unloaded. I offered him a ride in the O–1; I was about to direct an air strike about five miles out of town. His face went pale and he politely declined. He had flown a visual approach within the five-mile airport zone. The air traffic controllers never told him about VC and air strikes. Scottie later became a history professor at the Academy and eventually the air attaché to India.

After an early morning mission I had the rest of the day free. I browsed through the market and bought some hand-painted silk screens depicting typical Vietnamese scenes to send home. I still have them.

I then changed into my bathing suit and headed for the beach. The GIs were frolicking in the sand and surf, drinking beer, and centering their attentions on comrades who were fortunate enough to have Vietnamese girlfriends. Maybe they were bar girls, but to these GIs they were special people who cared for them and helped them forget the real reason they were in Vietnam. It was an opportunity for them to escape the hazards of the jungle and the drudgery of work details.

As I walked down the beach I thought of the many places that same scene was repeated—Cape Cod, Jones Beach, Ocean City, Myrtle Beach, Daytona, Fort Walton, Padre Island, Malibu, Newport, and Waikiki. All represent the common denominators of America's youth: sun, surf, and sex. The GIs deserved their fun; I wanted some, too. I approached a fisherman working on his nets, his junk anchored offshore in the knee-deep water. With rudimentary French and animated gesturing, I explained that I wanted to hire his boat for a sailing excursion. I thought it would be a great escape for some of us to sail to one of the islands off the coast. For a moment I forgot I was in Vietnam. Then, a patrol jeep with a mounted M–60 machine gun and two MPs drove along the beach. They waved as they passed. It had never occurred to me that the islands could be occupied by VC.

Another day, after landing at Qui Nhon from a FAC mission, I walked to the A–1 Skyraider operations tent for a cold soda. There I heard, firsthand, the incredible story of Jump Myers's rescue from the A Shau Valley Special Forces camp. On March 10, 1966, Jump's Skyraider was shot down while he was supporting the camp under attack by NVA troops. He crash-landed on the runway, outside the perimeter of the camp. As the NVA troops were closing in to capture him, one of the other pilots, Bernie Fisher, landed his Skyraider. He snatched Jump from sure capture or death and, amid a hail of gunfire, successfully staggered back into the air. He earned the Medal of Honor. Jump was the Skyraider detachment commander in Qui Nhon, the Surfs. Fate was to play with Jump again.

I had a day off in Qui Nhon. It was Sunday. I found my chino slacks, sport shirt, and loafers wrapped in a rubberized laundry bag crammed under one of the beds in the villa. I thought I would attend one of the Masses offered at the cathedral. Its location was unmistakable; the spires towered over the city. I walked to the church and climbed the steps two at a time, not bothering with the ornate iron railing. I slipped into a back pew, my eyes adjusting to the diffused light. The structure was majestic, Gothic, with high-vaulted ceilings and stained glass windows. It reminded me of the Protestant chapel at West Point, except the stations of the cross lined the walls. There was a refreshing coolness, a comforting serenity. The church was almost full, over 2,000 worshipers. The Mass began; I was startled by the unexpected high-pitched voices singing Latin. I was more accustomed to the deep Gregorian chant of the Western Church. At the solemn moments, I could hear artillery fire in the background and the hearty throb of the Skyraider engines as they lumbered into the air on yet another bombing mission. I prayed: "Dear God, do we have to launch these machines of death in order to preserve the world from atheistic Communism? Is this what You intended?" The bells tinkled from the altar. I recognized the Latin of the Consecration. "*Hoc est enim Corpus meum . . .* for this is my Body," prayed the celebrant.

I thought about the villages and hamlets I had destroyed in the last week. How many innocent civilians had I killed or caused to be killed? What was innocence? Do civilians really exist in this war? Did I have the right to judge where those bombs were going or was I just doing my duty? The Academy never told me about the morality of wars of liberation. We were warriors sworn to defend the Constitution. But here, in Vietnam?

The bells tinkled again. It was time for Communion. The priest turned, faced the congregation, and holding a Sacred Host aloft, intoned, "*Ecce Agnus Dei . . .* Behold the Lamb of God." I rose from my pew, and towering over the Vietnamese communicants, approached the altar rail. I knelt. The priest, standing in front of me and with a host between his thumb and forefinger, uttered the centuries old petition, "*Corpus Domini nostri Jesu Christi custodiat animam tuam in vitam aeternam . . .* May the Body of our Lord Jesus Christ preserve your soul to life everlasting. Amen." I extended my tongue to receive the host, the same tongue which only hours before had verbalized instructions to bring tons of bombs on a village, committing its inhabitants to the life hereafter.

I fled down the aisle, the dry host sticking to the roof of my mouth. I stumbled into the vestibule, clutching a stone column to steady myself. I began to perspire heavily. The stone was cool. I forced the host down my throat. My mind was confused. I was woozy. Was this a malaria attack? Had I been in the field too long? I couldn't concentrate. The closing words of the Communion verse drifted from the inner sanctuary. Escape! I pushed the outer doors open. I wavered on the steps, blinded by the sunlight. I grabbed at the railing. *Boom*! A howitzer fired in the distance and echoed from the mountain. Madness. Impatient parishioners filed from the church accompanied by the discordant sound of the Vietnamese recessional hymn. I clung to the railing.

A young seminarian, lifting the skirt of his cassock, climbed the steps and hesitantly approached me. He saw my discomfort and offered a handkerchief for my sweat-covered brow. I accepted it, thinking how Veronica wiped the face of Jesus. But I was an Antichrist—was this more madness? The seminarian talked to me quietly. I stammered an incoherent response, unable to concentrate. The dizziness passed and gradually I began to feel better. We conversed, lapsing between English and French. I welcomed the diversion. His family had fled the North and the persecution of the Communists. He liked the Americans. After we talked some more we exchanged addresses and said our good-byes.

As I walked away, I wondered where he came from. Was this God's way of consoling my troubled conscience? Was this political war a modern Crusade? The seminarian and I shared our thoughts in letters over the next several months.

The missions continued as we systematically destroyed the structures and bunkers in the valley. However, we were having flying problems. The upper command structure, probably Pentagon level, determined that all the aircraft in Southeast Asia should have a camouflage paint scheme. The logic was valid. This would make the aircraft more difficult to be seen by enemy gunners. But now the fighters couldn't see us. Gone was the silvery silhouette of the little O–1 skimming across the verdant jungle, yellow-green rice paddies, and brown rivers. Instead the fighters searched for a moving clump of bushes that looked like an O–1. Our best tactic was to silhouette ourselves over a body of water until the fighters picked us up. But there wasn't much open water in the mountains of I and II Corps. We were losing valuable time and the element of surprise. The VC had sufficient warning to either hide in their underground fortifications or occupy their gun positions, while we milled around trying to rendezvous with the fighters. Once the air strike was underway, the fighters had trouble keeping us in sight as they dove on the target. The stage was set for a mid-air collision. We had a couple of close calls, particularly with the jets because of their large turning radius.

Several of us went to the division ALO, our boss, the next time we were in Tiger Town. A senior captain was our spokesman. He was coming up for promotion and his next effectiveness rating could make or break his career.

"Sir, these camouflage paint schemes are dangerous and are wasting valuable rendezvous time. We need to do something," he said.

"Captain, that is the official paint scheme of the Air Force. We cannot change it," replied the major.

"Well sir, couldn't we put a white or silver stripe down the top of the wing, from wingtip to wingtip?" the captain suggested.

"No." Another FAC tried with the same negative result. My frustration was building. I tried.

"How about a band around the wing or the fuselage? Anything to break up the camouflage pattern."

"No. And that's final. We have a big operation coming up. We're moving some locations around. I'll keep you posted. That's all."

Now what do we do? I almost had a mid-air the previous day with a B–57 when even they lost sight of me. They had two sets of eyes, a pilot and a navigator, in the cockpit. Once out of earshot of the major, I turned to my fellow pilots and said, "I'll be in Qui Nhon tonight. I'll scrounge up some white, yellow, or silver paint. We'll paint the whole top of the goddamn wing the next time the plane stays overnight in Qui Nhon. I'll do it. I don't have anything to lose. He'll probably guess I did it. What's he going to do? Send me back to the field?" They shook their heads and walked away.

The next day we received a replacement airplane from the field maintenance depot in Nha Trang. It was camouflaged, but it also had a highly visible red stripe on the upper surface of the wing. Now we could go back to war—safely.

Tiger V was announced on March 22, 1966. It was a full-scale attack using the resources of both Korean regiments. The objective was unchanged, to seize and occupy the major rice-growing region of Binh Dinh Province. D-day was March 23. This was the major operation to which our division ALO had alluded. Although the operation came as no surprise, we still didn't receive much official warning. At least I knew the area; we had been bombing it for the past ten days.

I was to deploy to the division forward command post, or in Army terms, the "jump TOC." All combat operations would be channeled through the jump TOC. I was the acting division ALO and was pleased with the temporary appointment and position of responsibility. I was a first lieutenant functioning at the highest command level for one of the major operations of the war. Major Hong, the G–3 Air, was my contact with the division. I was in an awkward command position because the American ALOs at the regiment and battalion levels outranked me, as did the Korean G–3 officers. The Korean Army had been trained by the U.S. Army and, consequently, was very rank-conscious. However, I had two enlisted ROMADs, two radio jeeps, the partial services of Major Hong's batman, and I could wear my Aussie hat.

My ROMADs and I departed Tiger Town in mid-afternoon and were settled into our forward position before nightfall. Fortunately all our radios checked out; we were at the hub of the Tactical Air Control net. The Koreans had provided us with two-man umbrella tents. I had one to myself. No holes. Happiness was a tent without holes.

I was awake by 5 A.M. It was D-Day for Tiger V. There was a damp chill in the air. I pulled on my jungle boots and staggered to the perimeter of the CP complex to relieve myself. The Koreans were already bustling about, rays of light crept from under the tent flaps of the TOC. I entered.

"*Annyunhasimnikka, Jung-wi.* Would you like some coffee?" asked the assistant G–3 Air, a youngish looking captain.

"*Komapssimnita, Dai-wi,*" I replied. A cup of coffee appeared instantly. Major Hong's batman was at the ready.

"We will start with an artillery barrage to be followed by air strikes," said the captain. He handed me a sheaf of papers clipped to a board. It was the schedule of air strikes, fortunately written in English. They had been passed down from the DASC through Army channels during the night.

"Who else has these?" I inquired. "The regiments? The battalions?" I had to think big picture now.

"We don't know. We'll find out," the assistant G–3 responded.

I walked to the operations map that was mounted on a four-by-eight-foot plywood board. It depicted the entire valley and the forthcoming attack. During the night the staffers had plotted the order of battle. The 1st Regiment, my parent organization, was now on-line along the southern perimeter of the valley. They had moved into position during the night and would attack to the north. It was to be an infantry assault. Elements of the cav regiment had formed a blocking force along the western perimeter parallel to Highway 1. A full battalion, three maneuver companies, was to be inserted in pockets along the northern perimeter of the valley. Two of the companies were going in by helicopter assault, the third was moving by truck eastward from Highway 1.

It was a classic double envelopment with a blocking force. The forces were deployed in a horseshoe, with the open end to the east. I recognized the deployment from my classes in military studies. This time, however, technology was to play a role. One of the envelopments was in the third dimension—air assault. We were rewriting the principles of tactics using helicopters. The only possible avenue of escape for the VC was to the east and that was bordered by tidal rivers. The FACs and helicopter gunships were to patrol the rivers and attack any fleeing troops. It was free fire; if anything moved, kill it.

I looked at the order of battle and concept of operations. It was good, but there was one flaw. The air assault companies, the battalion from the cav regiment, would have their backs to the Phu Cat mountains. That was all VC and NVA. I knew it because we had chased some of them in there when I deployed with the 3rd Battalion. The Koreans could be hit from both sides.

"Lieutenant, we don't know if the subordinate units have the schedule of air strikes," said the captain. I glanced at the schedule. The first fighter TOT, time on target, was 0630 hours. There were seven flights, comprised of B–57s, F–4s, and F–100s, Canberras, Phantoms, and Super Sabers respectively. It was now 0530.

Boom! Kaboom! Boom! I raced out of the TOC. The first hint of dawn was creeping over the horizon. We were on a hillside facing north, overlooking the valley. I could also see to the east, toward the South China Sea. A four-foot muzzle flash appeared from nowhere. *Kaboom!* My chest shook from the concussion. The artillery barrage had begun. We were 50 meters from a 105mm howitzer battery and 75 meters from a 155mm battery. They were under camouflage nets and I never saw them when we pulled into the command post the previous twilight. More flashes against the sky. I could hear shells whistling overhead and a distant rumble. There was an eight-inch gun someplace in the vicinity. I was no longer sitting in a lecture hall at the Academy watching combat movies from World War II and Korea. I was in the middle of war and on the ground.

The crash of the artillery woke my ROMADs. They hastily emerged from their tent, startled, befuddled, half-dressed, their boots unlaced. They saw me.

"Lieutenant, what's up? What's happening?" they cried. They had probably enlisted in the Air Force to escape being drafted into the Army and now they were in the middle of an outgoing artillery barrage. I didn't have time to explain.

"Get on the air. Fast. Transmit this fighter data to everyone on the net," I ordered. I thrust the sheaf of papers at them. I may have been duplicating the communications channels, but now everyone would have the complete picture. "Let me know when you're finished." I would then explain to them what was happening. If our CP got hit and I was taken out, they would have to pick up the command and control responsibility. I reentered the TOC. Everything seemed to be on schedule. I returned to the radio jeep. The ROMADs had completed their transmission. There was a temporary lull. I updated them on what was happening.

"Ragged Scooper seven-zero, this is Yellow Bird six-one," crackled over the UHF radio. The lull was broken. It was the first flight of fighters checking in. The Yellow Birds were the B–57 Canberra light bombers based at Da Nang. I checked the schedule and target coordinates. They were to support the helicopter assault. I keyed the mike.

"Roger, Yellow Bird, your airborne FAC is Ragged Scooper seven-five. Contact him on three-one-eight-point-one; if no contact, return this frequency."

I turned to one of the ROMADs. "Start the other jeep. Bring the radios on the net. I want you to monitor all the hand-offs to the secondary frequencies. That way we'll know if the fighters are matched with the proper controlling FAC." The fighters were scheduled so tightly that any mistake would back up the entire operation. The artillery ceased firing. My head ceased pounding. I glanced at my watch. It was 0630. Boar 11, a flight of four F–4Cs, checked in. I handed them off to the Baron FAC. The sector FACs were helping us since we had only one Bird Dog and we couldn't cover all the air strikes. In they came: Yellow Bird 75 and 85, flights of two B–57s each; Demon 11 and 41, three F–4Cs each; then three F–100s, Dice 11. In two hours we had directed nineteen sorties on helicopter landing zones, trenches, and villages in direct support of the attacking Korean forces. The Korean commanders ensured their troops would have the maximum amount of fire support. It was one of the highest concentrations of air power on specific targets in South Vietnam. March 23, 1966, was our show.

We diverted Yellow Bird 75 from their original target to hit a machine gun and mortar position in the mountains. My suspicions were confirmed. The VC were in the Phu Cats and could take the cavalry regiment under fire on two fronts. At 1040 hours we received a request for immediate air support. The troops were unable to take a village. The request was submitted to DASC Alpha and we had a flight of three F–4Cs, Pogo 01, overhead within 20 minutes. However, our coordination channels broke down, exacerbated by the language problem, and the Korean troops never withdrew far enough to safely execute an air strike. We diverted the Pogos to a secondary target.

My ROMADs were literally working their tails off to keep up with the radio traffic. They were trying to monitor and record every message, every transmission, in their logs. It was impossible. With all four nets going nonstop, the volume was overwhelming, but I thought I'd let them try their best. The sun had climbed high, the temperature was over 90 degrees, and it was even hotter working in the jeeps and under the camouflage nets. They ducked into the open air whenever there was a lull. I noticed they had removed their fatigue shirts and were working in their white Air Force–issue T-shirts.

"Sarge," I said, "either put on your fatigue shirts or take off your T-shirts. And don't get sunburned." They thought I was being a real hardass because they were in their preferred work uniform, which was alright in the rear area, but not at a combat outpost. I knew those white T-shirts were visible for miles.

"Yessir, Lieutenant." They were pissed, but removed their T-shirts and put on their fatigue shirts. A compromise. The shirts became dark from sweat within minutes.

In late afternoon another ROK company was assaulting a village without success. They were stalemated and requested immediate air support. My ROMAD processed the request to the DASC. It was disapproved. I suspected a problem of command rather than nonavailability of fighters. I picked up the high-frequency radio mike.

"Ragged Scooper, this is Ragged Scooper seven-four. Please advise status of last request from seven-zero." I used my personal call sign rather than the division CP call sign.

"Be advised your seven-zero request was denied," was their response. Major Hong, who spoke excellent English, was listening to the conversation over the speaker. As the G–3 Air, he was being pressured from his command to obtain the air strike for the infantry so they could secure the objective before nightfall.

"Ragged Scooper, I need that request approved ASAP. The attack is stalled and nightfall is approaching."

"Wait one," was the DASC's response. I was running out of patience. I had been working 13 hours straight in the heat and humidity and under high stress. They came back with, "The duty officer wants to know if you'll really use them this time." Bullshit! They were apparently disturbed about the diversion of the Pogo flight in the morning. I lost my cool.

"This is seven-four. You're goddam right I'll use them. Stop jerking me around and get me some fighters." I was prepared to hitch a helicopter ride to the front lines and direct the strike myself from the company commander's location.

"Roger, your fighters are Spad zero-one, flight of two A–1s. Rendezvous is Quebec on primary strike freq. How copy?" The tone was professional; they were trying to be nice guys now.

"Copy all. Thanks," I responded.

Spad 01 flight arrived over Qui Nhon at 1815 hours with 28 100-pound bombs and 1600 rounds of 20mm cannon ammunition. The controlling FAC worked the flight for 55 minutes, virtually leveling the village and setting off five secondary explosions at coordinates CR028385. No wonder the VC wanted to retain control of the village. It was a major ammo dump. I watched the Skyraiders climb into the twilight and disappear into the last light on the eastern horizon. Their mission was complete. Mine wasn't. I had to finalize the air support for the next day with the battle staff.

I filled my canteen cup with some rice from the small mess tent. I didn't recognize any of the other Korean fare; I opened a C-ration can of turkey loaf and stirred it into the rice. I joined my ROMADs at one of the radio jeeps. They still had the other one operating as a spare. I told them it was OK to shut it down. They had rigged a shielded light in order to see their radio logs. Nightfall comes quickly in the tropics. They were transmitting the results of the last air strike to the DASC.

"Did you get any chow?" I asked as I wolfed down my supper. I had eaten a can of peaches for lunch.

"Yes, sir. We heated some C-rats on the muffler of the generator. We weren't too sure about the Korean chow. It looked like worms and eye-balls." In the red glow from the radio dials, they appeared much older than the 19 and 22 that they were. No one stayed young for long in Vietnam.

"OK. Swap the generator to a full can of gas and bring your radio logs and paper work to my tent." I walked toward my tent.

God, it was dark. I was thankful for the small amount of light that a distant flare cast over our camp. We were in total blackout with strict adherence to light discipline. We weren't looking for the VC to loft some mortar rounds or RPGs, rocket propelled grenades, into the command post. I heard the staccato of an automatic weapon. I didn't recognize the sound, but I noticed some of the ROKs carrying the old Browning automatic rifle, World War II vintage. I watched the tracers scoot across the rice paddies. Away from us. I found my tent and when I pulled the entrance open, I was welcomed by the cheerie glow from a gasoline lantern. My shared batman had readied my tent for night. I tossed my gunbelt and M–16 on the end of the cot.

The ROMADs arrived shortly, groping their way through the double flaps, their eyes adjusting to the white light of the lantern. They sat on the empty cot opposite mine. They had washed the grime from their faces, but their hair was still caked and reddish from dirt blown around by the vehicles and helicopters. The knotted handkerchiefs around their necks were soaked with sweat, their arms and faces sunburned. They kept their weapons handy and clean. Even though it was their first day in the field, they looked and acted like seasoned infantry, not radio operators in the Air Force. I was proud of them.

I pulled three Cokes from my flyers' kit bag. They thought I was a magician. My living with the 3rd Battalion in the field taught me that you acquire and hoard canned sodas at every opportunity. They gratefully accepted two of them and watched as I poured some Coke into my canteen cup and added an equal amount of water. I anticipated their question.

"Makes it last longer. Besides, I hate the water. Tastes like chlorine one day, iodine the next," I said. I extended my hand and they gave me the logs. I thumbed through them. "Can you give me a summary of the day's air operations? Just Tac Air," I asked. I handed the logs back.

"Yes, sir. But it'll take us a few minutes." They spread the papers on the cot and began copying information on a clean pad. They tallied up the numbers. "What we have, Lieutenant, is nine flights of fighters, total of twenty-four sorties. We missed the line-ups and BDAs for a bunch of them. They went to another frequency. We do have thirty-three hooches destroyed, nine damaged, five secondary explosions, and confirmed body count of two KBA."

"OK. That's fine," I said. I showed them how to set up a matrix to keep track of the sorties and results. "Try this. It should be easier. I don't need all the other radio traffic. Just keep track of the air requests and the results. Who's taking the first radio shift? If you have trouble staying awake come get me. Thanks for the good job."

"I'll take the first shift," replied the NCO.

"And try to find some olive-drab handkerchiefs," I instructed. "A sniper can pick those white ones out at five hundred meters," I warned. "I don't want to lose you guys." They unconsciously reached to their necks, sliding their fingers under the folded cloth. Now they understood why I made them cover up their T-shirts. They hadn't thought of that. Something else I had learned with 3rd Battalion in the bush.

"Thanks, Lieutenant," said the two-striper as he ducked out of the tent. I followed them out, waited for my eyes to adjust to the darkness, and headed to the TOC. I looked at the operations map. All the objectives had been reached. Surprise, helicopter mobility, firepower, and sheer determination by the Koreans had carried the day. We would rely on immediate air requests for the next day. I dragged myself back to the tent. Collapsing on my cot, I wondered what the VC had in store for us. I never took my boots off. I never heard the artillery fire. Day one was over.

Once I slept through the initial stages of exhaustion, I tossed and turned on the cot. It wasn't even 5 A.M. I thought about the air strikes on the previous day. I was impressed by the British-designed Canberras. The crews always located the target with a minimum of instructions, the aircraft carried a heavy load of bombs and napalm, had plenty of fuel to stay in the battle or hold overhead, and had machine guns and cannons. They were superb.

★   ★   ★   ★   ★

In 1988 I was talking to an Annapolis graduate who mentioned he had been a navigator in B–57s during the Vietnam era. He put me in touch with Ken "Slippery" Eells, a Canberra pilot from the same era. I called him on October 22, 1988.

"Slippery, Bill Palafox says hello, and he says you still couldn't find your ass with both hands without the help of a navigator. Tell me about the B–57s. Were you a Yellow Bird or a Red Bird?" I asked.

"Yellow Bird, 8th Tactical Bomb Squadron. The Red Birds were the 13th," he replied. "Why do you want to know?"

"I was a FAC in 1966. I worked a lot of Red Birds and Yellow Birds."

"I was in-country in 1966," he replied. "We were staging from the Philippines, spent sixty days at a time in Vietnam alternating with the other squadron. Wait a second. I have some notes. Let me get them." Pause. "Found them. What else do you want to know?"

"Slippery, where were you in March?"

"In Vietnam. Da Nang."

I looked at my notes, yellowing with age. "How about March twenty-third, a Wednesday?" I asked. "Did you fly?" I held my breath.

"Yeah, I flew that day. My notes say something about supporting Tiger V near Qui Nhon. My call sign for that mission was Yellow Bird eight-five." Silence. "John, you still there?" he asked. I swallowed. The lump stayed in my throat. I was relieved he could not see the tears welling in my eyes. So many fallen, so few left—another warrior found. I lapsed into the FAC jargon of 22 years ago.

"Roger, Yellow Bird, this is Ragged Scooper seven-four. I have you overhead. I'll be handing you off to your airborne FAC momentarily. What's your line-up and how—?" I was about to ask his fuel endurance, but Ken cut me off.

"You were the FAC!" he exclaimed over the telephone. "I remember it now. It was unusual to talk to a ground FAC. We usually contacted the airborne FAC immediately."

"Ken, for that mission, on the twenty-third, you only had half a bomb load, right?" I asked.

"That's right. We were even short of hundred-pounders." We talked for almost an hour.

"Ken, let me ask you one final question. Was it worth it?" He hesitated for a moment.

"At the time, I thought so, but we were led astray. John, we were duped. I remember all those night missions, working under our own flares, over the paddies, but that wasn't so bad. It was in the hills and karsts over the trail that was scary. Planes shot up, aircrews lost. We did our best, but it wasn't worth it. I wanted to win, but the politicians didn't want to win, so we got killed needlessly.

"Thanks, Ken. Anything else?"

"Say hello to Palafox for me; and, as I remember, I had to lead him around constantly. See you." *Click.* Twenty-two years had gone by; the camaraderie of warriors still existed.

★ ★ ★ ★ ★

Boom! Boom! Boom! I was snapped from my reverie. I peeked outside the tent. It was still dark; a hinting glow of light hugged the eastern horizon. The artillery had commenced a fire mission. We were still at war. Tiger V. Day two. My ROMADs were stirring, checking gas cans for the generators. They spotted me.

"It was quiet all night, sir. No traffic," the NCO said. This bothered me. I couldn't believe that such a concentration of VC would not probe the outposts. Activity was bound to pick up. The ROMADs were expecting a response. I was supposedly the expert on field operations. They were anxious and I didn't blame them; this was their first field deployment.

"Let's just wait and see. Let me talk to the Koreans," I said. I walked to the TOC and looked at the intelligence plots. The assistant G–2 gave me an update. Some night patrols had picked up VC concentrations near the Phu Cat mountains. An ambush had caught a VC squad moving along a trail. There was no doubt. The Cong were out there, repositioning and consolidating their forces, ready to counterattack or repulse the sweeping Korean forces.

In mid-afternoon all hell broke loose. The friendlies were pinned down in a mountain pass at coordinates CR038471—the Phu Cats. They had run into one of the VC concentrations. Division Artillery directed over 100 rounds of 155mm and 8-inch artillery, the biggest they had, to relieve the infantry. It didn't help. They wanted air support. We obtained a flight of three A–1H Skyraiders, Kilo 21, flown by Vietnamese pilots. They carried 500-pound bombs and 260-pound fragmentation clusters with daisy cutters. The conventional bombs blew the VC from their trenches and when they tried to flee, they were annihilated by the daisy cutters. The daisy cutters derived their name from their lethal shrapnel pattern. The frag clusters had six-foot pipes with contact fuses extending from their noses, which guaranteed an aboveground dispersion of the shrapnel. The enemy was literally cut down as if they were a field of daisies. The friendlies safely disengaged from the superior Viet Cong force. It was a classic battle of international cooperation: Korean infantry, American FACs, and Vietnamese fighter pilots.

March 24–25 (Night)—ROK troops on northern perimeter under night attack by reinforced company of VC troops. VC used civilian noncombatants as shields. Requested flare ships. Target coordinates CR045440.

Flare ships on station from 2130 hours until 0600; dropped over 250 flares. Call signs: Moonshine 51 and 52, Spooky 61, and Smokey Bear. FACs: Ragged Scooper 79 and 74. Attack repulsed.

It was a dark but clear night. Activity had slowed in the TOC; the tent flaps were seldom opened by people exiting or entering. My ROMADs and I sat on the hillside observing the occasional flare and monitoring our radios. It was quiet. No artillery, no machines guns, only the background rush from the four radios. The squelch was off; we didn't want to miss any transmissions. Suddenly, there was a flurry of parachute flares to the north. They were low on the horizon. I remarked to the ROMADs that they were probably hand-launched. This was followed shortly by an urgent radio call on the FM net.

"Ragged Scooper seven-four, this is Ragged Scooper seven-nine on Fox," came the terse voice. They wanted an immediate answer. The junior RO-MAD, the airman, grabbed the handset while the sergeant focused the red-lensed flashlight on the message log and began to record the traffic.

"Seven-nine, this is seven-four Mike. Go," replied the airman. A higher, brighter flare went off in the same vicinity. This one appeared to be launched from a mortar.

"Roger. One of our units is under attack. We can hear the shooting. It's near the flares." This got my attention, but we couldn't tell if the flares were two or five miles from us. I asked the airman to get the coordinates of the attack and any details. Artillery fired two rounds from the battery adjacent to our CP. Two more flares, these yet higher and brighter were illumination rounds. I ran to the TOC, stumbling in the darkness, looking for the fire support coordinator. He would have the coordinates for the fire mission. He didn't speak English. I went outside again, headed for the jeep, tripped and fell. I had lost my night vision in the lights of the TOC. I finally reached the jeep. Still no coordinates from 79. I picked up the handset.

"Seven-nine, seven-four. Give me the direction of the last flares from your location." I knew where 79 was and the flares were north of us.

"Approximately east-northeast," responded 79. Northeast was tangent to the Phu Cats. My NCO ROMAD held the flashlight as I drew two azimuth lines on my map. Oh shit. They intersected at the base of the Phu Cats, the same area where we put the two air strikes earlier in the day. Looked like CR045440 to me. Close enough for government work. I jotted down the coordinates and gave them to the airman. He looked at me, awaiting instructions. More illumination rounds popped open and floated to earth, swinging beneath their parachutes. My heart pounded. This is the way it started when the MACV compound was attacked in Phu Cat village.

"Call the DASC. Request a flare ship ASAP. Tell them to stand by for a possible air strike request. See if the A–1s, the Surfs, from Qui Nhon are available. Keep seven-nine advised of your actions. Keep pumping them for additional info."

I really didn't know what to expect, but suspected we were headed for trouble. The flares were in the heart of Charlie country. The bastards came out of the Phu Cats after dark to counterattack. We needed more candle-power. The Air Force Gooney Birds, relics from World War II, and the C–123 Provider cargo transports, carried big parachute flares, mega-lumens. For the Surfs, this was their backyard. We were only ten miles from down-town Qui Nhon. We could get a FAC airborne from Tiger Town in ten minutes. I thought I had all the bases covered. I was summoned to the TOC. My ROMADs continued executing my orders.

I was totally unprepared for what I learned in the TOC. First, the Koreans had also requested a flare ship through Army channels. OK, better dupli-cation of effort than no effort at all. Second, the VC were attacking from the Phu Cats. This I expected. *The VC were using civilians as human shields.* This I didn't expect. In the darkness, the Korean troops could not differ-entiate between the VC and the noncombatants. The small flares had been only marginally effective. The ROKs had been instructed to hold their fire.

That explained why we didn't get any updates from 79. The firing had ceased. But now it was critical. The VC were approaching the outer perimeter of the Korean positions. There would be a slaughter; innocent civilians, Korean troops, and, I speculated, a large number of VC. I was shocked, temporarily frozen, but I finally bolted into action. Darkness and caution be damned. I ran to the jeep.

"What info do we have on the flare ships?" I asked the ROMADs.

"Moonshine five-one is on the way, sir. ETA 2130 hours." It was now 2115, 9:15. Fifteen minutes to go. People could die needlessly in the meantime.

"Are they on freq?"

"We had them on Uniform, but lost them."

"Do you have a Fox Mike freq for them?" The FM had unpredictable capabilities, particularly at night. I had to try it. The NCO anticipated my request. He tuned up on the frequency, rotated the antenna selector switch, keyed the mike, and, satisfied that the radio cycled properly, gave me the handset. "Thanks, Sarge." I brought the ROMADs up to date. "The VC are attacking. We're gonna light things up a bit."

"Moonshine five-one, Ragged Scooper seven-four on Fox Mike," I transmitted. The speaker hissed at me, then a message.

"Roger, Scooper. We're on our way. Go ahead." We were in luck. Providence had answered my disjointed prayers in the cathedral. Innocent civilians—an opportunity to make amends.

"Moonshine, we're on the verge of an atrocity. We need help. Fast." I briefed the crew on the developing situation.

"OK, Scooper. We're going to METO power. Hang tough," they replied. I understood what that meant. They were pushing those old reciprocating engines to maximum except take-off power. This could literally tear the engines from the mounts or blow a jug, a cylinder; but, it would shorten the flying time by a few precious minutes.

"Moonshine, when you reach any part of the valley, five miles northwest of Qui Nhon, start dropping flares. Lots of them. We'll direct you from there." I intended to startle the VC; maximum impact, as much confusion as possible. I wanted that valley to look like a mid-summer lightning storm.

"We have a nav on board. Are the coordinates still good?" Moonshine inquired. "We have some small flares in sight. Near a mountain."

"That's it. Keep coming. Can you switch to UHF now? I need this radio to contact the other FAC, seven-nine." I saw the navigation lights to the east and a flare ignited. We swapped radios around, getting the two FACs, myself and 79, on Fox Mike, and all three of us on Uniform. More flares tumbled out, igniting at 3,000 feet, swinging from their parachutes, and gradually drifting across the valley. It was like daylight.

Moonshine held over the attack area. I gave the flare ship east-west corrections while 79 gave north-south corrections from his hillside vantage point. Several Korean officers had gathered around the jeep, watching the light show. After an hour, they told me the attack had stalled, the VC had withdrawn. Several VC had been picked off by sharpshooters. The civilians had been spared. My amends had been made.

We didn't need the Surfs, but we kept flare ships over the area the entire night. They dropped over 250 flares. I showed the ROMADs how to correct for wind drift and delegated control of the four flare ships, two Moonshines, Spooky, and Smokey Bear, to them. I had made them instant FACs. They were elated. I went to bed at 3 A.M. It had been a 22-hour day for me. My ROMADs never slept.

It was 20 years before the Air Force recognized the effectiveness and practicality of an enlisted FAC. We did it in Vietnam in 1966. The ROMADs eagerly accepted the additional responsibility and reveled in the recognition. We didn't pay much attention to conventional thinking.

March 25—Troops made heavy contact in fortified village at 1100 hours. Requested fighters; two A–1s, Hobo 01, and three F–4Cs, Demon 41. Ordnance was napalm, 500-pound bombs, anti-personnel CBUs, and 20mm cannon. Destroyed 50 structures, numerous secondary explosions. Coordinates: CR; 084389, 082397, 082395, 081394, 082409.

March 26—At 2330 hours (25th) Ragged Scooper 79 requested flare ship. Same company as previous night under attack in valley. Smokey Bear on target at 2400 to 0300, dropped 75 flares, VC broke off attack. Also Army flare choppers. Finally got to bed at 2 A.M.

At 1100 hours, DASC Alpha asked if we could use any fighters. Obtained: four F–4Cs, Sharkbait 31, and four F–4Bs, Congo 83. Ordnance was sixteen 750- and sixteen 1,000-pound bombs, respectively. Destroyed caves, foxholes, and structures.

The VC tried their night-time stunt once again, but the Koreans were waiting for them. They outflanked the VC and mowed them down from behind. The Army joined the action with a helicopter flare ship. They didn't want us to steal all the credit for the night-time show.

Our communications and coordination with the Koreans were now functioning smoothly. Even our mail was delivered. I received my first *Wall Street Journal*. When the DASC asked us if we could use some surplus fighters, we had a slew of back-up targets in our hip pockets. Artillery had been trying to knock out a complex of caves, structures, and foxholes at the base of the Phu Cats. Now we had ordnance perfectly suited for the target—big bombs.

This was one of the few times we had Navy birds in our area, the F–4B, Congo 83 flight. They were probably from the carrier positioned about 100 miles east from Cam Ranh, Dixie Station, in the South China Sea. Most of the Navy flying was into North Vietnam from Yankee Station in the

Gulf of Tonkin. We had heard there was a Navy carrier providing temporary support in the South.

I left the NCO ROMAD in charge while the airman and I drove up the highway to observe the airstrike. I had never seen a 1,000-pound bomb dropped, let alone from a Navy bird. We almost lost the strike. The airborne FAC, Ragged Scooper 75, had small smoke rockets, no big Willy Petes, to mark the targets. The Navy F–4s rolled in from outer space and they couldn't see the marks. By the time everything was squared away, they were low on fuel, and resorted to "one pass, haul ass." But they made a big noise. The Air Force F–4s, with their smaller 750-pound bombs, did some damage. My ROMAD was impressed. He would have a story to tell for the rest of his life. That is if we got out of here alive.

The major portion of Tiger V was coming to a close. For the first time we didn't need a flare ship during the night. However, a nearby U.S. Army artillery battery was hit during the night. The Army sentry, instead of using the M–60 machine gun, took potshots with his M–14 rifle at the VC infiltrator. As the GI crawled back to his foxhole, the VC launched a rifle grenade that killed the GI and wounded three others. The battery's S–3, a captain, who related the story to me had been to that location the previous day. There were few foxholes and trenches. He remarked how the American GIs don't like to dig, but they will now.

By late morning, March 27, the attack phase of Tiger V was officially terminated. Operational control of the division was transferred to Tiger Town. Our job was completed. The ROMADs packed the jeeps while I accomplished the required protocol with the staff officers. The ROMADs were tired, but I could sense their pride in a job well done. They had been in the midst of a full-fledged combat operation and in personal danger. They knew the results of the Air Force bombing strikes. I showed them the recapitulation of the infantry assaults compiled by the division G–2 staff.

TIGER V RESULTS

March 23–27, 1966—Binh Dinh Province, RSVN

Enemy Losses

VC killed	379	1 mortar plate
VC POW	6	40 medical packets
VC suspect	798	300 rounds small arms
Caves dest.	205	2 auto rifles
Grenades	136	7 Browning auto rifles
M–1 rifles	6	1 telephone
Carbines	8	1 pistol, 7 magazines
Machine gun	4	1 gas mask

| M–16 | 1 | 16 rounds, 60mm mortar |
| | | 1 lb. TNT |

Friendly Losses

| ROK KIA | 23 | 1 M–1 rifle lost |
| ROK WIA | 66 | |

My two ROMADs and I had been in the field for five straight days with minimal sleep, living on C-rations, rice, and kimchee. Our heads still pounded from the concussion of the artillery batteries. The ROMADs had experienced the tension, excitement, and risks of war. I had been in the field before on a sustained operation, but this was their first deployment; they were no longer "cherry." Now, all we wanted was a cold beer and some uninterrupted sleep. We pulled out of the CP complex and headed down the road. I knew every rut and ambush site between Phu Cat and Tiger Town.

As we approached Tiger Town, I noticed an O–1 turning base at the airstrip, only a half-mile away. Strange, our Division O–1 was parked in its usual tie-down spot. Maybe we were finally getting our second airplane. A slick jeep was headed to the airstrip to pick up the visitor. I really didn't give a damn. I could already taste the cold beer.

My ROMAD pulled the jeep up to the regimental operations' tent. The other jeep was right behind us. We unhooked the trailers and pushed them into their slots. The empty jerry cans were replaced with full ones. Bystanders were gathered in the tent and the sides were rolled up to let the heat escape. The regimental ALO wanted a complete debriefing of the operation.

"Yes, sir," I said as I flung my map on the table and ducked under the supporting pole that connected the two tents. I headed straight for the refrigerator, grabbed three cans of Schlitz and tossed two to my ROMADs. We were a combat team, had worked together, and we punched open our beers together, carelessly spraying the bystanders. We didn't notice that they now included the division ALO, a major; our boss, a captain; and a lieutenant colonel, the visitor in the O–1.

"Colonel Stewart, this is Lieutenant Flanagan," said the major, as the colonel wiped the beer from his flight suit. But he didn't seem to mind. "Colonel Stewart is the DASC Alpha ALO."

"A pleasure, sir," I acknowledged, as I shook his offered hand and then quickly withdrew mine—it was still covered with grease from the trailer hitch. Nice work Flanagan; guess it's back to the field for me.

Stewart began, "The preliminary reports from Tiger V indicate that the efforts were an unqualified success and the commander of 1st Field Forces Vietnam sends his personal congratulations to the entire Air Force contingent for the excellent air support." The major and my boss were absolutely beaming. Stewart continued with additional laudatory comments. I thought I was going to throw up. Where were these guys when I was catching static from the DASC because I had to divert the scrambled Pogo flight to a secondary target? I eased away and got another beer from the fridge, careful not to spray anyone this time. The request for the complete debriefing went by the wayside as the higher ranks hovered around the colonel. It didn't bother me any.

I prowled around the tent and found my mail. I sat on a cot in the corner of the tent, sipping my beer and reading my mail. Colonel Stewart came to me.

"I just heard how you put that flare ship over the VC and stopped their attack when they were using the civilians as a screen. Where did you come up with that idea?" he asked.

"I guessed at it, sir. The Koreans told me they didn't want to shoot at the noncombatants, but they couldn't see who was who. I figured if I could put some light on the scene, the Koreans would know what to do. The flares allowed them to outflank the NVA and pick them off from the sides and behind. I was with these guys on the ground for a month and I knew what they could do, particularly at night. Incidentally sir, those were not VC; they were hard core regulars, NVA. Probably part of the Yellow Star Division that had been hanging out in the Phu Cat mountains. They got their ass kicked by the 1st Cav up at Bong Son."

"How do you know that? It's John, isn't it?" asked Stewart.

"Yes, sir. We captured some local VC when I was at Phu Cat. They squealed on their Communist brothers. Said they were headed for the coastal mountains. They had a base camp in there. Apparently, left over from the Viet Minh days when they were fighting the French."

"How did you find this out? I thought the VC didn't talk."

"Look, sir, the Koreans are Oriental. They think and act like the Vietnamese. Our Western morality just isn't going to hack it when it comes to dealing with the VC. Besides the prisoners, I met these guys during one of the cease-fires. They're smart and they're tough. We bombed the hell out of them and they still kept firing. And they knew I was behind the whole deal. The Koreans understand them and they have ways of extracting information. I wasn't going to interfere."

"OK, John. I understand, but I wasn't quite sure what you were doing up by Phu Cat. Every time we turned around, your call sign was cropping up at the DASC. Ragged Scooper seven-four this and seven-four that. Fighters, recce, psy-warfare, weather reports, spot reports in the middle of the night. Fighter jocks giving debriefings about some FAC on the highway or on a hilltop, flashing mirrors and firing mortars. And then you turn up as the acting division ALO at the forward command post for Tiger V." I could hardly imagine what was coming next. Those two beers on an empty stomach and in the tropical heat were already having their effect. At least the colonel couldn't ask me to fly.

My boss, the regimental ALO, joined us. Colonel Stewart continued, "I was just asking Lieutenant Flanagan if he wanted to go to Tuy Hoa and fly with the 101st Airborne for a few days. They're a bit short-handed down there." No more "John," it was now "Lieutenant Flanagan." What a set-up. Looks like I'm headed down the coast to Tuy Hoa.

"I'm sure he would be glad to help you out, Colonel," replied my boss.

"Well, we'll be in touch with you in the next few days to confirm," said Stewart as he walked to the other side of the tent. I was right, Tuy Hoa and the famous Screaming Eagles of Bastogne. Those guys were nuts.

"John," said my boss in a voice loud enough for Colonel Stewart to hear, "Why don't you gather your gear and stay in the villa for a few days? You can fly some VR missions out of Qui Nhon. We've rigged a portable HF radio to communicate with the villa." Now I was truly suspicious, or someone was having a case of the guilts, which I doubted. However, I welcomed the opportunity to sleep in a real bed, take a hot shower, eat food from a plate, and drink from a glass. I wouldn't miss the noise and concussion of the outgoing artillery either.

I grabbed my gear, my civilian clothes from the bottom of my foot locker, and threw them into a canvas kit bag, large enough to hold an entire packed parachute. I couldn't find my personal survival radio. A disadvantage of being a FAC was the difficulty of traveling light: extra clothes, flying gear, webbed infantry gear, flak vest, rifle, steel helmet, and civilian clothes. I always wanted to be prepared for the next mission of opportunity, particularly a civilian clothes mission. I hopped into the jeep that was headed to town.

On the ride in, I tried to figure out what was going on. Was Stewart really up here to congratulate us, or was he just recruiting warm bodies for the 101st and I was the next sucker? Why did he leave us his airplane and jump on the C–123 shuttle back to Nha Trang? And why did he single me out? Didn't much care. Would be nice to see our female neighbors and share a Saigon tea with them during one of their breaks.

The shower was great and it felt good to put on some clothes other than fatigues. A couple of my fellow FACs had stocked the bar in the villa and our landlord would share ice with us. We didn't have a fridge, which was number one on our trading and self-help list. Two drinks with real gin and off to dinner. The three of us went to the local restaurant where American flyers usually hung out. No steak, but they had some fresh crustaceans that tasted like lobster from Cape Cod. That seemed a million miles away. I hadn't even thought about home or my wife or kids in ages. Some of the Army gunship pilots were at the table next to us. They had flown some support for Tiger V and were full of questions when they found out we were the FACs with the ROKs.

"Where do you find your targets?" they inquired. "We can never seem to find anything worthwhile to go after."

"Look," I said, "the entire Phu Cat mountains are loaded with targets and it's a free-fire zone. Just don't get shot down in there because you'll never be seen again. Are you guys flying tomorrow?"

"Yeah, we have to go at 0600 and another at 1000."

"What's your call sign and what freq can I get you on? I have all sorts of stuff circled on my map that the Koreans asked me to check out if I got a chance. I really don't want to go into those mountains alone and we only have one airplane. Maybe we can stir up something." That's where the NVA and VC launched their counterattack. I had a few scores to settle with those bastards for keeping me up all night.

"Scorpion. You can usually get us on 42.4 Fox Mike. That's if the Slopes haven't garbaged up the freq," they replied. It was an appropriate call sign for gunships, but I resented the derogatory term for the Vietnamese. We were, after all, in their restaurant and their country.

"I'm Ragged Scooper seven-four. You might try us on 116.0, Victor. That's our admin freq and you can get one of us on our ops. They can tell you if anyone is up. I'm supposed to fly tomorrow but I don't know what time. Talk to you."

We walked down the street and around the corner to our villa. The stench of the streets didn't bother me anymore. I thought it was rather practical to let babies and small kids wander around without any clothing on their lower halves. Sure beats changing diapers. Our neighbors were lounging in the street in front of their villa, chattering in their sing-song Vietnamese. Business must have been slow tonight. There were new faces and bodies. They spotted us.

"Hi, nee-bor. Come see me. We go inside," one of them teased and the rest of them giggled. She must have been the appointed one to try their new vocabulary. OK, my turn.

"*Comment ça va? Comment t'appèlles tu? Je m'appèlle Jean et je suis marié et j'ai deux enfants.*" A tall girl, by Vietnamese standards, took a couple of steps closer to me. I hadn't seen her before. She was attired in a Western-style silk dress that left little to the imagination. Her high heels accentuated her height. She put her arm around me and standing on her toes whispered in my ear.

"*Moi, je m'appèlle Gabrielle. J'ai aussi deux enfants, un fils et une fille. Mon mari est mort. Il a été tué par les Viet Minh. Entré avec moi et nous parlerons.*" God, she smelled good. I felt a tingling in my groin. I hadn't been this near a woman in over two months, and that had been my wife.

"*Non, merci. Je dois décoller à six heures du matin.*" I lied. Get yourself out of this one. Once inside with her it would be all over. She still had her arm around me. I carefully extricated myself and walked between the two villas to our main entrance on the side.

"*Au revoir,*" she called after me. We contacted division on the portable HF radio. I was scheduled for the second sortie, a nine o'clock takeoff. I collapsed into bed, but tired as I was, I had lingering thoughts of Gabrielle. She apparently had been educated by the French nuns, probably in Dalat, and taken a French name. The VC killed her husband. I could still smell her perfume and feel her arm around my waist. I had never been unfaithful to my wife.

I was airborne as scheduled from Qui Nhon and called the divisional command post at Tiger Town advising them I was headed for the Phu Cat mountains. If I were forced down, I wanted someone to know where to start looking for me. On the way to the mountains I overflew the valley that had been the scene of Tiger V. The rice harvest was continuing, except now the rice would move to the market in Qui Nhon instead of to the VC in the Phu Cats. I could see the Koreans patrolling the valley and vehicles traveling freely along the roads. I received no ground fire. What a difference from two weeks ago when we put all the air strikes in the valley in preparation for Tiger V. Another area was on its way to pacification. Maybe there's hope for this war after all.

I had been flying back and forth over the valley and gradually working my way north to the mountains. There were a series of small valleys, almost like fingers, that poked north into the mountains. I was choosing which of the fingers was the most likely access to the reputed VC complex. The Koreans had beaten them badly. This was the only possible escape route, so I knew they had to be in there someplace, nursing their wounded and trying to regroup. As soon as I crossed over the foothills of the Phu Cats, the entire complexion of the ground changed. There were no people visible, but, I could tell from an occasional wisp of smoke drifting over the jungle, that someone was down there or had been there over the night. The VC would build underground ovens and then channel the smoke up through the jungle at some distant location. I started to follow some trails that snaked into the mountains from the valley but would lose them as they disappeared under the dense jungle canopy. Occasionally, I could see the trail reappear where it skirted the edge of a clearing, or because I caught the proper angle, through the trees. Then I got the break I was looking for. I found a network of trails that were a different color from the others. Foot traffic had disturbed the grass and dirt, on the eastern slope of a towering north-south ridge line. As the trails wound up the mountains, the jungle canopy became thinner and the heavy elephant grass more prevalent. All the time I was gradually climbing, but there were still mountains that towered over me as I searched deeper into the Phu Cats.

I still couldn't see where the trails were going and suddenly I lost them. I searched higher up the ridge and farther north into the mountains. I knew they couldn't descend directly back down to the valley floor because the terrain was too steep. Suddenly the airplane gave a shudder. In my eagerness to find the trail, I hadn't paid attention to the airspeed and when I banked hard, the aircraft approached a stall. A stall in these mountains would be fatal. There was little room to recover and I would end up splattered against the rocks and trees, probably never to be found.

I was now thoroughly frustrated. I climbed higher thinking that a change in perspective might reveal the elusive trail network. No luck, but as I peeked over the the other side of the ridge line I saw a grass-covered tableland between the ridge line and the next spine of mountains. I noticed movement under the trees that bordered the grassland. Water buffalo! How did they get up here? Where there are water buffalo, people are not too far away. I saw hooches under the trees. Then I saw it. Fresh earth on the western slope of the ridge line, level with the tableland. The morning sun had not penetrated the trees and dried out the earth. It looked like a cave entrance. Wait a minute. I flew to the eastern side of the ridge line to where the trails disappeared. It was opposite the cave entrance, only it wasn't a cave—it was a tunnel entrance. This explained the mysterious disappearance of the trails. The clever and industrious VC had tunnelled through the ridge line and established a base camp on the tableland that was not accessible from below but only over the ridge line or through the tunnel. Both these avenues were easily defended. Even if a helicopter assault were attempted, the VC could trap the attackers on the tableland and annihilate them. No wonder the French never came in here pursuing the Viet Minh.

Then, I heard over my radio, "Ragged Scooper seven-four, this is Scorpion two-five X-ray, how copy?" It was the gunships.

"Roger, Scorpion. Come up your primary Fox Mike. If no contact come back to Victor, this freq," I responded. I quickly set 42.4 into my Fox Mike, and selected FM on my wafer switch. We could listen simultaneously to all three radios, but we had to select one on which to transmit.

"Scooper, this is Scorpion on Fox. We just lifted off the pad. Do you have anything for us?" they queried.

"You bet I do. Hooches, transports, and supplies. Give me a call when you reach the southern edge of the Phu Cats."

"Roger that."

I flipped back to VHF. "Ragged Scooper seven-zero, this is seven-four. I have hooches and material in the Phu Cats. It's a free-fire zone. No friendlies. Please advise the Alpha Lima Oscar that I am engaging with Army gunships."

"Roger, seven-four. This is seven-zero Mike. I will pass your message to the ALO," responded our headquarters operator.

"Scooper, this is two-five X-ray at the Phu Cats."

I flipped to the FM transmitter. "Roger. What's your lineup and how much fuel do you have? Keep heading north. I'm about ten klicks into the mountains. Stay high. The hills are over two thousand feet." I would use standard Air Force procedures and control the gunships as if they were fighter-bombers.

"We're a flight of two Huey gunships. Lead has four guns and number two has two pods of rockets. We can stay an hour or until we are out of ammo," they responded. That would be 7.62 millimeter machine guns, probably M–60s. Firing rate about 550 rounds per minute each gun. I could see the Hueys silhouetted against the sky. The rocket pods and guns appeared to be on mounts that extended from the fuselage. Everything fired forward. The ammo belts that fed the guns looked like snakes crawling from the fuselage. The pods looked small, probably seven rockets each. They were 2.75 inch, folding fin with high explosive warheads. Not bad.

"I've got a tally on you. I'm at your eleven o'clock, low. The target is some hooches buried under the trees just off my right wing, by the light green grassland. The weather is as you see it, winds from the north at ten knots. Use the Qui Nhon altimeter setting. No friendlies in the area. No ground fire. Cleared random direction passes. Copy?"

"Rog and we have you in sight. Are you going to mark?" Lead asked.

"Will do. Also, if you get in trouble the safest recovery is Qui Nhon. Closest is the valley to the south. Try to land near one of the ROK outposts. Target elevation is fifteen hundred feet. I'm in." I chopped the throttle to idle, pulled the nose up to kill airspeed, rolled right and kicked right rudder which sliced the nose down until it was well below the horizon and just below the target. A steep dive angle gave better accuracy. With my left hand I reached overhead and armed the left outboard tube, watched my grease pencil mark on the windshield rise up to the tree line, and I squeezed the trigger on the control stick. Whoosh! With the windows open, the sound of the rocket firing is startling. It's less than six feet from your head. The fiery red tail streaked straight to the target and a plume of white smoke blossomed through the trees. I punched the transmit button and said the words every FAC loves to say.

"Hit my smoke. You're cleared hot." Lead was in. The bullets tore through the trees and I could see pieces of thatched hut fly out. "You're right on. Two, put your rockets in the same place." Four rockets initially corkscrewed from the pods. As the fins extended, they stabilized and flew to the target. The HEI warheads penetrated the trees and slammed into the hooches, passing through the walls before exploding. Thatch, straw, bamboo, leaves, sticks, everything flew. This was the first time I'd seen high-explosive rockets fired in salvo.

"On your next pass I want you to move thirty-five meters north." Lead came around the base turn. I liked controlling the helicopters. Unlike the jets, they were never out of your field of vision and they could turn tighter than the A–1s. Three gunships would have kept a target continuously under fire. This time I was in position to watch the tracer rounds from the machine guns arc to the ground; every third or fourth bullet was a tracer. No straw flew this time.

"Two, go farther up the hillside. Twenty meters east of Lead's pass." Four more rockets. Again, grass, straw and rocks flew. A cave or tunnel entrance was camouflaged by a woven grass and straw mat. "OK, next pass. Right into the cave." The machine guns concentrated on the entrance. A puff of smoke erupted. They hit some ammo. The rocket bird headed right at the cave. It looked as if he were going to fly right into the cave and hand deliver the rockets. He was so close that the rocket motors had not burned out when the rockets hit. Two of them missed the entrance, sending rocks and earth skyward. The other two went down the throat, deep into the labyrinth, accelerating until they hit something. I feared the chopper had pressed too hard and was going to hit the mountain. I under-estimated these guys. The pilot virtually yanked the chopper around its own tail rotor. He missed the mountains.

Suddenly, a great cloud of white smoke came boiling out of the cave. Jackpot! The VC never expected us to find them and had left their stores close to the entrance. Back to the original tunnel. Maybe we would get lucky again. Now smoke rose from the hooches. The tracers had started a fire which had smoldered and was now burning brightly. Probably cooking oil. The water buffalo bolted from their hidden location and charged across the grassland. They had either broken from their corral or been released to escape the gunfire and rockets. We were in the midst of the proverbial "target–rich environment."

"Ragged Scooper seven-four, this is seven-zero Mike on Victor," came over my headset. Then the choppers called on FM.

"Scooper, Scorpion Lead. How about the buffalo?" They wanted to take them under attack.

"Stand by one, Scorpion." I selected the VHF transmitter.

"Go ahead, seven-zero."

"Roger, seven-four. I have a message from the Alpha Lima Oscar. You are not to use the gunships. Also, you are to recover at Tiger Town at the end of your mission. How copy?"

I keyed the mike, "Copy all." Now what? It's too late. I was already evening the score with the VC. What do I tell 70, if anything? What do I tell the gunships? They were orbiting the target area ready to pounce on whatever I wanted. I still couldn't see any personnel and we hadn't taken any ground fire.

I switched back to FM. "Lead, you have control of the flight," I trans-mitted. The FAC always has the option of relinquishing strike control of the flight to the leader, but under the rules of engagement, the FAC is ultimately responsible for the air strike. These rules apply when the FAC is controlling Air Force fighters. I was making up the rules when it came to controlling Army fighters. The gunships were on their own. I merely led them to the target.

I circled overhead and watched the rocket bird hit the tunnel while the gunship pursued the water buffalo. We were denying the enemy the ability to wage war by attacking his supply and transport base. Only moments before I had been elated by the results of the strike, but now I was dejected and confused. What was going on? We have targets that are cleared and in a free-fire zone. What difference does it make if the bullets come from Army or Air Force planes? It was too late; if the VC can use noncombatants as a screen for their attack, I could exercise my judgment and allow the gunships to take out a few water buffalo.

I recovered at Tiger Town as directed. Something was up. One of the jeeps met me and drove me to the regimental CP while the Korean ground crew refueled the O–1. The plane that Col. Stewart had brought up yesterday was tied down on the pierced-steel ramp. The division ALO was waiting for me. When he received my message about using the gunships, he was reluctant to approve Army helicopters for strike missions. So, like every good commander who wants to protect his ass, he avoided the decision and bucked it up-channel. He asked a colonel at DASC Alpha for a reading; the DASC colonel said no, because the helicopters weren't Air Force resources. I thought it better to just shut up and not tell him we had demolished a piece of the Phu Cats. Maybe I'd tell only the Korean G–2 staffers who had asked me to go take a look. I not only looked, but I found, confirmed, and destroyed: *Veni, vidi, vici.* That was my job.

I took a swig of water from my canteen. It was terrible. Stale. Tasted like iodine from the water purification tablets. I walked to the fridge for a cold soda. It still tasted like iodine. The ALO approached me.

"I want you to fly the other airplane to Qui Nhon this afternoon. Pack your gear for about a two-week stay in Tuy Hoa. Unless something changes, you're to fly there first thing tomorrow to work with the 101st Airborne," said the ALO.

"You mean you want me to take the airplane that Colonel Stewart brought, to Tuy Hoa?" I inquired.

"That's right." And I was right. I had been set up. The promised few days in the villa was two nights. The "you'll hear from us in a few days," was the next day and the few days of help was going to be two weeks. I hoped everyone else was working as hard as I was at this war. We might win and go home.

I rummaged around in the open case of C-rations and found some franks and beans. There was some water boiling on the gasoline stove. I took off my dog tags and using the opener I carried on the chain, a P–38, worked it around the top of the can and peeled the lid back. Holding it by the lid, I dropped it into the couple of inches of water. One of the guys once forgot to vent his can. The explosion blew beef stew all over the tent.

Another *Wall Street Journal* turned up. The Dow Jones had penetrated 1,000 for the first time. Secretary of Defense McNamara commented on how U.S. technology and ingenuity were the keys to winning the war. I wonder if we'll get another case of those ingenious green smoke grenades. They really show up in the jungle. Maybe we're supposed to hide under the green smoke if we get shot down. Ingenious, my ass. I finished off the franks and beans with some fruit cocktail that had been overlooked. The tent vultures usually sort through the C-rats and extract the edible components, like fruit cocktail and chocolate. They leave behind yellow-green eggs, salty brown ham, and dry pound cake that gets bigger in your mouth with every bite.

Back to Qui Nhon. My last shower for a while. Decided to have dinner at the same restaurant as last night. All the Scorpions were there. They had a great time in the mountains. They showed their appreciation by sending bottles of Vietnamese beer to our table. Another flight of gunships went back that afternoon with more rockets and hammered the caves and tunnels. We speculated the water buffalo would show up as beefsteak specials in the restaurants by tomorrow. We walked back to the villa. None of our neighbors was out in the street. Business must have been good. I was relieved that Gabrielle was not around. The temptation would be difficult to resist.

I fixed what I thought would be my last drink with ice for two weeks. A couple of my fellow FACs and I sat on the second-floor balcony, overlooking the street. We didn't have the usual wire mesh to keep someone from throwing a hand grenade in our laps. I told them about what happened with the target clearance for the gunships, but I also told them what I had learned about the capabilities of the gunships. We agreed that in a bind, the hell with the rules. We would use them just like fighters. We couldn't understand these petty rivalries. We thought we were all fighting the same war in support of South Vietnam versus the Viet Cong. We shot up a few water buffalo and burned some supplies just to let the Charlies know that even though Tiger V was over, we could return any time and harass them. We also accomplished some civic actions. The restaurants in Qui Nhon were short of beef and we supported the local economy.

This day of experience was invaluable. Later on in my tour, I worked very closely with the gunships in support of our troops, with a very high degree of success. Years later, the Air Force and Army would finally cooperate and develop joint attack teams that integrated rotary and fixed-wing close air support. We did it in a restaurant in Qui Nhon in 1966.

Tiger V was an unqualified success for the ROKs, the Air Force, and our new allies, the Army gunships. The Koreans were wresting the breadbasket of Binh Dinh Province from the Viet Cong, occupying and pacifying the territory after they conquered it. I had deployed new munitions, perfected the skills of controlling airstrikes, capitalized on opportunities, and wrestled with my conscience. I had skirted with authority, but did the job to the best of my ability and training. I was still alive and on my way to a new operation.

6

FACing with the Screaming Eagles at Tuy Hoa

I hitched an early morning ride with another ROK FAC from the villa in Qui Nhon to the airbase. He was flying a local mission; I was headed to Tuy Hoa. I tossed my weapons and kit bag in the back of the jeep. We always kept our weapons with us because we frequently shuttled between the villa and Tiger Town via jeep or airplane. I had everything but my civilian clothes in the bag. I wouldn't be needing them with the 101st. It was a mile's trip through the city's still-dark streets. I didn't have a specific take-off time so I browsed around the aerial port terminal and the Air Force administrative hooch. All quiet, no rumors. I drove the jeep to the approach end of runway 36; the first rays of the sun were sliding across the gentle waves of the South China Sea. It reminded me of Cape Cod Bay. I loved the peacefulness of the early morning, before the war started.

I returned to the opposite end of the 5,100-foot runway and to the general purpose tents of the Skyraider detachment, the Surfs. It was an appropriate call sign for the pilots, mechanics, and dozen airplanes from the seaside parent unit in Nha Trang. The pilots used one tent as an operations center, ready room, and a place to stow their flight gear. They let us use whatever little space we needed. The maintenance and armament people used another tent for tool boxes, test equipment, maintenance administration, and various beverage sales. Spare parts and munitions components were stored anyplace there was room. Their pet monkey was in his cage; he caused too much mischief.

The maintenance and ordnance sergeants had convened at the coffee pot. The birds were loaded, preflights were completed, everything was ready for war. They were waiting for the pilots to emerge from their mission briefing. We talked. There were shortages of replacement barrels for the wing-mounted 20mm cannons. The guns were worn and difficult to service; jams were becoming more frequent. There was an ammo shortage; two of the four cannons on each bird were loaded with target, ball, ammo. When they realized I was a FAC, they asked me to use the guns only when absolutely essential. Noted. They were getting more dud bombs. A young airman, who joined us, joked that he found a bomb fuse date-stamped before he was born. No big bombs were available. There were more 100-pound general purpose bombs, which were good for scaring jungle birds but little else.

The province ALO, Baron 20, was preflighting his O–1. He was one hell of a nice guy; he helped us on Tiger V. I talked with him as he did the inspection. Checking the rockets on the right wing, he mentioned that smoke rocket supplies were tight and not to waste them. I offered him some of our green smokes. We both laughed. When he saw the gear stacked next to my airplane, he asked me where I was headed.

"Down the coast to Tuy Hoa, with the 101st Airborne Brigade, for a week or two," I replied.

"Oh, that's Operation Harrison. I've seen the message traffic and intelligence reports. They're really mixing it up down there." I got a tight feeling in my gut. Here we go again. This time I hadn't volunteered; at least I thought I hadn't. He continued, "Well, I have to fly now. Oh, by the way, did you hear there's some flap about a FAC going into the Phu Cats and knocking out some supply complex? Used Army gunships and the Air Force thinks they should get credit for it. Good luck to you." He climbed into the cockpit.

I walked to my airplane in the adjacent tie-down spot. Yesterday, I was nearly reprimanded for an unauthorized air strike; today the Air Force wanted credit. I wanted out of town before I had to answer any official questions—honestly. I couldn't give an "All right, sir." I stowed my gear in the backseat and headed 40 miles south.

The runway at Tuy Hoa was a luxury; 3,700 feet of PSP, pierced-steel plank, with a dedicated O–1 and L–19 parking area. This was my first exposure to U.S. forces and their concept of operations. I introduced myself to Major Allison, the brigade ALO. He welcomed me, particularly since I brought a "new" airplane, fresh from major inspection. Major Allison would prove to be a capable leader—organized, aggressive, secure in his authority, and confident in his ability—different from the people with whom I had been working.

The 101st was on Operation Harrison and Fillmore. The unit was a separate brigade of the Airborne Division, had extensive organic helicopter support, and was designated as Airmobile. The soldiers were a mixture of straight-leg airmobile infantry, "a leg on a rope," and the elitist paratroopers. Units, ranging from squads of eight or ten men, through entire battalions of 600 to 700 men, were constantly shuttled in and out of the jungles, rice paddies, and grasslands on search-and-destroy missions. Long-range reconnaissance patrols, LRRPs, would spend days stealthily creeping through the jungles in search of the all-elusive VC and NVA. The overall mission was to push the VC from the coastal mountains and plains, into the central highlands. They were to deny the VC the benefits of the forthcoming rice harvest, much as the ROKs were doing in the Qui Nhon area.

I had barely settled into the operation when two Army Hueys were shot down near an isolated hill, ten miles south of the airfield. Helicopters, FACs, and surface convoys frequently passed by the hill, following the highway. We became creatures of habit. The VC recognized this and waited for a day of limited visibility and poor flying weather. They were in deep cover and looking for the right opportunity to nail a couple of aircraft. The VC caught the helicopters flying along the road at several hundred feet and opened up on them. The enemy apparently had crew-served machine guns, since the aircraft were virtually riddled with holes. By some miracle, the flight crews were unscathed. We put air strikes on the hill for two days, but I doubt if we hit anyone. The VC would slip away at night.

Maj. Allison, the ALO, and Capt. Willie Wilson, a FAC, had been forced down on a night FAC mission in support of a besieged fire base. Wilson was an old-hand FAC, while Allison was new in-country. They teamed up for this particular mission, Wilson lending an experienced hand. They related their story.

We were on a night air strike control mission supporting a fire base. We had a flare ship to illuminate the target. The strike aircraft were a couple of A–1s. Because of the darkness, we couldn't see the film of oil forming on the windscreen. We thought that it was haze due to the deteriorating visibility. In the midst of directing the fighters and watching out for the flare ship, we didn't pay much attention to the cockpit instruments. The cockpit lights aren't worth a shit so even if we did think of checking the gauges, we couldn't see them anyway. The engine froze and we force-landed in a river bed. Fortunately, we had some light from the flares. We piled out, ass-end-over-teakettle, and ran into the elephant grass. We were breathing so hard that we could hardly talk on the survival radio to the fighters overhead. The VC opened up with automatic weapons, spraying the grass. They didn't know exactly where we were. The fighters and the troops from the nearby Special Forces camp returned fire—tracers all over the place, arcing through the sky. It was a race to see who could find us first, the VC or the Special Forces. We were finally located by the Special Forces team. They took us out by helicopter at first light. Those Green Beanies were real heroes to come out looking for a couple of dumb-ass Air Force pilots.

Willie was a humorous guy and dedicated warrior. He had volunteered to take "one more mission." He left the next day back to the States. The O–1 was recovered by a helicopter. Examination showed a bad seal on the oil cap; the oil gradually siphoned out until the engine seized. I made a mental note to pay particular attention to the oil cap whenever preflighting the aircraft. I had lost my survival radio in one of my innumerable moves and would borrow one when flying. Sometimes I forgot to borrow one. I hoped I wouldn't need it.

We had an air cap, usually two A–1Es, to expend each day; some targets were lucrative and rewarding, others skimpy and frustrating.

One day I was scheduled to hit a suspected VC supply point. The terrain was flat, with no topographical features or man-made structures for reference. I had difficulty finding it or anything that resembled the target; not even a trail or foot-path crossed the area. The information came from an agent report—a figment that earned some woodcutter or farmer a few quick piastres from the intelligence-gathering network. Maybe the agent was a double, also working for the other guys. This was a crazy war.

On another day the target was a suspected staging area in the mountains. The fighters were three A–1E Skyraiders with bombs and napalm. Broken clouds hugged the mountain tops, obscuring the valleys beneath. I flew on the deck and in the valleys, leading the fighters to the targets. We were a mini-raid from the annals of World War II; I was the Pathfinder. I caught a lucky glimpse of the target, and the Skyraiders salvoed their load. We had a hit on a way station at the intersection of a trail and a stream. I observed a secondary fire creeping along the trail. Hidden supplies. Charlie usually felt secure in bad weather. Surprise!

Time passed rapidly. We were flying one or two missions a day, some of them running almost four hours, close to the O–1's maximum fuel endurance. Anything over that was pure luck. I landed one day with one tank empty and about ten minutes worth of gas in the other, but somehow it didn't bother me. It should have. Complacency kills.

The FACs rotated pulling a command post duty officer shift. The command post was located in a hillside villa overlooking the sea. Each Army section—administration, intelligence, operations, logistics, civic actions, fire support, and aviation—was located in one large hall. The Army concept of staff coordination was to put all elements in one room and let them fight it out. Each section had at least three radio nets that were on open speakers. During high combat activity, the volume of the blended transmissions rose to a crescendo as each section tuned its radios above the cacophony of the adjacent ones. It was like the stock exchange, where everyone was shouting orders at each other and the specialist was trying to maintain an orderly market. The problem was that there was no specialist to maintain order. The Army way was to wait until the market was closed, which was last light, let the traders sort their respective positions, and then hold a staff meeting to decide what to do next. Opportunities in the marketplace were lost. And to compound the problem, the tactical air planning request was 12 hours out-of-phase with the Army planning cycle. We had to guess at air support requirements.

FACs would return from flying, stop by the command post, and debrief the Army intelligence and operations staffs, the S–2 and S–3. The FACs were in the middle of the air-ground war; patrols, assaults, sweeps, helicopters, artillery, and air strikes. They kept track of everything and they would update the command elements before many of the situation reports and intelligence reports would filter up-channel. "Spotted new trail activity. Wisps of smoke at first light," and they rattled off the coordinates. "Good site for an ambush. The helicopters took fire here." The FAC was often the first to know about enemy activity since he monitored the various radio nets from his aircraft, as well as observing the deployment of forces, both friendly and enemy. He'd often volunteer to be the duty officer, "Take a break, I got it," or "You're flying this afternoon. Why don't you spend the time reviewing the new infra-red photos with intell?" People were recognized and appreciated for demonstrating extra effort. That was the atmosphere of leadership, responsibility, and initiative that Major Allison established and fostered.

One morning, while sharing the duty shift with a seasoned NCO, I did some command post "walking around." Intell map was current. Nothing on the radio net. No fire missions from the FSC. Aviation had most of the assault choppers on standby; only resupply choppers were flying. I snitched a cold soda from their ice chest. Aviators always find ice. Operations, S–3, was planning a force insertion in the afternoon. A company was to be helilifted in two waves and then sweep the hills to the north of the selected LZ. I remembered it had trench lines surrounding most of the perimeter and was the obvious place for a helicopter landing in the area. The rest of the area was heavy jungle while this was relatively open elephant grass. I suggested an LZ prep, using either the air cap or requesting additional aircraft from the DASC. The Army didn't think it was necessary. They were relying on the element of surprise. I went to Major Allison.

"Sir, they're planning a lift this afternoon. Two waves. The LZ can hold about five Hueys. You know the area. There's trenches and spiderholes all over the place. Fields of fire from the north."

"You're right, John," he replied. "In fact I was having a marksman contest with the artillery commander the other day and we drew some fire from the area. Let me see what I can do."

I was scheduled to fly that afternoon. I knew the coordinates and time of the lift. I would make myself available. After takeoff, I queried our brigade TACP.

"Eagle Ops, this is Ragged Scooper seven-four. Any change on that lift?"

"Negative," came the reply. The lift was still on and they were going in without any preparation. I flipped to the aviation frequency. I could hear the helicopters checking in on their radio net. I didn't recognize the call sign of any gunships. However, they were usually on alert.

I positioned the O–1 above and behind the Hueys as they approached the

LZ. They were in two elements of five and four aircraft, respectively. The command chopper circled the LZ and dropped a smoke grenade to mark it. The LZ didn't look big enough to handle five choppers. Something was wrong. I checked my map. This wasn't the LZ that I had marked on my map. Maybe the Army had changed the plan. No, they overflew the LZ and orbited while the C and C, command and control chopper searched for the proper one. It was two klicks away and this time they dropped two smoke grenades. The assault choppers were out of position. They had to overfly the LZ and make a second approach. So much for surprise. I could visualize the VC scurrying for their spiderholes and trenches, pulling the bolts back on their AK–47s to chamber a fresh round, snapping the safeties off, and sweeping their kill zone. I hoped there were no big guns on the hillside. The Hueys looked like big ducks in a shooting gallery when they came to a hover, their most vulnerable position. The elephant grass was too high for them to land cleanly, so they hovered and let the rotor wash beat down the grass as the troops jumped from both doors. When the troops leaped from the lead choppers, the entire tree line erupted with small arms fire. This forced a dilemma on the trailing helicopters. If they settled to a hover, they would expose themselves to intense ground fire. If they aborted the landing, they wouldn't have enough troops on the ground to suppress the enemy fire.

The worst of my fears was realized. A machine gun opened up from the hillside north of the LZ, pouring lethal fire into the helicopters. The gun was at the 12 o'clock position to the choppers, precluding the door gunners from returning direct fire. The rounds were smashing into the plexiglass cockpits. I could see chunks flying. The helicopters were getting chopped up by the machine gun, while the troopers were being picked off by the small arms fire from the tree lines. I admired the VC for executing a classic, murderous ambush. They had forced us to surrender the advantage of our three-dimensional warfare, and to fight them on their terms, in two dimensions. One bird rolled over like a great wounded bull elephant, the rotor blades still whirling as they chopped into the earth and then snapped, sending a chunk of blade boomeranging through the sky. Another chopper struggled vainly into the air, oscillated, then settled back into the elephant grass. A third lifted off, only to trail smoke across the sky. As the tragedy unfurled before their eyes, the tail–end helicopter pilots prematurely took off, forcing some of the troops to leap into the towering elephant grass. It cushioned their jump, but once on the ground, they were snarled by the grass and unable to accurately return fire. The gunships showed up. I selected the VHF radio. I wanted to talk to Maj. Allison at the CP.

"Eagle ops, this is seven-four on Victor. I need Eagle Lead."

"Wait one," was the reply. A pause, then, "This is Eagle Lead. Go ahead."

"The helilift is in deep trouble. The LZ is hot. There are two choppers down. The gunships are suppressing the small-arms fire. I can't raise the

C and C chopper due to the confusion. I need clearance to expend the air cap on a machine gun, three hundred meters north of the LZ. Can you get me the clearance at your location?"

"Stand by one," he replied. This was followed shortly with, "The Army wants to know why."

"Tell them that just as soon as they send in a medevac chopper or the second wave they'll know why. They'll double their losses."

After a short wait Allison replied with, "The Army doesn't know anything about a machine gun. Try the ground commander for clearance." Apparently, I was the only one who knew where the machine gun was. The choppers received so much fire that in the confusion of battle, the machine gun was not specifically identified. The gun wasn't firing at the gunships. The VC knew if they revealed their position, the rocket-armed gunships would attack them. These were some real cool bastards. They were waiting for additional slick helicopters to increase their kills. I radioed the air cap, the usual flight of A–1s, and had them orbit overhead at 6,000 feet. They could see the action from that altitude and they would be safe from helicopters, artillery, and ground fire. I briefed them and waited— and waited. The Army had stabilized the situation on the ground and were lifting reinforcements in and wounded out via helicopter. No fire from the machine gun. We dared them to open up, but they knew better. They probably fled. I handed the A–1s off to another FAC who had a target in another sector of the AO.

It was a tragic error. Lives had been needlessly lost. Helicopters were shot up, and command and control was temporarily lost. I had experienced what Clausewitz meant when he wrote about the "friction of battle." I should have been more insistent on an LZ prep.

The 101st continued to launch their searches and sweeps, moving continuously, leap-frogging about the entire area of operations. They were perfecting the concept of airmobile warfare using the mobility of helicopters to relentlessly engage the enemy. When the VC would break contact and melt into the jungle, the 101st would insert another unit along the avenue of escape and re-engage the VC. Some of the engagements were now with North Vietnamese Army regulars. They were attached to the local guerrilla units who knew the terrain and trails. The NVA possessed superior firepower and disciplined tactics with well-integrated command and control procedures. I suspected they were involved with the helilift ambush and were probably manning the heavy machine gun. That bothered me. That gun was still out there someplace, lurking in the jungle just waiting to shoot up some more helicopters or maybe FACs. Maybe even me.

On one close air support, CAS, mission, the VC were entrenched on a hillside and had the friendly troopers pinned down at the base of a ravine. Artillery fire was ineffective because the VC were on the backside of the hill from where the gun battery was located. The ground commander contacted me and asked for help. As soon as he gave me his position, I circled it on my map. Using a rule of thumb calculation, two-and-a-half klicks per minute, I gave an estimated time of arrival and directed the A–1 air cap to a rendezvous point close to the target. I located the ground troops, had them mark their position with a bright orange panel, and then describe the target's location. It was 200 meters above them on a hillside. I hit the target with a smoke rocket, confirmed with the commander, and cleared in the fighters. The A–1s took out the VC hillside position with fragmentation bombs and napalm. The elapsed time, from when the troops contacted me to the first bomb on target, was under 10 minutes. This was CAS at its best when it provided help for the beleaguered infantry.

On another occasion a patrol called me on FM. They were in heavy contact with some VC, dug into trenches and bunkers in a relatively open area. I had a Marine gunnery sergeant in the backseat with me, directing five-inch naval gunfire from an offshore cruiser. We contacted the patrol, and while the gunny took the target under fire, I requested some fighters. Within 15 minutes, the F–4C alert flight from Cam Ranh Bay was overhead. They had the now usual alert load of "snakes and napes," plus the 20mm Gatling gun. Snakes, or snakeyes, were the new 500-pound general-purpose bombs with retard fins that facilitated accurate delivery from low altitude, and allowed the aircraft sufficient time to escape the lethal shrapnel of their own bombs. Nape, or napalm, was the jellied gasoline mixture carried in canisters. Its size varied from 250 pounds to 750 pounds, 40 to 120 gallons. The F–4s usually had the larger cans. Napalm was most effectively delivered from low altitude, spilling fiery death across the ground.

Under cover of the naval gunfire, I had the friendlies move forward to observe the air strikes. I marked the target and cleared in Lead with the snakes. He took out two active bunkers on the first pass. Number Two followed with napalm, which spilled through the trench line, setting off a series of small secondary explosions of stored ammo. The ground troops were elated. They moved closer. Lead rolled in on his second pass. Suddenly, I saw muzzle flashes from the bunkers. The VC had decided to fight it out. Two more bunkers destroyed. The ground troops advised me that the fighters were taking ground fire.

"Two," I transmitted, "I saw muzzle flashes from the northern bunker. Friendlies confirm you're taking ground fire."

"Rog. Two's in on the north bunker," he replied. I was holding directly over the target; the fighters, streaking at 450 knots and a 50-foot altitude, passed beneath me. As the F–4 released the napalm, I saw flashes from the bunker and then a sudden flash on the wing of the F–4.

"Two's hit," he transmitted. "It's yawing bad. I'm gonna lose it." He pulled up right by me. I could see that the 370-gallon, underwing fuel tank had been hit. The tank had peeled back like a banana over the leading edge of the wing. The aircraft yawed from the sudden increase in drag. Fortunately, it was empty, or there could have been a nasty fire.

"Head for the water," instructed Lead. "I'll join on you and look you over."

"How's it look, Lead? Do you want a chopper?" I prompted. I was anticipating a bail-out by the two pilots.

"Looks OK. He's under control. No fire. We're headed for home plate." They were 60 miles, 10 minutes, from Cam Ranh.

The friendlies were now cautiously advancing on the bunker and trench complex. They wanted to know what happened to the fighters. I advised them that one had taken a serious hit and they were headed home.

"What's your situation now?" I asked.

"Everything's quiet, FAC. We're moving out. Tell the fighters, thanks. Hope they're OK."

"Rog. I'll pass your message. Call again."

So ended 30 minutes of combined arms and interservice cooperation of a Marine sergeant directing Navy guns and an Air Force lieutenant controlling Air Force fighters, all in support of an appreciative and concerned Army Spec 4. But it was all American warriors fighting bravely in a Vietnamese war.

The day following the F–4's hit, the command post contacted me while I was flying a visual recce mission. Some ground troops were pinned down by enemy fire near a village, Grid Square BQ9050. Another CAS mission. I was there in 5 minutes with fighters—two A–1Es, call sign Surf 11—right behind me. Their ordnance load was frags, napalm, white phosphorous (WP or Willie Pete) bombs and 20mm cannon. I was in communication with the ground troops, a small patrol of eight men sweeping the area. They had stumbled into a larger concentration of VC forces and the patrol was taking heavy fire. I contacted the patrol leader on the FM radio. Under the excitement of the situation, he would run his words together, and I had trouble understanding him above the popping noise of machine gun and automatic rifle fire. He was obviously genuinely concerned for the welfare of his troops. Once he spotted my O–1 overhead, his diction slowed and confidence crept into his voice. He described the general target area to me. I dropped a smoke grenade out the cockpit window and asked him to give me the position of the firing relative to the smoke. The VC were in a tree line about 25 meters from my mark. I left the immediate target area hoping to deceive Charlie into thinking he was unspotted and safe from air strikes. I wheeled back, marked with a smoke rocket, and cleared in the fighters. The element of surprise was one of the principles of war that had been drilled into me at the Academy.

I had developed a technique for this situation. With a soft target, I had the fighter carrying napalm drop first, followed immediately by the fighter with the frag bombs. Anyone running from the searing and suffocating heat of the napalm would be cut down by the larger kill radius fragmentation bombs. I usually had the fighters save their Willie Pete and guns, unless I needed the WP for target identification or smoke screening.

The patrol leader was overjoyed with the results, which was reflected in his entertaining commentary. The battle was turning in his favor. As the fighters rolled in on each pass, his FM radio transmissions were now interjected with:

"You got'em man!"—"Keep 'em coming."—"Good hit!"

"You got the sonofabitch on the run. He's goin' north."

From this encouragement, I gave specific corrections on the UHF radio to the fighters. Remembering that the A–1s were equipped with FM radios, I invited them to come up on the FM frequency and enjoy the continued colorful dialogue. There couldn't be any greater mission satisfaction than hearing, firsthand, the gratitude and enthusiasm of the patrol leader who, a few minutes earlier, had been in deep trouble and under heavy fire. Now the tables were turned and the A–1s were delivering his revenge.

There was one pocket of VC that had fled north across the trail into a patch of jungle. They had ceased firing at the ground troops and were now concentrating on the aircraft, most specifically myself. This was both a personal affront and a challenge.

"Surf," I asked, "what do you have left?"

"I have four Willie Petes plus guns," Lead replied.

"Same for me," his wingman added.

"Do you see the small clump of trees just north of where we had been hitting?" I asked.

"Roger." The Viet Cong had fled from the tree line and were now in an isolated clump of trees. They felt secure and had been shooting at us with impunity on our last passes. They had finally made a mistake.

"Let's surprise 'em. No mark. You have the target. I want you to close up your spacing and salvo your Willie Petes in one pass." Another principle of war—concentration of firepower. "Watch the friendlies. They have started to move out to the west along the edge of the trail." Wingtip to wingtip, in came the Skyraiders.

Pow! A direct hit! The eight bombs exploded simultaneously in the upper branches of the two-tiered jungle canopy. They showered glowing death throughout the clump of trees. The VC never had a chance to take cover. There was no escape. White phosphorus causes agonizing death. It burns, chokes, suffocates, and eats through flesh and jungle canopy as if it were butter. I didn't have the slightest bit of remorse. That'll teach the Charlies to shoot at us.

The Skyraiders still had their wing-mounted cannons. The request from the NCO armorers in Qui Nhon stuck in my mind. "Don't use the 20mm strafe unless absolutely essential." We saved the strafe. We did enough damage for one day.

I had been in Tuy Hoa a week when, one evening before dinner, Major Allison summoned me to his tent. We were living in umbrella tents that slept three guys with cots and gear. The floors were sand since we were in the coastal plain two miles from the sea. Major Allison had a tent to himself, complete with a hard floor—an aluminum 463L cargo pallet.

"How would you like to take 472 down to Nha Trang tomorrow for maintenance?" It was an order, not a question. He continued, "There's another bird ready for you to pick up. You've been a great help. Especially, spelling the guys in the command post. This will give you a break."

"Thanks, sir. I really appreciate it." I hadn't been to Nha Trang since I first arrived in-country, and that was over two and a half months ago. That's where I had met the FAC with the haunting eyes who'd been humping his way through the jungle. Now I understood what was behind those eyes. This would also give me the opportunity to replace my missing survival radio.

"And make sure you stop by the DASC. Colonel Stewart wants to say hello. The DASC has moved. Call them on the radio when you're ten minutes out and they'll send a jeep for you."

"Yessir. While I'm there I'll try to get to the BX." I needed the usual: shaving cream, tooth paste, razor blades, and some crotch powder. The damn crotch rash just wouldn't go away. "May I get you anything, sir? I'll have the enlisted troops make up a list and I can get some stuff for them."

"No thanks, John. Why not have one of the NCOs make a shopping list; save you some trouble. Let's go to dinner. We can make happy hour at the Officers' Club." We trudged through the sand to the O Club tent and entered a world of paper table cloths, dinner napkins, paper plates, plastic cups, ice, and quarter drinks from the bar. War is hell.

It was only a 40-minute direct flight down the coast to Nha Trang. I wanted to do some sightseeing. Remembering the ambushed choppers along the highway, I climbed to 4,000 feet, beyond reach of any hidden guns. The only clouds were scattered cirrus; the visibility was unlimited. I wandered along the coastline, following the line of the sea as it embraced the peninsulas along the shore. In some areas it reminded me of the coast of Maine and Canada where the mountains came to the sea. Other areas were flat and swampy with numerous streams and inlets, like the coast of the Carolinas. Everything seemed so peaceful, the war far away, as the 213-horse Continental engine powered me through the sky. I gazed across the landscape, my mind wandering.

The countryside with its beaches, flatlands, hills, and mountains was absolutely beautiful. The terrain and colors changed every five or ten miles. The deep greens of the rolling jungle, the light greens and browns of the patchwork paddies, the green and white of the elephant grass, the pale yellow-green of bamboo thickets, the harsh brown and gray of the mountain cliffs, the soothing aqua of the sea, the darker greens and deep blues of the sea over the coral reefs, the muddy brown of the rivers and streams emptying into the sea, all this passed under my wingtips.

But man's technology had destroyed nature's beauty. The red and brown earth was scarred by bomb craters, the jungle was blackened from napalm, rice paddies were pockmarked by artillery shells, and the swaths of trees were denuded where defoliants had done their damage; this too passed under my wingtips.

I drifted back to reality. Ten weeks in-country and I was still alive. There was a statistic that if you made it past the first few weeks, you would probably make it close to the end. Then carelessness, complacency, and false immortality took its toll. Forty-two weeks to go, but only ten minutes to Nha Trang.

"Ragged Scooper, this is Ragged Scooper seven-four. Ten minutes out," I transmitted on the DASC discrete frequency.

"Roger, seven-four. Transport will be waiting," was their response. Nice to know someone was actually expecting me.

I called Nha Trang tower for landing instructions. They put me on downwind for runway 12. I was so accustomed to flying from uncontrolled airstrips that it seemed strange to talk to a control tower. I flew over the Vietnamese Air Force ramp. It was covered with Skyraiders, many of them laden with bombs. They were pulling their weight in this war. I landed and taxied to the O-1 ramp. I logged one hour. The promised jeep was there.

I checked with the senior maintenance NCO. He gave me the tail number of the aircraft that I would fly back to Tuy Hoa. We transferred the flak vests, smoke grenades, and other loose gear to the replacement aircraft. I hung my rifle inside the cockpit, over the instrument spotlight. I wouldn't need that on-base. Map case, survival kit, headset, and gloves took care of the personal items. I kept my pistol, canteen, and knife.

I turned to the driver. "I would like to stop by the BX and PE [personal equipment issue] before we go to the DASC."

"Right, sir. Hop in." Off we went, and I bought some magic powder for my crotch rash. At PE I explained the loss of my radio. They said no sweat, and issued me a new one with a spare battery. I dropped off my purchases and equipment at the airplane.

I was totally surprised when we left the base and wound through the streets of Nha Trang, headed to the beach. DASC Alpha, as I remembered it, was on the airbase proper, in a couple of bamboo hooches built on a plywood floor, about two feet off the ground on stilts, so water could flow under the building and not through it. Wooden shutters dropped from above, to cover the screened upper portion of the outside walls, when the rains became near-horizontal. Nha Trang was a resort town with beautiful beaches, beachfront nightclubs, grand hotels and villas, and tempting restaurants. It reminded me of Atlantic City during the 1950s. It was also the headquarters for First Field Forces Vietnam (IFFV), the command element for all the U.S. forces in the critical II Corps area. DASC Alpha was the Air Force element that directed the air support for IFFV. This explained the magnificent, sprawling, five-story, beachfront hotel that contained IFFV and all its various support elements. Three hours earlier, I had 'performed' my bodily functions on an open-air two-holer; now I was approaching a structure that rivaled anything that the entire SHAPE Staff would have occupied in World War II. It was surrounded by neatly trimmed lawns, landscaped gardens, and gravel driveways. Vietnamese laborers worked on the flowerbeds. The military personnel were dressed in starched khakis or tailored fatigues. Wait a minute—what happened to the war?

The driver pulled the jeep around to the rear entrance. Apparently this was for the hired help or the poor combat slobs in the dirty fatigues. I climbed the steps and walked into the two-story high lobby. There was a check-in desk. I felt I should have brought my American Express card. Instead, I saw a sign: *Check All Weapons Here*. I kept mine; at least they acknowledged the presence of armed conflict. I climbed the winding marble staircase, searching for the location of the DASC. Upon finding it I poked my head in. One entire wall was given to plexiglass-covered maps and status boards. The war would halt if we ever ran out of multi-colored grease pencils for the status boards. Opposite the wall was a raised dais, on which sat the "lords of the DASC," dressed in khaki and green costumes, with gold, silver, black, white, and blue patches or ornaments either sewn or clipped on.

"Hi. I'm Lieutenant Flanagan and I'm looking for Colonel Stewart." No response. I didn't know the code word. I tried again in my best command voice. "I'm Ragged Scooper seven-four and I have an immediate air request for Colonel Stewart." That drew their attention. I stepped into the room, inviting the staffers' facetious epithets.

"So you're seven-four."

"You're the nut who keeps us up all night."

"You're dirty. This is a gentleman's office. Get out of here."

"Go back to the jungle. You stink. Is that gun loaded?"

"Lieutenants are the lowest form of life. 'Specially FACs."

A captain rose from his chair. His desk sign read Fighter Duty Officer. He walked over to me and extended his hand. I shook it.

"Hi. I'm 'Filthy' Brown, FiDO. Don't let those whoremongers bother you. That's their way of welcoming you." I'd heard of Filthy before—well-respected. He earned his nickname from his vocabulary. He introduced me to both the Army and Air Force members of the duty staff: airlift officer, recce officer, intell officer, fire support coordinator, assistant G–3 air, deputy director. Each briefly explained their responsibilities and how they functioned with Saigon, fighter bases, and radar sites. The view from the operations center overlooked the beach and the South China Sea. Junks were on the bay, weaving their way around the fishing boats.

"Colonel Stewart's office is across the hall. Just down from the admin section."

"Thanks."

"No more crazy requests, Flanagan, or we'll transfer you to the DASC for punishment." I held up my hands in mock surrender as I walked out the door. Great bunch of guys. I didn't realize how much I would depend on their resourcefulness in the months to come. I found Col. Stewart's office. I knocked, entered when invited, and saluted. He returned my salute.

"How do you like the 101st? Good outfit. Allison is a real tiger. Thinks highly of you." Rapid fire. He kept it up. "How are things with the ROKs? I thought you might want to see the command side of the operation so I suggested you come over. Have you been to the ops center?"

He never gave me the chance to answer directly so I interjected that I was learning airmobile tactics with the 101st, had met the DASC staff, and was particularly impressed by the communication links with the fighter bases and scattered radar sites.

"Fine," said Stewart. "Your airplane is ready. I've already arranged for a jeep and driver. I'll walk you downstairs. Do you want a soda?" He had a refrigerator in the corner of his office.

"Yes, please. A Pepsi, if you have it." He gave it to me.

We walked out, down the hall, then the staircase to the main lobby. I sipped my ice-cold soda as we walked. The building was cooled by the constant sea breeze. It was pleasant. He led me to the front door. I was suspicious of the solicitous treatment.

"We'll wait here until the jeep comes from the motor pool. I want to tell you about a special unit that's based in Nha Trang. They run hunter-killer and reconnaissance patrols in various parts of Vietnam. It's a bit risky, but nothing worse than what you've already seen. You live at a forward location for a couple of weeks and then return to Nha Trang for a week or so. They need a forward air controller. One of the two is going home. Would you be interested?"

Stewart was a super-salesman. He lured me from his office, with its uninspiring view, to proposition me overlooking an inviting beach. Then he flatters me by using the VIP entrance, but keeps me incommunicado from the other staff.

"Sure, I'm interested. What's the unit called?" The jeep drove up.

"Project Delta. It's part of Special Forces. It's nothing definite, but we'll keep you advised. Have a good flight." He saluted me as I climbed in the jeep. Colonels don't usually salute lieutenants. It's the other way around.

I had a great deal of respect for Stewart, but I thought I'd been duped again. We drove out between the flowerbeds.

I had a couple of hours before heading up the coast. The Officers' Club was near the flight line. The driver dropped me off and I enjoyed an American hamburger, served by an attractive Vietnamese waitress. She was tall, like Gabrielle. I finished eating, then walked to the flight line.

The flight to Tuy Hoa was uneventful. I took the direct route and didn't bother looking down. I kept mulling over Stewart's offer. Or was it an order? What was the unit? Project Delta. I recalled they were shot up at Bong Son and the An Loa valley.

The next day we rotated the other O–1 to Nha Trang for maintenance. The one I brought back was to perform the work of two aircraft, at least for a day or two. We kept a FAC airborne from first light to last light and then on alert for night missions. We still flew a minimum of three or four hours a day, helped out in the command post, and worked the next day's operation plan with the Army. I was in the command post, refamiliarizing myself with the battle scenario because I had missed a day while in Nha Trang. During the morning we lost radio contact with the airborne FAC. Thinking that he might be out of range, we asked some of the Army aircraft to raise him. No luck. Just as we were fearing the worst, the silver O–1 appeared overhead. No radio contact. He landed and I walked to the airstrip. I noticed the gunships were not on the alert pad.

"John, the damn radios went out. Nothing. No VHF, no UHF, no FM," said the pilot, Skinner Simpson. Skinner was a fellow lieutenant. I knew him. He was in the class behind me at the Academy.

"Could you hear us? We tried you on all frequencies."

"Nope. Couldn't hear anything. Not even background static. Even tried the backseat jack box." Major Allison joined us. Skinner turned to him.

"Sir, we have a real problem. Complete radio failure. Transmitter and receiver, all radios. There must be some common power source or bus that knocks out all the radios. Both seats."

Major Allison addressed us. "John, I want you to return to the command post and notify the DASC that our FAC plane is out of commission. See if they can expedite the return of our other bird or get us a replacement. Skinner, you stay with the aircraft. Maybe the Army avionics people can help us. Their L–19s aren't all that different from ours. I think they have some spare parts. Let's just hope we don't have to put in any air strikes until we fix it."

I advised the DASC. They would divert the afternoon air cap to another target. I advised our Army counterparts and hung around the CP. The clouds started to move in and the sky turned overcast and gray. An intermittent light rain started as I got some coffee. I walked to the Army operations center and listened to their traffic. Some unit was in a fire fight, location unknown. Another SITREP came in. They were pinned down and had some wounded. They had requested a medevac. I walked 20 feet to the other side of the room to the Aviation command section.

"Where are the gunships?" I asked.

"They've been detached to cover another mission," was the response.

"I understand. But where?"

"Cheo Reo or someplace to the west." That was over 50 miles away and it would be hard to determine their fuel or weapons status. I walked back to the operations net and listened. Apparently the medevac had tried to make the pickup, but had been driven off by ground fire. The FSC advised me they were conducting a fire mission with the 105mm howitzers to suppress the weapons fire. If the enemy fire was coming from anyplace near the coordinates in the SITREP, they wouldn't hit much. The entire area was honeycombed with trenches and deep bunkers. I asked our duty NCO if the O–1's radios were fixed. Negative. I picked up the telephone that gave us a troposcatter relay to the DASC and asked for the fighter duty officer.

Captain Brown, FiDO," said the voice on the end.

"Filthy, it's Flanagan. I need a favor. Can I get the air cap back for this afternoon?"

"I thought we told you no more crazy requests. Why? You got your airplane fixed?"

I could have lied. "No, not yet, but we'll work something out." I understood their command and control nets from yesterday's visit. I knew that if the air cap was anyplace in II Corps, the DASC could reach them either through a radar site or a FAC. "Send them to the 170 degree radial at 40 nautical miles off Channel 58. The weather is about 1500 overcast with light rain. Have them let down to the east of the rendezvous and listen up on primary strike freq."

"Hey, Air Force," someone shouted across the room, "Can you help us? The medevac didn't make it." This was apparently the second try. Brave men to go back in there.

"Filthy, you still there?"

"Yeah."

"Well, I got big trouble now. I need those fighters. Have them contact Ragged Scooper seven-four. I'm flying the mission. Call us on HF if you can't pull it off."

"You are fuckin' crazy." He was true to his sobriquet. I hung up the phone and shouted across the room.

"I got fighters. I need an L–19." I'd borrow an Army Bird Dog and direct the strike from it. The airplanes were virtually identical to ours. They had an extra FM radio. I ran across the room to the Army aviation desk.

"What's the tail number of an airplane that you have ready to go?" I asked.

"You can't fly it. It's Army. It's against regulations," said the captain.

I leaned across his desk and said quietly but forcefully, "There are guys out there dying. The medevac can't get in. I have fighters on the way and I intend to knock those guns out. I am going to the flight line and take one of your airplanes and the only way you're going to stop me is to shoot me or the airplane." I went to the S–3's desk and copied the call sign and coordinates of the waylaid troopers. The S–3 was an "old head" major and had anticipated what I was doing. The Air Force duty NCO shouted at me.

"DASC confirmed your fighters. Hobo two-five." My buddies from the 1st Air Commando Squadron. They were the best.

I raced out the door to my tent to pick up my flying gear. I threw my survival bag with my new radio over my shoulder, put my headset around my neck, and grabbed my M–16 and web gear. I tucked my map under my arm and buckled my gunbelt while I ran to the airstrip. I spotted the Army L–19. It was close to our O–1. I noticed the sky. The ceiling was dropping. I threw my gear in the airplane and started a fast preflight inspection. An Army lieutenant with aviator's wings on his fatigues showed up.

"The major says that I'm supposed to take you on an airstrike. He says that I should do whatever you ask."

Cooler heads than mine prevailed. I asked, "Have you ever controlled an air strike?"

"No. Only directed artillery fire."

"Okay. I'll hop in the backseat. You get this thing airborne and I'll take it from there. Let's go."

With the lieutenant flying, it gave me a chance to plan my mission. I circled the coordinates on my map and noted the terrain elevation of approximately 500 feet. The fighters had about 1,000 feet to work with under the cloud deck. It would be tight and we'd be well within the effective range of small arms fire. As we taxied out, the fighters checked in with me. They were still 30 miles away at 9,000 feet. I gave them a quick update. Friendlies pinned down. Enemy fire coming from bunkers. Trying to get wounded out. Weather not too pure. Need hard bombs. We taxied into take-off position.

"Roger, Scooper. We copy. We've been here before. All we got are some 250s and some frags. Don't think the Willie Petes will help much. Got some small napes, too," said Hobo. Lead was telling me that he was willing to work under the cloud deck, even though it was far below his optimum or approved altitude, and that maybe the antipersonal fragmentation clusters might be of help, since the only hard bombs he had were the small 250s. The bomb loaders in Qui Nhon had warned me about the scarcity of big bombs.

"Hobo, when you hit the rendezvous, start down on a heading of 090 degrees. That will take you over the water. If you don't break out by 1,000 feet, I suggest you climb back up. It's too risky." We were now rolling down the runway, my hand poised to grab the stick in the backseat. My feet were already on the rudder pedals, just to make sure we didn't lose directional control. I had never flown with an Army pilot in the Bird Dog.

The A–1s penetrated the clouds and broke out at 1,200 feet indicated altitude. The ceiling was still dropping, but the rain was only intermittent showers. I directed the fighters toward me. I contacted the friendlies. They were close to the coastline where the local terrain elevation was 300 to 400 feet. The fighters now had less than 1,000 feet of ceiling to work under. I pinpointed the VC complex—typical zigzag trench lines, interspersed with log-reinforced bunkers. There were no fields of fire from the bunkers themselves. The VC were apparently firing from the trench lines, and when the artillery fire would start, they'd hide under the overhead protection of the bunkers. When the artillery ceased, they would re-emerge and fire at the friendlies and the helicopters once again. I had a plan. The fighters called me.

"Scooper, this is Hobo. I can see the trenches and bunkers, but I don't see you. What's this Army L–19 doing in the target area? Are they going to fire artillery?" I forgot to tell them I was in the olive-drab Army bird. Nothing puts fear in a fighter pilot's heart faster than seeing friendly artillery hitting under him. The "big sky, small shell" concept did not always work, as several aircraft had been hit by friendly arty.

"It's me. I've changed services. Faster promotions," I joked. "Hobo, I need sustained target coverage on the trenches and bunkers. They're in the bunkers. Your 250s won't even make a dent. I want to bottle up the Cong while we slip a medevac chopper in. Napalm in the trenches will keep them from using their gun positions."

"Rog. We understand," said Hobo Lead.

I could hear the ground troops talking to the chopper on FM. I flipped to the FM radio to call the ground troops. Nothing. The Army bird had two FMs, so I tried again. Success. I was flying the aircraft now. I used the foot switch on the floor to control the radio transmission. Visibility from the backseat is marginal compared to the big windshield in the front seat. All I could see was the back of the pilot's head. This required me to stand the plane on its wing, look out the side windows, and then rack the plane in a series of violent S turns, to keep the target, friendlies, fighters, and helicopters in sight. I was displacing my aggression on the unfortunate front seater, as my violent manuevers threw the Army pilot from one side of the cockpit to the other.

I transmitted to the medevac, "Dustoff, this is Ragged Scooper, the FAC." They would expect the silver O–1. "Hold east of the friendlies as low as you can. When you see bombs and napalm, slip in, make the pickup—*you must stay low, under the fighters*." Dustoff acknowledged. The fighters were working well below their usual 5,000 foot, dive-bomb altitude. We had enough problems without a midair collision.

The plan was unfolding. I'd run the fighters from north to south, with a left-hand break. With the deteriorating visibility from the rain showers, this would enable them to keep the target, chopper, and friendlies in sight at all times. The only place for me to hold, where I could see, was to the west of the enemy. Everything was in place, or so I thought.

The Hobos discussed their tactics. They were unable to dive-bomb their ordnances, so they would level-bomb it. There was a problem. Except for the napalm, which was delivered in a shallow, dive angle, no one had ever tested level-bombing 250s and frags. The pilots didn't have any mil settings to put in their gun-sights, in order to calculate the proper release point. Also, they didn't know the safe envelope, to avoid being hit with the shrapnel from their own bombs, not to mention the VC ground fire. In order to save those wounded troopers, the two fighter pilots were improvising unproven bombing techniques that would have taken a dozen engineers six months to test in the States. And the Hobos might die doing it.

Lead advised Two. "I tried this once with 500s. Just as soon as the target went under the nose, I counted thousand-one, thousand-two, and pickled. I'll let you know, Two." With all this milling around, the VC must have gained a sense of security because I could see khaki and black uniforms running up and down the trenches.

As I gave back control of the aircraft to my front-seater, I said, "Put a smoke rocket in the trench line by the khaki uniform. He must be NVA. I have to give a positive target ID to the fighters."

He replied, "I don't have any. All I have is HE." High explosive. No smoke rockets. I forgot. We FACs use them, but there's a shortage, so there was no reason to expect the Army to have any.

"Gimme the plane back." I grabbed the control stick, pulled two smoke grenades from the seat pocket in front of me, pushed the nose down, and flew down the trench line at 20 feet. I threw the grenades out the window. Best to keep the Cong off balance by doing something unexpected. I pulled the plane up into a chandelle and stepped on the mike switch.

"Hobo, you're cleared hot," I transmitted on UHF and flipped to FM. "Dustoff, if the bombs are close, I want you to start your run. Do you see the smoke? That's where the fire will come from. Put your door gunners on it." The VC shoot at medical helicopters. We shoot back. So much for the Geneva convention and the rules of engagement.

A bomb landed 200 meters short. An unprecedented miss for the highly skilled Hobos, even with makeshift bombing techniques. "Hobo, what happened?" I asked on the UHF radio.

"I forgot to count." He said to his wingman, "Two, count to three and pickle." Number Two started his run. He dropped.

"Long bomb, Two, fifty meters. Maybe you should try two and a half," I said facetiously. They had it bracketed. The khaki uniforms had disappeared from the trench line. I switched to FM.

"Come on in, Dustoff. The water's fine." The Hobos would be on target with their next pass. The next bomb hit in the center of the bunker. It didn't destroy it, but the occupants would have some awful earaches. The Hobos had the technique. They alternated the frag clusters and napalm with the bombs. Dustoff picked up the wounded without taking any hits. The friendlies moved out as they flanked the bunker position. I gave control of the airplane back to the Army pilot.

The mission typified the unsung bravery that occurred routinely. The ground troops hung tough, protecting and supporting their wounded comrades. The fearless medevac pilots made numerous attempts to rescue the wounded. The intrepid fighter pilots relentlessly pursued a mission that clearly exceeded the bounds of regulations. The Army L–19 pilot was the bravest—I flew his airplane with reckless abandon, yet he never wavered during the entire mission.

The following day I flew over the same complex but at a higher altitude. The cloud deck had lifted. The bombs I'd considered misses revealed an extension of the trenches that I had not observed in the heat of the battle. Napalm had burned off some of the camouflage, exposing more of the network. As I passed, I happened to look over my shoulder. A VC had emerged from the camouflage and was shooting at me. He saw the opportunity to take a few cheap shots. I chopped the throttle, slammed the stick over, and pulled—a perfect split S. I armed a rocket, fired, and the VC disappeared in a cloud of white phosphorous smoke. Fair's fair. He took the first shot.

It was a clear morning. No fog. No mist. I had the first go. I was in the CP. I tore the frag order from the teletype machine. The mission listed three C–123s plus two B–57s, three cargo planes and two light bombers. That was an odd mix. I was the FAC. I looked at the target coordinates and plotted them on my map. They outlined a block of jungle that was 10 percent of our entire area. I was confused. We couldn't dent that target. Then it dawned on me. It was a ranch-hand mission. The C–123s were spray birds that were to spray defoliant on the jungle. The defoliant contained Agent Orange and the deadly chemical 2,4,5-T. But I didn't know about its potential gene-altering and cancer causing effects.

I flew to the edge of the target area. The C–123s had a navigator on board, they knew precisely where they were going. The B–57s also had navigators. This was simple—until the ground fire started. The prop-driven Providers, lumbering across the jungle at several hundred feet, were inviting targets for enemy gunners. The spray operator was in the center of the cargo compartment, encased in an armor-plated, unlidded box. As the aircraft took hits, he threw smoke grenades out the cargo doors. It was my task to search back from the smoke and find the gun. This was not a great idea. First, I knew the VC were accurate shooters because they had already hit the 123. Second, they hadn't put their guns away; they were looking for another chance to hit the spray birds. Third, they knew I would come back to look for them. But back I went, twisting through the settling and blowing defoliant mist, searching for the gun. More often it found me. That's why we had the very accurate Canberra escort. They would instantly pounce from their circling perch, swoop down as if to ingest the smoke from my marking rocket, and unleash the wrath of their guns, bombs, and napalm. The Canberra's attack reminded me of the Academy's mascot, the hunting Falcon. Many times I had watched that circling bird, at football half-time shows, plummet in a wing-tucked dive to unerringly snatch the whirling lure from the cadet handler. Even today, when I watch the Falcon strike, I am reminded of the shock wave of the bombs, reverberating through the jungle; I can still see the winking ground fire, and smell the burning napalm.

With the 101st, we worked very closely with the intelligence officer, the S–2. He had specialists in photo and electronic intelligence as well as a collection of information from paid agents. They had a recent SPAR, special agent report, reinforced by some recent IR, infra-red, photos of VC activity in the southwest sector. On my next FAC mission, I took the air cap A–1Es there to look. We searched for targets in the area. I noticed white smoke, similar to what we used for marking, rising three klicks north of the target area. I concentrated on the area of the SPAR and IR photos. I found a suspicious location and advised the Skyraider I was marking. Ten seconds later he advised seeing the mark, but I hadn't marked. White smoke was again visible, this time one klick from where I intended to mark. Someone on the ground knew our tactics. They were either trying to lure us off the target, or into a trap. I switched to a colored smoke grenade, had the fighter identify the color and then drop his anti-personnel bombs on the target.

After landing, I told the next FAC about the mysterious smoke. He went to the same area, encountered the same sequence of events, but he put the bombs on the deceiver's mark. This game of hide-and-seek was a draw; I hit my original smoke and the next FAC hit Charlie's smoke.

We debriefed the Army intelligence section. The S–2 officer had aerial photos that showed a possible radio antenna in the vicinity of the strikes. The enemy was apparently monitoring our UHF strike control frequencies. They understood English and our procedures. I suspected the NVA were involved, since we'd glimpsed khaki-uniformed troops in the area.

The Army chased us from our valley of mysterious smoke. It was no longer a free-fire zone. Allegedly, they were inserting a long-range reconnaissance patrol in the area and they didn't want us to drop any bombs on them. I think the real reason was the Air Force had uncovered a combined

VC and NVA marshalling and training complex. The Army was embarrassed they hadn't found it sooner. The operation was scheduled to close in the next few days.

My tour with the United States 101st Airborne Brigade was drawing to a close. With the exception of the Nha Trang trip, I had flown daily combat missions. Working with the Army staff officers, I had planned the missions and actively participated in the strategy and implementation process. Overall performance, whether successful or a failure, was difficult to measure. Assigning responsibility was easy; determining accountability was illusive. FACs, as individuals with the 101st, had a distinct advantage; they fought the same battles that they planned. Accountability, whether it be in planning or its execution, was identified with the specific FAC. Achievement was measurable—the defined mission was accomplished, the bombs were at the right place at the right time in support of the Army operation. On a higher level, however, unit performance by the Air Force was measured only by sorties flown and tons of bombs dropped in support of the 101st. Many of these sorties were superfluous and ineffective, which exacerbated the munitions shortages; but no one was held accountable.

At the Army unit level—whether it be company, battalion, or the entire brigade—performance was undefined. Success and failure had ambiguous measurements. Success was measured in enemy attrition and kilograms of rice captured, for which there was no quantified objective. Failure was never recognized. Missed opportunities and friendly casualties could be failures, but they, too, were never identified. Performance was subjective comparison, relative success versus relative failure, enemy versus friendly.

I still wonder if anyone was ever held accountable for the tragedy of the helicopter assault that I witnessed, for the failure to exploit the valley of mysterious smoke, or the defoliation mission that was clearly too late in the operation to be of value to the 101st troopers. In retrospect, the untimely spray mission reduced the exposure of the troops to Agent Orange.

The 101st was responsible for fighting a war of attrition, seeking out the enemy, closing, and then inflicting maximum casualties. "Find the bastards, then pile on." Their battles were fluid and opportunistic. Once contact was broken, the 101st would launch yet another pursuit. They would fight on the same turf, the same jungle and paddy, any number of times. Winning, in the war of attrition, was measured by how many of the enemy died. But no score card was exchanged; there were no referees; the 101st posted its own score. If the numbers were to be believed, the enemy had a high tolerance for dying, but that didn't make the 101st winners. The enemy threat would reappear the next day in the same area.

The Americans had the benefit of technology, the latest weapons, communications, unlimited helicopter and artillery support, and instant tactical air support. They were on the leading edge of developing and implementing airmobile tactics. Some commanders abused technology. Pilots were ordered to fly in unsafe conditions. Battalion commanders issued commands, via radio, to platoon and squad-level units, bypassing levels of commanders, countermanding their orders, and undermining the authority of the intermediate commanders. The incorrect smoke mark on the ambushed LZ came from a command helicopter, not a scout helicopter. The leader closest to the battle no longer led.

In balance however, the lowest unit leader was never denied the available resources, shortages notwithstanding, of the American war machine. He had artillery support and helicopter medical evacuation. We, as FACs, did our very best to support the ground troops, in spite of the shortages of bombs, smoke rockets, cannons, and FAC aircraft.

The strategy and tactics of the Korean Tiger Division were a marked contrast to the American Screaming Eagles. The Koreans were fighting a war of territorial occupation, a more classic war scheme. Performance measurement, either at the individual or unit level, or whether it be attributed to plan or execution, was more finite, more concrete. Whereas the Koreans took longer to prepare and launch an operation, their results were more permanent. They pushed out the VC by killing and capturing, then occupied the territory, fighting for it only once. The Korean forces maintained a presence in the pacified territory, working with the local villagers and farmers. Seized rice was directed into the open market, as were the subsequent harvests. They were products of a common culture and identified with the people. The VC were reluctant to return to, or challenge, the ROKs. Witness the planning, execution, and results of Tiger V.

Compared to the U.S. forces, the technical and logistical support for the Koreans was limited. They relied on the weapons they used in the Korean War, thirteen years prior. Helicopter support was rationed and prioritized, requiring more emphasis on conventional infantry tactics. The Koreans practiced detailed and systematic planning. Reflecting their Oriental culture, they were patient, foregoing the short-term opportunity to achieve longer-term results. They were masters of small-unit tactics—by the book with reliance on unit integrity and the chain of command. Whereas the 101st used helicopters and distant fire bases to probe and fix the enemy, the Koreans stole out of camp prior to sunset to stealthily patrol and set up ambushes. Tac air support was available, but on a lesser scale. Coordination was difficult at the squad or platoon level, due to the language differences. But they were tenacious fighters, schooled in discipline, and accustomed to hardship.

Each unit, Korean division and American brigade, was successful in its own way. The objective for II Corps was to prevent the VC and NVA forces from cutting the country in half, from the Laotian/Cambodian border, across the Central Highlands, to the South China Sea. The implementation by IFFV headquarters was opportunistic: the Americans used airmobile forces and enemy attrition; the Koreans used conventional infantry and territorial occupation. Central Vietnam was never cut in half, but victory never seemed to be achievable; it was undefined and unmeasurable.

Operation Harrison was finished. The 101st displayed, for the press, VIPs, and Saigon commandos, the captured equipment, supplies, and weapons. I looked through the materiel and found U.S. commercial medical supplies whose date-stamps indicated recent manufacture. I found medicines and bandages, of French manufacture, that were less than a year old. I wondered how this stuff was getting into the pipeline. I realized that as a nation at war we were not prepared to bomb or mine Haiphong harbor and cut off the supply source. Instead, we used America's drafted and professional GIs, humping through booby trapped jungle, to uncover some measly cache. I also realized we were engaged with a tough and determined enemy, one of knowledge and shrewdness. He knew our strike tactics and frequencies, deep in South Vietnam. I saw displayed for the first time a 12.7mm (.51-caliber) machine gun mounted on a tripod, with a 360-degree field of fire and antiaircraft sights. This weapon had twice the effectiveness of anything I had encountered; it would readily destroy an O–1, let alone a hovering helicopter. I was to personally tangle with one of these lethal weapons on my next operation.

I had had enough war for a while. I was anxious to return to Qui Nhon, to the restaurants, to the villa, and I wanted to sail.

7

Project Delta at Chu Lai; Flying the F–4

The Viet Cong never quit. With my gear in the backseat, I was leaving Tuy Hoa, flying to Tiger Town, when I received an urgent message from Eagle Ops to confirm a report of an ambushed convoy. The report was correct: a convoy had been hit on Highway 1, on its way to Qui Nhon, yet still in the 101st area. When I arrived overhead, the helicopter gunships were already spraying the roadside with machine guns the way weed killer is sprayed along a highway. The attackers withdrew, not anxious for a big fight. The area was supposedly pacified and secure. Someone forgot to tell the Cong.

The district intelligence network had channeled to the ROKs a report that I found very disturbing. We knew that the VC had captured a FAC far south from us—someplace in the III Corps area—and were moving him north through the jungle, probably to North Vietnam. Peasants had seen him in our vicinity. They described him as a skeleton of a man, shackled and shuffling, confined in a bamboo cage by day that he was forced to carry by night. The VC proudly displayed him as an example of the "invincible American flyers." We futilely searched the jungle for three days on the chance we might spot him. A nearby Special Forces camp doubled their patrols. No luck, but intelligence reports were not always accurate. I changed the last round in my revolver from tracer to ball ammunition. I wouldn't be taken alive.

Tiger Town was dullsville. The Koreans were still mopping up from Tiger V. They had pushed the Cong eastward to the sea. During my absence one of the FACs caught over a hundred VC at daybreak awaiting water transport to escape the pursuing ROKs. The VC navy never showed. The air strikes and artillery fire turned the water blood-red as the VC tried to escape using commandeered sampans. The Korean sharpshooters picked off the swimmers. The war was getting nasty. We deserved a mini-vacation—a sailing trip would do nicely.

The FACs in the villa welcomed the excursion. We needed an escape from the broiling heat. Ocean breezes were the answer. Our neighbors, eager to help, located the fisherman with whom I had the earlier discussions. Bringing soda, beer, and bathing suits, we bought fried plantains from the beach vendors, rolled them in rice paper, and with some raw fish proffered by our sailing captain, had our shipboard fare. Who cared about the war? Our neighbors wore sailing attire well. They enjoyed the time off as much as we did.

A message came through from the DASC. I was to be at Tiger Town on April 14. An airplane would pick me up. Nothing more. No details. It was only two days away. I waited.

On the appointed day, I drove one of the radio jeeps through the post-dawn mist from Qui Nhon to Tiger Town. The trip was now routine, although I always drove with the radios on to summon help if I were hit. An O–1 emerged from the murky sky and slipped into Tiger Town. No radio call. A jeep had already picked up the pilot when I reached the regimental tent. He was tall, six-foot one or two, dark hair, about my age, with one of the most engaging smiles that I had ever seen. He greeted me when I entered the tent.

"You must be John Flanagan." He could see my name tag on my fatigues. "I'm Jim Ahmann. I've come to pick you up. We're going on an operation." We vaguely recognized each other. He was a fellow Zoomie, a year ahead of me. The eavesdroppers in the tent listened with curiosity; Jim offered no further information.

"A pleasure to see you again. I heard someone was coming by," I responded, shaking his extended hand. He didn't have a name tag or rank on his fatigues. He wore a leather pistol belt, slung low on his hips like a gunfighter from the Old West. His fatigues were unlike anything I had ever seen—unmarked, black and shades of green in an irregular striped pattern, a tiger suit. A green beret stuck unobtrusively from the hip pocket; captain's bars shone on the exposed flash. My palms were suddenly sweaty. I had "volunteered" for Special Forces. "Let me get my gear," I said. He slipped into his web gear that had been slung over the back of a folding chair. I noticed that he had an inverted sheath knife attached to his suspenders and a D-ring sewn into them. He needed no further introduction. He was from Project Delta.

Project Delta, Jim explained as we drove to the strip, was an autonomous reconnaissance unit staffed by American and Vietnamese Special Forces, the American 281st Assault Helicopter Company, the Vietnamese 91st Airborne Ranger Battalion, and a USAF Tactical Air Control Party. The core of the unit was the American Special Forces, Detachment B–52, 5th Special Forces

Group. The missions he would explain later. We took off, heading north and paralleling the South China Sea.

Jim briefed me over the intercom during the 110-mile fight. We were headed for Chu Lai, a coastal Marine base, which had elements of the III Marine Amphibious Force and an associated Marine air wing. Project Delta would be operating reconnaissance patrols 35 miles west of the base, in the Annamite Range, rugged 5,000- to 8,500-foot mountains which formed the spine of the upper regions of Vietnam. It was a major infiltration route and staging area for the NVA and VC who threatened the coastal plains and cities. It was several valleys south of the infamous A Shau Valley and Special Forces camp of the same name.

As we passed over Phu Cat, I showed Jim where I had been on patrols with the ROKs. He mentioned that he had been on patrols with the 25th ARVN Division in III Corps. I did not envy him, and I respected his courage to patrol with the Vietnamese. They didn't have the combat reputation of the Koreans. We passed Bong Son, 40 miles up the coast from Qui Nhon. Jim confirmed the rumors that I had heard earlier. Delta had been badly shot up in the An Loa Valley. They had lost some teams, but I didn't know what that meant. The commander, a Major Beckwith, while flying on an aerial reconnaissance in a helicopter, took a 12.7mm round through the gut and was medevacked to Qui Nhon. He almost died; I knew what that meant.

Jim told me the Plei Me story in which Delta heroically reinforced the camp besieged by two NVA regiments. This was the first confirmed presence of NVA regulars in South Vietnam. They found enemy machine gunners chained to their weapons. I didn't like what I heard, but I was now committed.

We contacted Chu Lai tower for landing instructions. The field was swarming with Marine A–4 Skyhawks taking off and recovering from missions. The runway was aluminum matting laid over the sand. Heat shimmered from the surface. He landed and tied the aircraft down in a corner of the congested ramp. The heat penetrated the thick soles of our jungle boots. It was like walking on a frying pan. We were met by a Project Delta jeep.

We rode across sandy, rolling knolls covered with scrub vegetation. The Marines had tent communities everywhere—trim, perfectly aligned, but most of them exposed to the beating sun and blowing sand. The Delta camp was buried in a clump of trees, barely visible until the jeep was virtually on top of it. A Nung guard, a Chinese ethnic mercenary, slipped from behind a tree and motioned us through the concertina wire. The camp was comprised of a dozen or so tents nestled under the trees. Placement was functional; operations tents in one area, living tents in another, but all made maximum use of natural cover for concealment and shade. The GP mediums comfortably accommodated fifteen or twenty men with their gear and surplus cots for transients. The billeting was by organization: recon, aviation, Rangers, senior enlisted staff, officers, and camp workers. The commander, a lieutenant colonel, had a smaller tent of his own, as did the sergeant major. This was home.

Jim introduced me to the various members of the staff as we walked around the camp. Whenever we met a Vietnamese, Jim would say something in their language and they would smile or laugh and respond. Jim had lived with the Vietnamese for over five months in Tay Ninh where he had been a sector FAC before joining Delta. This was my first close contact with Vietnamese military forces. I was to grow to respect them.

Jim explained to me the operating concept of Project Delta. The core of the organization was the six-man reconnaissance teams led by a Vietnamese lieutenant with a team sergeant, two soldiers, and two American advisors. They were usually inserted into the jungle just prior to nightfall by helicopter. Their mission was to observe and report, and avoid physical contact with the enemy. In addition, Delta had teams of "roadrunners," indigenous Vietnamese who dressed in VC or NVA uniforms, carried enemy weapons and identification papers, and openly traveled the trails and explored the jungle way stations. To accomplish force recon and to serve as an emergency reaction force, one or two companies from the Airborne Ranger Battalion, the best of the Vietnamese Army, deployed with Delta. The primary mission of Delta was intelligence gathering, but it had the capability to destroy targets of opportunity with airpower. In support, Delta had its own Army helicopter detachment of Hueys, UH–1B Hog gunships, and UH–1D Slick transports, and two Air Force FACs with an O–1E Bird Dog. The dedicated air support, Army and Air Force, provided the flexibility and strike power which differentiated Delta from its distant cousins, the British SAS forces in Malaya and the French Berets Rouges in Indo-China.

This was Jim's first operation as the air liaison officer, the senior Air Force Officer. He had been the FAC with Delta for over three months. His predecessor was preparing to go home, which I found very encouraging. While Jim flew off to Da Nang to accomplish the coordination with the I Corps DASC, I familiarized myself with the maps, radio nets, and call signs. I met the officers and noticed that most of them, the captains and lieutenants, were younger than the sergeants, but well-qualified in their fields. I talked with some of the sergeants. They had been in Special Forces for years, some back to the 1950s, and had been fighting in Indo-China since the early 1960s. When I asked where and for whom, they just smiled; they later revealed they came from Laos and worked for the "Company," the CIA. They were experienced jungle fighters.

The first two reconnaissance teams went in at last light, inserted deep into the mountains by helicopter. They were followed the next day by a road-runner team, dropped also by helicopter, in the middle of a trail network. We maintained radio contact using radio relay aircraft. The SF communications technicians rigged the O–1 with an additional long, wire antenna extending from the wing strut back to the tail for the compact walkie-talkies that the roadrunners carried. A bilingual VN would fly with us.

I did most of the flying during the operation while Jim handled the liaison with the Marines, the DASC, and Delta command elements. I learned the special operating procedures, signals, map codes, and techniques that Delta had originated and perfected. The FAC had to develop a sixth sense working with the teams, knowing when to offer assistance, when to leave them alone, and when to take decisive action as dangerous situations unfurled. One of the teams had missed a scheduled radio contact. I was scrambled to attempt communication with them and in my haste, while taxiing on the congested ramp, I bashed a wingtip and aileron on a maintenance work-stand. I hopped out of the cockpit, bent the aileron back to its near-intended shape, disregarded the foot-long dent in the wing's leading edge, and took off anyway. The team was OK, but the plane wobbled slightly.

Meanwhile, in the exercise of his responsibilities, Jim was having command and authority problems. The Marines wouldn't give Delta permission to hit targets spotted by the recon teams or roadrunners. They wanted all enemy sightings reported directly to their tactical operations center and they would decide on the target disposition—infantry assault, helicopter envelopment, artillery fire mission, or air strike. This could endanger the teams and allow perishable targets to vanish into the jungle. To compound the problem the Marines would not allow Air Force fighters in their area of operations and we were dependent on the Air Force for our fighter support. We were victims of the command structure.

Jim made a decision. "John," he said. "Unless I can get this situation resolved, we're going home. We're not here to play radio relay for the Army or to give the Marines free reign in our area of operation. I'm going to talk to Colonel Warren." Lieutenant Colonel Warren was the commander of Delta.

"Sounds good to me. I'll wait for you." I was a political neophyte to offer any substantive advice. I took my dirty tiger suit, four of which I had received on arrival, to one of the Nungs for washing for a few piastres. Jim returned shortly.

"Warren wasn't too happy, but he understands. He's not pleased with the Marine arrangement either and is thinking of pulling all of Delta," related Jim. Weighty decision. "Let's go for a ride." We drove to the Marine operations center, a complex of three hooches located near the airfield. One of the buildings had a sign over the door, *III MAF—DASC*. We were in luck. The Marines had a DASC just like the Air Force.

A lieutenant colonel with pilot's wings—bristle haircut, cigar, squatty build, typical Marine—greeted us, looking for our rank and insignia. "Can I *hep* you boys?" he offered in a Southern drawl.

"Yes, *suh*," replied Jim. I suddenly noticed a Kentucky accent, his boy-hood roots. "We're from Project Delta and having a little problem with air support. The Air Force F–4s from Da Nang aren't used to working close to friendlies—." The Marine cut him off. Jim had completely skirted the issue.

"You boys came to the right place. We Marines perfected close air sup-port. Every pilot is combat infantry first. We use 250-pound snakeyes and napalm on the A–4s. Real accurate." The colonel was taking the bait.

"Well, sir, we've got some recon teams operating for III-MAF, west of here. They usually find targets—troops. Sometimes it gets real hairy if the team gets in a firefight and we have to pull them out under fire. KBAs," Jim continued. Enemy body counts made great press and the Marine fighters would get the credit. Jim kept dangling the bait.

"Here's our frequencies and call signs," said the Colonel as he exhaled a cloud of cigar smoke and handed preprinted cards to Jim and me. He was hooked. "We have birds on five-minute alert." Jim had pulled off the ultimate finesse. He had conned the Marines. They seldom committed their aircraft to the central allocation system run by 7th Air Force in Saigon. They retained control to support Marine operations only, but now we had a direct line into the Marine DASC with preapproved clearance in their airspace. "By the way, what do you boys do? Are you flyers?" he asked.

"We're F-A-Cs," replied Jim, spelling out the letters the same way that the Marine FACs identified themselves. "We've got an O–1E on the ramp."

"You guys are crazy. Like our FACs. Only one aircraft? Everybody flies in sections in I Corps, including helos and FACs. Too dangerous. Glad you stopped by." We shook hands and left. Jim and I looked at each other. We had beat the system. We had air support and target clearance. Now to see how Colonel Warren made out. As we rode back to the camp, Jim told me that the Air Force DASC had also cautioned him about flying single ship. The FACs in I Corps always flew in pairs for mutual support against ground fire and to maintain communications in the high mountains. We promised ourselves to be cautious and to maintain radio contact.

Colonel Warren had also resolved his problems with the III MAF com-mand. The tension in the camp disappeared, Delta was in full swing. The next two weeks were a blur of activity as teams were inserted and extracted. I was flying every day, long, intense missions, as Jim kept the precarious support channels open. On one mission, while searching for a team in the high mountains, a hidden 12.7mm gun opened up on me. This is what nailed the helicopters at Tuy Hoa. I recall the tracer rounds flashing across the nose of the aircraft; they looked like orange golf balls arcing through the sky. I was momentarily mesmerized, but rapidly recovered my senses and dove for the safety of the treetops. Close call.

On another day, two of the teams were simultaneously in deep trouble. One of the teams had snatched two local VC as prisoners and we were trying to get them out of the jungle with the helicopters. The other team had been compromised, spotted by the VC, and spent the day evading search parties. I spent ten hours and 40 minutes airborne, working with the teams and directing Marine fighters and Delta's helicopters. At one spell I never left the seat for six hours and 20 minutes. Jim had radioed the local FACs at a dirt strip near Quang Ngai that I needed a fast turnaround. The mechanics filled the gas tanks, dumped in a quart of oil, reloaded the rockets, wiped the windshield, taped the bullet holes, and gave my backseat Green Beret an armful of smoke grenades. We had relieved ourselves in empty grenade cans and traded them for two canteens of fresh water. All in less than three minutes.

We pulled one of the teams out with the enemy nipping at their heels, the extraction helicopter drawing fire as it lifted over the tops of the towering trees. The helicopter gunships were spraying the dense jungle with machine-gun and rocket fire—mostly to distract the enemy. I had two Marine A–4s holding overhead.

"Skyhawk, what's your load?" I asked, wanting to know their ordnance. They replied with a nomenclature that I didn't understand. I flipped through my checklists, not finding a description of the ordnance. The gunships came on the FM radio.

"FAC, this is Wolfpack. We've been taking fire about two hundred meters north of where the team came out. It's too thick to see anything. We're headed home. No bullets. Good luck."

"Thanks, Wolfpack." I switched to Uniform. "Skyhawk, we're taking some fire. I'll give you a mark. No friendlies in the area. Cleared for random passes. That ordnance you have, does it burn or go boom?" I wouldn't admit my ignorance, but I anticipated napalm or small bombs as the Marine colonel had promised.

"Goes boom," replied the section leader. Fair enough, I thought. It's a bomb. I slammed a smoke rocket into the dense jungle and set up an orbit over the target. "Cleared hot. Singles if you can," I advised the fighters, requesting their bombs one at a time. I watched the A–4s roll-in from 8,000 feet. They were small and difficult to see. I was too low, barely 1,000 feet, when I saw the first bomb separate from the fighter as he pulled out of his dive. I watched the bomb plunge earthward, growing larger and larger. It would pass right under me. It was the biggest goddamn bomb I had ever seen!

It hit. *Kaboom!* Kowabunga! The shockwave rolled from the epicenter. Trees crashed as if they were a bundle of pick-up sticks. Some were hurled hundreds of feet through the air, roots and all. Then the shock wave hit the O–1, sharply slinging it upward, our bodies painfully held in check by lapbelts and harnesses. The second fighter rolled in with his bomb. Another monster. I struggled for altitude, anxiously watching the downward path of the second bomb. *Kaboom!*

"What was that?" I asked Skyhawk.

"A thousand-pounder or so. We just got them," Lead replied.

"Nice," I said casually, trying to maintain my composure and thanking God that my airplane wasn't riddled with shrapnel or tree limbs. We dropped the remaining six bombs in the area of the groundfire, converting the jungle into a wasteland. Nothing could have survived; everything was literally blown into pieces. And I learned a lesson. I'd make damn sure of the munitions before I cleared a drop. I could have hurt some friendlies or blown myself out of the sky due to my stupidity and Irish arrogance.

More teams went in. There were signs of enemy activity but no major troop concentrations. One of the team members stared down a VC who was six feet away from him. The VC saw his raised rifle and fled. Another team member stared down a tiger, not wanting to shoot for fear of alerting the enemy. Colonel Warren went in with one of the teams, was separated upon insertion, and spent three days reconnoitering on his own—leadership by example. He had no radio; he flashed me with a mirror and we picked him up. Then a road-runner team's cover was blown; their radio, inoperative. I found them by chance on a trail and we got them out. Delta had some of the bravest men I had ever met in my life. I was in awe.

We had a couple of days when no teams were in the jungle. Several of us took this opportunity to go to the beach. It was absolutely magnificent—expansive stretches of pure white sand—the Marines even had a hot dog stand. Jim and I hit the Officers' Club. The Marine pilots lived in tents with sand floors, but the club rivaled anything stateside. They entertained themselves with games of raucous destruction—people and property alike. Carrier landings: a pilot, with a running start, attempted to slide on his belly the length of the sawdust-slicked bar top in a mock landing—or disastrous crash. Three-man lift: a subterfuge to lure an unsuspecting, and frequently pompous, visitor into a compromising position on the floor for a feat of strength, only to have pitchers of beer poured upon him by the devious bystanders.

The last teams were successfully extracted from the jungle. The *Stars and Stripes* carried a story about B–52 bombers going into North Vietnam. An Army intelligence officer, a fellow lieutenant attached temporarily to Delta to interrogate our prisoners, advised me that the flow of supplies was increasing from the North. I wondered when we would bomb Haiphong harbor.

Our initial difficulties with the Marine command structure were resolved, but it demonstrated to me the complexities of waging a war. Although Delta was an autonomous unit, it was dependent on operational authority from its requesting unit, in this case III MAF, who frequently had parochial interests. This, as I was later to discover, was endemic to the Vietnam War.

During the operation I learned more about Project Delta. Much of the credit for shaping the unit belonged to the persevering leadership of Major

"Charging Charlie" Beckwith. Jim Ahmann had worked for Beckwith before Beckwith was gravely wounded. Beckwith "cared for his men, expected a lot but really cared." (Beckwith recovered from his wounds, founded the counterterrorist Delta Force in the 1970s, and led the aborted hostage-rescue mission to Iran in April 1980.) The core of the Vietnam Delta was the sixteen reconnaissance teams who rotated on missions into the jungle. Depending on the threat, up to four teams could be in the jungle at any one time; that was the maximum number that could be safely supported. Delta was an all-volunteer unit with high esprit de corps.

But it, too, had ambiguities in the command structure. It took the joint decision of the American commander and his Vietnamese Special Forces counterpart to deploy the full resources of Delta. The support Ranger battalion was under the command of a Vietnamese general in Nha Trang. The unit was frequently deployed as a show of force to dissuade dissident political factions who threatened the authority of the Saigon government. Consequently, there was often a hidden political agenda. In spite of the shortcomings, the unit was structurally and conceptually suited to wage a jungle war: find the enemy and destroy them with firepower, or send a major conventional unit to do the job.

The operation closed and Jim and I headed back to Qui Nhon so I could collect my remaining gear. I would then join Delta at their permanent location in Nha Trang. I had passed my combat audition and as Jim stated, "The guys think you're all right. You've got your shit together." I was pleased. There was no higher compliment in Delta.

I arrived at Qui Nhon. My euphoria was short-lived. During my absence I had been reassigned to the ROKs. A colonel in Saigon learned about my transfer to Delta and determined that I wasn't eligible. The Air Force staffers had decided that the replacement FAC to Delta should have between five and seven months remaining in his tour. I had over eight months remaining. I would assuage my disappointment at the villa and the beach.

But that too had changed. We had been evicted from our villa. Some regulation had been invoked by the Army declaring our villa, which we paid for with our own money, as unauthorized. The open beaches, too, had disappeared. They were off-limits. The only authorized bathing area was a barbed wire enclosure staffed by gun-toting MPs who examined ID cards, denied access to Vietnamese, and confiscated beer. I was briefed on the other rules implemented by the Army general in command of the Qui Nhon Support Area. No more than four people and no less than two were to ride in a jeep. The driver had to be in uniform. No Vietnamese nationals were to ride in government vehicles unless they were U.S. government employees. No weapons were allowed within the city limits. All bars and restaurants were also off-limits, forcing all dining into the mess halls and military-run clubs. Unreasonable curfews were imposed and rigidly enforced; traffic tickets were given for the slightest infraction. We moved into three airless, depressing rooms in a U.S. contract compound that had apparently been a boarding academy.

Morale plummeted, but now we had a new challenge—how to beat the Army's system. We always kept an extra flight suit in the jeeps in town; the driver, officer or enlisted, pulled the suit over his civilian clothes. We knew where the secluded restaurants were and left the jeep in the approved parking compounds. We took our chances with the curfew, claiming we were en route to or from the airfield or Tiger Town when stopped. My seminarian friend from the cathedral told us about a leper colony with a secluded and secure beach one mile south of the airfield. A charitable contribution to the presiding prelate insured undisturbed beach privileges for ourselves, our enlisted men, and our Vietnamese guests.

Jump Myers, the Skyraider detachment commander, had several resourceful circumventions to the Army's rules. His mechanics worked long and hard keeping those ancient beasts flying. Crews pulled 24 hour alert, and Jump recognized their dedication. Since the Army controlled the beer distribution in Qui Nhon, Jump would dispatch a flight of A–1s to wherever beer was available and the birds would return with their cavernous bellies laden with cases of beer. Air Force flight suits were bartered for cases of steaks. On Saturday nights, the Surfs hosted a barbecue and beer bust at the airfield for all the Air Force personnel in the Qui Nhon area. This mandatory dining formation extended beyond the Army's curfew hours.

The Army was out to get the nonconforming Air Force. Rules were tightened and violations chronicled. Air Force commanders were openly criticized at joint administrative meetings. Relations were strained between the two services. The highest ranking Air Force officers in the area were majors and most of the personnel were involved in a combat mission. Compared with the Army supply staff, Air Force people were exciting and attractive to the Army nurses from the nearby field hospital. This further incensed the Army "bigs," culminating in the Army general bringing Jump Myers up on court-martial charges for an aggravated curfew violation. Fate had dealt another blow to Jump, who only a month prior had been shot down defending a Special Forces camp and then miraculously rescued.

Military lawyers, armed with brief cases and legal tomes, descended on Qui Nhon. The Air Force lawyers had commandeered one of our three rooms to prepare their defense briefs. It was Army versus Air Force; the battle had escalated to the generals in Saigon—an intractable situation. It was resolved only when Jump agreed to accept an Article 15, a nonjudicial punishment that would be prejudicial to his career. Jump had surrendered; that battle was over and the Army had won.

The entire atmosphere in Qui Nhon had changed. Work details for the GI were pure drudgery. The convoy drivers had nothing to look forward to upon their return from An Khe. The combat GIs, denied their anticipated fun-filled frolic, were bored and hostile. Our ROMADs were constantly hassled whenever they went into town, particularly since they carried their weapons and were conspicious in their bush hats. There were no smiles, no laughter, no escape, no girlfriends. A wedge had been driven between the Vietnamese townspeople and the GIs. I heard more frequently the terms *gooks* and *slopes*, replacing the more respectful term *Viets*. The MP jeeps made more calls to the GI compounds as drunken revelry and fights broke out among the frustrated soldiers. With no place else to go, officers drank themselves into stupors at the MACV compound Officers' Club bar. The commanders were unknowingly planting the seeds for the erosion of command authority and the proliferation of drug abuse in Vietnam.

In a sense, we were surrendering to the Viet Cong. We were being separated from the people we came to defend against Communism. On May Day, a traditional Communist holiday, the entire town was off-limits, giving the Communist sympathizers full reign to conduct their demonstrations and parades in the streets. We should have clogged the streets with American and Korean troops and vehicles, completely overwhelming and thwarting the demonstrators. The VC and their supporters were terrified of the Koreans. This was an ideological war, why should we just fight it in the jungles and rice paddies? I wanted out. I wanted back to Delta.

Col. Stewart appeared unannounced at the regimental tent. He was passing through Tiger Town on a field visit to the DASC Alpha TACP locations in II Corps. He sought me out and called me aside. I thought I was in for an ass-chewing because I had openly criticized my assignment debacle.

"John," he said, "I'm sorry about the assignment screw-up. I think you know what happened."

"Yeah, I think so." I skipped the "sir." I was still pissed; not at him, but at the system. "This place gives me a case of the ass." He was taken back by my crudeness, didn't recognize the Special Forces slang, but knew my feelings.

"The staff at Delta were pleased with your performance. More important, you fit. I assume you want to go back."

"Yes, sir!" I didn't hesitate with my response.

"OK. I thought so. Here's what we'll do." Stewart looked at a pocket calendar and continued. "Today is the first. On the seventh, move your gear to Nha Trang, and then report to Cam Ranh Bay on Sunday, the next day. I'll cut orders for you to fly in the backseat of the F–4 for a week, TDY. Then I'll transfer you, PCS, to Special Forces. How does that sound?"

"Great, sir. Thanks." May Day wasn't so bad after all. I would have the opportunity to do what I liked best: chase VC with Delta and get a chance to fly the F–4.

The week could not go by fast enough. I finally moved to the Delta compound in Nha Trang. We lived in hooches, with two men to a room. I hung my clothes in a closet for the first time in four months. This was my new home. The unit was deployed on an operation to War Zone C, in

III Corps. The next morning I hitched a chopper ride to Cam Ranh Bay. It was a short, scenic flight over the water. It was as beautiful as the day in early April when Stewart recruited me for Delta.

I had thought Chu Lai was an instant airbase by the sea. Cam Ranh dwarfed it, and it was still under construction. Like Chu Lai, the runway was interlocking sections of aluminum matting laid on the sand. Airplanes straying from the runway or taxiways were instantly bogged down in the sand. Walking was difficult except on the scattered boards. The expansive ramp was home to the 72 or so F–4Cs belonging to the 12th Tac Fighter Wing. Some of the F–4s were in revetments, while others were lined up wingtip to wingtip, waiting for the construction program to protect them. Where the Marines had tents and sand floors for living quarters, the Air Force had prefabricated, single-story, H-shaped barracks, divided into bunk rooms and a common lounge. I would bunk and fly with the 557th Tac Fighter Squadron, the Sharkbaits.

The program of having FACs fly as GIBs, guy in the backseat, in the Phantoms was well conceived and soundly executed. It was hassle-free, educational, and fun. I was fitted with a helmet, oxygen mask, G-suit, survival vest, inflatable water wings, and parachute harness. The Martin-Baker ejection seat contained the parachute itself. I was taught how to set up the inertial navigation system and operate the radar intercept system for air-to-air combat. I was surprised to learn the aircraft did not have self-sealing fuel tanks or armor plate. On my first mission, I felt uncomfortable strapping into an aircraft without my rifle. It had become an extension of myself and I feared being shot down without it, but, unlike the O–1 and A–1, there was no room in the cockpit.

We flew missions into Laos, usually in flights of three aircraft, and carried hard bombs. We'd contact Hillsboro, the airborne command post similar to a DASC, for a handoff to the FAC. Now I realized how dependent the fighter pilots were on the FACs to locate and mark targets, particularly in broken clouds and low visibility. We worked with the Tiger Hound FACs interdicting the flow of supplies south on the Ho Chi Minh Trail. We were looking for trucks but my FAC-trained eyes spotted some bicycles parked under the jungle canopy as we went in on a low-level snake-eye pass. Unlike the bicycles I saw near Qui Nhon, these were not heading to market with rice and produce, but were carrying boxes of grenades and rockets. We hit them. Seen from the cockpit, strafing with the 20mm Gatling gun was as impressive as from the ground. The pilot would nudge the rudder pedals, spraying the high explosive rounds about the target.

If we had to bail out at any time during the mission, I wondered where the nearest safe refuge was. As a FAC, we usually knew where the enemy concentrations were and we would plan to crash-land or bail out as far away as possible. Now I understood why the F–4 that took the wing tank hit near Tuy Hoa was so anxious to get home.

I'd fly the bird to and from the target area. I enjoyed flying formation again, and with the fuel burned down and ordnance gone, the F–4 could do some impressive aerobatics and max-performance maneuvers. I'd pull four to six Gs, just to feel the wings shudder as we approached a high-speed stall, knowing that our inflated G-suits would keep us from blacking out. Each mission lasted about an hour and 50 minutes, which was typical for an in-country or southern Laos mission.

I usually flew in the morning and spent the early afternoon wandering around the base, watching, listening to, and talking with people I met. Many of them wanted to know about the country and the people. Few of them had ever left Cam Ranh or even met a Vietnamese. Most of the construction workers were Filipino. The constant landings, usually to the north on the single north-south runway, were gradually sliding the entire 10,000-foot runway inches a day across the sand. Taxiway vibrations were jarring munitions loose on the aircraft. Work was being expedited on the parallel concrete runway. The mechanics and armorers, grizzled sergeants and adolescent airmen toiled for hours in the blazing sun or torrential downpours, readying the birds for the next mission. They followed their procedural checklists, even though it was not always the most efficient way to accomplish the task. An inspection team from Saigon had visited the flight line and noted that the men were out of uniform, they were working in the insufferable heat with their shirts off. They now kept their shirts on, griped, but kept working.

Late afternoon was beach time, Words could not describe the magnificence of the miles of pure white sand, clear, azure water, and gentle, rolling surf. I could wade a hundred yards into the surf and the water would reach only my waist. It was more beautiful than Nha Trang or Chu Lai, and much warmer than Cape Cod Bay. But Nha Trang had beach clubs, Chu Lai had a hot dog stand, and Cape Cod was in another world.

I looked forward to the evenings as an opportunity to renew old friendships and trade war stories in the Officers' Club and the Sharkbaits' lounge. But it wasn't the same atmosphere of fun and partying of Pleiku, Chu Lai, and Qui Nhon. I learned why. This is where I heard the other facets of the war: the tragedies, the frustrations, the deceits, and the hidden dangers. No one seemed to have any humorous stories.

I learned of the death of one of my Academy classmates, Terry Griffey, in an F–4 crash south of Qui Nhon. Terry was one of the few front-seat qualified lieutenants. The official cause was ground fire. I talked to a sector FAC in Qui Nhon who told me about the F–4 that virtually disintegrated as soon as the pilot released the snake-eye bombs. It was the same time as Terry's death. There was no ground fire in the area. There were fuse problems with bombs. Terry's loss was one of those unexplained tragedies.

Another tale touched me closely. A FAC had died in a mid-air collision over Laos. He was controlling a flight of F–105s that had been diverted from a North Vietnam target due to poor weather. The Thud drivers, unaccustomed to working with a FAC and forced to cope with marginal weather and the ludicrously camouflaged O–1s, lost sight of him. The radio transmissions overheard by the F–4 pilots were, "I think I hit something"— "Has anyone seen the FAC?"—"Oh my God! I hit the FAC." The FAC was Karl Worst. We shared rides to work during FAC school at Hurlburt.

Another classmate, Russ Goodenough, also a front-seat qualified lieutenant, had been shot down over Laos. He was on the ground for an hour, evading capture, before he was picked up by a helicopter. Russ was in top physical condition, but he said, "John, I was never so tired in my life, or thirsty. Every place I ran or tried to hide, it was full of troops. I jumped into a trench, armed only with my thirty-eight. Nothing but VC in the trench. They were as surprised as I was. I got out of there." To Russ, all enemy were VC. The official Air Force channels didn't acknowledge NVA troops in Laos.

A Sharkbait F–4 driver, Bernie Giere, was shot down over the southern area of North Vietnam. He bailed out and as he heard the jabbering of the armed militia searching for him, all he could think was, "It's fish heads and rice for dinner." He also was rescued. Bernie had two ejections in Vietnam. The other occurred when his bird ran out of fuel over the airbase. He was orbiting while a disabled aircraft was removed from the single runway. Running low on fuel, he advised the command post of his situation. They directed him to hold and not divert to an alternate airfield. He flamed out on downwind, ejected, and he and his backseater (it was his third ejection) completed the landing by parachute. The commander thought it better that they go home before their year was up. Bernie was jump-qualified, a graduate of the Army's rigorous parachute training course. He surmised that the "paranoid powers" thought he was earning his senior parachutist badge at the expense of the Air Force's F–4s.

The personal frustrations of the war were epitomized by the first lieutenants who were assigned to the backseat and unable to upgrade to the front seat. Many of them had more applicable experience and flying time than the aircraft commanders with whom they were flying. Reb Daniel and George Harrison, two other classmates, were in this situation. The Air Force, after several abortive attempts, finally implemented an in-theater qualification program, but not until they had thoroughly demoralized some combat-hardened junior officers.

I bunked under Doc Simmons, the squadron flight surgeon. Business, for him, was slow. He spent his time flying missions in the backseat. He became an accomplished GIB and the jocks were glad to have him along. The biggest complaint from his medical charges was the persistent crotch rash which the pilots developed from the constant dampness in the groin area. Having suffered from the same affliction, now cured, I passed along the advice the Project Delta medic gave me—stop wearing underwear; it traps fungus-fostering moisture on the skin. He laughed and said he would recommend it.

Every time I entered the Sharkbaits' lounge I was disturbed by the two hand-drawn posters that hung on the wall. One was a wooden cross of obvious religious connotation with the words *Kill a Commie for Christ* and the other was the American flag with the words *Fuck Communism.* I inquired about their origin and was told that they were drawn by American elementary school children in Okinawa and given to one of the pilots by the teacher. It frightened me to think of the impact that those posters had on the impressionable youngsters, and more significantly, the values of the educator who not only condoned but encouraged this irreverent and conflicting display of support. Our adult institutions were divided over the purpose, legality, and morality of the war, yet we were unwittingly distorting the values of our youth, undermining the foundation of our future. Maybe I overreacted, but after four months of combat, that's how I felt.

My week was over. I had enjoyed the air conditioning, fans, ice, American cooking, and washing machines. Except for the few pilots who had been on a FAC familiarization, the personnel were isolated from the country and its people. The American military were confined to the sprawling base, which covered the entirety of the peninsula. It was like flying from a stateside airbase except the bombs were always live, the range was bigger, and sometimes the planes didn't come back. I admired their flying and fighting credo; modest bravery was envied, timidity abhorred, recklessness forbidden, and sound judgment respected.

But I was frightened by the truths that I had learned and the frustrations of the men who were waging the war. I thought we had the logistical support of the government behind us when we launched on our jungle tracking missions, but we didn't. My thoughts, captured at that time, were disheartening.

The Defense Department is lying. There is an acute shortage of bombs. The F–4Cs previously carried six or eight bombs, now they carry only four; they used to carry four cans of napalm, now only two. They ran out of 20mm explosive bullets and are now using target practice ammunition. We can't get smoke rockets for our O–1s and the smoke grenades that we throw out the window are no damn good. Only one in four white ones go off. The other colors ignite more frequently, but who can see green smoke in a green jungle.

Jim Ahmann picked me up at Cam Ranh in an O–1 and brought me back to Nha Trang. Delta had returned from a successful operation in III Corps. One of the teams spotted a battalion of VC in an open section of jungle. Ken Kerr, the other Delta FAC whom I replaced, decimated the troops with air strikes. He had to borrow an airplane from the local FACs to fly the mission. They were upset when he brought it back shot full of holes. *C'est la guerre.*

Jim explained to me the machinations of my reassignment to Delta. Colonel Stewart discovered that the colonel in Saigon who cancelled my transfer was due for rotation back to the States. Stewart then kept me hidden with the Koreans, tucked me away at Cam Ranh, waited for the colonel to leave, and sent me back to Delta. Stewart's wars were different from mine.

I met the remainder of the Delta troops and staff who were not at Chu Lai. The project had its own club and mess facility, the Delta Hilton, which prided itself in the best of food served by comely Vietnamese waitresses. The club was for officer and enlisted alike and much of the off-duty time was spent there. The working relationships that I had experienced in the tension-filled operations were reinforced in the relaxed atmosphere of the Hilton and the hooches. They were based on mutual respect and dependency, intensified by danger, and resulted in extraordinary camaraderie and unit cohesion. I did not know how strong and sometimes painful this commitment was to become, but I would learn in the subsequent months.

Left: John Flanagan in Vietnamese-style tiger-suit fatigues at Nha Trang Air Base. The Ol-E Bird Dog, armed with smoke rockets under the wing, was the first aircraft used by the Air Force forward air controllers in Vietnam. *Right*: Deployed to a forward operating base with Project Delta. Note the deep drainage ditch and rolled-down tent sides that were typical for the monsoon season. The antenna on the rear of the MRC–108 radio jeep is for the HF radio.

Under the palms at Phu Cat with staff members of the Third Battalion, First Regiment, ROK Tiger Division.

Top: Briefing the brigade commander and staff of the 25th Division at Oasis. Many of Project Delta's displays were bilingual, as indicated on the map sheets. *Bottom*: Jim Ahmann, with his cowboy gunbelt, and John Flanagan, on his first Project Delta deployment, at Chu Lai. Note the larger warhead of the much-preferred white phosphorus marking rocket.

Top: One of the early Huey gunships from the 281st Assault Helicopter Company. The "hogs" escorted the Huey "slicks," which carried the troops. Note both rocket pods and M–60 machine guns extending from the fuselage. *Center*: From left, recon members Johnnie Varner, Gene Moreau, Norm Doney, and Street St. Laurent walk to the slicks at Tay Ninh. *Bottom*: Gene Moreau (foreground) and Johnnie Varner (right) prior to boarding the insertion helicopter with their Vietnamese team members. Moreau was killed and Varner was wounded the next day when they made contact with the VC in war zone C.

Top: Charlie Telfair (second from left), Russ Bott (right), who was later MIA, and the Vietnamese team members prior to insertion into war zone C, north of Tay Ninh. *Center*: The FAC, in his slow Bird Dog, was the link between the ground forces and the fast-movers. *Bottom*: A flight of fast-movers, the F-100 Super Sabres, headed on a tactical air-strike mission.

Left: Bernie Giere, sporting a handlebar moustache, flew the F–4C for the Sharkbaits out of Cam Rahn Bay. Note the underwing bombs and centerline gun pod. After Vietnam he became an airline pilot and eventually a colonel in the Reserve. *Bottom*: Rhodes scholar Bob Baxter flew the F-100 and was a member of the Dice squadron in Bien Hoa. His helmet is resting on an auxiliary fuel tank; the underwing pod contains cluster-bomb units. Baxter later became a White House Fellow and a brigadier general.

Top: Denny Hague is grasping the barrel of one of the four 20mm cannons on his A–1E. The arming propellers are visible on the noses of the 500-pound general-purpose bombs. Hague was a member of the Hobos flying from Pleiku and later became a partner in an insurance firm in Idaho and a general in the Reserve. *Bottom*: Jim Ahmann (left) just prior to one of his parachute jumps in Nha Trang. The primary chute was a backpack, with a chestpack as the reserve. Note the D-ring that activated the reserve chute.

Top: Lieutenants Flanagan and Simpson receive their parachutist badges from the commander of the Vietnamese airborne brigade. *Center*: One of the typical garrison hooches in the Delta compound in Nha Trang. Note the shutters to block rain and direct light. The sandbagged revetments had right-angle entrances to thwart gunfire and intruders. *Bottom*: Partying at the Delta Hilton: Jim Ahmann (at microphone), Joe Turner, John Flanagan, and Skinner Simpson. Note the highly visible regulation insignia on Ahmann's fatigues.

Top: Additional fun at the Hilton: Ron Deaton, Flanagan, Simpson, Ahmann, and Turner. *Center*: John Flanagan with Tommy Carpenter at Khe Sanh. Carpenter led the striker force that recovered the bodies of the FAC and his Special Forces observer ten miles north of the base. *Bottom*: Tommy Tucker and John Flanagan at Khe Sanh. Tucker insisted on flying with Flanagan during the height of the monsoon when they searched for a beleaguered reconnaissance team on the Laotian and North Vietnamese border.

8

The Central Highlands:
Battling Monsoons and VC

Project Delta ran local training exercises in Nha Trang. Part of their mission was to staff and operate a recondo training school for their replacement personnel as well as for conventional U.S. units that were expanding their organic, long-range reconnaissance patrols, LRRPs. As FACs, we would teach classes and cover the operations. It was an interesting concept of training; the enemy was real.

Delta was alerted for an operation. We were to deploy to the Central Highlands of II Corps, co-located with and attached to a brigade of the American 25th Infantry Division, the Wolfhounds. Our forward operating base, FOB, would be Oasis, 15 miles equidistant, southwest from the city of Pleiku and northwest from the SF camp at Plei Me. When we arrived, Delta was assigned an area of operations, AO, along the Cambodian border, 20 miles west of the FOB.

We were going into the heart of NVA country. The American 1st Cav had been badly bloodied in the nearby Ira Drang valley six months prior. Delta's teams were to recon there. The NVA had staged from the Chu Prong mountains which straddled the border and overlooked the Ira Drang. Teams would be inserted there, too. The monsoons were rapidly approaching which would hinder flying operations.

The monsoons and the airfield were to be as hazardous as the NVA themselves. The runway was 3,000 feet long, barely sufficient for the four-engine C–130s to shuttle supplies. The strip had been bulldozed through the elephant grass, sharply crowned for drainage, and covered with a rubberized membrane. The runway was so severely sloped that it was preferable to take-off downhill and land uphill, regardless of the winds. When the C–130s landed, the membrane would roll in a wave in front of the aircraft.

This wasn't dangerous on landing, but on take-off the Herky Birds were barely able to achieve take-off speed as they pushed the rubber bow wave, like a bubble in a carpet, ahead of them. As one Herky pilot told me, "I reached the end of the runway, unable to accelerate, saw nothing but towering elephant grass, trees, and ditch in front of me, pulled back on the yoke, and somehow it flew. We were at seventy knots, stalling speed, but we made it." Fortunately, the VNAF C–47, the Gooney Bird, Delta's primary re-supply link, required much less runway.

The monsoons flooded the dirt roads in the camp causing the Army vehicles to bog down in the axle-deep mud. They would then use the runway for travel from one end of the camp to the other. This covered the already slick membrane with mud, causing airplanes to skid off the runway into the ditches. An Army L–19 skidded off the runway, tipped nose-down, snapped the prop, and seized the engine. Combat operations were being curtailed; the U.S. Army was being strangled by its logistical tail. The runway was closed for reconstruction, also strangling Delta.

The first teams went in as scheduled on May 24. I staged from Pleiku during the day while Jim remained at the FOB. Fortunately the Army would reopen the airfield at night, allowing me to fly in at last light and receive a situation update. The NVA were hiding. One of the teams snatched a peasant for interrogation from the ill-defined Cambodian border area. He provided no information. The monsoon weather offered only marginal flying conditions with usually 1,000-foot ceilings in the operational area. Due to the differences in terrain elevation, the airfields at Oasis and Pleiku could be buried in the clouds, dangerously isolating the teams from FAC and helicopter support.

I was at the SF "C" Team compound in Pleiku when a radio message came through: "Launch Airedale ASAP. Recon team confirms battalion of VC. Air strike requested." Airedale was my personal identifier. The message was from Delta. The duty sergeant followed me out the door as we raced for the jeep. As we reached it, the skies opened with a torrential downpour; the height of the monsoons. It didn't slow the sergeant's driving. Vehicles, blinded by rain, had pulled to the side, clearing the road to the airfield. We skidded to a stop next to the O–1.

"Sarge," I yelled above the din of the pelting rain, "you get the tie-down ropes and chocks. I'll pull the pins." The Air Force crew chiefs scrambled from their hut, surprised to see anyone trying to launch an airplane. Lightning sizzled across the airfield, followed by the sharp crack of thunder. They recognized our urgency.

"Just get in, sir. We'll get it," shouted the senior crew chief. I was soaked while running to the airplane. A young airman pulled the cockpit door open and I piled in, smacking my knee on the door frame. He handed me the shoulder harness straps. I fed the lap-belt tongue through the harness loops and snapped the buckle shut.

"Here's the pins." The crew chief stuffed them in my seat pocket. The ropes were untied, one set of chocks already pulled. I slid the mixture control forward, turned the magneto switch to *Both*, hit the boost pump, and punched the starter button. I was flicking radio switches on before the engine even fired. The engine caught and someone pulled the remaining chocks, not waiting for my signal. The three of them stood there, absolutely soaked, hair plastered onto their heads, and as if on cue, extended their right arms, fists clenched, and gave me a thumbs up. I saluted them, pushed the throttle forward, and headed for the runway.

"O–1 taxiing southbound, say call sign," I heard in my headset. It was Pleiku tower calling me. I couldn't transmit because the radios hadn't warmed up yet. Receive, yes. Transmit, no. I pressed on, taxiing as fast as I dared, riding the brakes while I accomplished the magneto check. "Taxiing O–1, this is Pleiku tower. Be advised the airfield is closed."

"Rog, Pleiku. Say your active." The transmitter worked. The rain showed no signs of slackening. I looked to where the control tower was. I couldn't understand how they saw me because they were buried in the clouds. I came to a midfield intersection. My intended flight direction was west. I'd take off to the west. I proceeded up the taxiway, to the runway.

"O–1 taking the runway, be advised the field is closed. The weather is below minimums. State intentions." Another bolt of lightning flashed across the sky. I saw clearer sky to the west. The runway was flooded, 3,000 feet of lake remaining, and the O–1 was not amphibious.

"I'm rolling," I advised the tower. I urged the throttle full forward. The prop whipped the water to a froth, slinging it at the cockpit. I glanced down at the wheels. They were half-submerged, creating double waves as the aircraft barely accelerated. I pushed the stick forward, forcing the tail up and pulling the tail wheel out of the water. Acceleration increased but now the wheels were hydroplaning. The aircraft slewed down the runway as I struggled to maintain directional control, furiously pumping the rudder pedals. I couldn't see forward. I stole quick glances at the runway edges, keeping the aircraft equidistant between them.

"Say pilot's name and home station." The tower wouldn't give up. I hadn't filed a flight plan. They wanted to file a violation on me, but they couldn't if they didn't know who I was. I was finally airborne, water still streaming from the spinning wheels. I passed over the field boundary. I couldn't see anything.

I barely recognized the road at the edge of the field. It went southwest, through downtown Pleiku, the direction I wanted to go. I flew through Pleiku. I was so low that people ducked. I recognized the contraband for sale, stacked in doorways, out of the rain.

When I passed the other side of Pleiku, the terrain fell off and I had more ground clearance. By the time I reached the team's location, the rain had ceased and there was a 1,500-foot ceiling, good enough to work fighters with snakes and napes. Jim advised that a flight of two F–4s was holding over Plei Me, under the overcast. Every fighter jock that worked in II Corps knew where Plei Me was, only 20 miles from the Cambodian border. The VC used it for their live infiltration and mortar training.

I contacted the team and went searching for the illusive VC battalion. Unable to follow the VC safely, the team had lost sight of them. The terrain was flat grassland criss-crossed with numerous streams and small rivers, with dense trees and vegetation along the riverbanks. The F–4s had only four napes, two each, no snakes, but a full gun-load, 1,200 rounds, of 20mm HEI—the good stuff—and lots of gas. We knew the VC's direction of march, their approximate speed, and last known location. I briefed the F–4s on the situation, gave them a no-bomb line in order to protect the team, and turned them loose.

I fired a mark to get started. "We got your mark, FAC," said Lead. He continued, "Lead's in. Two, follow me through dry and take a look." They relished the opportunity to be their own FAC. I had challenged them and they were determined to find the VC. They hit major clumps of trees that could conceal a marching unit, alternating passes, dropping one can at a time, then searching. I flew at treetop level; they flew below the trees. I looked in the grass; they parted the grass. I had one pair of eyes per aircraft; they had two.

"FAC, we can't find them," said Lead.

"No flashes, no ground fire, no nothing. What do you think?" inquired Two. I could sense their frustration.

"I think we're up against a highly disciplined, well-camouflaged NVA unit who knows we're after them," I responded.

"FAC, we still got plenty of gas and the gun left." I cursed the shortage of bombs—risking four lives and two jet aircraft for four meager cans of napalm.

"Rog. Keep an eye on me. I'm going trolling. Watch for my smokes." I dropped down to the treetops, lowered the flaps so that I could fly slower and turn tighter, and started cruising the tree lines, weaving back and forth, trying to draw fire. Since it was a unit on the move, I didn't expect them to have any big guns or the opportunity to set them up. If they did, they would have gone for the fighters. I'd take my chances with a quick burst from an AK–47. I was crazy, but not stupid.

Now I was frustrated. To take off in a rainstorm, have an altercation with a control tower, terrify a village, chase a known target, try to get shot at, and then to come up empty-handed—it was too much. I started throwing smokes out the window into the most likely tree lines, concentrating on those bordering the wider and swifter streams. They would slow the NVA's march and force them into hiding during our search.

"Lead, have at it. Work the trees with the smokes. Keep in mind the no-fire line. Good luck." Working like a bird dog, I followed the fighters, scenting to flush the game, ready for the kill. Still nothing.

"We're Winchester, FAC."

"Rog. Thanks for the effort. Tell the Sharkbaits hello from Airedale. Stand-by for your BDA." I gave them their times, coordinates, and, regretfully, a negative BDA.

"Will do. We enjoyed the rat race. We don't get down in the weeds too often. Two, go button twelve." Number Two acknowledged the radio channel change and the F–4s disappeared through the overcast. I unslung my M–16 from the cockpit light and fired at the last smoke. It jammed on the second burst.

I landed at Oasis. There was enough usable runway. Jim met me at the airplane, wanting to know what happened to the battalion of VC.

"Jim, we lost them. They just disappeared. The team's okay. I need some coffee." I was still wet from the rainstorm at takeoff. We slid some new rockets into the empty tubes as the Army avgas truck pulled up.

"Fill it up, sir?" asked the young private. He moved the ladder into position and dragged the hose to the top of the wing.

"Yeah, both tanks." I couldn't resist adding, "and get the windshield, too, please." He smiled. Jim helped me with my gear.

"Where's your flak vest?" he asked.

"Under the seat cushion. Protecting the family jewels. Leave it there." He shook his head and we walked to the jeep as I extracted the jammed cartridge from my M–16. "Piece of shit," I mumbled. We headed for the TOC.

Delta held an afternoon briefing for the brigade commander, a one-star general. A separate brigade rated a brigadier general. His staff accompanied him into Delta's briefing tent. They looked surprised when they were greeted by a Vietnamese officer, Major Tut, who introduced himself as the commander. Technically, he was. We were advisors. The briefing charts were lettered in Vietnamese, another surprise for the Americans. The general took it in stride, but some of his staff were nonplused. I hung in the back as the briefing developed. It finally got to the inevitable question, "What happened to the VC battalion?" Vague answers came forth. The general pressed. He wanted an answer. I watched the S–2 squirm. He caught my eye, as if pleading for help. I walked to the front and, pointing to the map, explained our vain search. I suggested, based on the enemy's disciplined lack of response to the bombing and strafing, that the unit was NVA. The general agreed. He then wanted to know why it took 40 minutes from the original sighting to when an aircraft was overhead.

The communications sergeant replied, "The message came first to commo, sir. We passed it immediately to the intell section." The S–2 responded next, "We plotted the coordinates and verified the team's position with operations." The general fidgeted. The S–3 spoke. "We decided to send the FAC to check it out. We asked the ALO if the weather was good enough for an air strike." I was beginning to enjoy this. I edged to the side. I wanted out of the line of fire. The S–3 continued. "We sent a message to the C team in Pleiku to launch the FAC." The general promptly cut the charade off.

He fired, "What the hell was the FAC doing in Pleiku?" I sensed that he was gunning for the Air Force. I waited, expecting one of the general's staff to advise him that the field at Oasis was closed to fixed-wing aircraft. No one spoke up. After a polite wait, Jim stood and spoke from the far side of the tent.

"Sir, I'm Captain Ahmann, the ALO for Project Delta. The strip at Oasis has been closed for the last several days. Pleiku was the nearest secure airfield that we could stage from. The fighters were here within twenty minutes of our air strike request."

The general fired again. He advised his staff, emphatically and with ass-chewing vengeance, that the field would be open and if the engineers had to work on it they could do so at night, since his infantry fought at night as did the enemy. "Captain," he said, addressing Jim, "where is your airplane now?"

"On the field, sir." I was glad I had recovered at Oasis instead of Pleiku.

"Good. Now keep it there. Is there anything else for the briefing?" Pause. "Thank you, gentlemen." The general rose. "Keep up the good work. We'll get the bastards next time." His staff followed him out. That was my first personal exposure to a combat general. I liked it.

Jim and I exited the tent together. He handed me an envelope, postmarked Boston. It was an invitation to my graduation. I officially had my MBA degree. I had missed graduation; it was held that day.

The teams hunted and searched. Lots of signs on the trails, but no significant live sightings. One of the teams spotted a VC transportation squad with four elephants laden with munitions and supplies. Jim hit them with an air strike. The DASC wouldn't believe the BDA. He changed the elephants into transports. Then the DASC believed him.

I swapped flying lessons with the Army chopper pilots. I let them fly the O–1, which was a change for them since they were all rotary-wing qualified, and they taught me how to fly the Huey. I could take off and land it, but hovering was something else. This led to an offer from one of the chopper crew chiefs to fly a mission as a door gunner, if I would take him on a recce mission in the O–1. He checked me out on the M–60 machine gun. I donned the metal chest and groin armor, borrowed a helmet, and strapped in as the left-side door gunner on the reserve pick-up chopper. I fired a few bursts for practice as we skimmed across the jungle. Fortunately, we didn't have to make a pick-up. I respected those kids on the guns. They had it "all hanging out." That's one job they could keep.

The runway was closed again to transports. The monsoons were taking their toll in spite of the engineers. Delta was running low on supplies. The Americans borrowed from the 25th Division, but this didn't help our Vietnamese counterparts, who, including the Rangers, numbered several hundred. The VNAF slipped their Gooney bird under the low clouds and parachuted rice, live animals, and produce into the camp. They could parachute supplies as accurately as they could drop bombs. I met one pilot who had parachuted supplies to the French. They had years of practice.

Due to the marginal weather, Delta made changes to its proven procedures. As fog and rain moved over the elevated terrain of the FOB, teams had to be inserted during the most favorable weather conditions rather than waiting for the security of last light. Low clouds and fog were forecast for evening. A team was inserted in late afternoon. I flew cover, observing the insertion, ready to help if the LZ were hot. The choppers returned to Oasis while I orbited nearby until the team confirmed they were secure, and then followed the choppers home. The weather deteriorated as predicted.

A misty twilight settled over the camp. The tension of the day's activities gradually ebbed away. Jim and I had laid out the portable chess set in preparation for our usual evening game. Most of Delta had congregated around the mess tent, sipping beers and watching the Nungs cook the steaks on the open fire. Suddenly an urgent message crackled over the command net, freezing everyone in their place.

Ambush! Contact broken! Need help! The team was in trouble. We had to get them out. Plates flew, beer cans tumbled, and crews ran for the helicopters. Jim shouted instructions to our ROMAD, "Call the DASC. Get Spooky, with guns." We'd use flares and attempt a night extraction if necessary. Turbines whined and blades chopped through the wet air. The aerial armada, four slicks and three guns, lifted off and with the O–1 at the point, skimmed across the grass of the Highlands plateau, racing to the team's rescue. I quickly located the team—they had barely moved from their insertion LZ—and directed them to a new LZ. The original had been under surveillance and was now surrounded by enemy, strength unknown. One gunship, as a decoy, strafed the would-be ambushers while the other two covered the extraction.

In went the pick-up chopper. Out came the team. Delta at its best. Darkness closed in. With the O–1 now in the trail position, the fleet sailed across the treetops, following the streams leading to Oasis. The aircraft, invisible in the dark, appeared to be linked by their rotating beacons as if strung on wire, bobbing and weaving through the murk to safety.

I made a night landing, without lights, on the black, mud-slick runway, silently cursing the construction engineers. Scary. Our unfinished beers were still cool. The steaks were well done.

Time was running out. Frustrated by the lack of firm intelligence, one of the teams had been instructed to snatch a military prisoner from the border area of the Chu Prong mountains. Carrying with them an assortment of paraphernalia for sedating and extracting the prisoner, they planned to capture a loner or the last man in a patrol. "Lift him out just like a sleeping baby, FAC. He'll wake up and think he went to Buddha. We do it all the time."

The team advisor, realizing that the maps in the area were outdated and inaccurate, spent hours flying in the backseat with me, meticulously preparing hand-drawn maps of the uncharted area. He seriously invited me to go on the mission with him since he thought I knew the area better than anyone else. I was excited about the idea, but fearing I would be a liability on the ground, declined the invitation. In spite of their preparations, the team was unable to take a prisoner. By June 17, Delta had finished its mission in the Central Highlands. We packed our gear and skidded down the runway for the last time. It was back to the beaches and bars of Nha Trang.

Our military duties at the compound seldom took more than half a day. Write a report, sort through the latest bulletins from the DASC, fill out a questionnaire from the TASS, and teach an occasional class on air-ground operations to the Delta replacements and other SFers. All new SFers headed to the various A-teams and indigenous mercenary forces scattered throughout the country passed through the adjacent group headquarters. They seemed to know each other from Okinawa, Panama, Germany, or previous airborne units. It was like a fraternity of fighter pilots.

Among the more outstanding junior officers in Delta were two lieutenants, Jack Hamilton and Joe Turner. Jack was a former sergeant, served as a Ranger advisor, and loved to fight and party, in either order. He would serve another tour in Vietnam, would be badly shot up, but went on to lead an airborne battalion into combat at Grenada in 1983. Joe Turner was a college graduate, a good ol' boy from the South, who played professional football for a short while, and then was commissioned in the Army. Joe was the officer in charge of the reconnaissance teams. With Jim Ahmann, they showed me around Nha Trang—the bars, restaurants, shops, steam baths, and beach clubs. Nha Trang's diversions balanced the risks and hardships of the jungle. We were never at a loss for something to do, day or night. It was a good life, but we were cautious and listened to our Vietnamese counterparts. They sent us to the best restaurants—and the safest. It was a marked contrast to the containment, harassment, and paranoia of Qui Nhon.

One night, during dinner at a downtown restaurant, I mentioned to Joe and Jack that my M–16 had jammed again at Oasis.

"How many rounds do you put in the magazine?" Joe asked me.

"Only eighteen, max nineteen," I replied. I knew that if you loaded the full twenty, the first round would more than likely jam.

"How about cleaning it?" asked Jack.

"Before every operation. I field strip it. But it jams, even right after I've cleaned it."

"Yeah, I think I know what happens," said Jack. "There's so much dirt blowing around the cockpit, it picks it up. We're on and off the chopper so quickly, but you fly for hours."

"Too much oil and it'll jam. I carry a Swedish K. I don't trust the M–16," added Joe. "I know what. We'll get you a carbine, the M2, fully automatic. Doesn't have the velocity of the M–16, but it's tougher than shit. Thirty-round magazine. We've got a bunch of them in the weapons hooch. We'll get you one tomorrow morning."

"Thanks guys. Let's go over by the beach. There's a new singer at that French nightclub. The one by the villa where the guys that fly the weird C–123s live." I had a friend from Otis flying the black-camouflaged, unmarked Providers. He had a half-French girlfriend.

"Oh, you mean the ones that are dropping the Chinese mercenaries into North Vietnam. We trained some of them," added Joe. There were no secrets in Nha Trang. We went to the nightclub, which was on one of the streets that paralleled the beach. I remember that the singer wore a tight dress, I don't remember her voice.

The following morning I visited the Nung who ran the weapons cache for Delta. That's where they stored the Soviet and Chinese weapons, and about anything else you needed. He was expecting me. He had conventional stock and folding-stock carbines on the counter with a selection of 15 and 30-round magazines. I carefully loaded two new magazines, alternating as I did in the past, two ball and one tracer round. I took the weapons to the perimeter of the compound and squeezed off a few rounds, then a short burst on automatic. I liked the folding-stock weapon. I could fire it with one hand, and with the stock folded, it could be easily stowed and maneuvered in the cockpit. While the Nung armorer gave my new weapon a thorough cleaning, I reloaded the magazines, taping them together into pairs of two, 60 rounds a pair. I wouldn't have to grope around for extra magazines.

We hadn't been in Nha Trang a full week and Delta was alerted for an operation. The order was issued at 7 P.M. to leave the next morning, June 25, for Tuy Hoa on a five-day operation in support of the American 1st Cav and the 101st Airborne. I had worked with both units, but there was bad blood between Delta and the 1st Cav over the Bong Son operation. We were to travel light for the short operation. Jim had trouble getting an O–1 allocated from the DASC to cover the operation. He flew ahead by helicopter to establish the command and control channels, while I continued to pressure the DASC for an airplane. This was to become a recurring problem.

The DASC finally came through with an airplane. Since Jim had traveled with nothing more than a rucksack to carry on the chopper, I packed additional items for the both of us. I changed into my tiger suit, threw a couple of clean sets in a parachute bag and added shaving gear, socks, raincoat, poncho, poncho liner, air mattress, mosquito net, candles, and chess set. As an afterthought, I tossed in my helmet liner, steel pot, and an extra blanket. I buckled on my web belt with pistol, canteen, and knife, grabbed my flying gear, carbine, and flak vest, and laden with equipment, staggered from the hooch. The orderly room CQ drove me to the airfield.

I landed at the familiar Tuy Hoa airstrip, with its approach over a road and along a 500-foot hill. It was still a 3,700-foot PSP runway bordered by helicopters. This was Delta's rear base for the overnight parking of the helicopters; the operating base, FOB, was 18 miles northwest, at Dong Tre, an unsecure SF Camp with a 2,500-foot dirt strip and surrounded by mountains. That's where I found Jim, the commander, and his staff, and our now permanent ROMAD, Rudy Bishop, and his MRC 108 radio jeep.

Rudy had been a radio operator at the DASC, went looking for action, gave Oasis a try, and decided to move in with Delta. He was 19 or 20 years old, had completed a year of college and joined the Air Force. Now he was fighting a war. As he told me at Oasis, "Lieutenant, I don't want to be here, but as long as I had to be, I thought I'd join up with you guys and the Special Forces. I didn't know Captain Ahmann, but the other operators knew you when you were a Ragged Scooper. They said you were OK." The enlisted men kept a running scorecard on the officers as we moved about II Corps.

"Gottcha on base, Airedale. Park on the west end." I recognized Rudy's voice over the radio. He had spotted the O–1 as I popped over the top of the mountain and turned base leg at Dong Tre. I bounced across the rutted dirt strip, the prop blowing a cloud of dust at the tents as I added power to get over the furrows. Rudy met me and guided me to a level parking spot. He handed me a cold soda.

"That's it, Lieutenant. This place is nothing but dust, and hot. What you see is what you get."

"Thanks, Rudy." He inserted the rocket safety pins into the tubes.

"Want me to check the oil? No gas, here, Lieutenant."

"No thanks. Checked it at Tuy Hoa. How'd you learn to be a crew chief?" He was now busying himself, checking the additional long-wire antenna installed by commo.

"Watched the Army mechanics and talked to some Air Force guys in Nha Trang. Everybody has a mechanic for their airplane, except you and Captain Ahmann. So I thought I'd be your mechanic, too."

"Rudy, you are unbelievable. Let's go to the TOC." Short, rotund, and jocund, he was easy to like. And damn competent.

Delta was to insert teams in an area centered about Dong Tre in a 270-degree arc, clockwise from the southeast to the northeast, at a radius extending to five miles. Dong Tre was so small, even by SF standards, that

Delta set up its few tents and sandbags outside the camp perimeter. The camp was nestled in the horseshoe of a river with steeply rising terrain on all sides—except for the narrow river valley that snaked for 18 miles to the sea. Within a mile of the field the terrain climbed to 500 feet; at two miles, 1,000 feet; and at ten miles, 3,000 feet. Elevated plateaus covered with thick and towering grass—over ten feet—linked the jungle-covered ridge lines. It was not only rugged, but it was outside the range of supporting artillery. It was a typical Delta deployment, but without any amenities.

The first teams were inserted within 24 hours of Delta's arrival; one of them at first light. I monitored the insertions and recovered at Tuy Hoa at night with the helicopters and other support personnel. Jim and Rudy spent the night virtually on the edge of the jungle with the skeleton command staff. There was barely room to sleep in the TOC. Rudy slept in the jeep. Jim was thankful for my air mattress and blanket. I would make do with the poncho liner and borrow a cot from some of my friends in the 101st.

It was still dark when I took off from Tuy Hoa for the 12-minute flight to the AO. Climbing to 3,000 feet, I could see the first rays of the sun emerging from the edge of the sea. There wasn't the slightest hint of dawn in the steep mountains and deep valleys as I circled over Dong Tre. Everything was quiet. I landed at the camp to share my first cup of coffee. Delta's copters were ten minutes behind me. As soon as the sun peeked over the hills, the radio messages from the teams started. By now, June 27, four teams had been inserted. It was a maximum effort to find the VC.

"Where's the FAC?" transmitted the first team. I was in the TOC listening to the radios.

"Is the FAC up?" chimed in another. On this operation the teams were close enough to the FOB for their transmissions to reach the TOC directly.

"We need a fix. We've moved." Yet another had moved their location during the night and wanted a position verification. It was time to go to work. I walked to the aircraft, my map under my arm, trying not to spill my coffee.

I started the engine and monitored the FM radios. "All stations stand by. Does anyone have any urgent traffic?" transmitted the operator at the FOB. He had taken control of the net. No response. I advanced the throttle; he saw the cloud of dust from the prop. "All teams be advised the FAC is taxiing out now."

As I approached the general location of each team, I gave them a brief coded message that I would be overhead. I'd position the aircraft between the team and the sun to facilitate a mirror signal. The mirror was directional, could be seen for miles, and was the best way to precisely locate a team without compromising its position. A quick flash from the jungle, a glance at my map, a cross check with a prominent topographical feature, and I would transmit the team's location in code. If the FOB could hear the radios, they too would update their maps with the respective team's location, or wait until I landed. The code was an overlay on our maps, known only to Delta. The team had the code exclusively for their patrol area; I had the entire area. Using this technique, unless the team were severely lost, their position could be verified in less than a minute.

I learned to recognize their voices over the radio. Each call sign was not an impersonal code, but the voice of someone with whom I had shared a beer, a funny story, a picture from home, or a secret desire. From their voices, I knew when they were safe, when they were threatened, or when they were fleeing for their lives. Isolated in the jungle, two intrepid Americans and four stalwart Vietnamese, reaching out, "FAC, gimme a fix," verifying not their location, but their link with the outside world. I tried never to let that link be broken; it was an awesome responsibility.

And they, too, looked after the FACs, always ready to fly in the backseat with us, to lend guidance and support; and as they confided, to look after us if we were forced down. This concern was not limited to the flying missions, but extended to their reconnaissance patrols.

I was flying, at a safe 1,500-foot altitude, across a grassland area three miles northwest of Dong Tre, peering down, looking for signs of the elusive VC. I was startled by a sharp radio call.

"FAC, are you alright?" It was Joe Turner's voice, the OIC of recon. He had gone in with one of his teams.

"Rog, I'm OK. What's up?"

"A couple of AKs just opened up on you. We got a fix on them. We'll get 'em." The tenor of the message was "how dare you bastards shoot at our FAC." I never heard the ground fire, the snap of the bullets, or saw the muzzle flashes. As Joe later described the incident, several VC had emptied their magazines at me, hurling some 40 or 50 rounds of .30-caliber fire at the O-1. Joe's team altered their patrol route, pursuing the fire, but found only dozens of spent cartridges in the trampled grass. Sometimes bullet holes would be found in the aircraft and we would have no idea where they had come from.

The sun had climbed high into the sky. There were a few scattered clouds above at 8,000 feet. The heat was simmering from the jungle below as I followed the valleys, tracing my flight path on my opened map. The area was so rugged that the tightly packed streams and mountains began to look alike, blending together into a single mass of green mountains, slashed by rock cliffs and tumbling waterfalls.

"Airedale Pup, this is Airedale." It was Jim Ahmann calling me on the VHF radio, which we reserved for tactical and confidential traffic. We used personal identifiers when we wanted to talk directly to each other. As the junior officer, both in rank and responsibility, I was naturally "Pup." Jim was at the FOB, the pulse of Delta's operation.

"Roger, 'Dale. This is Pup. Go."

"We have a reported sighting of two or three hundred VC moving in the open. It's our Alpha Oscar." He gave me the coordinates. I scribbled them on the window with a grease pencil. "Would you check it out?"

"I'm on my way." Wow, I thought, I've never known the VC to be so careless. I plotted the coordinates on my map and racked the Bird Dog to the new heading. Rudy called.

"Fighters are on the way. The sighting was made by an Army Foxtrot Oscar. Will advise." He was already on top of the situation. I wondered about the forward observer. He didn't belong to Delta. What was he doing in our AO? Was he in a Loach or an Army Bird Dog? The little observation helicopters were impossible to see. I needed to locate him.

"Copy, Rudy. I need freqs and call signs. Fighters and observer," I implored.

I could imagine what Jim was experiencing at the FOB. Jack Warren, a lieutenant colonel, Delta's strong-willed commander, impetuous and aggressive, would be anxious to take the target under fire. It was beyond ground artillery range. The choices were Air Force Tac Air and/or Army ARA (aerial rocket artillery), a euphemism for massed attack helicopters.

I reached the coordinates. There was nothing there; no sign of the enemy or the FO. I searched the vicinity. Still nothing. Maybe the FO was in a Loach and had landed.

"Airedale, this is Pup."

"Stand-by one." It was Rudy.

"Go-ahead," said Jim.

"There's nothing here. Nothing." I heard fighters checking in on the strike frequency on the UHF radio. "Jim, have the fighters hold high. Save fuel. I need some time. Rudy, I need the 101st freqs, Fox Mike. Quick." In times of stress, as frequently happens, call signs are abandoned. Also, the FO was apparently working with the 101st Airborne and I wasn't privy to their signal instructions.

Rudy quickly came back with some frequencies for me to try, but no call signs. It was like working with the Koreans again, except everyone spoke English. I saw a swarm of helicopters pass under me, and then turn in a large arc, as if they were searching for something. I looked again. They were gunships, but there were too many to be Delta's Wolfpack. Now I feared for our teams. We had rogue helicopters loose in our area.

"Army Bird Dog, this is Air Force FAC, over." No response. I switched frequencies and tried again.

"Roger, FAC, this is Sundance X-ray."

"Who the hell is he?" I thought. "Sundance, are you a Fox Oscar and do you have a target?" I transmitted.

"Roger. I got three hundred VC in the open and I'm trying to locate the Alpha Romeo Alpha." Success. Charley was about to get his ass ripped. Gunships and tac air. The FO confirmed the coordinates, same as I had. He was lost. Now to find him before the target disappeared.

"John. This is Jim. What's the status? Our six is pushing." He was on our discrete Victor radio. Jim was getting pressured from Warren to turn the fighters loose.

"I've made radio contact with the FO. As soon as I find him we'll have a go."

"Rog. Also be advised there is a third set of fighters on the way." Timing was now critical. I was anxious to get started before fighters started running out of fuel. I switched back to FM.

"Sundance, describe what you see beneath you." He described a meandering river with numerous bends and some specific ridge lines. I tried to match his description on my map.

"OK. I think I know where you are. Follow the river north until you come to a junction from the west. I'll meet you there." It was the edge of our AO. I spotted the Bird Dog, high and silhouetted against the sky. "I've got you. I'm low, at your one o'clock. Lead me to the target." I glanced over my shoulder. The choppers had also spotted him and were following us. I traced our path on my map. We were now outside Delta's AO.

"Down there, FAC. Along the light green field. They were heading west and disappeared in the trees." It was low elephant grass and light jungle. Relatively easy marching. I checked my map. Something was wrong. We were ten klicks, six miles, from the original coordinates.

"Are you sure this is where you saw them?" I asked. I circled over the location, maintaining a safe altitude.

"Yes." As he spoke the words I saw the serpentine column, on the backside of a rolling knoll, moving through the grass. He was right, there were maybe 200 or 300 troops, all with packs, and as I flew closer, I saw that they were in a hodgepodge of dark-colored uniforms. VC attire. Something wasn't right. They must have seen me, but didn't flee, take cover, or fire. We knew, however, that VC, caught in the open, would frequently behave like friendly troops, even to the point of waving at passing aircraft.

The gunships, enfiladed for the attack, closed in on the target. It was my opportunity for a sharper look. I chopped the power and headed for the grass, opposed to the copters and abeam the column, expecting to be riddled with bullets at any moment. They were Vietnamese troops ... carrying American carbines ... wearing colored scarfs. They were friendlies!

"*Abort! Abort! Abort!*" I shouted over the radio. I was nose-to-nose with the lead gunship. They kept coming. They couldn't hear me; they were on a different frequency. I slammed the control stick full over and pulled. The aircraft shuddered as it entered a steep bank and the ensuing stall. I released some back pressure and rolled out in front of the gunships, positioned between them and the friendlies. They couldn't fire without hitting me. I tried again.

"Sundance, get the fucking helicopters outta here. They're friendlies." Somehow the message got through. The choppers broke off the attack. I climbed for altitude and switched to the VHF radio. "Airedale, this is Pup. Divert the fighters. The troops are friendly." I gave Jim the coordinates. I noticed that my hands were shaking.

"Roger, John. See you on the ground." The Army pilot followed me back to Dong Tre. Jim met me when I landed. I was soaking wet from perspiration. We met the Army pilot, a lieutenant younger than Jim or I, new to the country, and now visibly upset as he realized what had transpired. I showed him where he had erred; the detail topography of both locations was similar, but he had lost track of the big picture. It was an honest mistake.

Jim related the particulars of the incident as they had unfolded at the TOC. Intelligence reports had indicated there was a major VC force in the area of the sighting. The visual sighting confirmed the earlier information. Warren wanted the target hit, attempting to coerce Jim to order me to hit the target. Jim deferred. When I transmitted the correct coordinates, they were plotted in the AO of the II Corps Mike Force, located on Delta's flank.

In the relative tranquility of Dong Tre, the series of fortuitous events which nearly resulted in a calamity were reviewed. An indigenous striker force had almost been annihilated by friendly fire, and through the adherence to the rules of engagement, and admittedly, Providence, a tragedy of war had been averted. The event had attracted the attention of the corps head-quarters in Nha Trang. Colonel Warren confided to Jim that he now fully appreciated the power and mobility of tactical air support, and the requirement for a disciplined control system.

I was to receive the Distinguished Flying Cross for that mission. It meant more to me than all the other awards. Unlike the others, this award was for not killing someone.

The teams prowled through the jungle. We ran aerial reconnaissance in the areas inaccessible to the teams. Still no sign of the VC. Orders came down from Saigon; Delta was to extend beyond the original five days. The S–4 sent an urgent message to Nha Trang; the Vietnamese C–47 showed up the same afternoon with cots and ice chests. Delta didn't mind fighting the war, but as they told me, "There's no sense being miserable while you do it." I liked their philosophy.

The teams, once inserted and secure, quickly became bored when there weren't any "Charlies to fuck around with." They invented a game called Challenge the FAC. They would position themselves where they could precisely identify their location, interpolating their maps to the nearest ten meters. They would pace the distances from streams, or climb trees to shoot back-azimuth compass readings from prominent terrain features and then lie in wait for me; "FAC, gimme a fix." They never hesitated in letting me know when I was wrong, which, by their standards was always, since it was impossible to simultaneously fly and achieve a ten-meter accuracy.

But I got even. I dropped them six-packs of soda, rolled in any cushioning material we could find to prevent the cans from rupturing. My backseaters were delighted when I "just happened" to drop the soda on the other side of the stream or in the middle of a bamboo thicket. Our average was four out of six cans remaining intact, and Coke out-sold all other drops.

I saw Skinner Simpson again. He had FAC'd with the 101st on their deployment to the Cambodian border and was now back at Tuy Hoa. The three of us, including Jim, rehashed stories from our Academy days and speculated on what kind of football team the Academy would have in the fall. Since Skinner had been the captain of the 1962 team, we expected him to be the expert prognosticator. We would parlay this into a betting advantage against the West Pointers we kept meeting. I left Skinner and Jim talking together. Jim was telling Skinner about Delta. Jim was due to go home in three weeks and I surmised he was recruiting Skinner to join Delta.

After nine days at Tuy Hoa and Dong Tre, Delta pulled out. No VC.

We arrived at Nha Trang tired, sore, and frustrated. The monsoons had ceased temporarily during the operation. I didn't know which was worse, the chilling rain and gooey mud of Oasis, or the insufferable heat and parched earth of Dong Tre. But it didn't matter now. We were in the comparative luxury of our tin-roofed hooches and the welcoming smiles— for some, arms—of the Vietnamese girls, the *cos*.

I had received the alumni newsletter from the Academy. The most graduates killed in Vietnam were FACs in the O–1. And that didn't include Chuck Franco, a classmate and FAC who had been killed only three weeks earlier. I was half-way through my tour. I didn't like the percentages, but if the numbers were to be beaten, Jim was on the verge of doing it. It was already mid-July and he was scheduled to depart on the nineteenth. He had successfully recruited Skinner, who checked into Delta on the fourteenth, Bastille Day. I welcomed Skinner to Delta and a new aspect of the liberation war caused by the French. Skinner had left the Americans, the 101st Airborne, and would now fight with the Vietnamese with Project Delta.

We also received our alert order on the fourteenth. Delta would be leaving in three days, to return to the Central Highlands and the border area. I thought that maybe I should apply for a Cambodian tourist visa.

Delta deployed to another base hacked from the jungle. This one was Buon Blech, located half-way between Pleiku and the city of Ban Me Thuot, and situated on a feeder road that connected with Highway 14. Highway 14 was the major north-south road that extended down the spine of the Central Highlands. The French Groupement Mobile No. 100, with the 1st Korea Battalion as its main combat force, had been slaughtered by the Viet Minh one mile north in the Chu-Dreh Pass.

Skinner and I overflew the rusted hulks of the French vehicles. The ambush trenches were still visible. We touched down at the FOB at noon on the July 17, exactly 12 years after the French battle. The airstrip would be another challenge, 3,100 feet long with an elevation of 2,100 feet. It was

400 feet shorter and 400 feet higher than Oasis. The length was no problem for the O–1, but the elevation insured that we would be flying in the clouds more often. The central monsoons were at their worst. During the monsoon season there would be two or three days of steady rain with low clouds and fog. On each side of the steady rain there would be one or two days of marginal weather, separated by a clear day, and then the cycle would repeat itself.

The C–130 pilots, the big cargo birds, would be flying on the edge of the performance envelope. The runway was covered with an identical rubberized membrane to Oasis. As we taxied down the bubbled surface, I saw a C–130 hopelessly mired in the mud at the end of the runway. A portable weather station was positioned near the runway, manned by an Air Force observer. The parking and unloading area was slick and steeply pitched. Jeeps would slide off the edge with their brakes locked. The ingenious GIs found a solution. A passenger would leap from the skidding vehicle and throw a sandbag under a wheel, bringing the jeep to a permanent halt. We used a similar technique for the aircraft.

This was my first operation as the ALO. I accomplished the necessary coordination with the American brigade to which Delta was operationally attached. They had FACs, mechanics, and one or two airplanes located at Buon Blech, with ample fuel and spare rockets. Rudy was disappointed. His responsibilities were limited to radio operator, with no refueling or rocket loading tasks.

A quick hop, 45 minutes, to Pleiku facilitated coordination with the II Corps DASC. I laughed to myself as I taxied to the ramp at Pleiku. The last time I was there, I had taken off in the monsoon storm with the field closed. I was glad that we changed call signs every operation. I'd remain unidentified. The DASC staff remembered our previous deployment and would serve as our alternate air request net. Like DASC Alpha, they operated 24 hours. They promised to keep all strangers, other friendly aircraft, out of our area. They couldn't promise the same for unfriendly aircraft. They warned me about the sighting of mysterious aircraft along the Cambodian border.

Jim Ahmann had hitched a ride to Pleiku from Nha Trang. He wanted to say good-bye to the men at the FOB. He flew in the backseat with me to Buon Blech. We landed in a rainstorm so heavy that I couldn't see. Jim looked out the side and told me when to flare the aircraft.

The next nine days were a battle against the elements and a continuous challenge to maintain contact with the teams. On the eighteenth, Teams 2, 5, and 6 went in, followed on the nineteenth by Teams 7, 8, and 12. The weather was marginal and since it also affected the helicopter pilots, the teams were unsure of their insertion location. Swollen streams and flooding in the AO made land travel difficult and navigation impossible. The teams required position fixes every day. The weather sequences were 400-foot broken clouds with 1,000-foot overcast; another day, 300-foot overcast and two miles visibility with fog and rain. Skinner landed with cloud ceilings of only 100 feet and visibility of an eighth of a mile. Some flights were as short as ten minutes when we were forced to return to the airfield by poor weather. All of this flying was done completely visually; we had no instruments or navigational aids for all-weather flying. Without a transponder, it was impossible for any radar site, a CRC or CRP, to pick up the weak radar return in the rain. The storms would block out their scopes. We routinely violated every possible Air Force flying regulation. But we never lost contact with a team or roadrunner, or failed to find them when they needed help.

Living conditions were not any better. Rain penetrated the canvas, creating a mist under the tent. Water flowed through the tents; occupied cots would settle into the mud, stopped only by the hinge of the crossed legs. We stored clothes in rubber bags and ignited chunks of C–4 explosive to heat iced-tea mix in canteen cups to ward off the wind-driven cold. Sweaters, shorts, ponchos, and jungle boots were the preferred camp uniforms. Water seeped under our ponchos and down our necks. Fatigue trousers were instantly soaked, acting like icy wicks that shriveled testicles to the size of peanuts.

In the middle of this, Team 8 was engaged in a firefight and required extraction. I used the helicopter gunships to break up the fight and cover the extraction. Two days later, July 24, a gunship crashed in the weather; no injuries. Another gunship spotted some fleeing deer and took them under fire; we had venison steaks for dinner.

Word reached us at the FOB that a helicopter with Delta people on board had crashed. We subsequently learned that a ferry flight from Pleiku to Nha Trang had taken off in the fog and rain, and the Army aviator, not qualified to fly in the weather, became disoriented and slammed into a mountain five miles south of Pleiku. Jim Ahmann was on the helicopter. He survived the crash and was on his way home. He was the only one of the nine occupants who had not been medevaced to the States with severe spinal injuries and burns. Jim always had an aversion to helicopters.

Somehow a chaplain found his way to the camp and held an open-air Mass for the Catholics at Buon Blech. A score of us gathered on a hillside overlooking the airfield. We were deep in mud, but the rain had ceased enough for us to remove our ponchos. The altar was fabricated from sandbags and discarded shell boxes. The priest donned his field vestments and approached the altar. It was too low. It had sunk into the mud. "Just a minute, Father," said an artilleryman, "we have another fire mission going. We'll have more boxes to raise the altar." We would kill more so that we could pray better. Madness. I offered a private prayer. I didn't stay for the Mass.

As mysteriously as a chaplain appeared, so too did secret and top secret classified messages find their way to me. Some required an equally classified response within 12 hours or sometimes sooner. Regulations required that classified documents be retained in a locked safe with controlled access. Here I was, in the middle of mud and elephant grass, with no way to store the documents, let alone answer them through secure channels. I showed them to Skinner. We laughed at the absurdity. We decided we would burn them before the paper became too wet to burn. Our next alternative was to eat them, which appealed to neither of us.

The weather won. Delta pulled out of Buon Blech on July 27. With the exception of the gunships, we never fired a shot in anger or dropped a single bomb or can of napalm. Skinner and I threw our filthy and soaking gear into the back of the airplane. Skinner climbed into the backseat and we launched at 1300 hours enroute to Nha Trang.

By 1400 hours, only one hour later, we were in the middle of a battle. As we approached Nha Trang, I switched to Delta's FM frequency, intending to advise the base of our arrival and to request a jeep to meet us. Instead, I heard automatic weapons fire, grenade explosions, and the cry, "Any station, any station, this is Recondo One. We've been ambushed and need help."

"Roger, Recondo, this is Airedale. Can I help?" I answered.

There was a pause and then a transmission. "Red Baron, is it really you?" The men of Delta had assigned me the unofficial call sign of Red Baron. The voice sounded like Tommy Carpenter, one of the recon sergeants from Delta.

"Sure is, Tommy. Give me your coordinates." He did. He was in Delta's training area for the recondo school. They were on a three-day training exercise that was required for graduation from the school. "Skinner," I said over the intercomm. "Call the DASC, Ragged Scooper, and get fighters. Don't worry about target clearance. We own this area." This was all new to Skinner. I looked over my shoulder. He nodded.

"Recondo, what's your status?"

"We ran into a nest of Charlies. We've broken contact, but we have two wounded. They're looking for us." I thought quickly. All the helicopters and gunships were still at Buon Blech, but there had to be some support at Nha Trang that put the team in. I called the base.

"Get some choppers. We'll pull the team. I have fighters on the way."

"Roger, Airedale. We've advised the 281st. They're getting crews now." We were lucky. We'd get some of the assault helicopter pilots that were experienced with Delta operations. I had feared we would get the take-the-colonel-to-Saigon pilots.

"Skinner," I shouted. "Where are the freakin' fighters? It's been twenty minutes. Cam Ranh's only twenty miles away."

"I'll check."

"Tommy, how're you doing?" I didn't need his answer. I heard the gunfire again.

"We're hurting, FAC. The fuckers found us." Shit! We were getting a team shot up in our own backyard. No caps and gowns. Some of the graduates would be in body bags.

"Airedale. This is Boxer zero-one. We're at Nha Trang." I glanced at the cockpit clock. Twenty-five minutes to scramble the alert flight. Two F–4s. Piss-poor performance.

"Boxer, follow the river that's on the north edge of town. I'm six miles west, just where the mountains start. What's your load?" He started to give me some authentication code word, followed by call sign, mission number, fuel, and so on. He was a new guy reading from his checklist, determined to do everything by the book. That explained the delay. I was curt.

"Boxer, just give me your goddamn bomb-load. Now!" He did. Four snakes and four napes. The bomb shortage was partially over.

"Tommy," I said on FM. "I got F–4s with snakes and napes, but I think I got some new pilots. I'll need smoke from you and your heads down. The Clydes know where you are anyway."

"No sweat, Red Baron. Lay it on them. One hundred meters west." I knew where Tommy was from the coordinates he gave me. He was one of the best we had. I saw his red smoke. I positioned two marking rockets in the jungle, bracketing Tommy's description.

"All right, Boxer. Napalm. South to north. Right break. Between my smokes. Friendlies are east, at the red smoke. Any doubts, go through dry. Cleared." I saw the pick-up helicopters following the river. There were only two of them.

Boxer might have been new guys, but they were determined to hit where I told them. They followed with the snake-eyes and the helicopters made the pick-up without taking a single round of ground fire. It was a job well done. We landed at Nha Trang, but the mission wasn't over. Some equipment had been left behind: a radio, code books, maps.

The Vietnamese Ranger reaction force was to be inserted to mop up and recover the equipment. Skinner FAC'd the mission, using a diverted flight of four F–100s for air support. It was just an average day for Delta; a team was ambushed, safely recovered, the reaction force committed, and six fighter sorties expended—in less than three hours. The only problem was, this was less than five miles from the Delta Hilton and in a "pacified" area.

Nha Trang was comfortable. We thought we would have a week or two until our next operation. The Ranger force that was committed for the recondo training was back from the field. They suffered three wounded, none serious. We had a graduation party in the Delta Hilton for the recondo class. The team and the Rangers profusely thanked Skinner and me for the air strikes. They thought we had a sixth sense to appear overhead when they were in trouble. I had to caution the non-Delta attendees that FACs don't miraculously appear. You have to ask for them.

Skinner had the opportunity to meet the other members of Delta who kept the operation running so well. He had barely checked into Nha Trang when, two days later, we left for Buon Blech. He was the new guy on the operation. Just as I had to prove myself on my first Delta operation at Chu Lai, so too was Skinner tested at Buon Blech. The men of Delta expected Jim Ahmann to select only the best replacements, and I inherited that same responsibility. Skinner was good and now one of us. But I didn't know yet how good he really was.

We traded stories and experiences from the last operation. The consensus was the operation was better suited for the Navy SEAL (sea-air-land) teams. They could have swum in and out of the operations area. Air boats could have replaced helicopters. We could have then hunted more deer.

Once again I enjoyed the conviviality of the Hilton, the laughter and joking with the petite and attractive Vietnamese waitresses and barmaids. They always welcomed us back, but for good reason. Business would boom and they would get bigger tips. Our mess sergeants always found a way to come up with juicy steaks that we charcoaled over the 55-gallon drums that had been cut in half lengthwise, mounted on angle-iron cross legs, with a grill fashioned for the top. Our Nung workers could do anything. I'm not sure how we always had such good food and plenty of beer. I suspected that our constant supply of Montagnard artifacts, particularly the copper bracelets, blowguns, and crossbows, brought a good price on the barter market. Viet Cong flags were manufactured anywhere, and customization with appropriate bullet holes or chicken blood was easy. Delta deserved the premium food, and the rear-echelon types brought home authentic souvenirs to attest to their combat experience.

I learned that with every position of responsibility came administrative tasks, after-action reports, and conferences. The after-action reports I didn't mind, since I assumed that someone must be reading them and we were doing a good job. Delta was searching, locating, and killing the enemy without taking heavy losses. We were deploying precision tactical air support on purely military targets. We were using American technical and logistical superiority to help the Vietnamese win their war. I trusted that the chain of command above me recognized this from my reports, and that in some small way I could influence the strategy of the war. History would show how naive I was.

The after-action reports for Delta were factual results, compiled much the same way the Koreans reported the results of their operations. Individual performance reports, the efficiency ratings, were to an individual what the after-action reports were to the unit. My boss in Qui Nhon, fulfilling the requirements of the regulation, had accomplished an ER on me based on my performance with the Koreans and with the 101st Airborne. He gave me the highest marks, but his superiors, who had to endorse the ER, balked because it was "too high." They based their criticism on the fact that I had never been a fully qualified fighter pilot, and therefore could not be an outstanding FAC. Apparently performance didn't count; the ratings were based on subjective criteria prejudiced by the attitudes of the higher ranking officers. However, in 1966 I didn't care. The Koreans, the 101st Airborne, and every member of Delta trusted me. Their trust was the more important reward. My boss persevered; the rating stood. He chose the difficult right, instead of the easier wrong.

The DASC director convened a two-day conference in Nha Trang for all the ALOs who were operationally responsible to DASC Alpha. This included the unwieldy American units, the 1st Cav, the 101st Airborne, the 25th Infantry, and the Allied units, the Koreans, who were under the command of First Field Forces Vietnam. I worked for DASC Alpha, but Project Delta didn't work for IFFV. Delta was a joint command; it worked for the Vietnamese and the Americans, but under the direct command of Saigon. Regardless, I attended as ordered.

I sat in the back of the conference room, which was arranged like a movie theater. I looked for Colonel Stewart, my mentor, but he had rotated to the States. I was the only lieutenant from a combat unit among the twenty-five or thirty attendees, most of whom were majors and lt. colonels. Some were from the support organizations and I thought, mistakenly, to listen and learn about the needs of the combat units in the field. It was not a discussion conference. It was a self-serving assembly for the promulgation of policy and edicts from the DASC and the support units.

For two days I listened about reports, classified messages, efficiency ratings, and the "magic words" to get a medal approved. Ironically, the awarding of specific decorations had a higher correlation with the submittal words rather than the act or performance. I wondered why every time a major or colonel got shot at he was looking for a medal. Most of the captains and lieutenants I knew were thankful to be alive. The enlisted personnel would get a rubber-stamp end-of-tour medal processed by the DASC. The attendees were grateful for this. It relieved them of unwanted responsibility and additional effort. I was glad the enlisted men would get some recognition, particularly the ROMADs. However, no one explained why there were light bomb loads, bad fuses, shortages of O–1s, operational conflicts with maintenance, and ridiculous classified messages to the field requiring immediate replies.

I did learn something about airlift, particularly for the American units. When the Army wanted airlift that couldn't be handled by their helicopters, they naturally went to the ALO. He represented the Air Force. Wrong. This was the age of specialization. The ALO was tactical air, not airlift. The fortunate ALO might have one airlifter on his staff to handle emergency resupply, but not relocations of entire units. The Air Force eventually added more staff to facilitate local load planning. But the airlift resources, the C–130s, didn't work for the Air Force general in Saigon, the commander of the Seventh Air Force. They worked for a command in Hawaii and Japan. When an Army division commander, a two-star general, wanted to move his unit, he expected it to be moved immediately. Delays were not tolerated. He didn't give a damn about for whom the airplanes worked, and he directed his frustrations at the nearest Air Force officer, the tactical ALO. Consequently, the entire airlift system in Vietnam could be temporarily disrupted as hundreds of C–130 sorties were diverted to move the Army unit. I took pride in knowing that a couple of Air Force C–130s and the VNAF C–47, shuttling for a day from Nha Trang, could move Delta to anyplace in Vietnam.

Eventually, I lost interest in the conference. I could have created a reason to leave, but I stuck it out. I was fighting a much different war, a war of small patrols, indigenous forces, Vietnamese paratroopers, and clandestine operations—a war unrecognized by the others. I made a few pointed comments addressing critical operational problems. Since ignorance was expected of lieutenants, my comments were attributed to my inability to grasp the big picture. I had no fear of being relieved of my command. No one else wanted it.

The conference closed. I drove from the opulent, beachfront hotel, through the potholed and fetid streets, to the modest, paddy-bordered Delta compound. The contrast was the key; it was the institutional military that couldn't grasp the big picture. They had created a war that wasn't there, destined to be fought from a Kafkaesque script. Not so the Koreans; they understood the war and wrote their own script. And the Vietnamese. It was still their war, but I realized the Americans were determined to wrest it from them.

We had some fun. Touch football on the beaches of Nha Trang with Green Berets was more like Texas versus Oklahoma, or Giants versus Redskins. Everyone sincerely believed they could play for any pro team. We had a few who had. Skinner demonstrated his skills as former captain of the Air Force Academy team. I still remembered some of the plays, so we put them to good use. But it wasn't "touch" football by any stretch of the imagination. Body blocks were bone crushers.

During our stand-down between operations, we trained new people and refined our military skills. The Delta troopers perceived an obvious gap in the Air Force's qualifications, an obstacle to be overcome; we were "legs," or non–jump qualified, in an airborne unit. SFers were always suspicious of legs. The sergeants were determined to put us in opened parachutes.

I defended myself. "But Sarge, I'm a pilot and it's against my principles to jump out of a perfectly good airplane."

"Don't make no difference, Lieutenant. You gotta jump. Report to the pit after breakfast tomorrow. We'll work on your technique." For the next two days I practiced parachute landing falls (PLFs) under the tutelage of the most exacting professionals ever to exit an airplane: front falls, side falls, back, stand-up landings, hot sun, sand pit; up the ladder onto the platform, ready, jump; up the ladder, ready, jump; ready, jump; ready, jump.

"Well, Lieutenant, you're looking better," said my instructor. "Tomorrow we'll give it a try. The Ranger battalion is on the first jump. You can go with them. C-47."

I was to jump with the Vietnamese! If I didn't go through with it, I would lose face. They were carrying weapons. The drop zone was on the outskirts of town and not always secure, "sometimes we get some sniper fire." The Gooney Bird lumbered into the air. They never closed the door, "in case something goes wrong we can get out faster." The gear and flaps had been barely retracted when the jump lights came on. The commands were shouted in Vietnamese: Get ready... hook up... stand in the door ... go! I tumbled forward, then was jerked upright by the opening shock. I looked up; I had a good canopy. I looked around; I was falling faster than the lighter Viets. I looked down. The DZ was a graveyard! My SF buddies had the last laugh.

I survived and made another jump. That stick was all Americans. I followed Joe Turner out the door. He said something about we were the wind dummies as we leapt into space. He made a stand-up landing and I collapsed in a lump. So much for PLFs. I was jump qualified.

The warrior spirit and professionalism of Delta had affected the assigned Air Force personnel. Jim Ahmann earned his jump wings with Delta; he made over a half-dozen jumps. Skinner qualified, and our ROMAD, Rudy Bishop, or "Heavy Drop" as the SFers called him, also qualified. We were proud of those wings and everything they stood for. Delta. Airborne. Vietnam. Commitment. The Air Force, through their regulations, prohibited us from wearing them except in Vietnam. Jim later convinced some personnel type to convert his VN wings to American. He beat the system. He told me that in 1989. I was jealous. I had worn mine on the inside of my uniform.

The mood in the Delta compound had transitioned from returning relief, through the tedium of training, and was now one of restless uncertainty. We had dried out on the beaches, chased the girls in the nightclubs, conducted training classes, and parachuted from airplanes. The helicopter company was bored with flying local "ass and trash" missions, and the gunships, the Wolfpack, were eager for a workout. They had jury-rigged a six-barreled mini-gun on one of the Hogs and were looking for live targets. Everyone had become accomplished with the 40mm M-79 grenade launcher, the Blooper, and was anxious to try it from the air. Ten days had elapsed since we had returned from the monsoon swamps of Buon Blech.

Now, postprandial conversations were hushed and speculative. Nights of drinking at the Hilton deteriorated into raucous singing and feats of craziness. One recon sergeant, cross-trained as a medic, intentionally smashed a beer bottle against his forehead, opening a three-inch gash, then extracted a needle and thread from his fatigue shirt, and casually sutured his own wound. Like high-strung horses, these thoroughbreds were anxious to reenter the race of war. It wasn't long before Delta was summoned to the gate; post time—two days. We were going to III Corps for a month.

9
Project Delta in III Corps: Song Be and Tay Ninh

Operation 10–66 for Project Delta was split in two phases. Initially, we were to deploy to Phuoc Long Province and operate from the small town of Song Be. We would be working for the 5th ARVN Division. In the second phase, we would relocate to Tay Ninh Province and operate from the Tay Ninh West airstrip, which was three miles from the city of Tay Ninh. We would be working for the U.S. 25th Infantry Division. The Tay Ninh deployment would entail operations in war zone C. Both locations were adjacent to the Cambodian border. The need for a Cambodian tourist visa, initially facetious, was now becoming fact.

Skinner had worked some of the areas northeast of Phuoc Long with the 101st Airborne. He had been in Quang Duc Province operating out of Nhon Co, a border base to where I had flown a mechanic back in May. We headed 237 degrees from Nha Trang, cutting across the lower Central Highlands of Vietnam directly to the city of Dalat on the first leg of our two-and-a-half hour flight to Song Be.

Dalat was a resort city unmarked by the war. The government had a training academy there. There were also civilian educational institutions established by the French in the city. Gabrielle had been educated there. The most remarkable feature of the city was its distinctive architecture. It looked like a Swiss village in the Alps with multi-storied structures of white stucco, dark timber beams, porches, and high-peaked roofs. The bright orange roofs stood out from the contrasting green of the surrounding jungle. We then swung due west until we could see Nui Ba Ra, the 2,372-foot mountain that rose from the flat of the jungles and plantations. The plantations amazed me. They were tremendous estates with rows of rubber trees that extended for miles. Virtually every estate had a swimming pool, whose aquamarine coloring was in stark contrast to the surrounding red earth and green trees. The panorama was completed by tennis courts and long, loping roadways free of bomb craters and tank tracks. The plantation owners were keeping their tax payments current—to both governments.

As we approached the mountain, we could see the village and the runway barely a mile north of the mountain. The government publication of *Aerodrome Index for Southeast Asia* aptly described the airfield.

SECURE. Normal ops for lt acft only. C–45 and larger acft use Song Be, 1.5 mi W of mtn. 2400' mt 1 mi prior to app end Rwy 36. City hall 300' fr app end Rwy 18. 20' high power line and barricades 100'–200' prior to app end Rwy 18. Public road crosses app end Rwy 36. Prkg area N end E side for 6 O–1 acft. Heli prkg and refueling close to rwy W side midfld. 130' radio twr NE of fld. Extv heli tfc. Uncontrolled auto and pedestrian tfc.

The airfield was a 2,200-foot runway that was the main street of town. It was guarded by a mountain on one end, and the town hall and barricades on the other end. There were power lines and radio towers. I'm certain the FAA would never approve this field for anything. We had very carefully described the helicopter parking and refueling area for the Viet Cong. We also told them precisely where we would park our aircraft. The VC didn't need spies. All they needed was a subscription to the U.S. Government (DOD) publication.

We buzzed the street/runway, which was our way of saying we were going to land. The last of the pedestrians cleared the runway and Skinner slipped the bird in. I noticed a large Catholic church on the east side and immediately adjacent to the runway. We taxied up to City Hall. There was no mayor to greet us, only an Air Force mechanic.

The Delta advance party had already erected our tents along the west side of the runway and just south of the helicopter refueling pit. Not the safest location from a mortar attack. We stowed our gear in the tents, and Skinner attended to local coordination details with the ARVN and sector FACs. Rudy already had the radio jeep set up and sandbagged in. He stretched a couple of ponchos over the top for protection from the sun and rain. This was Rudy's shop and he ran it well.

I jumped in the airplane for the one-hour flight to Bien Hoa, to accomplish the corps-level coordination with the DASC. We had arrived at Song Be at 11:30, and by 1:30 I was in the air again. I never trusted message traffic and published task deployments. For all I knew, our entire ops plan was buried under a stack of papers on some staff desk. I would ensure that when we needed air support for our teams, it would be immediately available and no questions asked. It was equally important that the corps headquarters staff knew where we were and what we were doing. Since we were working for the 5th ARVN Division on this operation, I wanted to verify that they had advised their American counterparts. Also, when the Army would receive Delta's intelligence reports, they would target particularly lucrative sightings for radar bombing missions or artillery fires. The Army was responsible for targeting, but they frequently neglected to check on the location of the information source. I didn't want any errant bombing missions or artillery fires near any of our teams.

The III Corps Headquarters was a joint headquarters, staffed by Americans and Vietnamese. The DASC was also joint and handled all the air requests for both American and Vietnamese forces. This was different from II Corps, where the Corps DASC in Pleiku handled only Vietnamese requests, and DASC Alpha in Nha Trang handled only American and Korean requests. Delta always received the highest priority in II Corps, and I wanted to ensure the same in III Corps.

Lt. Col. O'Grady was the III Corps DASC director. I found his office in the corner of a sprawling, single-story stucco building that housed the headquarters. The facility was a far cry from the relative opulence of the grand hotel that First Field Forces used as their HQ in Nha Trang.

"Good afternoon, sir. I'm Lieutenant Flanagan, the ALO assigned to Project Delta."

"Come in, Lieutenant. Is that the Special Forces unit that was up in Tay Ninh back in May?" That was the operation I missed, due to my temporary reassignment to the Koreans before I could rejoin Delta.

"Yes, sir."

"I remember you caught a VC battalion in the open. Wiped them out with air. Impressive. We were talking about it for weeks. How's, uh, Ahmann, I think it is?"

"That's right. Jim's back in the States now. Had a close call. Survived a helicopter crash on the way back from his last operation. Ken Kerr, the other FAC who directed that strike, is also gone." I walked over to the 1:250,000-scale map sheets hung on the wall. They covered III Corps. I pointed to the northeastern portion along the Cambodian border. "We'll be operating out of Song Be City until twenty-three August. We have our reconnaissance teams, helicopter support, and the Viet Ranger reaction force. I flew down to coordinate the tactical air support."

"Good. Come with me," said the colonel as he got up from his desk. I followed him down the hall to the operations center. It was similar to the one in DASC Alpha, except there were numerous Vietnamese staff members. He introduced me to some of the staff.

"This is Major Blumer. He's the senior duty officer. This is Captain Olson, the assistant corps ALO. Over there is Sergeant Bomar, the radio operator. You'll probably want to get with him later. Please continue with what you started to tell me in my office. You can use the operations map." The ops map had the various sectors within the corps delineated, as well as the areas of responsibility for each of the maneuvering units. I walked over to the map. One of the Army sergeants from the Tactical Air Support Element, the Army portion of the DASC, joined us.

"As I was telling the Colonel, Project Delta will be conducting reconnaissance patrols in the area immediately north of Song Be and extending west to the Cambodian border." I unfolded a tissue trace of our area from my fatigue shirt pocket. The sergeant lifted the plastic overlay and we slipped the tissue underneath. He began to trace the outline of our area on the plastic with a felt pen. I continued, "We are a self-sufficient unit except for air support. We usually operate outside of artillery range and are, therefore, totally dependent on tactical fighters and our own gunships. We also want to make sure that no one drops any stray bombs in our area. Please insure that our area is a no-fire zone to everyone, except ourselves. We'll be in there through the twenty-third.

The colonel nodded. The sergeant cross-hatched our area on the overlay with heavy blue lines, and wrote in the dates. It was now a restricted fire zone. By this time I noticed that several Vietnamese had gathered around. They were jabbering away and pointing excitedly to our area on the map. I couldn't understand them, but they anticipated my question and said in English, "*Beaucoup* VC. Number ten." In the next two weeks, that was to prove to be one of the all-time understatements.

I was about to mention the second phase of our operation in war zone C, but I thought better of it. I had been warned about VC sympathizers who had penetrated the command elements and were just looking for intelligence to pass on to the VC. I walked over to Sgt. Bomar, who was half-hidden by the radio rack. He removed his headset and we introduced ourselves.

"Sergeant, I need to know your call signs and frequencies. I'm going to be operating out of Song Be for the next couple of weeks."

"Yes, sir. That's Tangerine three-one. We're Tangerine. We use code letters for the HF frequencies. Charlie is 7474, Echo is 4946, and Foxtrot is 6694, all on the upper side band. Foxtrot is reserved for Americans only, so if you get in a real bind, call us on that freq. Today, we're on Sheet ten of the crypto throwaway pads."

"Thanks, Sarge; but we'll be operating autonomously from Tangerine three-one and the local Viper FACs. Our request identifier will be Airedale and the FAC call sign will be Typhoon, with no numerical suffix. I would appreciate it if you would process our requests ASAP, even though they may not have all the required information. I have only one ROMAD and he gets awfully busy."

"Wilco, sir. And welcome to III Corps. I've already been talking to Airedale Mike. We didn't recognize the call sign." Good old Rudy. That young two-striper had already found a way into the radio net.

Major Blumer called me aside. "Thanks for stopping by, Lieutenant. To tell you the truth, we didn't know a damn thing about your operation until you came in. Our coordination with the Viets is not the best, but then it could have been our own Army troops who screwed up. Did you get all the information you needed?"

"Yes, I did. Thanks."

"How about rendezvous points and strike frequencies? Do you have those?" I shook my head and took out my little notebook. He continued, "Off channel seven-three, Bien Hoa, the big mountain by Song Be is zero-one-two degrees at five-five nautical miles. The abandoned air strip to the north which the 101st used, Djamap, is zero-one-seven at seven-one." Skinner had told me about Djamap. All the fighter pilots recognized it.

"How about off Saigon? Channel three-eight, I think," I asked.

He queried one of the other officers. "Zero-one-eight degrees at six-three miles should put you over Song Be. Primary strike frequency is 271.0."

"Thanks a lot, sir. You've been a great help."

"And Flanagan, watch yourself up there. Intell tells me there's lots of activity along the border. We lost a FAC a few months ago. Pressed too hard in the weather, we think."

By four o'clock I was in the air again, headed back to Song Be. I certainly didn't like the sound of things. Even the Viets admitted it was bad territory. They should know. They've been living and fighting here for years. We Americans transferred in and out every year.

Skinner and I started our rotation of flying the team sergeants over the area in the backseat of the O–1. The VC were accustomed to Bird Dog overflights; Hueys created suspicion. There were many signs of enemy activity along the river that formed the border with Cambodia. Logs that could be used for bridges were hidden along the banks. The trails showed signs of heavy traffic. I spotted cart tracks in open grassy areas, indicating that heavy supplies were being moved. There was an intense schedule planned for the insertion of teams.

As was customary, either Skinner or I would attend the team's formal briefing to the staff. The team would propose their primary landing zone and an alternate, in case it turned out to be hot or they were spotted going in. They would then present their planned route and observation points, where they could observe trails and suspected way stations. They always had an exfiltration zone in mind, should they be compromised or ambushed and need immediate extraction. They presented their escape-and-evasion plan, their last-ditch effort for survival.

After the formal briefing, one of us would meet with the Vietnamese team leader and the two American advisors, and review specific aspects of the air operations. Yes, we would be airborne at first light, weather permitting, to give them a position fix. In marginal weather and poor light, the helicopter pilots frequently had difficulty inserting the team where planned. The team wanted a positive ID of their location; if they didn't know precisely where they were, their sightings of enemy troop movements and base camps were of little value. The knowledge and experience that I gained with the Koreans was invaluable. From my patrols through the paddies and jungle, I could now relate to the difficulties and hazards facing our recon teams. The teams were usually outside the range of artillery batteries. For support, they were virtually dependent on the helicopter gunships, tactical fighters, and the reaction force; all were contingent on weather suitable for flying.

We reviewed the emergency procedures with the teams: If you are compromised, come up on the radio and we'll give you the compass heading to the nearest clearing where the helicopters can land or take you out with ropes. If you are being pursued, drop a red smoke grenade, continue in your direction of escape, and drop a yellow smoke to indicate to me your direction of travel. We will direct air strikes perpendicular to your path and will keep advancing the strikes as you drop alternately colored smokes, which should effectively cut off your pursuers. If you want air strikes forward of your moving position or if you are static, you will have to come up on the radio and state your request. If you are forced to E and E, we will search your intended escape route. Signal the airplane with whatever device you have available: smoke, mirror, panels, or flares, or wave your arms if you are in the open.

Although these were standard operating procedures for Delta, I think the teams appreciated the personal attention. If there were any misunderstandings, I wanted to clear them right away, not in the middle of the jungle when they were in a firefight. I wished them luck and told them I'd be talking to them on the radio.

The next twelve days was one of the most intense combat periods for Project Delta. We were stretched almost to the breaking point: we couldn't handle any more operational crises, whether they involved recon, the Rangers, the helicopters, or ourselves as FACs.

August 10—We flew two VRs over the area. Much activity near the border. Teams 10 and 11 went in.

August 11—Flew two VRs, one at first light to give a position fix and the other in preparation for a Ranger operation. Teams 6 and 8 went in.

August 12—Marginal weather, but airborne at first light. Gave three position fixes. Team 10 had an injured man who was successfully extracted.

August 13—Initial sortie at first light. In the afternoon, Team 11 spotted a squad of VC in huts. It took 45 minutes to get the air strike; Eagle 01, flight of two F–100s with four napalms and eight cannisters of CBUs. They delivered the ordnance under a 1,000-foot ceiling with visibility of only two miles in rain showers. One hut was destroyed, another damaged (the napalm cans actually hit on each side of the hut), killing five enemy. The team also found blood trails and C-ration cans.

Unfortunately, one of the fighter pilots became disoriented, was 20 degrees off heading on his bomb run, and hit one of the friendlies with some CBU pellets. The team was extracted due to a "slight wound in the arse," as they described the incident over the radio. The Green Beret had no hard feelings toward the fighter pilot, but it demonstrated to the fighters the importance of not releasing bombs unless they were absolutely sure of the target and position of the friendlies.

Our O-1 developed a crack in the engine cowling that was spreading and the rockets were misfiring. Skinner took the aircraft to Bien Hoa for repairs. He returned the next morning, before the first rays of the sun poked over the horizon.

August 14—The Rangers launched a sweep with the local CIDG forces of an area not more than two miles east of Song Be. The Ranger advisors were Lieutenants Ron Deaton and Jack Hamilton. [Jack, a combat veteran, was to lead a battalion of paratroopers in the 1983 mission in Grenada.]

Our forces suffered two killed and eight wounded. We directed four F-100 sorties and three VNAF A-1H sorties in support of the operation. The ground troops confirmed three enemy KBA and captured one Browning automatic rifle, plus several other weapons. They found the arm of a VC alongside a weapon near a bunker. It was not included in the body count.

In the middle of the air strikes, I lost my radios. It was Tuy Hoa all over again when Skinner and I first met and he lost his radios. Fortunately, I spotted a radio cable that came loose under the seat and we were able to repair it in the air. I could see the church in Song Be as I directed the air strikes. Strange way to spend a Sunday.

August 15—Team 10 located a VC work party on a log ramp at a river crossing. The river crossing was at the Cambodian border. The Phantom 31 flight of three F-4s dropped 11 cans of 750-pound napalm right on them. The team was compromised and extracted without incident. The VC had their hands full after that air strike.

August 16—Teams 6 and 8 had been in the jungle for five days and had successfully reached their exfiltration zone. Team 6 was picked up without incident. Team 8 spotted a weapon-carrying VC who was observing the pick-up zone. We hit him and any of his friends with napalm and CBUs delivered via F-100, Dice 05. The team came out unscathed. Teams 7 and 12 were put in at last light.

There was always an early morning fog at Song Be. The town was in a horseshoe bend in the Song Be River, and the fog spilled over from three sides, smothering the airfield. We usually didn't pay much attention to it. We just took off and climbed through it, a matter of only a couple hundred feet. If we were to suffer engine failure after takeoff, it would be virtually impossible to dead-stick the airplane back on the runway. The city hall, the church, and numerous other buildings adjacent to the runway precluded any attempt at a blind landing. Our alternative was to put the plane in the rice paddies and hike back to the field before the VC found us. I was always glad to have one of the SF troopers in the backseat with me. He was much more skilled at ground warfare than I.

This particular morning we were going to pick up the two teams, so I waited until there was sufficient visibility for the helicopters to get out safely. I contacted Team 6 first.

"Spook, this is Typhoon. What's your status?"

"We're at the LZ. We've been observing since yesterday. Negative activity. LZ is secure."

"Roger, Spook. Copy all. I'll be back to you." That was one less worry. Now for Team 8.

"Peeper, this is Typhoon. Are you on?" I knew they would be. They always had their radios on in the morning, if for nothing more than to say hello to us or to check up on their fellow teams. They could usually hear my side of the conversation, due to the aircraft's altitude. Also, this was "go-home day." Their spirits would be high. They wouldn't want to miss their ride out of the jungle.

"Roger, Typhoon. We copy loud and clear. How me?"

"Five by. What's you status?" I inquired.

"The LZ was secure yesterday afternoon, but some dude moved in overnight. He's got a gun and he's sitting on the opposite side from us. We can't tell if he has any friends. He's wearing khaki and web gear." Oh shit, I thought. Here we go again. The LZ guards were usually local VC, but this guy was hard-core NVA. We were sitting virtually on the river, and the other side was Cambodia.

"Stand by one, Peeper. Let me snoop around." I flew over to Cambodia. There were open trails that were more like dirt roads in the States. I could see cart tracks leading from the road and into the elephant grass and jungle. There were boxes stacked in the open and under the trees. Some were covered with tarps. There wasn't the slightest attempt to hide or camouflage anything. The river bank was heavily trampled and showed marks, as if boats had been dragged to shore. The Vietnam side had dense jungle, steep banks, and showed no signs of traffic. I looked at my map. I had circled where Skinner hit the log ramp on the river yesterday. It was downstream. Now it made sense. This was a transshipment point, a freaking terminal. The boats were loaded here and floated downstream to the ramp, where they were off-loaded. I bet they were stamping bills of lading and issuing dock receipts.

I came back to the Vietnam side of the border. The presence of supplies meant troops. I wasn't going to take any chances. I was going to take that guard out. Maybe he was just skating from a work detail. I'd teach him to goof off. For all I knew, we could even run into trouble with Spook, Team 6.

I transmitted on VHF, "Airedale Mike, Typhoon, over."

"Roger, Typhoon. Go ahead." It was Rudy's voice.

"I need some fighters. We may have a problem. Hold them at Song Be. Call me when you have an ETA." He acknowledged my request. I switched over to FM and called Delta's forward operating base. "Dancer, this is Typhoon. You can start the choppers. Spook looks OK. Peeper could be a problem. Will advise."

"Roger, Typhoon. We heard your fighter request." The commo guys had been hanging around Rudy's shop again. I formulated a plan. As soon as I had confirmation on the fighters, I'd get the choppers airborne. Pick up Spook first. If we run into trouble, I have the fighters. If it's clean, then I can use the fighters to cover Peeper, where I expected the problem. That sequence reduced the risk of leaving Spook stranded, if all hell breaks loose with Peeper. I called Dancer and gave them the plan. The commanders of Delta were very accommodating. They let the FACs run the air show, including the helicopters. Delegation of authority and unity of command made things much easier.

"Typhoon, Tangerine confirms Dice 05 at the rendezvous in one-zero minutes," Rudy transmitted on the VHF. Good service from the DASC. Rudy continued, "I've advised Dancer. Alligators are lifting off now." If I could only teach Rudy to fly, I could retire; or at least swap jobs with him.

"Typhoon, this is Spook. You didn't tell us you had fighters." They had overheard my Fox Mike transmission to Dancer and now they were jealous. The teams loved air strikes and they would go to all extremes to find a suitable target.

I switched back to FM. "Sorry about that. Maybe next time."

"Typhoon, Dice zero-five at the mountain." Over to UHF.

"Stay on the same radial off seven-three, and come out to six-eight nautical." They should stay on the same course from the Bien Hoa Tacan, and 68 miles on their distance-measuring equipment would put them right over me. "Don't cross the northeast-southwest river. I'm just southeast of the river. We're supporting a recondo extraction. No fire yet, but we anticipate some. What's your line up?"

Rudy cut in on VHF, "Two F–100s just went over. They should be yours." At least I knew the fighters were on course.

"We're two F–100s with four napes and four CBUs plus twenty mike-mike. We can stay about forty-five minutes." What a luxury. When the Sabres went up to II Corps, they were almost at bingo fuel.

"Stay at eight or ten thousand and orbit southeast of the river. I've got choppers down here and we're going to pull some guys out of the jungle. I've got you in sight. Looks good." Switch to FM.

"Spook, get ready. Choppers are three minutes out."

The pick-up chopper, Alligator 3, transmitted, "Typhoon, will you mark the team for us?" I did this by circling the team in a tight bank at treetop level. The low wing of the aircraft became a pointer directed at the team. This allowed the team to stay in concealment until the last possible minute. It did, however, expose us to ground fire and a dangerous flight envelope. While the choppers were occupied picking up Spook, I climbed back to 1,500 feet and headed for Peeper.

"Peeper, is your friend still there?"

"Affirmative."

"OK. Keep your heads down. He's history." I would take him out before he could give any signals. I planned to walk the CBUs through the LZ and tree line opposite the team, and then work the fighters toward the river where I saw all the activity. The river was only 300 meters away.

"Dice, you're going to hit on the northwest side of an LZ that I'm going to mark. I want your passes from southwest to northeast. Parallel the river with a right break. Stay out of Cambodia. We know we have one VC in there and the purpose is to dissuade any others from joining him. We're going to bring a chopper in during the strikes. I want CBUs only—for now." The napalm would obscure the LZ and make landing difficult.

"We copy." Two clicked his mike button twice, indicating he copied. I rolled in with a smoke mark in the center of the LZ. "You're cleared. Hit the tree line twenty meters northwest from my mark." The CBUs came out in a string with the F–100 and gave excellent area coverage. Each softball-sized bomblet had a lethal radius of about fifteen meters and they came out by the hundreds. This was a new weapon to Vietnam, similar to the Willie Pete CBUs I'd used near Qui Nhon.

Peeper was on the radio right away. "You got 'em. He never knew what hit 'em. Keep it coming, FAC."

"Dice, ground troops confirm on target. I want you to make multiple passes on the same heading. Move each pass forty meters northwest, toward the river. I'm bringing choppers in now from the southeast." I'd been monitoring the progress of the pick-up of Spook on the FM radio. I breathed a sigh of relief when I heard that they had the team and were returning to base.

I called the lead helicopter, "Alligator Lead, Typhoon on Fox."

"Go ahead," replied Lead.

"Bring your Alligators about five klicks northwest. You'll see some smoke and fighters. Stay southeast of the fighters. They're dropping CBUs. We have sanitized the LZ. I'll mark the team when you get closer. Break, break. Peeper, choppers are about three minutes out. Get ready." I was a half-mile, just under a klick, south of the team.

"Roger, Typhoon. Tell the fighters they're taking ground fire the closer they come to the river." I turned northwest to investigate. Switch to Uniform.

"Dice, you're taking fire. You must have stirred something up. Hit the same area on your next pass."

"Lead, I think I just took a hit," transmitted Dice 06. "Everything looks okay. I'm rolling in." The helicopters would be in range of the guns. Back to Fox Mike.

"Alligator. This is Typhoon. Orbit in your present position. We're taking fire in the vicinity of the LZ and the river. How's your fuel?"

"We've got a good forty-five minutes." That's a help, while I sort this thing out.

"Lead, I think I see them," said Dice 06. "I saw something flash about a hundred meters to your left on the last pass. Near the small hill."

"Dice, go high and dry," I directed. No acknowledgment. Wrong radio. Switch to UHF. Retransmit. Acknowledgment. I looked over the area. I asked my back-seater Green Beret if he saw anything.

"Looks to me they have some troops and guns camouflaged in that thicket of bamboo. The one that's in the depression just this side of the small hill," he said. I saw where he meant. I would have looked on the hill, since it gave a better field of fire, but in this case concealment was more important. I flew over the thicket. No ground fire, but I didn't expect any. The NVA were too clever to fire at a high-flying FAC. They knew I was waiting for them to give their position away. Their chances of hitting me were pretty slight unless they had some big gun, but it looked suspicious.

"Dice, this is Typhoon. We think we found the guns. All small arms. Set up for napalm. I gotta talk to the Army before I can mark." I went back to FM.

"Peeper. Typhoon. What's the status on the LZ?"

"Everything's quiet, FAC. Ground fire's stopped too. We want a beer." They were anxious to be exfiltrated. I didn't blame them, but I wanted them out safely.

"Alligator. Typhoon."

"Go ahead."

"We think we found the guns. They're two hundred meters northwest of the pickup. We're gonna hit 'em with napalm. You can use the napalm for a reference. The team is two hundred meters southeast of the napalm. Hold a 345-degree heading and you should fly right to them. They've moved to the south side of the LZ. It's the only one in the area. Stay as low as possible. Copy?"

"Rog." Back to UHF.

"Alright, Dice. Sorry for the delay. Let's go to work. Choppers will be coming in from the southeast. I told them to stay low. Because of the border, you'll have to pull up over them. Friendlies are in the same place. I'll mark in ten seconds. Target is close to where you thought." I honked the Bird Dog over, rolled wings level and smashed a smoke rocket into the heart of the thicket. "Same heading as before. Lead, I want you to hit twelve

o'clock, thirty meters. Two, you hit six o'clock, thirty meters. Cleared."
This would give Two a chance to avoid the smoke and fire from Lead's
hit.

Everything was looking good. Lead hit ten meters long but it was still
in the thicket. Two was right on. The entire bamboo was engulfed in flame.
I saw a cloud of white smoke boil up through the orange flame, and black
smoke from the napalm. A secondary explosion. My back-seater was right.
There was something in there. The choppers were coming in.

"FAC, you're taking fire. *Watch Out!*" It was Peeper. I started jinking
right away, in order to confuse the gunners. I switched to FM.

"Abort! Abort! Abort!" I had to stop Alligator from going in for the
pickup until I could find out where the fire was coming from.

"Typhoon, this is Dice. I think I took a hit on that pass." Back to UHF.
After a slight pause he continued, "Everything looks good in the cockpit.
We've only got twenty mike-mike left."

"Dice, could you tell when you took the hit and from which side?" I
asked. I climbed for some more altitude.

"I took it coming down the chute. On the port side." He got hit on the
left side as he was heading northeast. The light suddenly turned on. Was I
stupid. The fire was coming from Cambodia. I turned the nose there. Sure
enough, wispy gun smoke clouds were hanging over the jungle on the other
side of the river. Now what? Could I risk bringing the chopper in, hoping
it didn't get hit? Send the team to another LZ? Put an air strike in Cambodia?
I needed a plan—fast!

I couldn't risk getting a chopper shot down. How would we ever get it
out or rescue the crew as long as the NVA sat in Cambodia and fired away
from their sanctuary? There wasn't another LZ nearby for the team. Besides,
it would put them at great risk to move. They were probably low on
rations, and with all the activity, the NVA knew they were in there someplace. Air strikes were forbidden in Cambodia. It was a neutral country.
Apparently only neutral for me. Back in February I signed a document to
that effect. I could have the fighters strafe in Cambodia and if anyone asked,
I could deny it. Strafe doesn't leave evidence like bomb craters or napalm.
However, with all those supplies stacked along the river, we would probably
set off a secondary explosion that could be seen all the way to Saigon. Or
Washington. My career was at stake, but so were the lives of the team and
the pilots.

"Dice, I want you to make dry passes along the river. Stay high. I want
you to be visible. I'll tell you when I want a hot pass with the mike-mike.
Be prepared to come in from either direction, parallel to the river." That
should keep them out of harm's way and accessible when I needed them.
The VC will be following the flight path of the fighters, never knowing
when they would drop a bomb. Changing direction might confuse the

enemy gunners. The noise of the jets would screen out the Whup-Whup-Whup of the helicopter rotor blades. I switched to FM.

"Alligator, this is Typhoon. I found the guns. We'll take care of them. Call when you are a mile out from the LZ." I didn't want to tell them the guns were in Cambodia. I was taking a calculated risk with their lives.

"Peeper, when Alligator calls at one mile out, I want you to pop a smoke. The color of the smoke is the color of a coward. Do you understand?" I learned my lesson about smoke colors when the VC monitored our radios in Tuy Hoa.

"Roger. It's the same color as Dorothy's brick road." Who ever said Green Berets were a bunch of uncultured, snake-eating Visigoths? I selected intercom and talked to my back-seater.

"Look in the seat pocket. Find all the red smoke grenades you can. Give me two. You keep the rest. Be prepared to drop them out the window one at a time, just as fast as you can when I tell you. Pull the pins on a couple of them and hang onto them." If he dropped one we'd have a cockpit full of red smoke. I switched to UHF.

"Dice, I'm going to put out a string of marks along the river. I want you in hot ASAP, with strafe. Multiple passes. Hit between the marks and the river. Stay parallel to the river, either direction." I paused. "The marks will be the same color as a returning buoy on your right. Disregard all other marks."

"Typhoon, I don't understand the color." Oh, no. I must have a mid-western fighter pilot who's never been near open water, let alone sailing.

"Try the color you see when you are angry." I heard two clicks on the radio. He understood. I sat in an orbit north of the team and just inside the border. From this vantage point I could observe the team, helicopters, fighters, and the source of ground fire on the river.

The pick-up helicopter, flanked by the gunships, was approaching one-and-a-half miles from the team. They were on course. It was time to execute my plan. I had only one chance. It had to succeed. I shouted over the roar of the engine to my back-seater, "Get ready. We're going in." I chopped the power, rolled inverted, and sucked the nose down through the horizon. As the nose went through 30 degrees, I rolled the aircraft right-side-up and hit the mike button.

"Dice, I want you hot on the next pass." I was at treetop level, 50 meters from, and parallel to, the river. I put the control stick between my legs and pulled the pin from the smoke grenade. I dropped the pin to the floor and re-grabbed the stick, holding the safety handle firmly. I didn't want premature ignition. They burned hot. The second grenade, still safetied, was hooked on the instrument panel. Alligator called one mile out. The plan was working. I shouted to the sergeant, "Now," and he dropped his burning smokes from the rear window. He was holding them in his bare hands out the window. When they hit the jungle, they instantly blossomed into a deep-red cloud of smoke. I threw mine from the front window and he followed immediately with two more, as I groped with the pin and tossed the sixth grenade. I jammed the throttle forward and yanked back on the stick, as I put the Bird Dog into a climbing wingover. I looked out the top window and saw Dice rolling in on final for his strafing run. I ran out of airspeed at the apex of the wingover, kicked bottom rudder and sliced the nose downward. I reached up and armed my last two smoke rockets. I could see the yellow smoke rising from Peeper's location and Alligator was tracking on the smoke. Now for the grand finale.

I fired the rockets into the river bank on the Cambodian side. I couldn't direct air strikes in Cambodia, but nothing was said about marking targets and deceiving the enemy. I avoided hitting supplies or touching off explosions. The fighters were now strafing the river bank. On the legal side. The red smokes had screened the pick-up helicopter. My smoke rockets sent the enemy diving for cover, unable to fire at the choppers or fighters. Did I stretch the rules? Yes. Was it wrong? By 1968, U.S. forces could cross into Cambodia if "in hot pursuit" of their adversary. The determination of right and wrong in this war was as evanescent as the smoke dissipating over Cambodia.

August 17—Team 7 found a concentration of VC just prior to sunrise. They called for an immediate air strike, which was followed by another when the team was spotted and pinned down by enemy fire. The attack was broken and the team successfully exfiltrated. We followed up with three additional air strikes. In the afternoon, we returned with yet three more strikes. We expended a total of 26 fighter sorties, both American and VNAF, killing a conservative estimate of 95 VC and destroying three automatic weapons. Teams 4 and 9 were put in at last light.

Team 7, led by Lt. Vu Man Thong and Sgt. Norm Doney, were inserted just before dark and moved several hundred meters away from the LZ, unsuspectedly toward the center of a major VC bivouac area. They settled in for the night, within the sound of a burbling creek. In the early morning hours, they were awakened by the rythmic banging of sticks from the opposite side of the creek. They interpreted this as a signaling device that carried long distances in the jungle. Also, Doney had spotted smoke, indicating a VC base camp, and he wanted an air strike on it. Skinner Simpson, the FAC, who had taken off before dawn in order to be in the vicinity of the teams at first light, immediately passed the word back to Bishop at the radio jeep in Song Be. Bishop contacted the DASC, and they diverted to us three F–100s, loaded with napalm, CBUs, and bombs. The DASC response was much better after I had complained about the 45-minute wait on the thirteenth.

The first morning after insertion was the most critical: If the VC spotted or heard a low helicopter, they would try to determine if and where it landed and begin a search. The helicopters used masking techniques to confuse the enemy. But by now, they knew Delta was operating in the area.

Skinner spotted Doney's mirror, reflecting the first rays of the morning sun. It was fortunate, since Doney's location was 1,500 meters from where the helicopter pilot thought he dropped the team. While Doney and Skinner were conversing on the radio, the Viet team sergeant crept down to the creek to investigate the signal sticks. What he saw was utterly amazing. The signal sticks were keeping the beat for a physical training class. There were over 100 VC in a clearing under the jungle canopy, barely 75 meters on the other side of the creek. He scurried back to tell his lieutenant, who was the only Viet who spoke English.

Doney quickly got on the radio and told Simpson to cancel the smoke target and hit 75 meters north of the creek. The fighters were already on their base leg, waiting for Simpson's marking rocket. Skinner adjusted his aim and put a rocket in the middle of the formation. The team barely had time to get their heads down when the first jet came in. The sound from the signal sticks was still echoing through the jungle when the first strings of winking cluster bombs blew their thousands of pellets through the formation. Now with a good reference, number Two put his snake-eye bombs on the edges of the formation where the concussion and shrapnel of the bombs knocked the fleeing troops to the ground. Three came in next with napalm, its effectiveness limited since it detonated in the top of the jungle canopy. Doney and the other team members could hear the cries of confusion and agony from the enemy as they tried to escape the air strike.

As the team started to move out, they observed a heavy concentration of khaki uniforms to their south, on the same side of the creek. The team had become preoccupied with the PT formation and had not noticed the enemy to their south. They advised Simpson they were virtually surrounded and to get them out of there. The presence of khaki uniforms indicated the same hard-core NVA.

Meanwhile at Song Be, Bishop and I could hear the radio traffic between Skinner and the fighters and Skinner's half of the conversation with Doney on the ground. Many of the base camp troopers had gathered around our radio jeep to listen to the battle. During a short lull, Skinner asked for the pick-up choppers and more air support. We had already called the DASC and requested an additional flight of fighters. With the ensuing emergency, I'd asked them to divert everything they had to us. We couldn't wait for them to scramble alert aircraft; we needed already-airborne jets streaking to us. I understood the system and would make it work for us.

The second flight of fighters showed up and Skinner immediately directed them on the khaki-clad troops that were surrounding the team. As soon as the bombs tore into them, they ran in panic through the jungle. A trio ran within five feet of Doney and never saw him. Skinner directed the team toward an LZ and tried to sterilize the area around the team. The few enemy who had seen the team were now occupied with other concerns—survival from the deadly accurate air strikes. The NVA, trying to rid themselves of the killer bees that rained havoc on them, now turned their weapons on the fighters. This gave the team the opportunity to move again to the LZ. Once they reached the LZ, they formed a defensive perimeter in order to ward off any enemy attacks. Skinner directed the helicopter gunships onto the tree lines surrounding the clearing. Another flight of fighters orbited overhead, which Simpson held at-the-ready. The pick-up chopper slipped in amid a hail of enemy fire, as the door gunners hammered away at the tree lines with their M–60 machine guns. Miraculously, the chopper got in and out without wounding a single crew or team member. Back at Song Be, the crew chiefs counted 23 fresh bullet holes in that Huey. They were one brave crew.

As the Huey lifted out of the heavy elephant grass of the pick-up zone, Skinner saw three machine guns send tracers arcing toward the chopper. The fire was coming from the north side of the creek in the vicinity of the first air strike. Without friendlies on the ground to worry about, Skinner cleared the fighters for random passes on the guns. Random passes were the most difficult for the enemy to counter. They never knew from which direction the fighters would come next, as Skinner continued to mark the targets with smoke rockets and smoke grenades.

Doney landed at Song Be. We had two more flights of fighters on the way and I wanted to ensure we hit the best targets. I grabbed him as he scrambled out of the chopper. He speculated they had been on the periphery of a regimental-size complex, less than two miles from the Cambodian border. This correlated with the air strikes we had put in on the fifteenth and sixteenth at the border. He suggested we keep working outward from the site of the PT formation. It appeared to be a central gathering point and training center. I passed this information to Skinner as he picked up the two additional flights of fighters. He transmitted to me on VHF.

"Airedale, this is Typhoon on Victor." I keyed the mike.

"Go."

"They're all over the place. Some 500-pounders just uncovered another complex of hooches." These must be the sleeping platforms that the team briefly mentioned. He continued, "They're not even trying to hide. They're just standing there shooting back at us." They were disciplined NVA troops, demonstrating to the local VC trainees the importance of concentrating small arms fire at aircraft. The battle was on. I picked up the HF handset.

"Tangerine, this is Airedale. I want your Foxtrot Delta Oscar, over." I wanted to talk directly to the fighter duty officer at the III Corps DASC.

"Wait one." A pause. "This is FiDO, over."

"Rog. We have uncovered an NVA complex. We have no idea how large it is. It's full of troops and close to the border. I'm afraid they'll slip back to Cambodia tonight. I have no friendlies in the immediate area. Send me whatever you have."

"We'll try our best. For the record, do you have the coordinates of the complex?"

"Roger. Vicinity of grid square Yankee Uniform 220360." I didn't bother to encode the coordinates. The NVA knew that we knew where they were.

"We'll get back to you. Out."

Skinner landed shortly thereafter and came dragging over to the jeep. He was exhausted from stress and soaking wet from perspiration. He looked like he had just played the toughest game of his career. In a sense he had. He had been flying over three hours, all of it in intense combat and ground fire. Doney came over and shook his hand.

"Thanks, FAC." Skinner grinned from ear to ear. In his unmistakable drawl and typical understatement he replied, "It was fun." He turned to me. "They're everywhere. Every time we made a pass, some new area would start shooting at us. I didn't know where to hit next."

"What kind of BDA are you giving?" I asked him.

"Hell, John, the canopy is so thick that it's tough to see the bodies. We hit the muzzle flashes and smoke. I knew we hit them, but I was conservative. I was giving maybe ten or fifteen estimated KBA per flight. Depends on whether it was a two-, three-, or four-shipper and the number of passes."

Doney was standing with us. He confirmed Skinner's speculation. "You must have hit at least fifty of them before the chopper took us out. You wouldn't believe what chaos it was down there. They hadn't even shed their packs, they were so surprised. They were bleeding from their ears and mouths from the concussion. The CBUs turned them into limp rag dolls."

I shuddered at Doney's words and found myself sickened by the description of the carnage. Then I thought about the people we lost and the rows of body bags and stacks of coffins I had seen. Okay, Charlie. I can hang tough.

"Norm, Skinner. I've ordered more fighters. We're going back before they get away."

Doney took off in a chopper back to the target area, while Skinner and I awaited confirmation from the DASC for additional fighters. They diverted three additional flights in the afternoon. These were maximum effort flights of four aircraft, each with heavy bomb loads. One of the flights was our F–100 friends from Bien Hoa, while the other two were VNAF A–1Hs with all 14 wing stations loaded with bombs and napalm. One flight of A–1s yielded a total of 56 munitions, and with their long fuel endurance, we were able to drop their ordnance, one at a time, on precise targets. Although it was Skinner's day to fly, I took one of the mid-afternoon flights of VNAF Skyraiders. This gave Skinner a break and also allowed him to do some detailed target planning with Doney, after he returned from the recce in the chopper. We later learned that Prime Minister Nguyen Cao Ky personally led one of the strikes. A former air vice marshall, he was an accomplished fighter pilot with thousands of missions. It's not very often you find the chief political figure of a country leading bombing missions.

I, too, was amazed by the size of the complex. It was my responsibility to find the appropriate targets under the jungle canopy for the VNAF pilots, who never missed. I vividly recall, after one 500-pound bomb was accurately dropped, seeing NVA troops in khaki uniforms, scurrying out from under the trees and into the center of the bomb crater to recover their dead and wounded. They looked up at me defiantly, daring me to hit them again. I did. Then I had an ominous, fleeting thought: What would happen if I were shot down or if my engine quit? Years later, while flying a similar plane in the Reserves, I had a catastrophic internal-engine failure that tore the engine from its mounts. If I'd had that failure on August 17, 1966, I am positive the NVA would have had some "special treatment" for me.

With the new inputs from Doney's recce, Skinner went back to the complex with the eighth flight of fighters for that day. Doney found fresh troops. They were setting up gun positions, and others were dragging bodies to the creek bank. Skinner hit them with another flight of A–1s. At the end of the day we tallied up the results. We had expended four flights of U.S. fighters and four flights of VNAF fighters for a total of 26 fighter sorties. We flew four FAC sorties in the O–1. Skinner had flown six hours and five minutes, and I flew one hour and forty minutes, directing air strikes. We estimated killing 95 NVA, and we knew we knocked out three machine guns. Doney went back once again in the helicopter just before sunset. He found a cortege of about 50 sampans along the creek where he had been that morning. They were preparing to take their dead and wounded back to Cambodia. We left them alone. We had done enough killing. We had decimated the likes of a NVA battalion.

August 18—ALO airborne at first light. Team 4 compromised first morning after insertion. Broke contact. Compromised again by VC platoon. Team located gasoline-powered generator. Two air strikes, Eagle 51, three F–100s and Eagle 01, two F–100s expended on platoon and generator. VC tried to climb trees to escape air strike. Five KBA. Team extracted. Teams 1 and 3 inserted at last light.

August 19—Team 1 surrounded at 0530 hours. FAC airborne at 0600. Team became separated. FAC directed choppers and gunships to rescue team. All extracted, two WIA. Air strike conducted Sharkbait 21, three F–4Cs. Team 3 made contact at 1100 hours. VC observed in bamboo. Air strike conducted, Eagle 41, two F–100s. Team OK, all ordnance on target. Team 9 spotted two platoons VC. Two airstrikes, Eagle 71, two F–100s, and Boxer 01, two F–4Cs. Negative BDA due to foliage.

We had been operating in the jungle along the Cambodian border for ten days. We were having trouble keeping the teams intact and out of danger. The NVA were fully aware we were patrolling in the area. They had observers posted on virtually every potential landing zone. As soon as the teams were inserted, the NVA and VC would begin tracking the team. After a successful extraction, one of the team members told me of the VC searching for them all night with flashlights in the jungle. Another team member had his wrist stepped on by a searching VC. He showed me the bruise.

The teams were finding plenty of targets. The problem was, the area was so densely infiltrated with enemy troops that the teams could not withdraw to a safe distance for us to conduct concentrated air strikes. We could not have the teams mark their position because of the danger of disclosing their location to the enemy. We relied on directional-signal mirrors on sunny days, but on overcast and rainy days we were positioning the teams almost by feel and intuition. Skinner and I had been working with the teams long enough that we could almost sense where they were. We could usually give the team their position within 100 meters, but for us to get more accurate necessitated our flying at almost treetop level. This, in turn, could compromise the location of the team, as the VC would intensify their search efforts wherever they saw us flying.

Skinner and I worked with the teams to improve our target identification techniques, particularly in marginal weather. The teams improvised, using lengths of fuse cord to detonate smoke grenades. They would light the cord and stealthily creep away, while we circled overhead waiting for the grenade to detonate. It only worked sometimes because the cord and igniter would get wet. We tried wrapping them in plastic. The cord also burned with a whisp of smoke, which could be both smelled and seen. But we tried.

Under the situation we had at Song Be, the most valuable target identification was debriefing the teams after they were extracted. They would describe in minute detail the dimensions and composition of the installations. The most prevalent was clusters of sleeping platforms. The bamboo floor was elevated about three feet from the wet and insect-laden jungle earth, and the side poles supported a sloped and interwoven latticework of bamboo and leaves. Each platform could accommodate four or six soldiers and their equipment. Since the enemy usually moved at night, the best time to hit them was in the early morning hours or during the early afternoon rest period. The midday heat was so intense that activity was suspended for a couple of hours. We would be more than willing to interrupt their rest time, or "phak," with an air strike.

The enemy complex we were probing measured several miles on each side and was contiguous to the Cambodian border. Every time we thought we had its dimensions, we'd find another offshot or series of clusters. The generator site and two platoons that we hit on the eighteenth were 12 miles from the border. We had an area target that called for saturation bombing. We couldn't dent it with the A–1s, F–4s, and F–100s. The entire concentration was only 70 miles from downtown Saigon.

After consulting with the intelligence officer of Delta, who had been meticulously plotting the sightings and formulating the enemy order of battle, we decided to ask for some heavy air strikes. The United States was in the midst of a bombing campaign, Rolling Thunder, directed at the logistics heart of North Vietnam. Rail yards, petroleum storage areas, and bridges were the primary targets. All were heavily defended by radar-controlled antiaircraft guns and surface-to-air missiles. Ships in Haiphong harbor were still off-limits. Waves of 36 and 48 aircraft, high–bomb capacity F–105s, were being launched almost daily from Korat and Takhli airbases in Thailand, to Hanoi. Why go there to hit heavily defended targets when we had numerous companies of enemy troops and their supplies on the doorstep of Saigon? The bridges in North Vietnam weren't going anywhere. Conversely, our targets were perishable, and our sporadic but inadequate bombing would only force the NVA back into their Cambodian sanctuary. Concentrated and timely bombings by the F–105s, however, would annihilate the NVA before they could flee. I'd submitted numerous preplanned air requests, looking for a portion of those Thunderchiefs with their 750-pound bombs. I was naive. I had no concept of the convoluted politico-military strike approval process. My requests were categorically denied.

It was three days later, when I personally visited the DASC at Bien Hoa, that I learned the truth: I had submitted by requests to the wrong place; the requests had to go to the White House! The F–105s were being targeted from the White House, bypassing Pacific Theater Headquarters in Hawaii, the next command level from Vietnam. I couldn't believe it. Maybe I should have dropped those bombs in Cambodia. That would get White House attention. I also learned there was a political prohibition to using Thailand-based aircraft for air strikes in South Vietnam; North Vietnam and Laos, however, were fair game. That logic escaped me. The enemy on the ground, shooting at me and the teams, was from North Vietnam. What difference did it make whether the bombs originated in Thailand or Vietnam? The enemy was the same to me. Let Buddha sort it all out after I dispatched them to the hereafter.

The DASC did offer some help while we were at Song Be. They thought I might get a B–52 bomber strike approved. In a high priority, it could be done in 48 hours, but would require the approval of COMUSMACV, General Westmoreland, to change targets. I told them thanks for the thought, but to skip it for now. In 48 hours, the enemy would be gone and so would Delta.

We had a surprise. We made the front page of *Stars and Stripes*, the military newspaper. It proudly announced the success of the elite Project Delta in killing over 120 enemy soldiers with air strikes on August 17, 1966. The article identified the FAC in the Song Be vicinity operation as none other than First Lieutenant Carlton S. Simpson. I was in trouble. The commander wanted to know, in no uncertain words, how a clandestine, secret operation managed to make the headlines.

"Skinner, where are you?" I called over to the officers' tent.

"Leave me alone. I'm tired of flying," he shouted back in jest. I walked to the general purpose tent from the commander's tent, a distance of about 60 feet. I had the copy of *Stars and Stripes* in my hand. As I ducked to enter the tent, I saw he was playing cards with Deaton, Jantowski, and Hamilton, the Ranger advisors, all combat-hardened lieutenants. "Besides," he continued, "I'm finally beating these sons-of-bitches at hearts." There was always friendly rivalry between the Air Force and Army. He looked up from his seat on the cot. I showed him the paper.

"Did you see this?" I asked.

"No. Where'd that come from?" He glanced at the article.

"One of the chopper pilots brought it back from Bien Hoa."

"At least they spelled my name right. Got the numbers wrong. We added only 90 or 95. We probably killed more. Just like the press though, to exaggerate."

"No, Skinner. The old man wants to know how it got in there."

"Beats the shit outta me. Wait a minute. Pollock was in one of those flights of Huns. He recognized my voice. We were roommates at the Academy." Apparently some enterprising reporter from the *Stars* was hanging around the bar and listening to the guys talk. We know that the fighter pilots were excited about the missions on that day. His next stop would have been to pry some of the info from the intelligence section at Bien Hoa where they collected all the BDAs. The reporter was picking up the info secondhand. That would explain the inconsistency of the KBA numbers. We doubt he could have picked it up at the formal MACV press briefing in Saigon, the Five O'Clock Follies. Something as secret as Delta's operation would have been scrubbed from the briefing.

I went back to the commander and told him what had happened. He accepted the explanation and asked us if we could be more careful in the future. I made a mental note to talk to the fighter jocks in Bien Hoa. Fortunately, the press article didn't appear when we first arrived in Song Be. It would have compromised the entire operation. Personally, I was pleased we were spotlighted for deserved recognition, but I was cognizant of how dangerous it could have been. In a free society the press is a way of life. But in this case, it was irresponsible press.

August 20—Teams 3 and 9 both in difficulty. Team 3 unable to move. Extracted. No positive target for air strike. Team 9 escaped and evaded the enemy. Two airstrikes on battalion position concealed under trees. Silver 05 and Dice 81, each a flight of two F–100s, carrying 500-pound bombs and napalm. No CBU available.

August 21—Weather marginal. Team 9 spotted two platoons of enemy in the open. Team became surrounded. FAC directed gunships to suppress ground fire. Slick helicopter shot down. Helicopter crew and team successfully extracted. One WIA. Three airstrikes, Saber 09, two F–100s with eight napalms, Whiskey 21, four F–4Cs with 16 napalms, and Red, three VNAF A–1Hs with eight napalm and ten bombs. This was a light bomb load for the A–1s. They could have filled a total of 42 bomb stations.

The operation on Sunday morning, August 21, 1966, was one of the most intense, integrated, small-arms encounters for Project Delta or similar recondo force. It was only through the skill, tenacity, and bravery of everyone involved, that what could have been a tragic disaster was a successful rescue and extraction. On March 5, 1989, at Lackland Air Force Base, near San Antonio, Texas, I recorded that mission as Skinner Simpson remembered it and flew it almost 23 years earlier. Jim Ahmann was also present. They both retired from the Air Force as soon as they were eligible, with the rank of lt. colonel. This was the first time the three of us, the Project Delta FACs—Air Force Academy graduates of 1961, 1962, and 1963—had been reunited since July 19, 1966, when Jim left Buon Blech in the Central Highlands on his way home. This is Skinner's tale.

It was absolutely miserable weather. The field was a little a bit higher than the surrounding terrain, so after I took off I descended to follow the river. It was early morning, barely sunrise. We hadn't heard from the team and it was important to talk to them. I was in and out of the clouds all the time, just picking my way along. The team was on the whisper radio. The VC were all around them. They wanted an exfiltration point. The clouds were really bad, about 500 feet. There were holes up to 10,000 or 15,000 feet. The team started to take some shooting. You could hear the popping noises on the radio. They were all over the place and they started shooting at me. They usually didn't open up until you knew they were there. The team is now running to an exfiltration zone and I'm trying to get the helicopters in. They're having the same problem we are with the weather. I was trying to rendezvous the fighters. They were at 20,000 feet and I'd climb up through some holes to get them in-between the layers of clouds.

I finally got the helicopters to the zone. Troops were taking heavy fire. I sent the gunships along the tree line. Time is moving on. Very tense. It's been two and a half hours. We're just trying to keep the bad guys off the good guys and get the good guys out. Gunships were taking severe hits. We tried for a pickup and the slick got shot out of the sky. The slick just crashed right there. Everyone got out; now we had the six-man team plus the chopper crew on the ground. The weather was getting better and the fighters could see. The sergeant in the backseat with me is firing the grenade launcher out the window. We were having just a good old time.

We finally got fighters in with napalm that I put in the tree lines behind the troops. The gunships were running out of ammo at this time. With the combination of the gunships and slicks we got everybody out, got another flight of fighters to blow up the helicopter so the VC couldn't get anything out of it. I had been up four hours before we got them out of there. I was running out of fuel. I had a two-hour bladder; it got so bad that I had to take a leak in my canteen. On one pass by the VC, I threw my canteen out the window at them. "Here, take this. Piss on the enemy." I hope they drank it. I needed a helicopter escort back and I got as high as possible. I flew a flameout pattern in case the engine quit. I was just happy to be on the ground. Only minor injuries, shrapnel for one of the guys on the ground.

We looked at the aircraft. There weren't any holes in it! I couldn't believe it. That's why you wouldn't give me any medals, because there weren't any holes in the aircraft. I should have gone out there and shot it—a couple of holes, at least.

When Skinner first joined Delta, we had agreed that the airplane or pilot would have to take a hit to be considered for a serious medal. Years later, I admitted to Skinner that I had deprived him of some medals when I realized how prostituted the system had become. Other pilots were getting medals for the risks that we were taking on a routine basis at Delta. Our standards were much higher than what the others were using.

After that exciting morning, the commander announced we weren't putting in any more teams. We were redeploying to Tay Ninh. It was Sunday and we were to be in position by Wednesday. We would get a few days off. I was relieved, not to think how the teams felt. I walked the quarter-mile across the field and the runway-street to the church. I went to Sunday Mass. I didn't even take my guns with me.

We had put in 25 air strikes, most of them in the last week under harrowing conditions. We had expended 67 sorties of fighters, every one of them on confirmed military targets. We lost a chopper, but no teams or crew members. We had lost two Rangers and had several people wounded, none seriously. We had killed an untold number of enemy and had disrupted major staging areas. We were off to Bien Hoa for a few days of fun and frolic, before heading to war zone C.

It was a welcome respite to sleep in a real bed with sheets, take a shower from water taps, and shave in a real sink. A porcelain commode was sheer luxury. Air conditioning and ice from machines were overwhelming. This was Bien Hoa, a bustling Air Force base and the home of the Third Tac Fighter Wing and its four squadrons of F-100s. These were the guys, together with the VNAF, who had given us most of the air support over the last ten days. We became the cause celebre; many of the pilots had flown at least one mission in support of us. Our Typhoon call sign was as unique as tiger-suit fatigues were on Air Force pilots. We met the jocks who flew the missions when Skinner hit the PT formation. It was, indeed, led by his roommate from the Academy, Rob Pollock. His wingman had pressed the attack so intensely that he brought back a three-foot section of tree in the leading edge of his wing. They agreed it was the most rewarding mission they had flown in combat. We thought it was rather significant ourselves. Another pilot wanted to know why I was talking in riddles and why I needed all the red smokes. I didn't care to disclose I was playing with the rules of engagement in order to protect the team and the helicopter.

Some pilots prodded us for more details about what we were doing, but after the unfortunate publicity gained through the *Stars and Stripes* article, Skinner and I were circumspect with our comments. The pilots were trying to document what they called "significant missions." What I didn't realize was they were looking for facts to support documentation for medals, primarily Distinguished Flying Crosses and in some cases maybe even Silver Stars. If they had told us why, we could have helped them without compromising the security of Delta. We probably denied deserving pilots medals they earned. If everyone makes the same salary, it's difficult to recognize achievement without medals. The worse part is I probably caused some pilots to compromise their values when they wrongfully embellished another mission to obtain the recognition they rightfully earned in flying combat for Delta. It is undeniable, the teams could not have survived without the close air support of the fighters. We used close air support in the true meaning of the word.

I met a couple of pilots who had been instructors in my pilot training class. One of them had been involved in the marching punishment incident in Oklahoma. He still hadn't been promoted. Maybe his combat record would atone for his prior error in judgment.

While in Bien Hoa, I flew a strike mission in the backseat of the F–100, a two-place F-model. I had previously flown in the Hun when I was a cadet. It brought back fond memories, except this was a combat mission and not a joyride over the California desert. It gave me an appreciation for the fighter pilot's perspective of the jet air-ground war in III Corps. It was a noneventful mission. Now I understood why the pilots were challenged by the Project Delta close air support missions. Our missions required the utmost of concentration and accuracy in a tension-filled hostile or emergency situation. That brought out the best in the fighter jocks. They thrived on competition with their peers, and our missions presented that environment. Fear was not in their vocabulary, but judgment and skill were. I enjoyed flying formation again and flew the traffic pattern to the touchdown. I needed a little help from the front-seater to give us a smooth landing. I could now add the F–100 to my Vietnam repertoire of A–1E, F–4C, Huey, and L–19 aircraft; and parachute jumps.

I went to the DASC to debrief the completed phase of the operation and to open the next phase. This time I needed no introduction to O'Grady, Blumer, and Olson. They had kept a separate tally sheet of our air strikes and results on large display boards. They were as proud as we were of the results. I admitted our BDAs were probably understated, but it was very difficult to obtain a confirmed body count with a six-man team in the middle of a NVA complex. They were welcome to send the 5th ARVN Division in after us to tally up the score. I sat with the intelligence staff, both Army and Air Force, and described to them in detail the complexes and the various peripheries that extended along the Cambodian border. I recognized that the Army was responsible for all targeting in South Vietnam and I wanted them to clearly understand the enemy order of battle. I plotted coordinates and drew traces on their tissue overlays. I gave suggested headings for B–52 carpet bombings that would give the best coverage. I took some good-natured ribbing on my requests for F–105 fighter-bombers based in Thailand. How was I to know they were the play toys of President Johnson and Secretary of Defense McNamara, and reserved for some North Vietnam bombing escalation strategy with Ho Chi Minh? I had NVA troops only 70 miles from Saigon, not strategy.

I discussed the next phase with the DASC staff. We would be working for the 1st Brigade of the 25th Infantry Division out of Tay Ninh West. Our area of operation was the infamous war zone C. I gave them a tissue trace of our AO. We were going right into the heart of C. I just hoped we came out of it.

Using the same large map that I used on August 9, I proceeded with my briefing. We would be there until September 5. The same procedures applied. It's a no-fire zone for everyone but ourselves. I asked for a suggested rendezvous for the fighters that everyone was familiar with. We decided on Nui Ba Dinh, the 3,235-foot mountain. The TACAN was 302 degrees at 44 miles from Channel 73; closer to Saigon than Song Be. The TACAN for the field was 295 degrees, same distance. Sounded tough to get lost. The primary strike frequency was the same. I asked if there was anything else I should know. Affirmative: the location of COSVN—Communist Command Center in South Vietnam. That should be fun. One more item: Please try to keep it out of the newspapers, at least until the operation is over. We shook hands and they wished me well.

I spotted Sgt. Bomar, the radio operator supervisor.

"Thanks, Sarge, for the efficient service. You were there when we needed you. Same thing, except we'll be at Tay Ninh."

"Oh, yessir. That's Tangerine two-seven. They'll help you if you get in a bind."

"Thanks. We'll stop by on our way back."

On Wednesday, August 24, Skinner and I said good-bye to our fighter buddies at Bien Hoa. They invited us back. We implored them, please no more press articles. We threatened them with a "short round" report, which is the report a FAC submits when a friendly gets hit by an air strike. Our instances were rare; besides, Skinner and I were not much for paperwork.

It was a pleasant flight from Bien Hoa to Tay Ninh. Afternoon thunderstorms had not yet developed. We flew beneath the scattered deck of puffy stratocumulus clouds. Visibility was great. We could see Nui Ba Dinh from 20 miles away. Everything else was flat. We were more accustomed to the hills and mountains of II Corps, or the monster mountains of I Corps.

Even Song Be had some hills and depressions. But not this section. We overflew our base at Tay Ninh and advised Dancer that we were going to take a quick tour of the area. Skinner and I never flew together tactically. A lucky hit would take us both out and leave Delta stranded. But we looked at this flight as an administrative flight, with a visual recce tacked on the end.

"What do you think?" I asked Skinner over the intercomm. He was looking down from the backseat and shifting from the left side to the right in order to get a broader perspective.

"This stuff is thick," he said referring to the jungle canopy. "There are no holes except where the jungle is growing back in some of the grassland area." Some parts of war zone C had apparently been cultivated at one point. Now the dense elephant grass and bamboo were reclaiming any open areas. But 90 percent of the area was double- and triple-jungle canopy. There were virtually no landmarks, no roads, and only a few jungle trails, some of which were shown on the maps. The villages depicted on the maps didn't exist. Our maps were old, some of them dating back over ten years to the French.

"Skinner, this is going to be a real bitch to navigate and give position fixes." I glanced at my map and tried to locate our exact position. It was difficult. You couldn't even see the streams that were marked on the map. "Notice the change in color of the vegetation," I continued. "The new jungle is a lighter color and it shows as grassland on the map. The contours are the same." They never taught us this in cartography and geography at the Academy. They gave us the big picture: Vietnam was green for jungle and brown for mountains. Period.

"John, what's that over there? At two o'clock." I oriented myself. We were flying south. Two o'clock was toward Cambodia. I turned west. As we approached the border, we could see white stucco and red-tiled buildings. And streets. And pagodas. It all stopped very abruptly at the border. It was a different world on the other side. We were at the "twilight zone."

"Let's land. I've seen enough. I want a beer," I said, as I banked the little craft toward the airfield. The runway was 3,800 feet of tightly packed and rolled laterite with a PSP-covered area for parking and tie-down. What a luxury. There was a C-130 unloading and helicopters buzzing all over the place. A little Bird Dog could get blown right out of here. We parked in the 25th Division area. They had a fuel truck and a soldier who was topping off an Army L-19. We shut the engine down, climbed out, threw some chocks under the wheels, and installed the rocket safety pins. Skinner tied the wings and tail wheel down, while I filled out the forms. Rudy walked over from the Delta tent area and helped him.

"Hi, Lieutenants," said Rudy in his usual cheerful tone. "I bet you guys just screwed off in Saigon while I had to get the jeep loaded on a C-130 and hauled over here."

"Rudy," said Skinner, "you wouldn't believe us if we told you we stayed on the base. A jeepful of guys got grenaded on the highway to Saigon, so we stayed put. How's the food?"

"Great. We got our usual chow. But you can go over to the division mess hall and eat. Real American chow. Tables and chairs, food trays. Kool-Aid. Officers have plates. It's screened so the bugs don't eat everything." Now I know why the SFers called Rudy "Heavy Drop." "Let me get the fuel truck for you," he offered. Rudy loved ordering the Army around. They had no idea what rank he was, since Rudy also wore unmarked tiger suits while on the operation. A helicopter taxied at a hover down the runway, covering us with red dust.

"I'm getting sick and tired of these helicopters," said Skinner. "They don't give a damn who they're blowing dirt on. I'm gonna get one of them some time. Look, the same sonofabitch just blew a tent down." Sure enough, he did.

"Skinner, did you see we only have twenty-five hours left on this bird? I thought you were going to check it out in Bien Hoa." I had been filling out the log book, the 781, and noticed that the aircraft was coming due an inspection.

"I tried, John. Same old story. They're short airplanes and don't have any available." I suspected as much. We had a II Corps high-time airplane and I wouldn't expect Bien Hoa to give us a low-time III Corps airplane in exchange. "Maintenance said they would do the inspection in one day for us, if we gave them some advance notice." That's a help.

"Let's go find the division ALO and say hello. I have some names from the DASC. Rudy, do you mind staying with the aircraft until they finish refueling? Also, it might take a quart of oil. There's a case behind the seat." Skinner told me he stole it from maintenance, when he got mad because they wouldn't give him a new airplane.

"No problem, L. T. Would you see what's for chow? The Army posts a menu." Boy, was Rudy getting spoiled. He was making up for Oasis and Buon Blech when we almost starved.

We found the Air Force contingent assigned to the brigade, which was the level below the division. They knew we were coming and they gave us the freqs and call signs for all the local players: Cottonmouth Control, Cottonmouth 11 X-ray, Sonar Shopper, Square Lobster, and Lancer Forward switch. I wondered who dreamed up the ridiculous call signs.

Our Nung laborers cooked a supper of hamburgers, french fries, and beets over an open fire. Not fancy, but it was good. There was a certain tension in the air as the guys sat around sipping beers and sodas. Team 2 would go in the next day. It was like playing in a major football game. The tension of the locker room would disappear as soon as you made that first contact. Except in our game, that first contact could be fatal.

I'd been with Delta just over four months; Skinner barely a month and a half. We'd been truly tested in Song Be, and we emerged as an elite, cohesive and proud fighting unit. War molds relationships of endurable bonding, a camaraderie that cannot be duplicated anywhere else among men. I felt it that evening in Tay Ninh.

August 25—Flew two VR missions for familiarization. Team 2 inserted at last light.

August 26—Airstrike for Team 2. Dice 07, two F–100s with eight 500-pound bombs. Five were duds, fuse problem again. Teams 5 and 10 inserted.

August 27—Airborne at first light. Weather poor. Landed and returned. Gave position fix. Team 5 in fire fight, broke contact, AOK. At 1530 hours air relay aircraft spotted smoke in vicinity of Team 2. ALO scrambled, team was separated and pinned down. American body was in the middle of clearing that VC were trying to reach in order to booby trap and mutilate. Protected body and kept VC at bay with three hours of constant fighters, total of eight F–100s (Ramrod 01, Silver 03, Saber 01, Buzzard 09). The Ranger reaction force was committed to rescue the team. Spooky 43, C–47 flare ship with Gatling guns [sometimes called Puff because of the dragon-like spouts of machine-gun fire that rack down on the jungle] stayed overhead through midnight until the VC withdrew. Losses: one U.S. KIA, one U.S. WIA, one VN KIA, one VN captured. The remaining two VN were unscathed.

Somebody dropped six stray bombs in our area of operations during the night. The DASC had no knowledge of the mission. It was a radar-controlled Sky Spot mission.

When I arrived over Team 2, my worst fears were realized. They had no radio contact. I buzzed the figure in the clearing—it was an American. There was no movement; he was either dead or gravely wounded. I saw a feeble wave from the north edge of the clearing—another American. I spotted a signal panel in a bomb crater to the west—two Vietnamese. That's four out of six accounted for. I transmitted on VHF, anger welling up within me.

"Rudy, get me air. Fast and lots of it." Over to Fox Mike, "Dancer, Team's been hit. Coordinates XT460788. I can account for four personnel. They are separated and close to an LZ. I have requested air support."

"Roger, Typhoon, copy all. Stand-by this push." I gave two clicks of the mike in acknowledgment. Now to find the VC. I doubt they would show themselves when I was overhead. I would guess they were on the south or east side of the clearing, or they would have attacked our survivors by now. I was concerned about the American on the north side. If the VC were behind him I wouldn't have any way of knowing it in the dense jungle. The two Viets were OK. I could see them clearly and anyone approaching them would have to come into the open. The same for the prostrate American in the clearing. I saw movement in the elephant grass along the south side of the clearing. Was it one of the missing team members? No, it had the black shirt and trouser pajama uniform of the VC. He was slithering through the grass, trying to reach the American in the clearing. I saw another. The American still hadn't moved. The VC were after the body and the radio.

Just as I removed my stowed carbine from the cockpit light, I heard, "Typhoon, Ramrod zero-one, over." Sweet words; it was the fighters. I re-stowed my carbine.

"Ramrod, I want you to go to burner now—three-two-two radial, forty-five miles, channel seven-three." Lead recognized the urgency in my voice. I had the TACAN radials and DME drawn on my map. The afterburner would push them close to supersonic and shave a few precious minutes from their flight time.

I heard Lead transmit, "Two, go burner. Typhoon we have six napes and two CBUs plus the guns. What's up?"

"You know who we are. We just had a team ambushed. The VC are crawling to one of our men. I want CBUs first. When you hit forty-three miles, turn east for your downwind and come back in, just as fast as you can. I'll mark. You'll see the man in the center of the grass clearing. He may be dead, but the VC are after the body. Probably booby trap. I got another friendly on the north side of the clearing, and two more in a bomb crater to the west."

"Lead, this is Two. My TPT's creeping up." His tailpipe temperature was rising from the sustained afterburner use.

"Lead, I have you now. I'm at your one o'clock low. You can slow it down and start your turn. I'm in on the clearing. Hit along the south side." I put my mark on the edge of the jungle and cleared in the fighters. As soon as my mark hit, the VC broke and ran into the jungle. "Lead, hit in the south tree line. Charley just ran in there." Lead made his run and pulled off the target.

"I saw the body. It wasn't moving," he transmitted

"Thanks. Let's go to work with the napalm. A can at a time. We'll take each piece of that jungle apart around our troops."

I spent three hours and fifty minutes in the air, directing strikes to protect the remnants of the team and to prevent the VC from moving any reinforcements into the area. Skinner borrowed an Army L–19 and relieved me when my fuel ran low. The Rangers were inserted and dug in for the night. Skinner got the Spooky gunship squared away, to provide flares and firepower for the guys on the ground. He landed at Tay Ninh using jeep lights to mark the runway. It was quiet in the Delta camp that night.

We had a short service the following afternoon. Gene Moreau was the American killed. The medics cleaned up his body, but it was difficult to hide the ravages of the AK–47 rounds that ripped through him. We gathered around, our heads bowed while a chaplain said some words. I didn't hear them. The sweet smell of death lingered in the hot, humid air. You almost hoped a chopper would fly over and stir the air. The dust wouldn't seem so bad now. Johnny Varner, who was medevaced to a rear area, would recover.

Gene Moreau's death touched me personally. Not that I didn't feel close to Terry Griffey or Karl Worst, but Moreau was different. Back on May 21, the recon sergeants had presented me with a green beret. It had belonged to Gene Moreau, who'd made the presentation. They felt I had earned the privilege to wear it. I was honored. Now Gene was dead. I still have the beret.

August 28—Team 5 and Rangers extracted. At 1815 hours Team 10 was compromised and extracted. An unmarked Twin Beechcraft was spotted by the teams, flying over their position. Skinner and his back-seater killed three VC on a trail with the M–79 40mm grenade launcher. We painted three stick figures on the aircraft.

August 29—No flying by us. We were saving aircraft time. Teams 6 and 11 inserted.

August 30—Team 6 surrounded by VC company-sized unit on trail to south. Located team and hit two automatic weapons positions with napalm delivered by Ramrod 01. Team confirmed positions destroyed. Follow-up airstrikes with Buzzard 09 and Saber 07, more F–100s with snakes and napes, 80 percent target coverage. Team extracted. Team 11 compromised but continued with mission.

August 31—Air strike conducted for Vietnamese road-runner team using auxiliary walkie-talkie radio and interpreter in the backseat. Eight F–100s dropped their bombs and napalm on a VC company and command post. Team confirmed ordnance on target. Conservative estimate of ten KBA with 80 percent target coverage.

Our aircraft, tail number 489, ran out of flying time and Skinner flew it to Bien Hoa for maintenance. No replacement aircraft available

Events were stacking up against us. The teams were programmed to stay in the jungle for five days before extraction. They were compromised within one or two days. It was their choice whether they wanted to continue with the mission or be extracted. After the loss of Team 2, they were extremely cautious. Our FAC aircraft was out for maintenance and we were dependent on what we could borrow from other units. We could overfly the scheduled maintenance inspection, but I didn't want to risk a mechanical failure in the middle of an air strike over enemy territory.

In order to avoid publicity, Skinner and I were giving conservative bomb damage assessments, resorting to a percentage of target coverage. It was a legitimate reporting procedure, but understated our mission effectiveness and the accuracy of the fighters. Only the VC really knew how hard we were hitting them. The recon sergeants also knew. They had been on the ground and knew the effectiveness from firsthand observation. Their enthusiasm and support never waivered.

There were always volunteers to fly with us. Some of the guys were jealous of those monopolizing the flights. (They listened to the radios, anticipating the FAC missions. A rotation schedule solved the problem.) As soon as I picked up my map and put on my scarf, they would scramble to get their web gear and grab their M–16s. By the time I had my gun belt buckled and carbine slung over my shoulder, they would fall in step with me as we walked to the airplane.

"Going flying, FAC?"

"Yeah, sure. Wanna come?"

"Yup. Bring the M–79, FAC?" referring to the 40mm grenade launcher, which they loved to fire out the rear window at targets of opportunity.

"No, not today." They usually brought it anyway, "just in case, FAC."

"We got fighters, FAC? We gonna hurt some Clydes? I like the CBUs best—and napalm—that's good shit."

I could sense their feeling toward the enemy by their choice of vocabulary: VC, Victor Charley, Victor Charles, Mr. Charles when in awe, Charley and Clydes in light speech, and occasionally just The Cong. The North Vietnamese Army was NVA, November Victor Alpha, or Hard Core. They respected their enemy. They never used the derogatory terms I would hear elsewhere: gomers, slopes, dinks, gooks, zips, slopeheads. They were professional warriors.

September 1—Team 11 was spotted by the VC. VC sent search parties out. I borrowed an Army L–19 and was airborne by 0700. Directed team's extraction. We hit the VC search platoon at XT430853 with napalm and 500-pound snake-eye bombs. Buzzard 01 did the job from 0805 until 0825, before most people have a second cup of coffee. Road-runner team went in. Skinner brought our airplane back from inspection. Fast work by Bien Hoa.

September 2—Flew VR for next day's Ranger operation. Teams 4 and 8 inserted at last light.

September 3—FAC airborne at first light. Team 4 had been inserted 6 klicks, 3.6 miles, east of their intended area. They were compromised and pursued by a VC platoon. Buzzard 09 hit the platoon with snake and nape, team was extracted.

The 2nd Company of the 91st Ranger Battalion was helilifted into an adjacent area to assess the results of a B–52 strike. During the lift, Team 8 got in a firefight, fighters were diverted from the LZ prep and used to break up the fight. Team was extracted. Fighters and gunships hit target again. B–52s hit center of battalion complex. Found documents and extensive trenches. Found equipment, including sandles, lying in center of complex, but no bodies. Skinner flew six hours and twenty minutes. I flew three hours and thirty minutes in an Army L–19. Team 12 was inserted.

September 4—ALO airborne at first light. Weather completely undercast, right on tops of the trees. Team 12 compromised and ambushed on the way to the extraction zone. One WIA. Used helicopter gunships and four fighter sorties, Silver 03 and Ramrod 91 flights, to neutralize ambush. We saw one body, estimated killing five more, started a secondary fire, and covered 80 percent of the target area with ordnance.

It required five hours and thirty minutes of high-stress combat flying to find and support Team 12, secure and guide the helicopters, neutralize the ambush, and clobber the VC with air strikes. It was typical of our operations in III Corps since our arrival at Song Be on August 9. We were finished. There was no question or doubt that our teams had infiltrated into two of the highest areas of enemy concentrations, NVA at Song Be and VC at Tay Ninh. We hit the enemy as the opportunity presented itself; now was the time for major assaults by massed armies to capitalize on our gathered intelligence.

Skinner and I hopped into 489 to accept our open invitation to Bien Hoa. While Skinner headed to the fighter wing to find us some bunks for the night, I went to the DASC to debrief the intelligence staff. We hadn't found COSVN, but we had them worried. We must have found everything else. Our scorecard for the last month: 42 air strikes consisting of 103 fighter sorties plus Puff the Magic Dragon, all under a close air support and precision bombing environment; estimated 120 enemy killed by air, seven KBA body count; six automatic weapons destroyed, and innumerable casualties on area coverage targets of complexes and troop concentrations. Our Delta losses were one U.S. and one VN killed in action, four U.S. and two VN wounded, one VN missing, and one helicopter shot down, unrecovered. We saw some of the same friends and faces at the Bien Hoa Officers' Club. We relived the missions and shared the triumphs and tragedies. I met the Ramrod pilot who led the first mission when Moreau's team was ambushed on August 27. He made some notes. I hope he got the medal he and his wingman deserved.

Before falling asleep that night, I had to wonder where we were going with this war. I saw more and more U.S. troops moving in. It was not only a U.S. air and logistical war; it was now a U.S. ground war. I was frustrated by the lack of response to the perishable targets we had pinpointed in Song Be and war zone C. And I felt our prohibition to hit enemy complexes in Cambodia to be an unreasonable tactical constraint, an irrational command decision, and an unconscionable policy of the government. The command structure was a mess. I couldn't get heavy air strikes. There were still stray bombs dropping in our area, and some party had been flying electronic surveillance, mistaking our signals for those of the enemy. On a local level, I was still begging and borrowing airplanes in order to accomplish the mission. The fuse problem was still with us, but maybe the Dice flight with five dud bombs was a training and supervision problem. I was seeing a lot of young faces on the flight line. I was old at 26.

On the two hour and ten minute flight from Bien Hoa to Nha Trang, Skinner and I relieved our boredom and challenged our proficiency by dropping useless smoke marks from 10,000 feet. We aimed at the empty swimming pools and tennis courts on the plantations, tracking the grenades' green gossamers as they plunged earthward. Maybe we hit some.

10

Search for F–4 Pilot;
Return to War Zone C

It was pleasant to return to Nha Trang. It was like coming home from a long trip. The Song Be and Tay Ninh deployments had been demanding and costly. Even though Delta was a finely honed fighting machine, we lost people and helicopters. The VC were tough adversaries. We needed time to re-group and train new people. The recondo school was in full operation and I was lecturing on close air support tactics in a jungle environment. We were the masters of the techniques. Skinner found a cancellation on a commercial R and R flight to Hawaii. I told him to take it while he had the opportunity. With Delta's erratic deployment schedule, we never knew when we would get time off. It was highly unlikely that we would be deployed for at least a couple of weeks. I would cover the training courses and the local training patrols.

The manager of the Delta Hilton had booked a touring Filipino show with singers and dancers. Our parties, although raucous and at times raunchy, were still the best in Nha Trang. We always invited the nurses assigned to the field hospital in Nha Trang. They came in groups for mutual protection; they knew our reputation, but didn't want to miss a good time. I chatted with one of the nurses during the show's intermission. She was a few years younger than I, maybe 22 or 23. After college graduation, she was commissioned in the Army, received her initial military training, and was sent to Vietnam. She was a big girl, about five-foot-nine, with a pretty face. She found her work very demanding, but also rewarding. She told me how she was initially shocked and horrified at the number and severity of casualties, and now she had become inured to it all. I asked her if I could visit her ward. She gave me directions to her ward and told me she was finishing her shift at midnight the next night. I was to meet her between 11 and 11:30, just before she came off duty.

I kept the appointment the following night. Since I was visiting an Army installation, I thought it better to wear my fatigues instead of civilian clothes. I swung my jeep through the hospital gate, returned the MP's salute and found the appropriate ward. The wards were a network of interconnected semi–permanent canvas Quonset huts. I waited for my nurse friend. I hardly recognized her with her hair pulled back and dressed in jungle fatigues. She looked a bit fuller in the fatigues than in the civilian skirt and blouse she had worn when I met her the previous evening. She wore the same perfume.

It was quiet in the wards. We walked silently down the rows of beds. Medical apparatus were suspended everywhere. Arms and legs were in various states of traction. Wounds draining. I saw the empty space under a blanket where a leg was missing. We moved to another ward. It was less encumbered by apparatus; the site for malaria, dysentery, leech sores, fungus growths, immersion foot, and any number of undiagnosed fevers and infections. If the VC didn't get you, the jungle would. She was one brave lady. I couldn't handle it.

She wanted to continue our conversation of the previous evening. The town was off–limits due to the Vietnamese elections, but we slipped off to one of the Vietnamese beach clubs, which stayed open all night. We toyed with our beers and listened to the small combo play American songs. It brought back memories of the States. We walked down the beach and found a comfortable spot under the palm trees. We didn't need a blanket. Jungle fatigues were made for sand and dirt. The half moon reflected off the South China Sea. We talked. I knew about her job, she wanted to know about mine. It was difficult explaining the role of a forward air controller. Our goals were different; she was a healer, I was a killer. The common bond was that we both swore allegiance to uphold the Constitution of the United States and we were in Vietnam. The night slipped on. Rosy-fingered dawn crept over the edge of the shimmering sea. It was the same dawn of eight months ago when I overnighted in Nha Trang on the way to Qui Nhon. It meant a lot more to me now. I was thankful for every first light.

Our differences evaporated with each exchange of thoughts and feelings. We were both committed to helping the Vietnamese in their struggle against oppression. We were at different ends of the spectrum, but we were both warriors. She was brave in her way, I in mine, and we each sought and respected honesty and integrity. We left each other that morning knowing we would never meet again, yet satisfied that two people had shared the intimacies of common values through the night.

Murphy's Law struck. One afternoon Delta was alerted for a mission on one day's notice. Skinner was still in Hawaii. We were to deploy the next day with minimum equipment to Cam Ranh Bay and search for a missing

Air Force F–4C pilot. The emergency beacon signal from his parachute had been picked up in the mountains, eight or ten miles southwest of the airfield. Delta was given the task of searching for him, or determining the sources of the beacon signal. Cam Ranh was only 15 minutes from Nha Trang by helicopter. I immediately called the DASC and advised them that I would need an airplane early the next day for approximately three days, in support of the Air Force's 12th Tactical Fighter Wing.

Before dinner we congregated at the Delta Hilton bar to speculate on the mission. When we were in garrison, if we were not in town at our usual two or three night clubs, we would be at the Delta Hilton. The recon team members were excited about the operation. Quick and simple. The Air Force fighter-bombers had bailed them out of many tight situations, and now they had the opportunity to reciprocate.

I attended a postprandial staff briefing which covered the concept of the operation. The helos from our own 281st Assault Helicopter Company were the sole transport source, with departure from Nha Trang at 1000 hours the next morning. The search party would be an all-American team of twelve members of recon; no Vietnamese. The party would be accompanied by a skeletal command and communication element that would establish an operations center at Cam Ranh Bay. The only equipment was what could be carried in the helicopters: personal equipment plus the portable communications gear and one small tent for the ops center. Upon arrival at Cam Ranh the next day, the team leaders would be given a situation briefing by the Air Force intelligence staff. The team would then develop and plan its concept of operation and search patterns. They would be inserted late that afternoon and search until they either found the pilot, or determined that the signal was spurious. It was a mission of mercy, not of battle.

The team composition was unusual. It was twice the size of the normal team and it was completely American. It was a formidable search force, twelve of the very best that Delta had to offer. I was proud of Delta. The Air Force needed help, and the MACV hierarchy called on its best warriors and jungle trackers to take the mission. They were ready to go into the jungle in less than 24 hours. No impedimenta to slow them down; a lean and mean patrol, not looking for a fight, but capable of an accounting if they met resistance.

The fire support was to be the usual helicopter gunships and tactical air. Once again the team would be operating beyond the range of artillery support. I called the DASC night duty officer to inquire about the status of an O–1. He knew nothing about it. Call back in the morning. I walked to my hooch to get some sleep. I lay awake on my steel cot, surrounded by the mosquito net that was suspended from two T-shaped bars fastened to either end of the cot. It gave a false sense of security. I had to remind myself that mosquito nets stopped only mosquitoes; it was ineffective against the shrapnel of mortar rounds or grenades. The Delta compound hadn't been hit in months. I think the VC knew better, especially if they hit the Delta Hilton. I focused my mind on the forthcoming operation. Rudy Bishop and his radio jeep weren't going with us. How was I going to get air support if I couldn't get into the air request net to the DASC? I'd be too far south and in the mountains to contact the DASC directly from the airplane. I finally fell asleep thinking about my nurse friend. I knew I would never see her again socially; I hoped I would never meet her professionally.

The Delta compound was abuzz with early morning activity. A different mission to break the monotony of garrison, excitement for a couple of days, and then back to the Hilton bar. Weapons and web gear were stacked outside the hooches.

"Hey, FAC," called one of the Delta troopers. "We're going down with some of your kind. You know anybody down there?"

"Sure do. Flew with them in May."

"When are you leaving, FAC? We gonna see you there? We're going by chopper."

I called the DASC. Still no word on my airplane. The choppers were warming up. They lifted off, headed for Cam Ranh Bay, their passengers anxious to help the Air Force. Here I was, stuck in Nha Trang, no airplane, while my unit was going to war. What the hell was going on? My gear was all packed and ready to be thrown in the backseat of an O–1. But I didn't have an O–1. Maybe I should have taken a portable radio and prepared to go in with the team on the ground. Too late now. I hung around the orderly room, wishing for the phone to ring. How about if I went to the flight line, found an O–1 that was in commission and just took it? Then it would be someone else's problem. What could they do? Court-martial me? Send me to war? Send me home? The field phone finally rang. The duty soldier answered it and turned to me.

"Lieutenant, it's for you. It's DASC Alpha."

"Hello," I squeezed the handset to talk. "This is Lieutenant Flanagan. I can't hear you very well. Call me back." I hung up and the phone rang again.

"Hello. This is much better. What do you have for me?" It was one of the assistant duty officers. "I'm to what? Direct a demonstration air strike for some VIPs in Nha Trang and then take the aircraft to Cam Ranh? What time is the air strike? You don't know? It's after they finish lunch—maybe what? 1400 to 1500 hours." I was furious. "You don't understand; my unit is going in this afternoon. I have to be there." He didn't understand. "OK, what's the tail number? Four-eight-nine. Thanks." I hung up. Damn. I forgot to ask the coordinates of the air strike target. The rest of the information I could get over the radio. Rudy Bishop walked into the orderly room.

"What's up, L. T.? You look angry."

"You're right, Rudy. Do me a favor. Call the DASC, ask what the coordinates are for this goddamn demonstration air strike. It's this afternoon. Get a TOT, call sign, and frequency. Tell them I'll use Airedale for my call sign."

"What's this demonstration air strike? *Today?*"

"Yes, today, around 1400," I replied.

"But I thought you were going to Cam Ranh to support recon. Somebody has their priorities all screwed up."

"No shit!"

"I'll get the info for you, Lieutenant, and bring it to your hooch."

"Thanks, Rudy." The young duty soldier was noticeably surprised by the casualness of the conversation between an officer and an enlisted man. Sorry about that, not everything is done the Army way.

I directed the demonstration air strike and arrived at Cam Ranh just as the team was loading onto the helicopters. They waved to me as I taxied between the rows of F–4s parked in their revetments. The Delta ops tent was close to the flight line. It had a direct field phone to the fighter wing operations center. I called fighter ops.

"Duty officer here. Can I help you?"

"Yes. This is Lieutenant Flanagan. I'm the FAC with the search team that took off about fifteen minutes ago." I was monitoring the radios in the tent. I wanted to hear if the team was inserted without any problems. "What do you have on alert?"

"Two F–4s on five-minute alert. They are backed up with birds on fifteen- and thirty-minute alert."

"Okay. Thanks." I snapped the phone back into its cradle. I'll just sit tight and see what develops. The choppers came back, the team went in without any problem. Now maybe I could get my act together. I still didn't know how to get fighters if I were airborne, but at least I knew they were available. I walked across the sand to the wing operations center. Since May, my last time here, boardwalks had been laid over the deep sand to facilitate walking without stumbling. The white sand still glistened in the sun, and the azure sea stretched to the horizon, but this time, with hardly a ripple. Some off-duty airmen were splashing in the crystal clear water. Still no hot dog stands.

I reached the operations center and gained access to the command post, the nerve center. I was in luck. Colonel Lew Allen, the wing DO, deputy for operations, was there. I introduced myself. He gave me a genuinely warm welcome and expressed his gratitude for our prompt response.

"Who's the missing pilot, sir?" I asked.

"He's not actually a pilot. He's a flight surgeon who flies in the back-seat on a lot of missions. Doc Simmons," replied the Colonel.

"From the 557th? The Sharkbaits?"

"Yes. How do you know?"

"That's the unit I flew with in May on the F–4 orientation flights." I had met Simmons and had slept in the bunk under his. Now I was involved in searching for him, the first flight surgeon to be lost in combat since World War II.

"Sir, I understand you have birds on five-, fifteen-, and thirty-minute alert."

"That's right. As soon as the five-minute flight is scrambled, the others move up in the order and a new crew takes the thirty-minute slot." A call came in on the UHF radio in the command post. That gave me an idea.

"Colonel, I have a problem. I have no radio operator or jeep with me. If the team gets hit, I'll need air support fast. I have to get into the request net to the DASC. I know you have a land line with the DASC, so maybe I could use your command post as my requesting agency to relay to the DASC."

"Well," he responded, "I think I can do you one better. We appreciate what Delta is doing for us. Doc Simmons is a great guy and we'd like to find him or at least come up with some definitive information. How about two F–4s on alert, cockpit alert if you want it, for instant scramble. They're yours. No one else can get them. I'll keep them out of the system." He was an innovative commander, a leader with conviction and purpose.

"That's great, sir. That is the best. I can scramble them directly through the command post here, either on UHF if I'm airborne, or by the field phone from our ops tent."

"That's right. We'll put a special instruction in the duty officer's operating procedure book."

My problems were solved. I had air support, my very own, with instant response. We had streamlined the command and communication channels by cutting the DASC out of the loop. I wish I could have briefed the team on this before they went in. The field phone rang. The duty officer answered it.

"Is there a Lieutenant Flanagan here?" he called out. My heart skipped a beat. Colonel Allen, sitting next to me, sensed my alarm. I feared the team had been hit. I'm sure the VC knew they were in there since the team was inserted in broad daylight. I leaped over the railing that separated the colonel's staff area from the ops center area and grabbed the phone.

"Lieutenant Flanagan here." It was the duty NCO at the Delta ops tent.

"Sir, we just received a message from the team. They've run into some bad terrain problems. They want a position fix and some help getting to the objective before they secure for the night."

Colonel Allen followed me, going around the railing. I overhead him briefing the duty officer on our scramble procedures, "That's right. The airplanes are a dedicated resource. They won't be reported available to the DASC or TACC. However, we will maintain our normal alert commitment."

I continued with my phone call. "Tell the team I will be over their position in one-five minutes." I turned to the colonel and duty officer. "Everything's okay; team's met rough terrain. My call sign is Airedale. Is this your frequency?" I asked, as I pointed to the UHF control head's tuned frequency.

"Yes, it is." I copied the freq in my pocket notebook.

"I'm going flying sir. Want to come? I'll show you the best flying just short of World War I open cockpit and World War II Mustangs." A big smile came across his face.

"No, thanks, John. I've got some paperwork to attend to." How did he know my Christian name? The duty officer looked familiar. I had met him on my last trip to Cam Ranh.

"My alert birds," I asked, "Can you put flares on one of them for tonight?" I continued, "Fifteen-minute alert is fine. I can't get to the area any faster myself. Fifteen minutes tomorrow is okay unless I see a problem, then we'll upgrade the alert status. Snakes, nape, and gun should work. See you, and thanks, sir."

The tower expedited my taxi and take-off request and I was airborne in only a few minutes. Other aircraft held for me as I taxied out for an intersection departure. Had someone made a phone call to the tower and given me priority? I don't know, but I appreciated it. It allowed me to get to the team that much quicker.

"Searcher, this is Airedale." The team came up on the radio immediately. They were expecting me. I continued, "Let me see if I can find you." The shadows were deepening in the high mountains. A mirror signal wouldn't work. "Give me some vectors and maybe a panel." They spotted me.

"Fly three o'clock, FAC." A pause as I banked hard. "Okay, twelve o'clock. We have a panel out. We're near the top of the ridge."

"Gotcha." I marked their position on my map. I had plotted the approximate location where the emergency beacon had last been heard. Now to work out the best way to connect the two points. Looking at the steep mountains, dense jungle, and plunging ravines, I wondered how they could get to the beacon position.

They were on the southern slope of an east-west chain of mountains that dropped sharply over a thousand feet into a valley and then rose up the other side into another chain. The chains of mountains were connected by a saddle at the western end of the valley. It was almost a box canyon. I continued to survey the terrain.

"Searcher, your path is blocked by two deep ravines that run to the valley floor. Even if you could cross them, there's no cover or concealment. I suggest you climb up the ridge line, move west about two klicks and then start down. That should put you just above your destination."

I stayed with the team for over three hours, guiding them from my aerial observatory. It was now dark and they advised me they had set their night security. "Roger, Searcher. If you run into trouble, we have fighters on alert with flares. We could take you out at night, terrain permitting. See you in the morning."

"Roger that. Out." It was a firm voice, without fear.

I recovered at Cam Ranh. Our helicopter crews were sleeping in their birds. I found a bunk with the 557th Fighter Squadron. Reb Daniel and George Harrison were still around, trying to be upgraded to the front seat. I left word with the Delta duty NCO that if they wanted me, to contact the command post duty officer. He could track me down by telephone, or, if necessary, send a runner if the phones were knocked out. I told the duty officer I would be at the Officers' Club and then with the 557th. I ate some food and was tempted to join the revelry. Fighter pilots party and drink like no other humans, except maybe Delta. But Delta is a separate category. We had a team in the jungle; I had learned my lesson at Oasis when I relaxed prematurely and the team was hit at last light. I stumbled through the darkness to the Sharkbaits' barracks. The two posters were still in the pilot's lounge. I sacked out. It was Doc Simmons's bunk.

I was airborne at first light. The morning fog hovered in the valley. A steamy mist was rising from the jungle-covered mountainside as the morning sun heated and cooked the moisture-laden vegetation. Some overnight rain clouds still clung to the top of the higher mountains. It was a typical morning in the coastal mountains of Vietnam.

"Airedale, this is Searcher. We hear you. Sounds like you're far away and to our north." I was. The team was alright. I was checking out the other side of the mountain. If the VC were following my flight pattern, which they could easily do from any number of mountain-top observation posts, I wanted them to think there was more than one patrol, or that Searcher had moved to the other side of the mountain. Searcher hit me with a mirror. I gave them their coded location. They agreed. They were making good progress in spite of the terrain and vegetation. They wanted to complete the mission and get out of there.

I flew toward the saddle that connected the two mountain chains. The previous evening the saddle had been in deep shadows and I had been unable to observe much. Now I was surprised. Exactly on the crest of the saddle was one of the heaviest log and earthen bunkers that I had ever seen. It commanded a view of both valleys as well as the mountainside. If it were occupied, there was no way they could have missed the helicopters landing the previous day. Depending on what kind of weapons the VC had in that bunker, they could make the extraction of the team extremely hazardous. The team reported hearing sporadic rifle fire. Single shots, probably signals. The VC were looking for them. It would be afternoon before the team would reach the objective. That big bunker still bothered me. I sensed an impending ambush or firefight.

* * * * *

In 1989 I was talking with a business associate with whom I did some executive search work. He had been a FAC in Vietnam in 1971 based at Cam Ranh Bay. I mentioned to him about the search mission into the valley. He said, "Oh, that's the Toe Hop Valley. We never went in there. The ARVN sent a couple of patrols in there and they got mauled. In fact, a FAC got shot down and was never found. We heard he eventually wound up in the Hanoi Hilton. That valley was all triple-canopy jungle and nothing but VC. Eventually it was turned over to the Koreans and even they wouldn't go in there. We kept the ridge lines clean with air strikes and artillery to keep the VC from dropping mortar rounds and rockets into Cam Ranh."

* * * * *

I landed at Cam Ranh and debriefed the Delta command element. I told them about the rifle shots and the bunker. The commander of the helicopter detachment winced when I described the bunker. They had apparently flown right over it after making the insertion the previous day. They never saw it, nor did they take any fire. This led me to believe it was unoccupied, but that was yesterday. Today could be much different. Also, if the team couldn't make it to the planned extraction zone, we would have to take them out with ropes from small clearings. There were no other areas in which you could land a chopper without hiking a day or two. It would be suicide to return to the original LZ. The VC would have set up an ambush.

I trudged through the sand, taking a short cut, to the wing command post. My colonel friend was there.

"Sir, I'd like you to change the bomb load on our alert birds. I'd like one aircraft to have thousand-pounders, or at least seven-fifties. We may have to blast our way out of the jungle by creating a mini landing zone, at least big enough to lower our extraction slings." We had 40-foot ropes that could be lowered into a small clearing from a hovering helicopter. They could take three men out at a time using that technique. I continued, "The other aircraft should have snake-eyes. I spotted some bunkers that might give us a problem. Napalm won't work. Also, we'll probably need five-minute alert status this afternoon. Just to be on the safe side." He made some phone calls.

"John, I've got good news and bad news. We can change the bomb load, but we don't have any big bombs. The F–105s and B–52s in Thailand have priority on that inventory. I can give you more Mark 82s, 500-pounders, but they'll be slicks. We ran out of retard fins. The other aircraft will have snakes. Five-minute alert is no problem."

"Thanks, sir." Here we go again. I'm really beginning to hate this war;

particularly the leaders, the system responsible for giving us the tools to fight the war. Maybe my young nurse friend was right. The whole thing was absurd. People are destroyed, we patch them up, and send them out to destroy or be destroyed all over again. She felt that Vietnam would destroy everyone, one way or another. I think she was right.

The usual scattered afternoon clouds began to settle around the mountain tops. The team was almost to the objective. They were in a brief firefight and had either driven off or killed two VC. They were pushing on. They were not slowing down to follow blood trails. It was time for me to go back to work. One of the enlisted Ranger advisors had flown from Nha Trang that morning on the resupply chopper. He wanted to fly with me. We took off and headed for the valley.

The team had reached the objective and fanned out, searching the entire area for any signs of Doc Simmons. No parachute. No tracks. No equipment. Nothing. The beacon signal had been spurious. The war had claimed a healer.

The team reassembled to push the last 300 meters through the jungle to the extraction zone. More signal shots. Now it was a race to extract the team before the VC closed in. Speed, not stealth. I could see them slide and tumble when they lost their footing on the severely pitched mountainside. My back-seater estimated it would take them about an hour to reach the zone. I called the operations tent.

"Delta ops, this is Airedale. Searcher should be at the Lima Zulu in six-zero minutes. Please advise the choppers."

"Roger, Airedale. Copy all." I flipped to UHF.

"Fighter ops. This is Airedale. I'll need my fighters in three-zero minutes." May as well relieve the anxiety of the flight crews. Were they going to scramble? Now they knew. My plan was to have the fighters available, in case the team ran into an ambush or they wanted the extraction zone prepped. The noise of the jets would screen the noise of the choppers until they got close to the zone. I wasn't sure what I was going to do about the bunker on the saddle.

I called the sector FACs on VHF. I told them where I was and that I needed clearance for an air strike. They came back to say it was all VC territory and not to worry about it. So much for the rules of engagement. About 20 minutes later, I got a call on UHF.

"Airedale, this is Fighter ops."

"Go."

"Do you still want your Sharkbaits?"

"Rog."

"On the way." It was that simple. Five minutes later, two bomb-laden F–4s were holding over the valley. They barely had their landing gear up and their take-off flaps retracted, when they were overhead. The team came up on Fox Mike.

"Airedale, we see your fast friends. They look good." I could tell by the elation in his voice that the sight of the fighters was a morale booster for the team. The Ranger advisor, a seasoned jungle fighter, transmitted to me from the backseat.

"FAC, you should get the choppers now. I know what it's like. When you see those jets overhead, it gives you a real shot in the ass. Those guys will be to the LZ before you know it."

"Thanks, Sarge." I switched to Fox Mike. "Delta Ops, this is Airedale. Crank the choppers now. Have them hold at the mouth of the valley." I wanted to keep them out of reach and sight of the saddle bunker. The advisor was right. Barely ten minutes had elapsed when I received, "Airdale, this is Searcher. We're on the LZ and checking it out now. Looks secure. We heard some rifle fire again. It's closer."

"Rog, Searcher. Choppers are on the way. I'm going to put some bombs on a bunker about a klick west of you and just south. Shouldn't bother you." If the LZ was secure, I may as well neutralize that bunker. The signal shots could be for the bunker occupants. Over to Uniform.

"Sharkbait, this is Airedale. I've got a bunker that's right in the middle of the saddle that overlooks the valley. I want you in from the east to the west. Friendlies are on the ridge line that's on the north side of the valley. Who's got the slicks? I want pairs." Two bombs at a time.

"Lead does. We have the target in sight." I was getting bounced around by the wind turbulence barrelling over the ridge lines.

"You're cleared hot, Lead." The first F–4 came streaking up the valley. The dive angle looked too shallow to be dropping slick bombs. The bombs came off and I could see the retard fins open. Snake-eyes! I was expecting slicks. The bombs were long. They missed the saddle, and even with retardation, they flew 400 meters down the valley. I hit the mike button.

"Lead, what gives? I thought you had slicks."

"Sorry, Airedale, that was Two who dropped." Lead proceeded to give Two the worst tongue-lashing I had ever heard over the radio. He told Two to get back in position and stay there, and if he repeated the stunt, he would personally shoot him down. Wow! There was no doubt who was in charge.

I directed the choppers up the valley and told them to hug the northern ridge line. It was secure since the team had just traversed the area. Their flight path minimized the silhouette of the five helicopters from any gun positions in the valley and from the opposite ridge line. Searcher popped a smoke and the choppers homed on it. I needed that bunker neutralized—fast.

"Lead, you have your flight sorted out?" I asked.

"Affirmative."

"Cleared, Lead. Same bunker target. Watch the choppers coming up the valley beneath you." Lead rolled in with a steep dive angle, 45 degrees, the helicopters settled into a hover. I saw the bombs come off the F–4. The team broke from the wood line, firing. I followed the flight path of the bombs—the team clambered onto the choppers—the bombs hit the firing slit of the bunker. The helicopters lifted off, the team safe. The bombs were the most accurate that I had seen dropped in my entire eight months in Vietnam.

But the bombs didn't go off. It had to be those goddamn fuses again. This was the aircraft that had been reconfigured that morning. The F–4s dropped several more bombs near the bunker, partially destroying it. If any one were in there, I'm sure they were either crushed by the 500 pounds of iron from the first bombs, or they fled fearing time-delay fuses.

I recovered at Cam Ranh. I had to pick up my gear and I wanted to attend the intelligence debriefing with the Sharkbait fighter pilots. I walked into the debriefing room. Two was obviously chagrined. He didn't say a word. I told Lead about his perfect bombs that didn't go off. His name was Leon J. Plotnitzski. I was to meet him again. In 1971, he was the full-time Air Force advisor assigned to the Air National Guard unit in which I flew. I was to recount this story with pride.

The Ranger advisor had waited for me in Cam Ranh. He didn't want to go back to Nha Trang on the choppers. We skimmed across the South China Sea at 50 feet, buzzing the junks and sampans. The flight took only 15 minutes.

The next day, in Nha Trang, I had a phone call from the DASC. They wanted to know how I got the fighters at Cam Ranh. I told them the truth, that I had scrambled them directly via the command post. They wanted to know why I didn't go through them. I told them I didn't have foolproof communications.

I later unraveled more of the story. The number crunchers in the TACC in Saigon couldn't figure out how the 12th Tactical Fighter Wing actually flew two more sorties than scheduled available on September 10, 1966. The wing DO was chastised for making those two additional sorties available to cover the Project Delta search mission. It didn't make sense to me. We had a mission to accomplish and the wing DO and I orchestrated a way to make it work. A colonel and a first lieutenant, resourceful and flexible— the traditional strengths of the American fighting man—got the job done. But we went outside the system, and the system came back to bite us.

From today's perspective, I respect Lew Allen even more. I more fully appreciate the vicissitudes of command responsibility. He was a brave leader who took an action he believed was right without concern for his personal position or advancement. He was honest. He recorded his decision, so that the duty officers were fully aware of the purpose of those additional alert birds. But most of all I admire his integrity. Delta came on short notice to find one of his downed crew members; we had absolutely no responsive heavy-fire support and he came to our aid without any equivocation or reservation.

Nha Trang settled into a routine garrison environment for a couple of weeks, but it was still combat. I gained an appreciation for training. We continued to run long-range reconnaissance classes for MACV and for the new members of Delta. The graduation requirements included a live patrol mission of at least two days in the Nha Trang area. The students were required to run a dummy air strike, which frequently was live when they made contact with the VC. Our constant physical surveillance of the surrounding hills of Nha Trang precluded the VC from setting up mortar or RPG (rocket-propelled grenade) positions. We would protect the Delta Hilton at all costs.

Norm Doney came up with a diversion for the troops. With the exception of the two-day mission in Cam Ranh, "a short walk in the hills," we were in our third week in Nha Trang. They had run out of new bars and bar girls, and even the old standbys were losing their appeal. Norm conned a transportation detachment into providing a boat and crew for a Delta fishing trip. The boat was actually an amphibious LARC which I first saw in Qui Nhon, unloading the ships in the harbor. The FAC was invited to go, along with a dozen or so guys from recon and the Rangers.

A Delta fishing trip was an experience in itself. Everyone brought their weapons, "just in case we wanted to stop off at a couple of islands and check it out for some Clydes." They were inveterate warriors. There were cases of beer and soda and food from the Hilton. Ammo boxes packed with ice made great coolers. There were also several cases of hand grenades, M–16 ammo, smoke grenades, and flares. They brought a PRC–25 radio, "in case we need an air strike, FAC." But no fishing poles. Hand-held nets, but no poles or bait. This looked more like a marine recon trip, except everyone was in jeans, cutoffs, or bathing suits.

Once we got out to sea, everyone had a different opinion of where the fish were. The obvious solution was to ask the FAC. "FAC, where are the VC? FAC, where are the fish?" After a few beers it was all the same to them. I suggested we look where the birds were feeding, which would indicate the presence of small fish, which in turn attracted larger fish. "Great idea FAC. Where did you learn that?" Cape Cod. Empty beer cans thrown overboard were instantly cut in half by M–16 rounds. We found the fish. "Open the fish hooks, hurry," came the cry. I was confused until I saw a barrage of hand grenades launched into a school of fish. "Fish hooks by DuPont, FAC." What a melee. Geysers of water, fish flopping and floating, birds diving on prey, nets scooping up the fish, and Doney admonishing the troops not to kill any more than they could eat. We took only the big ones to cook at the Hilton. As soon as the local fishermen in their junks and sampans saw what we were doing, they followed us, dragging their nets and capturing the fish we left behind. We darted from school to school, enjoying great sport and pleasing the Vietnamese fishermen. This was a bonus catch for them. It reminded me of the water buffalo kill with the gunships in the Phu Cats. We had a nice fish fry in the Delta Hilton that night.

The following day, I wandered over to the Air Force compound. The 21st Tactical Air Support Squadron (TASS) had been transferred from Pleiku to Nha Trang. They had not seen me since my initial in-country check-out seven months ago in Pleiku. This was the official Air Force unit to which all FACs in II Corps were assigned. They handled the administrative record keeping and the all-important maintenance of the aircraft.

The office walls were lined with the ubiquitous status boards, showing the respective locations and assigned Army units for the aircraft, pilots, and mechanics in the Squadron. In an obscure corner was the cryptic entry "SF A—Flanagan, Simpson." Nothing more. We were an enigma.

The personnel had rotated. I didn't know anyone. There was a major standing by the status boards with his back to me. I drew his attention and introduced myself. He was the squadron operations officer, the second in command.

"So you're Flanagan. We really didn't believe you existed. The mechanics would see you, and we knew about Simpson. We just cut him orders for R and R in Hawaii. Everytime we asked the DASC about you two, we got vague answers." We shook hands.

"It's a pleasure to meet you, sir. I guess we are a bit different," I responded. He went on to describe how much better the facilities were in Nha Trang and how they were gaining administrative control over the Squadron members. My interpretation was that Nha Trang had beaches and no snipers, and they were building an empire. I looked around. I noticed the ceiling fans to relieve the oppressive heat. There were a dozen desks with clerks, typewriters, and filing cabinets. No guns. No grenades.

"We now have a FAC school in the Delta region, down in IV Corps," he explained. We do the initial qualification there, and about half-way through your tour, we send you back for a standardization-evaluation check-ride and ground school testing." He looked at another status board. Blank by my name, except for the date I arrived in-country, January 28, 1966. I was long overdue the check.

"That's nice, sir. When would you like to send me down there? And Simpson too?" Those stan-eval purists would have a field day with us. I carried a nonstandard automatic weapon, loaded my revolver with tracers, and elected not to wear a flak vest, survival vest, or parachute. I took the safety pin out of the trigger on the control stick as soon as I was airborne, not just before the air strike as the procedures stated. I usually armed my rockets when the team said they were in trouble or had a target, not waiting for the final dive as the procedures also stated. The ground school exam probably included a lie detector test to determine if I had violated any of the rules of engagement, including border incursions. I continued, "By the way sir, I never attended Snake School in the Philippines. Could we include that in the package?" If I played this right, with the travel time and all, I could get a month off. "But please, Major, make sure you have someone to cover the Project Delta operations while we are gone. You know, those locations that don't show up on your boards."

His look was incredulous. He got the point. The subject was dropped. He was to come to my much-needed assistance two months later, when I had an altercation with the supply squadron over some missing equipment.

Several days later, I was walking from lunch and gazing at the sky. No usual afternoon clouds. Hot as hell.

"Hey, Skinner, Jack", I called to Simpson and Hamilton, as they walked ahead of me down the PSP path that extended behind the revetments from the Hilton to our barracks. "Want to go to the beach? Maybe we can go to that new beach club that just opened, the one by the field forces head-quarters?"

"No, thanks. We're going downtown. I ordered some shirts from that Indian tailor on Duc Lop Street, where we got the Delta shirts," replied Skinner. "Besides, Hamilton says there's a new steam bath and bar that opened up, and he wants to check it out."

"Okay. See you later." They were headed for fun and mischief. The orderly room clerk came out of the administration hooch that was across the street from our barracks, and cut me off on my way to changing into my bathing suit.

"Lieutenant Flanagan, there's a phone message for you. You're to call some lieutenant colonel at DASC Alpha. Says it's urgent. Here's the number." He handed me the message. I recognized the number of the DASC director. I was patched through the three switchboards it took to reach his office.

"This is Lieutenant Flanagan. I was told to get in touch with the colonel." I was talking to the administration officer, a fellow lieutenant.

"John, can you come over here? Right away. The colonel wants to see you."

"Okay. Take about fifteen minutes." There goes my trip to the beach. I drove the Air Force radio jeep to the DASC. I almost never took it out of the Delta compound. The VC would love to booby trap that vehicle but this trip was to a secure military location. I went out the gate behind Skinner and Jack. They were in mufti. I was right. Fun and mischief for them.

I pulled into an empty parking space behind the field forces headquarters. It still looked like SHAPE headquarters to me. It had been five months since Lieutenant Colonel Stewart had sold me on joining Delta. What now, I thought. I climbed the expansive staircase and walked down the wide hallway. I was now familiar with this place. I went by the DASC operations center. "Filthy" Brown was on duty. He spotted me. I feigned pulling the pin from a hand grenade and tossing it at him.

"Here, catch, you DASC weenie. This will end your war sooner."

"Get out of here, Flanagan. I told you I was going to transfer you to the DASC."

"Screw you, Filthy. See you later." I continued down the hall to the director's office.

"Lieutenant Flanagan reporting as ordered," I said, as I rendered a half-decent salute. In the field, salutes were not de rigeur, but this was garrison.

"Sit down," he invited. I took a seat next to his desk. This looked serious. He began, "The concept of Project Delta is being expanded. MACV is forming two similar units. One will operate in II Corps, the other in III Corps. The II Corps unit will be under the joint command of the commander, First Field Forces, and the Vietnamese II Corps commander. The air support will be coordinated by this DASC." Oh great, I thought. This ought to be another organizational mess. The Vietnamese corps commander is in Pleiku; the American forces counterpart is in Nha Trang, 120 miles apart. Air support, regardless of whether the unit was under Vietnamese or American command, would be under the direction of DASC Alpha, the American part of the joint command. He continued, "I want you to prepare a list of requirements to support the new unit. I need it by Wednesday. Deliver it personally." Today was Monday.

"Yes, sir," I replied, and inquired, "What will be the structure of the units? Will they be similar to Delta, a special B-team? What is their unit designation?" If I could obtain that information, I could nose around the 5th Special Forces Group headquarters and get some idea from my SF buddies what the table of organization and equipment would be on the Army side. I could then match the Air Force requirements using Project Delta as a comparison base.

"That information is not available. You are not to discuss this with anyone else," directed the Colonel.

"Yes sir." I saluted and walked back down the hall. I passed the DASC operation again. "Hey, Filthy, is that transfer a promise? I might want it."

"You don't want it. Believe me," said Filthy. I drove back to the Delta compound and put some ideas on paper. I wanted to talk to Skinner before preparing the report, and he was downtown someplace.

That evening Skinner and I were hanging around the Hilton. The atmosphere was relaxed, rumors were flying. The recondo training classes were going well, but we were anxious to get our next deployment order. Sure enough; the SFers had picked up some information about the expansion of the Delta concept. The II Corps unit was Project Omega, the III Corps unit Project Sigma. The new "Greeks" were to be formed by transferring some people from Delta and adding volunteers. This fit with the information that the DASC director had given me. Skinner and I discussed it over some beers.

"What do you think, Skinner?" I asked him. "I think we're going to get squeezed. I don't trust that colonel," referring to the DASC director.

"Look, John," Skinner replied, "here's an opportunity to go on record for what we really need. He wants a report. Let's include the requirements for Delta with Omega. We're running the training operation here as a live exercise, yet we don't even know from one day to the next if we have an available airplane. It's bullshit."

"Good idea." We finally had a mechanism with which to surface our problems and to have them resolved. We agreed on the requirements. We needed two permanently assigned ALO/FACs and a permanent ROMAD for each project. TDY or augmentees were not familiar with our procedures. Untrained people jeopardized their own lives and those of the members of the respective units. It was obvious the projects could be deployed simultaneously and in separate geographic regions. For equipment, we needed two dedicated airplanes per project whenever deployed on an operation. We had missed too many target opportunities and risked the safety of the ground troops on too many occasions, when the aircraft was grounded for maintenance problems or when we needed constant air support. Skinner almost ran out of fuel at Song Be and I had stretched the limit at Chu Lai and Tay Ninh. In I Corps the FACs always flew in pairs, due to the high-threat environment. Jim Ahmann and I were lucky not to be shot down when we flew single ship in I Corps back in April.

We also needed a dedicated radio jeep for each project, one that was in top operating condition that the ROMAD could call his own, rather than relying on just any jeep from the DASC pool of vehicles. We never had a single problem with the jeep that I had for a month in Phu Cat with the Koreans. My ROMAD took personal pride in caring for that vehicle. Our lives depended on it. Finally, we agreed that we needed an aircraft on standby whenever we were running the live training patrols in the jungle around Nha Trang. We already had instances of teams being hit in our own backyard. We also needed it for contingencies such as the short-notice search operation in Cam Ranh. We had the report typed in proper staff study format. Skinner and I thought this would go a long way in resolving our problems. Little did we know they were just beginning.

I personally delivered the report to the director on the appointed day. He read it and proceeded to ask me questions, the answers to which were explicitly contained in the report. I was having serious doubts about his mental faculties, but maybe he was just reinforcing his comprehension. I gave him the benefit of the doubt.

Days passed. Nothing happened regarding our staff study. Still no response to our recommendations for additional equipment and personnel.

Skinner was assigned to Omega; I would stay with Delta. Delta was alerted for a deployment. Rumor had it that we were going back to Tay Ninh and war zone C. Skinner was working with the staff of Omega, organizing the unit. They expected a mission order shortly. At least they would stay in II Corps. This was familiar territory to Skinner. Lieutenant Colonel Stewart, our mentor, was no longer at the DASC. We had no one to talk to. Skinner still lived in the Delta compound. We saw each other regularly.

"Skinner, let's hang out at the Air Force Officers' Club. Some of the DASC staff might show up for dinner. Maybe we can pull the director aside and see what's up. I nosed around the TASS and learned they were expecting a couple more airplanes. Maybe they're for us."

The command and support structure for the ALOs and FACs was split in three elements. In the Air Force, we were assigned to a tactical air support squadron. They owned the pilots, the ROMADs, the airplanes, and did all the aircraft maintenance. However, we took our operational orders from the DASC. They assigned us to the respective Army units, and allocated the airplanes, jeeps, and support personnel. On the Army side, we would take orders from the Army commander regarding the day-to-day management of the battlefield. It was also the Army's task to feed us and give us a bunk. We had no single command element that could be held accountable for our well-being and support requirements. Somehow, the system functioned, but only because individuals, like Lieutenant Colonel Stewart, made it work. Now it was the responsibility of two first lieutenants, Skinner and myself, to unscramble the convoluted mess and secure the support we needed, before someone was killed.

Skinner walked into the Officers' Club first. We were both over six feet, and with Skinner's infectious smile, dark hair, and good looks, we never had a problem being recognized by the hostess. She showed us to a table. Luck was with us. The DASC director and some of his staff were having dinner. He recognized us.

"Let's go over there," said Skinner.

"No, wait. Wait until they've finished. Let's see if he'll come to us. If not, we'll chase him down as he leaves." He finished his dinner and joined us. His companions remained at their table. I opened the conversation, "Good evening, sir. How are you?"

"Fine. What brings you two over here? We don't see much of you." True. When we were not in the jungle making war, we preferred the Hilton or downtown—more fun.

"Well, sir, Skinner and I prepared that staff study of requirements. We wanted to know what the status was. Delta's been alerted for an operation and Omega is sure to follow shortly. It's critical that we train a couple of FACs and a ROMAD before we deploy." MacArthur's quotation, on the irrevocable penalties for employing untrained personnel, went through my mind.

The colonel responded, "We don't have any people. We might be able to give you a ROMAD. We will send you some TDY FACs."

"But sir, TDY people are ineffective. We have special techniques and procedures that take a while to learn. Our codes are unique to our operation," said Skinner.

"Well, you'll just have to cope."

"Colonel," I said, "I learned at the TASS that a couple of additional aircraft are being assigned to II Corps. Are they for us? We desperately need two aircraft when we deploy. When we are in garrison at Nha Trang, we don't need them. We only need one to support the recon training school."

"Those aircraft are not available for you," he responded with finality. "We'll be in touch." He walked back to his table. His entourage rose and followed him out the door.

I turned to Skinner, "We've been had. I'm going to kill that sonofabitch before he gets us killed. We can cripple him. They'll think the Vietnamese street cowboys did it." Skinner put his had on my arm restraining me, calming me.

We surmised what had happened. He had used our requirements study to justify with command staff in Saigon the need for additional aircraft and personnel. It was clear that Skinner and I weren't getting those airplanes or FACs. They were going to another unit, probably a more conventional American unit. The additional resources would enhance the director's image in the eyes of the army generals. Special Forces was still considered a maverick unit by the straight-leg Army. We went back to the Delta Hilton.

I surreptitiously surveyed the airbase for FACs who appeared to have free time. I decided to recruit on my own. Whenever the O–1s went through an inspection or major repair, it had to be flown on a test hop. Occasionally, when I was in Nha Trang, I flew the test hops myself. One pilot seemed to be the permanent test pilot. He had been in my FAC class at Hurlburt, but I really didn't know him. He also ferried aircraft from one location to another. He delivered spare parts and personnel to the remote field locations. I thought his function was superfluous, so I asked about him. He had been assigned to a combat unit, and in the last month was transferred to Nha Trang. I asked some more. He was never able to find the hot targets, or, his aircraft would develop some mysterious malfunction that couldn't be verified after the fact. It appeared he was afraid of combat. He didn't shirk his duty in a war zone; he just couldn't handle danger. Personally, I could understand that. Bravery, under fire, either is there or it isn't; its presence is unknown until it's tested. This FAC wouldn't fit into Delta or Omega. Skinner and I were still on our own.

My apprehensions were realized. The operations order was published. Delta was returning to Tay Ninh and war zone C, where we lost Gene Moreau and the two Vietnamese. Skinner and I had to split up. He was deploying with Omega to an operation in II Corps, and we had no trained or assigned replacement personnel. I didn't have an airplane once again. Since Delta was working in III Corps in support of the 196th Light Infantry Brigade and Operation Attleboro, I was directed by the DASC to pick up an airplane at Bien Hoa. I was assigned a FAC on loan from the 196th. At least he knew the area and his parent organization. I would have to familiarize him with our Delta procedures. He met me in Bien Hoa and we flew the airplane to Tay Ninh, but it wasn't ours. We were the delivery pilots and we had to borrow one from his parent organization, which left the 196th one aircraft short. Skinner was apparently getting the alloted Delta airplane to cover the simultaneous Omega operation.

The Tay Ninh airfield was even busier than the last time we were there. C–130s were providing major resupply efforts for Attleboro. Helicopter traffic had increased threefold. The place was dangerous, particularly for O–1s and Army L–19s. We established our base camp. Delta was going back to war. The teams were going in.

September 26—Arrived Tay Ninh at 1600 hours due to delay in getting aircraft. Teams 3 and 9 went in.

September 27—Airborne at first light. Teams AOK. At 0915 hours Team 9 compromised. They were in the middle of a VC battalion complex and being tracked. Team extracted and four F–100s expended on complex; Buzzard 01 and Yellow Jacket 01 flights of two each. Difficult to assess damage, estimated five KBA and started major secondary fire in the center of the complex. Requested radar bomb mission (Sky Spot) on same target for that night.

September 28—Sky Spot dropped 150 meters short of target. Team 3 requested air strike on VC bivouac area. Saber 01 flight, two F–100s with CBUs and napalm. Estimated three KBA, secondary explosion from ammo cache, one storage structure destroyed. Team AOK. Requested two more Sky Spots on Team 9 target with instantaneous fusing. L–19 pilot killed in crash at Tay Ninh.

September 29—Sky Spot on target. Team 3 made contact, air strike conducted, team extracted. Ranger force inserted and made heavy contact with VC; required reinforcements, numerous air strikes, and Puff gunships all night. Total of five airstrikes and three C–47 gunships expended.

The two Sky Spot missions hit the same area during the night. They were on target, but the fuses were wrong. I requested instantaneous fusing to destroy the surface hooches and supplies. The bombs had a split-second delay, which directed the explosive energy into the earth. This was effective for deep bunkers and tunnels, but ineffective against the confirmed assembly area. All we did was scare the VC, maybe hit a few, and create some shallow wells for them.

The commander of Delta decided to send a stronger recon force into the area where Team 9 had located the battalion-sized complex. The team had spotted electrical wires, strung through the jungle. Intelligence suspected they were onto something big. Similar to the last time Delta was in war zone C, the teams were quickly compromised and tracked by small VC patrols of two or three men. Once the teams were compromised, it became a game of hide-and-seek, and they were ineffective in gathering intelligence and observing enemy movements. By sending a stronger unit of Vietnamese Rangers, platoon or company-sized, plus American advisors, the unit could engage the VC and then proceed with a recon in force. By the time the VC could assemble a force strong enough to engage the Rangers, their mission would be accomplished and they could be extracted. Panther 91, a flight of two F–100s, prepped the LZ, destroying an occupied bunker, and the Rangers went in without incident shortly after sunrise. I wouldn't let Delta make the same mistake I witnessed the 101st Airborne make at Tuy Hoa in April, when they were ambushed on the LZ.

Team 3 made contact with a VC unit that was pursuing them. We scrambled the Saber flight from Bien Hoa. I directed the team toward an extraction zone, alerted the helicopters, and the team started dropping smoke markers per standard operating procedures as they raced through the jungle. The VC followed the smokes, hoping to catch the team as the choppers came in. They didn't know we were luring them into our trap. The Sabers were sitting overhead with napalm and CBUs, as I waited for the team to call the right moment. The team reached the zone.

"OK, FAC. Hit them now. We can hear them right behind us. They're just coming up on our last smoke. We got our heads down," he panted over the radio. I had prebriefed Saber on what to expect; they were to hit perpendicular to the alternate colored smokes. I would call the ordnance.

"Saber, now! With napalm. Hit the red smoke." I didn't have to mark the target. The team had already done it. Lead pickled two cans of napalm precisely on the smoke. No sense in wasting ordnance. "Two, come through dry."

"Rog, FAC. What's wrong?" inquired Two. The team was on the FM radio immediately to me.

"Beautiful, FAC. Beautiful! Three crispy critters that we can see. Maybe more." I chuckled. War is inuring. I was insensitive to the gruesome description.

"Nothing, Saber. The team confirms three KBA on the first pass. Stay around and let me see what else I can get for you." It was 15 minutes from when the team confirmed they were in trouble to when we annihilated their pursuers.

I asked the team how they were doing. "Do you want to come out ASAP or stay there a bit? Choppers aren't here yet. They've been busy with the Rangers. They had to refuel."

The team responded, "We're okay, FAC. It's gonna take Charles some time to get his shit together after that hit."

"Okay. Give me everything major you've seen. Give it to me in grid code," I requested. While they were preparing the information, I switched over to UHF.

"Saber, the team's been in there three days. They have a few addresses for us to make some deliveries to Mr. Charles. Just bear with us." The team gave me a half-dozen sightings in Delta grid code. "Okay, Saber. I have the addresses. Just save your twenty mike-mike in case I need it when we extract the friendlies." For the next twenty minutes, we delivered either napalm or CBUs on every target the team had spotted during their walk through the woods. The VC thought they were impervious to air strikes when hidden under the triple-layered jungle canopy. We gave them one hell of a surprise. Even though the team could not observe the enemy, they could see some of the fighter passes. I advised, "Okay target number two, or target number three," and the team would confirm the precision and location of the fighter's pass. We took the team out without further incident. The major portion of a bivouac area was destroyed.

I'm sure these VC didn't want to tangle with us anymore. Any survivor from the pursuing VC patrol probably had a major session of *khiem thao*, self-criticism, admitting his failings. He would have borne the blame for the air strikes and failure to stop the team. He probably wished he had been killed, instead of incurring loss of face and the displeasure of the cadre political officers. But other VC were preparing to get even. They knew where we were, and our methods of operation.

The Rangers continued with their force-recon mission. They were probing the periphery of what was thought to be a battalion-sized complex, less than five miles from the Cambodian border. Team 9 had lasted only overnight in the same area before they had to be pulled out. The VC allowed the Rangers to penetrate the complex with nothing more than sporadic resistance. Major supply huts were found. Concealed under the jungle canopy were fully enclosed structures that could house fifteen and twenty men. These were not isolated structures; each one was within ten or twenty meters of the next. It was a complete city, spread out through this section of war zone C. Had they found the elusive COSVN, the Communist command center? But where were the enemy troops? The Rangers confiscated documents, smashed typewriters and sewing machines, and destroyed crude tools for manufacturing booby traps. The Rangers themselves didn't encounter any booby traps. This was Charlie's home and he didn't expect any unannounced visitors. The VC had fled. The Rangers saw oil slicks on the streams and could hear gasoline-powered generators, whose sound was trapped under the canopy. By mid-afternoon the resistance stiffened. The VC had concentrated their forces. The Rangers were pinned down. They were taking casualities. The Delta commander and his Vietnamese counterpart committed a reaction force of additional Rangers. We had a pitched battle on our hands.

The ever-diligent Rudy Bishop started the air requests. Once again the Sabers, followed by the Skoshi Tiger F–5s, and then the Eagles in their F–100s, joined the fray. I had the Rangers mark their position with smoke grenades. They were huddled together for mutual support, but the jungle canopy was so thick the smoke was trapped under the trees. I finally had them fire some flares so I could locate them. The VC were closing with the Rangers, in order to avoid the air strikes. I could sense panic setting in on the ground. They were asking me to bring the air strikes on their own position. This was a last resort, and I was not willing to use it. The senior Ranger advisor who was requesting the strikes was new and overreacting. If Jack Hamilton or Ron Deaton, seasoned jungle fighters, had requested the strikes, I'd know they were in deep trouble. I would have directed the napalm and CBUs on their position without any hesitation. Instead, I gradually worked the fighters closer and closer to the Rangers. This precluded the VC from moving reinforcements into the battle, and forced the VC to get closer to the Rangers and expose themselves to the concentrated small-arms fire. The battle was a stalemate, but we thought the VC would wait for the impending darkness to overrun the positions.

"Rudy, get me some Spookys," I requested over the VHF net. I wanted the venerable old Gooney Birds with their side-firing Gatling guns. They could put a bullet every six inches in a football field area with a five-second burst. They also carried parachute flares for target illumination.

"Already got one, Airedale. Spooky 41 is over the field now. I'll send him up your way." That two-striper was utterly amazing. He had been listening to the battle, anticipated our needs, and requested the DASC to scramble the C–47 early. The gunship had enough time to orient himself in the twilight, before the pitch black of the moonless tropics obscured all landmarks. I orbited over the Rangers while Spooky put a few preliminary bursts into the jungle. The Rangers, although surrounded, had broken contact with the VC and were able to establish a perimeter defense around a small clearing. Some brave Vietnamese Ranger had crawled to the center of the clearing and spread a luminescent panel that was visible only from the air. Spooky had a reference point. Every time the Rangers saw movement or heard noise outside their perimeter, they directed Spooky on it. Three Spookys, in turn, maintained station over the Rangers throughout the night. The VC wanted no part of Puff the Magic Dragon. I made a night landing at Tay Ninh with only the headlights of a jeep marking the end of the unlit runway.

It had been a tough but personally rewarding day. I had flown nine hours and forty-five minutes, directed five separate air strikes in a very intense, close air support, life-or-death environment. I left the battlefield knowing the Rangers had a reasonable chance of surviving the night. As exhausted as I was, I would wake up every hour, walk to the radio jeep, and listen to the traffic between the Rangers and Spooky. Rudy never slept the entire night. Maybe he dozed, but he never left his jeep and the radios. I wondered if these kids, the draftees and enlistees like Rudy, would ever receive recognition for the selfless dedication they put into their jobs. Delta recognized it, I recognized it, but did our institutionalized military and government leaders recognize it? How about their peers? In retrospect, they were frequently ridiculed by their peers when they returned to civilian life. They demonstrated their own form of bravery. Twice.

September 30—The Rangers were successfully helilifted out. Casualities were light considering the intensity of the combat. Complex was confirmed, regimental size; it could assemble and bivouac over 1,000 troops.

We went to work on the complex, six flights of fighters, total eighteen sorties (Tiger 21, Devil 51, Green, Demon 71, Houseboy, Tiger 71, the Greens and Houseboys were VNAF A1Hs). The results were seven major secondary explosions, innumerable smaller explosions, five fires, five huts destroyed; that's what we could see.

Teams 6 and 11 were inserted at last light.

I was standing outside the operations tent, observing the airstrikes in the same area where the Rangers had been. The DASC at Bien Hoa had diverted every heavy-fighter mission they could to our target. The TDY FAC from the 196th was controlling the air strikes. The complex was 15 miles north of us and we could see the heavy, black smoke clouds boiling up to 3,000, even 5,000 feet. We listened to the strikes on the jeep's UHF radio and heard the exclamations of the fighter pilots as they touched off gigantic secondary explosions from ammunition and rocket caches.

"God, look at that one go."

"Sierra Hotel." (Shit hot.)

"Two, this is Lead. There's another hooch next to the one that's burning." A pause. "You missed. Get it, Three." The FAC was allowing the Lead pilot to control his flight. It wasn't very often, due to the stringent rules of engagement, that the FAC could delegate control to Lead, but now Lead could be totally accountable for the performance of his flight. The pilots were elated.

"FAC, how did you find these targets?" inquired a fighter pilot. These were not toothpick and monkey-killer missions.

"Never mind. Just bomb," replied my helper FAC from his position in the O-1 over the target. I was relieved by his response. I had visions of *Stars and Stripes* headlines, once again compromising Delta. Some Ranger advisors walked up to me.

"Thanks, John. It was tough in there. We were outgunned. The senior advisor panicked. He's been transferred from Delta." Another one said, "You don't know how good it was to have Spooky up there all night. It calmed the Vietnamese right away. It gave us the psychological boost we needed." A couple of guys from recon joined us. They had just come out of the jungle and had also been on patrol the last time we were here.

"FAC, this is suicide. It's crazy. Look at that smoke," said one. Another gigantic black cloud erupted over the jungle as a flight of fighters streaked overhead to the target. The other trooper continued, "We don't have a chance in there. We found all this shit last time, and now they send us back in again. It's not our job to come back and destroy it. That's why they have conventional units. We're recon, not search and destroy." He was right and I could sense the uneasiness in the camp. The upper command elements in Saigon were abusing the mission of Delta, and the troops recognized it immediately. This was the first time I ever saw a deterioration of the morale in Delta. These men were sharp, bright, and the very bravest, and they resented being abused and misdirected. Yet they kept going.

I walked into the operations tent and went to the back section where Intelligence, S–2, had set up their shop. They were sorting and cataloguing stacks of documents the Rangers had captured. I found a training manual on antiaircraft firing. One of the illustrated training aids depicted a suspended model airplane that could be pulled along a wire between two trees. With this device, gunners practiced firing at aircraft. Primitive, but effective. No wonder our loss rates were increasing. I was joined by one of our medics. He was thumbing through a VC first aid book.

"How you doing, FAC?" he asked.

"Fine, O'C. How about you?" It was Paul O'Connor. Red-haired and freckled, slight of build, mid-twenties, typical Irish. He intended to join the family mortuary business when his tour was up. One of the medics always rode the pick-up helicopter. It was a high-risk mission, but if anyone was wounded they would receive immediate care while the chopper flew back to the base camp.

"As good as to be expected. Did you hear about the L–19 crash on Wednesday?" Today was Friday.

"Heard about it but no details."

"I saw it, FAC. The L–19 had just taken off when a helicopter flew over the top of him. The rotor wash nosed him right over into the runway. I ran to the crash. The pilot was unconscious. No pulse, but I couldn't see any injuries until I looked at his head. He had the imprint of the compass in the middle of his forehead. Crushed his skull. Died instantly." I shivered. The standby compass protrudes from the top center of the windshield. Apparently the inertial lock on the pilot's shoulder harness had failed and he was thrown forward into the compass. I never wore a helmet, because they were too hot, too heavy, and restricted your vision. I promised myself to always manually lock my harness and never rely on the inertial lock. No crushed skull for me.

October 1—Airborne at first light. Team 11 requested an air strike. They had a VC Company performing PT. Silver 01, two F–100s with napalm and CBUs scrambled. Estimated 20 percent casualties.

This was my opportunity to duplicate Doney's and Simpson's feat of August 17 in Song Be. I held the scrambled fighters over Nui Ba Dinh, a mountain, well out of sound and sight of the VC. The team had located a company of VC performing early morning calisthenics. I knew where the team was and the target was 100 meters north of them. I quickly plotted a heading for the fighters from the mountain to the target. It would take them about two minutes to reach the target.

"Silver, set up for CBUs. You'll be hot on the first pass unless I abort you. Fly a heading of 320 degrees precisely from the mountain. At one-minute thirty-seconds, start looking for a red smoke. Lay your CBUs from the red smoke to the yellow smoke on that heading. Call me when departing. Friendlies cannot mark their position. They are one hundred meters south of the target. I need a hard right break off the target to avoid Cambodia. Confirm."

"We copy, FAC." A pause. "Departing now," said Lead. I punched my clock and called the team on Fox Mike.

"Get your heads down. Fighters will be coming from the southeast in two minutes. If it doesn't look good, call me immediately." I dropped the first smoke 150 meters short of the target, and the second one 100 meters past the target on a 320-degree heading. This would allow for the reaction time in the fighter cockpit, from when the pilots saw the smoke to when the first CBUs would drop. I had aligned myself with the mountain at my six o'clock position. The VC were accustomed to O–1 overflights and they felt secure under the jungle canopy. They wouldn't be able to see the smokes and if I kept my wings level, they would think I was on a routine visual reconnaissance patrol.

After dropping the second smoke grenade, I started a gentle turn to the south toward the team. I knew if the fighters were coming at me I would have to abort the pass. They would be too far south and close to the team. It was all hanging out, right here. High risk, but if it worked, high reward. God, I couldn't see the red smoke. Was it a dud? My Green Beret back-seater saw it. "Looks okay, FAC. Here come the fighters," he said over the intercom.

The team confirmed, "Looks good, FAC." I was scared. One minor error at 450 knots and we would kill my buddies on the ground. We had hit a team in Song Be when the fighters strayed off heading. As the scenario unfolded I could see the fighters were on heading. The yellow smoke popped above the jungle. "Go, go, go," I shouted above the roar of the engine, to relieve the tension. *Bam, Bam, Bam, Bam.* The first CBUs started to trickle out of the underwing pods and then cascaded like a waterfall. On target! We did it!

"Same place, Two," I transmitted. Lead hesitated momentarily after passing the yellow smoke and racked into a 90-degree bank. Appears he did go into Cambodia. So what, he didn't drop any bombs there. "Watch the border, Two," I cautioned. "You're cleared second pass, Lead." The team came up on the radio.

"You got 'em, FAC. More, more, more!"

"Rog." My heartbeat went back to something more normal. After the second pass, I had Silver hold high and set up for napalm, while I went to take a look. In spite of the jungle, I could see enemy troops, prone and moving. We had achieved the element of surprise. I fired a smoke rocket into the center of the formation and cleared the fighters in with napalm. Same devastating results. I asked the team for an update.

"Well, FAC, they just cancelled PT class. It's now a first-aid class. They're looking for blood donors. We're moving out to the west." What comics. Here they were in the middle of war zone C, and they were making jokes.

I was pleased with the results of the air strike, but my flight almost came to a tragic ending. I flew back to Tay Ninh and turned onto a short final approach for landing. I was flying slower than normal. I was set up for a short field landing, to avoid taxiing back up the runway to my parking spot adjacent to the runway. Just as I was about to touch down, a hovering helicopter crossed the runway from the refueling pit to the helicopter pad. It cut right in front of me. I struggled with the controls as the rotor wash killed the lift over my wings. I crammed the throttle forward, desperately trying to gain air speed. The aircraft slammed into the runway and the spring-steel landing gear rebounded me into the air. Fortunately the engine caught, I regained control, and was flying again. I pulled up onto a closed downwind and accomplished an uneventful landing. I hastily shut the engine down and leaped from the cockpit. I was seething. I ran to the helicopter. The rotor was winding down, the pilot was still in the seat. His helmet was off. I reached through the right-hand window and grabbed him by the collar with both hands.

I screamed, "You sonofabitch, you do that again and I'll put a rocket up your ass and blow you out of the fucking sky! You've killed one Bird Dog pilot with your undisciplined flying but you're not going to get me." He realized what he did and was visibly shaken. I walked away and returned to my airplane. He came over and apologized. I, in turn, apologized for losing my cool, and we agreed to meet later for a beer. He was not one of the Delta chopper pilots. I'd never had any problems with our guys. He must have carried the message to his fellow pilots; they didn't even blow any tents over during the remainder of our stay.

October 2—The Rangers were going in again on a Force recon. Yellowjacket 81, three F–100s prepped the LZ. The Rangers found one VC body on the edge of the LZ and a trench blown up. Brought them out same day.

October 3—Put two VNAF flights of A–1Hs (total six sorties) on the regimental complex. I personally saw the secondary explosions throw smoke and debris over 800-feet into the air. The rectangular shape of the burning and exploding structures was clearly visible under the trees. The VNAF were good. Locate the target and they would take it apart by themselves. We cut a supply road from Cambodia with 500-pound bombs.

Team 11 was extracted. No target. They did enough when we hit the PT formation on the 1st.

October 4—Team 6 was extracted. We took no chances and pounded the extraction zone with two flights of F–100s before we directed the team and helicopters to the zone.

Delta's role in Operation Attleboro came to a close. In nine days, we directed 21 air strikes consisting of 52 fighter sorties. In addition, we used the Gooney Bird gunships, Puff, all night. We also used radar bombing at night, to hit the targets found by the teams and the Rangers. The Rangers ran sweeps and force reconnaissance patrols, and almost got themselves wiped out. The quick response of reinforcements and the use of airpower averted a potential disaster. Delta was not configured to fight sustained battles. We were glad to get out of there on October 4, 1966.

★　★　★　★　★

Operation Attleboro continued through November 24, 1966, involving 22,000 Vietnamese and American troops. The observations of the Delta recon troopers were apocalyptic. War zone C was for pitched battles with conventional forces, like the ROKs fought. In February 1967, Operation Junction City was launched into war zone C, with 30,000 American troops committed to that operation, the largest of the war. In 1969, the loss rate for FACs in the Tay Ninh area was 60 percent, according to a FAC widow. Her husband, a West Pointer, arrived in September 1969 and was dead by November. By 1971, the war spilled into Cambodia, adjacent to Delta's operational area of 1966. According to Sundog 45, Tom Maguire, a FAC in 1971, a French-speaking observer who flew along with him was in contact with a Cambodian government representative to "preserve the architecture."

★　★　★　★　★

Throughout the operation, the aircraft plight had not improved. In the nine days at Tay Ninh, I had four different airplanes assigned. I didn't know from one day to the next if I could cover the targets and the teams. However, I had become quite adept at borrowing airplanes from other units, whether they be Army or Air Force Bird Dogs. I still didn't have an assigned FAC to Delta. Fortunately the TDY FAC was an excellent performer, but he had no interest in joining Delta permanently. I really couldn't blame him. I hoped Skinner was making out better than I in his manning requirements.

I flew to Bien Hoa to visit the staff at the III Corps DASC, to thank them for their support and to debrief them. I mesmerized the intelligence staff with my descriptions of the VC regimental complex and the tremendous explosions and fires that we started. We virtually burned out sections of a village hidden under the jungle canopy. They were beguiled by the oil slicks on the jungle streams. I traced the ones I could remember on their maps. I told them about the antiaircraft training manuals. I regretted not having torn out several pages to show them. Hitting the PT formation had been briefed at the Seventh Air Force commander's daily operations update. The DASC staff had reminded the briefers that this was the second time we had achieved this feat. They laughed when I related the team's comment about the PT class becoming a first-aid class. They would eventually receive copies of the formal intelligence report, but I was adding some advance color. They asked me when we would be back. I replied honestly, "Never, I hope. At least not back to C." I remembered the SFers' caution about Delta not belonging in the middle of a conventional battle. I explained to the Army and Air Force intelligence staff why we didn't belong there. They acknowledged my reasoning, understood my reservations, but reiterated that any future Delta deployment would be controlled by the corps commander and the Saigon hierarchy, not them. Period.

I made a command decision: I was taking a mini-leave, to party in Bien Hoa and Saigon. It was old home week at the fighter base. I could now tell the fighter pilots how we found the targets in war zone C. We relived the missions, the PT formation, the gigantic secondary explosions. I also met the Skoshi Tiger pilots. They were conducting a combat test of the Northrop F–5. The United States eventually gave the F–5s to the VNAF.

I had buried a pair of civilian slacks, a couple of shirts, and some loafers in the bottom of my canvas A–1 bag. I thought they should see some service. They were a wrinkled mess, but one of the hooch-maids pressed them for a few piasters. The fighter pilots introduced me to a local French restaurant. Dinner was clams baked in garlic butter, French onion soup, lobster Newburg, buttered peas, all washed down with a quality Bordeaux.

The following day I met Bob Baxter, a classmate from the Academy who was flying F–100s at Bien Hoa. Bob was one of those phenomenal individuals who excelled at everything. A native of St. Louis, he was an honorable-mention All-American tackle in his sophomore year, but gave up football for academic interests. He was Dean's List, Cadet Wing heavyweight boxing champion, a member of the Cadet Wing staff, and Rhodes scholar. Now he was killing VC with me.

We went to dinner in Saigon. We started with cocktails at the Caravelle Hotel, where the journalists and correspondents created and reported their version of the war. A couple of them tried to engage us in conversation. We were new faces at the bar, obviously military with our short haircuts, and younger than the usual Saigon staffer. They smelled a fresh news source, but we assiduously avoided them. I couldn't fathom Delta featured in *Time* or *Newsweek*. Bob would have been a story in himself. Pete Dawkins, the West Point Rhodes scholar and footballer, was up-country serving as an advisor to a Vietnamese airborne battalion. The press stayed close to him. The enemy sought officers of notoriety to funnel to Hanoi and exploit politically.

We followed cocktails with dinner at Maxim's. We enjoyed the china, silverware, fresh linens, delicious food, and plush atmosphere. We had shared several classes at the Academy in economics and political science. Our dinner conversation focused on politics, his student experiences in Europe, and existentialism, particularly in relation to the Vietnam War. I felt we, as individuals, were isolated in a war indifferent to man. We felt military commanders were reluctant to make decisions, fearful of consequences. The war was at an impasse, philosophically and militarily. We adjourned from dinner and took the obligatory walk down Tu Do Street, peering into the nightclubs and bars. Lots of action, but none for us.

We'd had the foresight to reserve a room in a Saigon hotel, to avoid the 10 P.M. travel curfew to Bien Hoa. Before retiring, I complimented Bob on his choice of restaurant. He had selected it for quality of food and ambiance, whereas my criterion was usually on the recommendations of the Vietnamese members of Delta. They advised me to stay out of restaurants where you didn't see Vietnamese customers. In Maxim's, most of the clientele were Vietnamese and French, a comforting mix, considering the VC's disposition to restaurant bombings. We returned to Bien Hoa on the first bus in the morning. Bob took off in his supersonic F–100, and I in my 100mph O–1. But our paths would cross again on several occasions after Vietnam.

I landed at Nha Trang in the tail end of a torrential rainstorm. During the two weeks we were gone, the northeast monsoons had settled along the entire east coast of Vietnam. The water was half-way up the wheels as I taxied off the runway and headed to the O–1 parking ramp. The brakes were marginally effective since the brake assembly was partially submerged. The crew chiefs drove out to meet me, stepping into the ankle-deep water. One of them had a practical solution; he wore nothing but shower clogs with his fatigues rolled up. They welcomed me back and inserted the rocket-pod safety pins, while I sat in the cockpit and filled out the log book. They were surreptitiously looking for bullet holes. They didn't know I had flown four different aircraft during my absence, and had managed to distribute the holes accordingly. This bird was unscathed.

A Delta trooper pulled up to the aircraft. He looked sharp in his green beret. Rendering a crisp salute he said, "Welcome back, Lieutenant. Want your gear in the jeep, sir?" I reached into my tiger suit pocket, pulled out my green beret, adjusted it, and returned the salute. Air Force regulations prohibited the green beret, but they couldn't take away my pride in being a member of Delta.

"Yes, thanks. Stay in the jeep," I instructed. I climbed from the cockpit and stepped into the water. I immediately felt the cold water seep through the ventilation holes of my jungle boots. I reached into the cockpit and passed my map case and flak vest to the trooper. I hefted my A–1 bag from the backseat and passed it to him. He tossed it in the back of the jeep. The crew chiefs had started the post-flight inspection. Apparently one of them was new to the aircraft. I reached back into the cockpit, unslung my carbine, removed the magazine, unchambered the round, deftly catching it as it flew out. I tossed the round to the new crew chief. "Souvenir, Sarge. Unauthorized weapon in the Air Force." I reinserted the magazine, turned to the trooper and said, "Let's go." We started up the street on the airbase, headed for the gate and the entrance to the Delta compound. It was a half-mile trip.

"Any news or rumors? How's Omega doing? Where's Delta going next?" I asked.

"Omega left on an operation a week ago. Not much news. Speculation has it that Delta is going to I Corps, maybe in a week or so," he replied. This was critical. Delta still needed another FAC. If we were going to I Corps, I wanted two airplanes this time. He continued, "FAC, a DFC came through for you and the old man recommended you to the Air Force for a Silver Star. If you don't mind me saying so, sir, we're glad to have you with us."

"Thanks, Sarge. I'm pleased to be with Delta," I mumbled, but my thoughts were elsewhere.

The rain started again. We hit a large puddle. Muddy water splashed onto me. A tremor shot through my body. I was on the verge of panic: I Corps, hard-core NVA with big guns, a new, untrained FAC. We desperately needed another aircraft. Delta had barely survived war zone C for the second time in a month—bloodied. I was struggling to stay alive, and the system could only give me medals. We were headed for deep shit.

11

Battle at Khe Sanh:
FAC Shot Down

I missed Skinner in more ways than one. Omega had in fact deployed to someplace in the Central Highlands, adjacent to the Cambodian or Laotian border. I never said good-bye to him. We spent so much time along the borders, I often wondered why we didn't cross them. I had routinely overflown the ill-defined border, finding it much easier to locate the exposed source of the supply trails, and then follow them through the impenetrable jungle to the camouflaged terminals and hidden caches in Vietnam.

Skinner was also my alter ego; together we'd fought the VC, testing and developing combat tactics, as well as the command bureaucracy, to secure airplanes and trained personnel. But now we were separated, our strength divided, and the foreboding prophecy of the Delta trooper was to come true. Project Delta was deploying to I Corps, once again under the operational control of the III Marine Amphibious Force. The FOB was Khe Sanh, a Marine outpost situated ten miles east of the Laotian border and 15 miles south of the North Vietnamese border. The area of operations would be the northwestern corner of South Vietnam, contiguous to Laos and North Vietnam.

There was good news when I packed my gear on October 13 for the expected 30-day deployment. An additional FAC, experienced, would be permanently assigned to Project Delta. He would report early the next day. But there was bad news, too. We would be going to I Corps with only one airplane. I queried the DASC. The reason given was that Omega was also deployed and there weren't enough airplanes to support simultaneous operations. The recommendations of our staff study went unheeded, as did my spontaneous request to borrow an additional airplane from I Corps.

We departed Nha Trang early on the morning of October 14. The new

FAC, also a Zoomie, class of 1959, was in the backseat. I didn't know him when I was a cadet; he was in a different group. Since he was a captain, and outranked me, he would be the ALO. That was fine by me. I had only three months left in my tour and I was pleased to relinquish my command responsibility.

After a three-hour flight along the coast, we stopped at Da Nang to coordinate the tactical air support for Delta Operation 13–66, the official title. I met the DASC director, Lieutenant Colonel Parker, and his assistant, Lieutenant Colonel Brewington. Some of the staff vaguely remembered our previous deployment in mid-April to Chu Lai, but since we relied primarily on the Marines for air support, their operational memory was short. The colonels assured us they would give us their fullest support and briefed us accordingly. Their call sign was Water Pipe and they would be our primary request net; the Marines had a DASC located at Dong Ha, ten miles south of the DMZ, call sign Land Shark Bravo, for backup; and finally there were the Tiger Hound FACs located at Khe Sanh, base call sign Baton Rouge Nine. I didn't know there were Air Force located at Khe Sanh but I made a note to visit them.

As we were leaving, I asked the staff to please keep all others, particularly aircraft with bombs, out of our area. I also remembered my near-fatal encounter with Marine ordnance loads and nomenclature. The fighter duty officer gave me the latest information: Delta 24 was a gun pod; Delta 9 was napalm, size unknown; Delta 4 was small snake-eyes, 250 pounds; Delta 5 was a rocket pod, size unknown. That was enough. I'd fix those smart-ass Marine pilots the next time they rattled off their indecipherable ordnance.

We flew north along the coast, and then headed inland, almost due west, to Khe Sanh. The weather was good, scattered clouds, with five to ten miles visibility. Smoke rose from the village cooking fires and the charcoal kilns of the ubiquitous woodcutters, reducing flying visibility as the haze spread across the sky. I could see the mountain mass, with its towering peaks of 4,000 and 5,000 feet, rising steeply from the coastal plain of marshes and rice paddies. The Quang Tri River led across the plain, to the mountains, and directly to Khe Sanh, as did the sometimes parallel Highway 9. But they were unusable for transport; it was Charlie country. All resupply was by air which explained the SeaBee-built 3,900-foot aluminum matting, first-class runway. As we approached Khe Sanh, I noted that the highway was usable in the vicinity of the combat base, extending west to the village of the same name, through the coffee plantations, and then to the Special Forces camp at Lang Vei, a few miles short of the border. The airfield was on a 1,600-foot plateau, the eastern edge of which plunged steeply into the Rao Quan River. The river flowed south and intersected the Quang Tri River a mile below Khe Sanh. In bad weather, there were enough roads and rivers that led back to the base. The problem would be to avoid smashing into the plateau, which would be buried in the clouds.

The parking area for light aircraft was on the north side of the east-west runway. A couple of Air Force O-1s were snuggled in the corner of the revetment. Delta's camp was 200 meters east from the revetment, outside the Marines' perimeter defense, and on the northeast side of the runway. The Marine CP and fortifications were on the south side. Our Nungs, with the supervision and assistance of the SFers, rapidly constructed defensive positions, strung concertina wire, and deployed appropriate command–detonated and trip-wire munitions. Rudy had arrived with the radio jeep a couple of days earlier and had sand-bagged it in. I introduced him to the new FAC, now ALO. The Nungs helped me dig a deep foxhole adjacent to my cot. I recalled how the American artillery battery had suffered casualties during the Koreans' Tiger V because they hadn't dug in. I covered it with pierced-steel planking and sand bags.

We examined the situation map in the TOC. Although located on a plateau, we were surrounded by high ground on three sides, with lower terrain to the west, toward Laos. Delta's AO was centered ten miles north of the base. It was a rectangle measuring 13 miles east from the Laotian border, parallel to the North Vietnam border, and 8 miles south from North Vietnam. It was 100 square miles of steep mountains, river valleys, jungle, and some grassland, containing the major NVA routes to the coastal population centers and Marine bases. This was also their access route to the infamous Rockpile battlefield on the edge of the coastal plain. I saw nothing but red plots, indicating enemy forces, and big trouble.

The ALO and I walked across the field to visit the Tiger Hound FACs in the Marine compound. They worked the Ho Chi Minh Trail in Laos and the western borders of North and South Vietnam. Their primary job was to locate the truck parks and staging depots that were along the network of trails and roads that comprised the trail. They never knew what they would run into; anything from a bicycle supply squad, to quad-mounted antiaircraft guns on the back of a truck or dug in along a trail. Their call sign was Covey. I recalled working with them and the airborne command post, Hillsboro, a specially configured C–130, on my F–4 missions to Laos.

We stumbled into their dimly lit bunker. There were a couple of pilots and several mechanics and radio operators munching on some C-rats. They noticed our tiger suits, mistaking us for SFers.

"No, we're Air Force FACs assigned to Project Delta. We're from Nha Trang," I said.

"Oh, we thought you were some new guys from SOG," said a captain wearing an Air Force flight suit. He had a spreading handlebar mustache that was the vogue among fighter pilots and FACs. I had even noticed some in-country transport pilots sporting them.

"What's SOG?" I asked, my curiosity aroused.

"Studies and observation group." It sounded like a field research team from a university. "They're Special Forces with local Montagnards running patrols in Laos. We get good target information from them," said the other pilot. They were apparently a cross-border Delta.

"We do similar missions, except in-country only. We have Viet SFers with the Americans." They briefed us on local procedures, call signs and frequencies, handing me a preprinted card with the essential info. One of the mechanics spoke up.

"We'll look after your airplanes, sir. Just park them when you land. We'll re-arm and fuel them. We have some spare parts."

"We only have one airplane, Sarge. It'll be easy."

"You're crazy!" simultaneously exclaimed the FACs. "You'll get your ass killed," continued one.

"The NVA have big guns," advised Captain Handlebar. "They shoot at fighters. They love to catch lone FACs. We don't do it. Two aircraft missions. Radio contact missions, maybe. But never airstrikes or recce." I didn't like what I heard.

"We'll be careful." I looked at the card they gave me. "Are these your strike frequencies?" I asked. I recognized only a few of them.

"Yes. Those are the channels," replied Handlebar. The UHF radio in the O-1 had twelve crystal-controlled frequencies, with no tuning capability. I Corps used different strike frequencies from II and III Corps. "Anything wrong?" he asked.

"Yeah. With the exception of the two common freqs, my radios are incompatible. I'll have my ROMAD monitor the discrete strike frequencies and then switch the fighters to my freq." I was, once again, thankful for Rudy's competence. Captain Handblebar turned to the mechanic.

"Isn't one of our birds coming up on its one hundred-hour inspection?"

"Yes, sir. It has to go to Da Nang."

"Don't you think Sarge, that maybe our airplane might not get to Da Nang with its original radio?" Handlebar smiled at me. They'd pull the radio and switch it with mine.

"Gottcha, sir." The mechanic then looked at me. "Just check the frequency card in the cockpit, sir. You'll know when I swapped 'em. We really don't want to make an entry in the 781. Nobody would understand." He wouldn't make a false entry in the maintenance log book. He just wouldn't make any entry.

"Thanks, guys." I rose from the folding chair and hit my head on the roof of the bunker. They laughed. I rubbed my head. "I guess this takes some getting used to. By the way, do you have a Lima-Lima?"

"Sure do." They gave me the switch connection to call them on the land line. Delta had a switchboard that connected with the Marine switch.

The teams and roadrunners went in and the monsoons started. We had the worst of worlds, plus a new commander. The intelligence estimate indicated concentrations of enemy forces as formidable as war zone C, except these were organized regular forces, not irregular guerrillas. We had

survived the southwest monsoons, which deluged us in the Central Highlands during June and July. We were now faced with the northeast monsoons, which dumped their winter torrents on the coastal plains and the
abutting mountains. It seemed that every rainstorm was equipped with a
Tacan navigational radio and would home in on Channel 58, Khe Sanh. I
recorded the situation and my perceptions in a letter of October 22, 1966.

It has rained for the last five days; no airplanes have come in or out. We have run
out of fresh food and are resigned to eating C-rations. I managed to fit in one flight,
but the weather has been so poor that I couldn't put in an air strike. I've gotten a
bit more cautious. I'm disappointed with the Army (Delta); we've had four commanders in the last four months, each trying to outdo the other. It's gotten to the
point where the extraordinary has become commonplace and expected, but I'm
damn tired of being pushed. The helicopter pilots feel the same way; we have formed
a tacit agreement—no more unnecessary chances!

In the middle of the night our tent blew down. What a mess, but rather humorous
as four grown men groped about under this great sheet of canvas, attempting to
find their way out. . . .

In the book *The Warriors* by Professor Grey of Colorado College, he wrote about
what makes men fight and why he seeks danger, either consciously or subcon-
sciously. I have experienced this . . . on many missions I am frightened or maybe
just scared enough to make me keen and sharp. . . . when I am in the thick of an air
strike, directing choppers, or zooming low, searching for a machine gun, I am light-
headed. . . . every bit of the male instinct surges through me and I land, elated and
inebriated from the thrill of battle. . . .

But I'd trade it all to be back home safely right now.

Whenever the weather would lift enough for flying, a team or roadrunner
patrol would be inserted or extracted. The teams were highly cautious,
avoiding enemy contact, conducting surveillance only. If they were ambushed, or spotted a target for an air strike, they would invariably have to
evade on their own, or delay the strike for more propitious weather. We
needed at least 1,000-foot ceilings and two or three miles visibility to conduct
an air strike using jets. Team 5 located a heavily reinforced gun position,
either artillery or antiaircraft, in their area. The team was extracted on
October 20. We waited until the twenty-fifth before we could hit the target.
Swiss, a flight of two F–4s, destroyed the position, triggering a secondary
explosion of stored ammunition. The targets were there; we needed the
weather to hit them.

We kept going, supporting the teams to the best of our ability. The new
ALO was learning the operation, but just as he was attaining proficiency,
he was inexplicably transferred. He had been with Delta a week. Rudy and
I were on our own. I had the greatest of faith in that stalwart airman. I had
to; my life depended on him as did the lives of many others.

The DASC in Nha Trang sent us a replacement FAC. He arrived on one of the C–130s that shuttled supplies into Khe Sanh. I walked the half-mile across the field to meet him. The transports kept their engines running. The Marines and loadmasters skidded the pallets of ammunition and food down the sloped ramp. Passengers, laden with equipment, a photographer among them snapping away, followed the pallets. Outbound, able-bodies and walking wounded quickly took their place—minimum ground time.

"Welcome to Khe Sanh. I'm Lieutenant Flanagan with Project Delta," I shouted over the engine roar. I saluted the captain. He half-heartedly returned my salute. He was looking beyond me, at the work detail feverishly slinging body bags on the now level ramp of the Hercules. "Let me help you with your gear. Our camp is across the field. We can walk down the runway. Less mud." I could sense he wasn't overjoyed with Khe Sanh. Maybe it was the body bags.

As we walked, I told him about the Marine base. I pointed out the command bunker and beer hall. The beer hall was the only aboveground structure of any substance. I started to ask him questions.

"How'd you learn about Project Delta?"

"I didn't. They told me to pack my gear and go to Khe Sanh. I don't know anything about any Delta Project or whatever it's called." I didn't like the sound of what I was hearing. First, I was disappointed that he didn't bring an O–1. Second, he knew nothing about us.

"Well, didn't anyone tell you this was an all-volunteer unit?"

"Listen, Lieutenant, they didn't even have time to cut my TDY orders. I flew here as an augmented crew member."

"You mean you're TDY? Not permanently assigned to Special Forces?"

"That's right." We stepped off the runway and sank into the mud. He looked suspiciously at our Vietnamese. He must have been with an American unit. I took him to the officers' tent and offered him a couple of empty cots. As he unpacked his gear, I noticed that he didn't have a mosquito net or air mattress. His rifle was dirty.

That was it! I'd been deceived enough. The teams were uptight. I was one of the few familiar faces they could talk with. I was also flying the SOG teams on radio contacts. I now had a TDY FAC who had never been in the field. I had no idea what his skills were, but I'd be damned if I'd risk the lives of the teams. I suggested that he get on the next transport out of Khe Sanh, which he eagerly did.

I expected all hell to break loose. I had slapped the disjointed Air Force chain of command in the face. But nothing happened. Nobody gave a rat's ass, or so I thought. I had sealed my own fate. Rudy and I were alone again until November 7, Monday, mid-morning, when the C–130 shuttle delivered Captain Charles F. Swope.

Charlie was in his early thirties, short in stature, but stocky in build. He was an Annapolis graduate, class of 1957, who opted for an Air Force commission. Like Jim Ahmann, he came from Kentucky. Like Skinner

Simpson, he played football, but the 150-pound variety. Not much hair, but that didn't bother me. I was losing mine rapidly. He had volunteered for the Greek teams and had been indoctrinated by Skinner with Omega. The weather broke. It was a happy day.

Charlie had barely settled into the tent and stowed his gear when I had his maps ready and sent him off on a couple of visual reconnaissance missions. I wanted him to become familiar with the area while the weather was good. The Rangers were planning a company sweep the next day in the Khe Ta Bong Valley, eight miles north of Khe Sanh. The Marine pilots, who would provide the heavy-lift assault helicopters, moved into the tents with us. We had requested supporting air strikes for the next day.

We launched early Tuesday morning, with Charlie flying and me in the backseat to check him out. We prepped the LZ with a section of Marine A–4s. We were ready for their ordnance: two dozen Delta 4s, small bombs. The combat assault was professionally executed by a diverse but kindred aggregation of players: an Annapolis graduate, controlling Marine A–4s, supervised by a Zoomie in an Air Force plane, in support of Vietnamese Rangers, with Special Forces advisors, helilifted by Marine CH–46s, with Army gunship escorts. Multi-service units, living, planning, and executing together; it worked at the basic fighting level.

After two hours, Charlie and I landed. The Rangers pushed through the jungle, following the river and exploring its tributaries. The surrounding mountains were so steep that enemy camps would have to be located at the edges of the rivers and streams. They virtually waded into the middle of a bunkered village and immediately began taking fire. The Rangers were divided on both sides of a stream, unable to concentrate their forces, pinned down by raking machine-gun fire. Charlie took off. He was on his own, while Rudy and I requested fighter support.

We pounded the NVA all afternoon. I listened on the radios to Charlie's intrepid orchestration of the air support. Apparently some big gun opened up on him, but he ignored it since it didn't threaten the Rangers. When Charlie ran low on fuel, I took off in an Army Huey and controlled the air strikes from the front seat of the chopper. The door gunners marked the targets with tracer fire and smoke grenades. We had a bad bomb; one of the fighters dropped too close to the friendlies, deafening the Ranger point man and bloodying his nose. Charlie was controlling the strike. He felt badly about it; it was his second day on the job. We submitted an incident report. If there was fault, it was the fighter's. Charlie sent him home. We brought in Puff with his flares and Gatling guns, to keep the Rangers company through the night. Charlie and I stood at the perimeter of the concertina wire at Khe Sanh, watching the flares drift between the mountains, illuminating the valley where the Rangers were.

"Charlie," I said. "You did good. I think you'll like Delta. What was that big gun all about?"

"Thanks, John. I don't know. The Rangers told me they heard a single heavy recoil, but nothing hit their position."

"Let's get some sleep. I think we'll have some fun tomorrow. If the weather holds." Charley walked to the tent. I went to the TOC to check the message traffic. Routine. That is, if war ever was routine.

I was airborne as soon as the early morning fog lifted over the field. Mist still lingered over the rivers and streams, but there was blue sky overhead. The NVA forces had broken contact with the Rangers and fled west a thousand meters across the Khe Ta Bong, a swiftly flowing ten-meter wide stream. The Rangers had now regrouped and were in the middle of the virtually invisible village. Once they told me where they were, I could see the occasional outline of a hooch under the trees. They found supplies: rice, cooking oil, and utensils fashioned from spent napalm cans, and signalling devices made from bomb casings; and gore: pieces of limbs and flesh, and blood-soaked bandages and sheets. Sandal tracks and blood trails indicated the direction of escape, terminating at the stream's edge.

I landed and briefed Charlie on the situation. We surmised that the NVA had another camp, similar to the one the Rangers found, on the west side of the stream and at the base of the mountain. There was a visible trail network that I had sketched on my map that started in the DMZ, led over a saddle, and disappeared three klicks above the stream. Charlie would look there as well as surveilling along the DMZ. Sergeant Art Glidden, also new to Delta, would ride in the backseat on the afternoon mission. I headed for a Marine CH–46 to observe the Ranger extraction.

Charlie had been airborne about an hour when Rudy came to the officers' tent. I had returned from the helo ride and was reading *Up the Down Staircase*, reliving my high school experiences.

"Lieutenant, I haven't heard from Captain Swope in over a half-hour. I can't raise him," said Rudy. I got up from my cot and walked to the radio jeep with Rudy.

"When's the last time you heard him?"

"Shortly after takeoff. He was talking to the Rangers." That made sense to me. He went to the Ranger extraction first and then probably headed to the trail network.

"He's probably along the DMZ. The mountains would block any transmissions," I advised Rudy. We tried a couple of calls on each of the radios, thinking that maybe one of the receivers in the airplane might be inoperative. Nothing. "Keep trying, Rudy." It had now been an hour since we heard from him. If he had radio problems, he would have landed. Maybe he had an engine problem and went into one of the strips toward the coast.

I walked to the TOC, some 50 feet from the jeep, and called the Tiger Hound bunker on the land line.

"This is Lieutenant Flanagan, with Project Delta across the field."

"Yes, sir. What can I do?" It was one of the communications sergeants. He remembered my visit.

"I can't raise our FAC. He took off almost two hours ago and we've lost contact. Can you have the Coveys try to raise him? Also, can you get a ramp check for me at Dong Ha, Quang Tri, and both Hues? Tail number is 472." Besides initiating air-to-air calls, he would contact local airfields for a physical check for the airplane.

"Will do, Lieutenant. I'll also call a couple of the other fields we know about. We keep a current list."

"Great. And will you get back to me?" I gave him the switch connection.

"Sure will." I returned to the jeep and told Rudy what I had done. He still couldn't raise Charlie. I walked to the aviation tent. They always had a duty officer for the helicopters. I told him the FAC was missing and I might need some help. I expected we would find him an another base with a bad engine. I went back to the jeep. The S–3 came by, Jim Lundy.

"Understand you've lost contact with the new FAC," said Jim.

"Yeah, Jim. But I expect we'll find him at another field. He doesn't have any way to contact us. We don't accept collect calls." Jim smiled. I was making inane jokes to suppress my anxiety.

"Let me know if I can help."

"Thanks." A specialist in the commo van, adjacent to the jeep, leaned out the back. In addition to the radios, he had the telephone switchboard in the van.

"Red Baron, I just put a call through the TOC for you." These guys knew more than my gossipy aunt who'd eavesdropped on the party line when I was a kid. I headed to the TOC. The open line was waiting. I squeezed the press-to-talk.

"Lieutenant Flanagan here."

"No good news, sir." It was the Tiger Hounds. "No luck on the radios. Nothing on the ramps. I asked the TASS in Da Nang if they knew anything. Sorry, sir. Our birds are low on fuel, but the captain here says we can start a search as soon as they land and refuel."

"Thanks." I was shaking. Reality was creeping in. Charlie and Art were down, someplace in the jungle. Jim Lundy was standing next to me.

"Jim, I need that help." Delta moved into high gear. The helicopters took off, separating into a grid search pattern. A recovery team was assembled; six of Delta's best, ready to go into the jungle, followed by a reaction force if necessary. I prayed silently, "Please, God, let them be alright."

A chopper spotted the wreckage, near the saddle, crumpled under the trees at the edge of a clearing. A wisp of smoke had eked above the jungle, attracting the crew's attention. The recovery force went in. I listened on the radios. There were no survivors. I was too late with my prayer.

The chopper landed at Khe Sanh. The medics unfurled the body bags, placing the charred remains inside. They sealed and labeled them. *Requiescant in pace*: May they rest in peace.

Sergeant Tommy Carpenter from recon had led the recovery team. They had been on the ground only a few minutes, just long enough to recover the bodies. He had but a quick look at the wreckage. The fuselage was upright, but canted. The entire cockpit area had been destroyed, burned and almost broken in half. There had been an intense fire. I told him that the fuel tanks, which were in the wing roots above the cockpit, had probably ruptured, spilling burning fuel over the occupants. He had found some large holes in the wing, .50–caliber sized, but they could have been made by tree limbs or rocks as the aircraft plunged, tumbled, and skidded. We later recovered the wreckage and weapons experts closely examined it. The entire cockpit area was riddled with hundreds of holes, smaller than .22 caliber. They deducted that the aircraft had been hit by a large weapon, possibly a 57mm recoilless rifle, firing cannister rounds. The resourceful NVA had shot at them like hunters at ducks. Mercifully, Charlie and Art had died instantly.

I walked to the Tiger Hound bunker. I had to send a report through Air Force channels officially notifying Saigon, the TACC, and Nha Trang, DASC Alpha, of Charlie's death. The glowing red sun was slipping into Laos. I wondered how something could look so beautiful in the midst of death and war. I kept walking. Charlie had arrived on Monday; he was dead by Wednesday. He was killed on his fifth mission with Delta. I had over 200. The Coveys helped me fill out the message form, encrypting sensitive information. The standardized form focused more on the disposition of the aircraft; the death of a pilot and observer was almost incidental. They tried to console me, which I appreciated. It was dark when I left their bunker.

The dampness of the monsoon season had settled over the plateau. I slipped on my jungle sweater to ward off the cold. I entered Delta's mess area. It was covered with several large tarps, open-sided, with rough benches and tables. The Nungs worked over open fires, buried in the earth, the glowing coals invisible from a distance. Huong, one of the cooks, had saved me some supper. He somehow kept track of me, when I was flying, saved meals for me, and did my laundry and errands. I paid him lavishly by Vietnam standards, a couple of U.S. dollars, or piastres. I had noticed that whenever there was an alert, he would materialize beside me, his weapon and grenades at the ready. I learned that he had assumed the responsibility as my personal bodyguard.

"I sarly, *Trung-Uy. Dai-Uy mort*," said Huong, mixing English, Vietnamese, and French as they often did. Although Charlie and Art were new to Delta, the entire camp felt the loss, including the Viets.

"*Cam on. Merci*," I replied. I appreciated his caring and the integrity of these simple people. I finished my supper. Rudy joined me as I sipped my coffee. I didn't want to go back to the tent and face Charlie's empty mosquito net. A flare popped south of the Marine sector.

"I got through to Ragged Scooper like you asked, L.T.," said Rudy.

"Good. What did the assholes have to say?" I was bitter. I didn't trust anyone at DASC Alpha.

"You get a new airplane tomorrow. Someone's flying it up from Nha Trang. And Water Pipe has some fighters for us."

"Great. One airplane again. Is it my turn to get shot down?" I got up and walked to the tent. I had been too abrupt with Rudy. It wasn't his fault everything had turned to shit. It was dark in the tent. I ignored the empty bunk.

The early morning weather was suitable for flying. There were no friendlies in the vicinity of the downed O–1. Two local FACs, Trail 60 and 66, directed a flight of B–57s, Yellowbird 15, into the area and beat it up badly. The NVA didn't show their big gun. A second flight, F–4s, was cancelled that afternoon due to weather. The NVA would expect us to retrieve the aircraft. We spoiled their ambush.

The air strikes were over. I could procrastinate no longer. I had to pack Charlie's personal gear for shipment. I knew little about him except for his military life. I had to intrude into his other life. I found a letter from his wife. There were no other letters. He had mentioned a son to me but I didn't know if he had any other children. I threw out the odd cans of C-rations, dirty socks, and underwear. He had a couple of paperbacks I hadn't read. I kept them.

I thought about his now-fatherless son. I found a form for awards and decorations. I recalled the magic words from the ALOs' conference in Nha Trang. I'd try them—a Silver Star. At least his son would know his father had died with honor and valor.

A major walked in the tent. I didn't recognize him; he was new. He introduced himself as Jim Lindsey, the ALO to the 5th Special Forces Group. I finally had a boss; he was the first Air Force field grade officer to visit us at any FOB. He had delivered the replacement airplane. I wanted to ask him if it were to be my coffin, but I thought better of it. I gave him the recommendation for Charlie's medal. Or was it his son's? Together we composed the letter to Charlie's widow. It was the second toughest thing I'd had to do. The toughest would be to carry the guilt of Charlie's avoidable death for the rest of my life.

The replacement airplane was new. Actually, it was built in 1950, but it had been completely remanufactured—engine, radios, cockpit, instruments, structure. Sparkling silver paint. I took it up and wrung it out; loops, rolls, split S, clover leaf, stalls. Most of the maneuvers were prohibited by the flight manual, but most FACs were illiterate. It was a dream to fly.

Instead of caution, I flew with reckless abandon. I had become fatalistic, launching in any kind of weather. I didn't care anymore, daring gunners to shoot at me. I berated fighter pilots for not pressing attacks or for shying from marginal weather, chastising them when they missed easy targets. The teams, roadrunners, and chopper pilots performed to extraordinary levels; I expected the same from the fighters. We sent radar-controlled bombing missions into the Khe Ta Bong Valley almost nightly and in bad weather, challenging the NVA to reclaim occupation.

After losing Charlie, Rudy ensured that I checked in every 15 minutes with coordinates and next expected location. I took a VNAF helicopter pilot, who was supporting SOG, into Laos to reconnoiter an LZ; I took the Delta commander with me on an air strike control mission to knock out a team-confirmed gun position in weather so marginal that the fighters almost hit a mountain on their bombing pass. I wanted him to experience what we were enduring. He never asked to fly with me again. The gathered recon and Ranger advisors endorsed my action by teaching me how to fire an 81mm mortar—elevation, traverse, increments—"good to 3600 meters, FAC." They cheered when the round came out of the tube and cheered again when the binoculared spotter declared a hit.

At 3:30 one morning, a TPQ radar-controlled bombing mission dropped bombs 200 meters from a team. Rudy was on the radio instantly, aborting any subsequent missions. Somehow an unauthorized mission had slipped through the command approval channels at the corps and MAF level, narrowly missing Team 11. It was Rudy and I, completely on our own, fatigued but committed, bedraggled but resolute, doing the best job we could. But we were cracking.

My hands shook. I couldn't speak coherently unless I was on a radio. Each flight was getting more difficult. I was tired of fighting incompetency and educating the stupid. I had risked my neck too much—I had been recommended again for the Silver Star—disapproved by the same colonel in Nha Trang. Rudy's jovialism and optimism had disappeared with our isolation and pressure. Intelligence reports, our own and those of the Marines, indicated that the NVA were creating a noose around Khe Sanh, waiting for the hanging. The Delta commander asked me to extend my tour for six months. I declined. But finally good news came. We were to stand down for a week, while Saigon decided if Delta was to redeploy or continue the mission. Rudy and his jeep would get out on a C–130. I fled Khe Sanh on November 17, taking off on instruments, swallowed up by the clouds, blindly straining for altitude to get over the mountains.

I slipped into Nha Trang at twilight on Thursday. En route, I had made a quick administrative stop in Da Nang and lost my flying scarf there.

Major Jim Lindsey had done it all. On his overnight delivery trip to Khe Sanh, he had recognized what Project Delta was all about. His subsequent visit with Skinner and Omega had shown him more. He knew that I was burned-out; I had been reduced to a flying robot. I had combat fatigue, but I did not recognize it until Friday, when I went to DASC Alpha. I was unable to function outside of the jungle, outside of an airplane. I was paranoid, short-tempered, fearful, could not stand still, and could not sleep. Everything had been arranged—special flight orders, currency vouchers to obtain U.S. dollars, and time to get some clean clothes. The SF medic gave me some pills. "Here FAC, take these. You'll feel better." By 6:30 Saturday morning, I was on my way to Bangkok in a C–130 on an unofficial leave. It was my first real break in the ten months I had been in Vietnam.

Bangkok was a wonderful reprieve. Friendly people, clean atmosphere, nice hotels, cultural and historical sights, excellent shopping—I took advantage of them all. I saw the Emerald Buddha, the palace, the market (similar to Les Halles in Paris), the zoo, and I was there for the Asian Trade Fair, a small-scale world's fair. I ate Thai food, Chinese food, Hungarian food, Kobe beef, and French cuisine. I saw native Thai dancing, which was as beautiful and expressive as any that I had seen. I viewed a staged but frightening sword fight in a dinner theater; the audience was protected by a wire mesh curtain. Thai boxing also was not lacking for action; the participants used their feet and knees as well as their hands and elbows, paced by a fast-tempo drum beat. I had an escort for the week who looked after my needs. Her name was Sansouk, which means "I am happy." So was I.

But I had to return to Vietnam. My one week of escape was over. I returned from Bangkok on Friday night, November 25, the day after Thanksgiving. I once again felt like a human being. I had only seven weeks remaining in my tour. I promised myself no more unnecessary chances. It was ridiculous to have made it this far and then to get wiped out.

While I was in Bangkok, Delta had returned to Khe Sanh, as I had expected. Intelligence reports, including Delta's from the last operation, indicated that the NVA and Viet Cong were undertaking a force buildup. My new boss, Major Jim Lindsey, was covering the operation. I was glad he was still around, considering his ominous introduction to Delta. Charlie Swope crept into my mind, but this time it was fleeting thoughts of his widow and son.

The most comforting news was that there was an O–1 coming out of periodic maintenance at Nha Trang, and I was to fly it to Khe Sanh. At last, we would have two aircraft to fly in pairs for mutual protection. The gunners would have to get both of us. DASC Alpha had finally conceded that flying single ship in I Corps was absolute suicide.

The next best news was a large brown envelope on my bunk, addressed to me with a Da Nang APO return address. It contained my red flying scarf with the embroidered Project Delta emblem, and a note from the Marine helo pilots that supported us at Khe Sanh: "John: I hope this catches up with you. It was found at Da Nang and we knew it could only belong to you. Fly safe. See you soon. /s/ Shea."

I was glad to get that scarf back. It had become a talisman to me, more valuable than my flak vest. I also had some bad news. Rudy Bishop had asked to be reassigned to the DASC when he had returned from Khe Sanh. I couldn't blame him. He had been with me and Delta for over five months, living and working under some of the harshest conditions imaginable. He would pull shifts with the SF Commo staff and had earned their respect, particularly when he voluntarily parachuted with them. He was exposed to as much combat as anyone. Sitting in the jeep with the four radios, he was in the middle of every battle. He could hear the gunfire and excited calls from the ground troops and the helicopter crews. He listened to the command net as the battle strategy unfolded. He was the first to know in the forward base when someone was shot, an ambush sprung, a helicopter downed, a fighter hit, or a team lost. He lived in the Delta barracks and socialized at the Delta Hilton. To him, virtually every call sign had a name and a face. His was a conjured battlefield, but the losses were real. I wondered if the scars of vicarious battles would outlast the wounds of the flesh.

I drove to the DASC and personally thanked him for his outstanding work. It was 20 years later that the Air Force fully recognized the capabilities of our enlisted men and created an Enlisted FAC (E-FAC). Regardless of the rules, we did it in Vietnam in 1966.

I had to replace my flying and survival gear that had been in the backseat of the O–1 when it was shot down. I drove to the base equipment management office at the Air Force compound. I usually drove an Army jeep with the Delta symbol on the bumper. It made parking easier. Everyone knew that we were crazy; we'd park the jeeps anyplace with impunity.

I located the personal equipment sergeant. "Sarge, I'd like to draw some new flying equipment."

"Yes sir," he responded, "what would you like?"

"Just give me the basic load and we'll go from there." He looked at me as if I had two heads.

"The basic load, Sarge," I repeated. No response. I realized we were not communicating. I had been with Special Forces so long that I spoke a different jargon. I had lost touch with the administrative Air Force.

"Sorry, Sarge. I need a headset, survival radio, spare battery, personal medical kit, collapsible canteen, survival ration packet (to supplement the plastic ration bags of rice from the Vietnamese), waterproof match case, small compass, pen flare gun, strobe light, day/night signal flare and signal mirror. I also need a flak vest, extra large (I still intended to sit on it), a gas mask, leather flying gloves, size 9, and a handful of .38 tracer rounds. Oh yeah—a packet of condoms." They were recommended as emergency canteens. They also made lethal water bombs for fights in the hooch.

"Right, Lieutenant. I understand." He gave some orders to his helpers. They started pulling the materials from the stockroom shelves, and a small pile of equipment and boxes was spread out on the counter for inventory. I looked at the strobe light. It had a hooded shield with a bluish lens over the high-intensity bulb.

"What's that for?" I asked, realizing it would reduce the intensity of the signal light. It was difficult enough to find a downed pilot in the jungle with the standard issue strobe. A young airman with a new guy look— unfaded fatigues, unscuffed jungle boots—responded, "Well sir, at tech school they told us that the strobe lights had the same cycle rate, 100 to

150 per minute, as a heavy antiaircraft gun. They came up with this fix. It looks blue instead of white." He demonstrated it to me.

Oh, Christ, I thought, how many of our downed pilots have we splattered with CBUs thinking it was a gun emplacement? And how is someone to recognize a bluish tint when the entire area is engulfed in smoke, haze, muzzle flashes, and red tracers? I pushed the strobe light back over the counter.

"Thanks, I won't be needing it." Put that in your savings account, Secretary McNamara.

I fiddled with the switches on the survival radio. They were different from my previous radio. "We're not authorized to give spare batteries," said the sergeant. "Bring the old one in and we'll replace it."

I didn't say a word. I could just see myself being forced down in the jungle. "Time out Mr. VC, my batteries are running low so I can't bring in any more air strikes on your heads. I have to go back to Nha Trang and get some more batteries but I'll be right back."—"Fuuuck me!" as Jim Ahmann used to say. Only seven more weeks and I'll be out of here, but our own people are making it tougher.

"We don't have any survival rations," he continued. "But they put some chocolate in the medical kit. What do you want with the gas mask? They're only for the airport security force."

I didn't want the gas mask anyway. I was going to remove it. I wanted the canvas bag and webbed straps, but they couldn't issue the bag alone. I would put my survival gear in it as I had in the past. It was more convenient to put everything in a single bag and sling it over your shoulder or store it in a jeep or airplane. The survival vest, with its pockets and protrusions, was hot and cumbersome. I had been carrying the canvas bag ever since I had been patrolling with the Koreans back in February.

"Skip the mask, Sarge," I replied. "Just show me your latest in Brooks Brothers survival vests."

He hauled out a carton of survival vests which were standard Air Force issue. As I picked through them I found what I was looking for—one made from camouflaged light-weight canvas rather than the green nylon and mesh that was standard for flight crew members. I thought the camouflaged vest would blend better with the tiger suits and jungle if I were forced down. Besides, since I looked and dressed no differently from any of the other SF troopers—no rank, no insignia—I'd be damned if I would make it easy on the VC to determine that I was a pilot, much less a FAC. FACs were not winning any popularity polls with the VC.

"We don't have any tracer rounds for the .38," said the sergeant. They were scarce. I had bartered a 30-round carbine magazine for a handful of tracer rounds in Qui Nhon. I realized that if I were on the ground and needed to signal a rescue chopper on a cloudy day, the only way to signal through heavy jungle canopy was with a tracer round. The five tracer rounds that were in my revolver were seven months old and I wanted some fresh ammo. The sixth round was fresh ball-ammunition. I hadn't changed my mind—the VC weren't taking me alive. Bangkok seemed light-years away. I was mentally transitioning back to the world of war.

The sergeant spread a file on the counter, shoving some of the equipment aside. "Sir, we've pulled your records and they show you've been issued this equipment at Tan Son Nhut in January." He went on to tell me that he couldn't reissue the equipment without higher authorization. I tried the supply officer for the authorization. He didn't believe that my aircraft had been shot down and the equipment destroyed. Someone had to officially certify the loss. In exasperation I called the major, the ops officer, in my parent squadron.

"What can I do for you, John?" he asked. He remembered me. I explained my predicament to him. He understood. I was in luck. "Go to the Officers' Club, have some lunch and I'll call you there," he instructed.

"And by the way," I squeezed into the tail end of the phone conversation. "When is my airplane coming out of maintenance? I want to get to Khe Sanh ASAP." Lindsey hadn't flown any hard-core missions with us. I didn't want to lose him when I finally had a champion to fight the political wars at DASC Alpha.

"I'll check on it," he replied. I walked, instead of driving, to the Officers' Club. It was lunch time on a weekend. I knew there wouldn't be any parking spaces.

The air conditioning hit me with a frigid blast. I hadn't been in the Nha Trang Air Force Officers' Club in months. I looked around. I knew these lunchers were rear echelon. They wore starched fatigues with regulation blue and white insignia, name tags, and appropriate badges; impossible to hide in the jungle. Also, the VC snipers couldn't miss the shiny wings, centered over the heart.

It was crowded. Screw lunch anyway. I hadn't eaten an American hamburger and french fries in so long that I would probably barf it up. I ordered a beer and sank into the corner of the Club and watched the parade of shills. The majors were kissing the lieutenant colonels' asses. They in turn kissed the colonels' asses. There was a general and his entourage from Saigon enjoying a weekend at the beach. Everyone was kissing his ass.

That started me thinking. I had better kiss some ass and find out the status of my assignment to the States. A month prior, I went through the forecasting process in Saigon, completing paperwork to reassign me to Otis with my old unit, then into the pipeline for graduate school and the Academy.

Another beer, and the paging system announced my name. Everyone looked up—what the hell—hadn't they seen a lieutenant at lunch before? Or were we all supposed to be out fighting the war? The ops officer was on the telephone. I should go back to BEMO; everything was taken care of. Also, my plane should be ready Monday night for my flight to Khe Sanh on Tuesday morning. The weather was forecasted to remain shitty for the next few days. He suggested that I get as far as Da Nang and wait for a break in the monsoons before trying to slip through the mountains to Khe Sanh. He was an OK guy.

When I walked back into BEMO, my gear was stacked in a box. The sergeant had the paperwork for me to sign. He grinned lasciviously. "You can get the condoms from the clinic. We're not authorized." Like hell I would. All they wanted to do was give a blood test for VD and put a letter in my personnel file, which would get a pilot grounded and scheduled for six hours of counseling with the chaplain. It didn't matter whether the test was positive; they sent the letter anyway. Actually the procedure made sense. No one would like to be interned in a VC or NVA camp with a case of social disease. But my medic buddies at Delta had a better procedure. Massive doses of penicillin; no records, just cures.

When I got back to the Delta compound, things were quiet. The jungle fighters were at Khe Sanh, and the admin and supply people were the only ones left around. I walked to the communications hooch to check the message traffic from the field. The continued miserable weather at Khe Sanh precluded any flying and therefore no teams had been put in. The Marine Amphibious Force was pushing for some intelligence. I didn't like the scenario, particularly since I was still in Nha Trang.

I went back to my hooch, spread my gear on my cot, and tried to figure out how I would rig my new survival vest. I wanted everything placed so that I could reach it with either hand, and to reach my medical kits with my teeth if necessary. The kits were now taped shut with waterproof tape that took two hands and daylight to open. With a razor blade I slit the tape open, resealed the kits with dripping candle wax, and rolled them in a sheet of plastic. I still couldn't reach them. I obtained a bandage pack and morphine syringe from the SF medics. I put it in a top pocket of the vest that I could reach.

I had to store the ammo for my carbine. With my gas mask bag, I had left the double 30-round magazine sticking out the top so that I could slide it out without danger of losing any of the contents of the bag, and could do it with one hand while flying or firing with the other hand. But I discovered that the vest had a pocket across its back, much like a game pouch. I could now fit two double 30-round magazines in the pouch. When seated, they were uncomfortable in the small of my back, but it was comforting to know they were there. I had increased my personal firepower from 120 rounds to 180 rounds. As soon as the O–1 came out of maintenance, I would be prepared for war once again.

I spent the next day checking on my rotation assignment. There was no record of my forecast, so the system assigned me to McClellan AFB, near

Sacramento, to fly the same aircraft that I had flown in Massachusetts. What an absolute screw-up. My family was in Massachusetts. This would require a relocation to California, only to return to Boston eight months later when I would start graduate school. The system would waste taxpayers' money and my time with needless relocations. I finally convinced the personnel assignment people of the folly of their ways, and they said they would make every effort to get the assignment changed. I didn't need that aggravation.

The airplane that I would fly to the Khe Sanh came out of maintenance as scheduled on Monday afternoon. I drove to the maintenance area and chatted with some of the NCOs and airmen. Nothing had changed. These guys were still working outdoors, in revetments with makeshift canvas and tin roofs, and standing in water over their ankles. The O–1 ramp seemed to be the lowest spot on the field. My plane to be, tail number 498, was on a test hop.

I approached the senior NCO. He was one of the old heads that had been around Nha Trang as long as I had. He apparently didn't recognize me. I was dressed in olive drab jungle fatigues with black insignia, instead of the usual camouflaged tiger suits that I wore on operations. I remembered the looks of dismay on the maintenance troops' faces when I would taxi-in, returning from a month in the field, with the aircraft mud-spattered and filthy inside. However, when they saw the bullet holes, the cockpit littered with spent rifle cartridges, M–79 shells, and grenade pins, and smelled our jungle-rotted clothes and gear, they would look at me or Jim Ahmann or Skinner Simpson and just say, "Welcome back sir. We'll take care of everything." They understood.

The NCO finally recognized me. A big grin spread across his face. "Hi, Lieutenant," he said as we exchanged salutes. This was a true compliment because the NCOs around the flight line stretched the regulation on saluting officers. I didn't blame them. "How was Bangkok? Heard you found some work on the railroad—laying Thais," which brought a laugh from the other mechanics. He introduced me to a couple of the new people who had just joined the unit.

Some of the men had gathered around. "Understand you're going up north again. Major Lindsey told us. Heard about the deep trouble you got in last time, Lieutenant. We knew it was bad when they told us to drop 472 from the records. You got a real good bird this time, 498." Each one of the specialists came up to me and, in turn, offered his personal description of the work he had accomplished on my airplane.

The armorer, a big black Sergeant who flung the rocket tubes around as if they were matchsticks, said, "Sir, I checked those tubes myself. I had to adjust the starboard one, but you put that sight on Charlie's ass and I guarantee you'll get 'em. All the circuits checked out."

The avionics technician spoke next. "I put a new jackbox in because the wafer switch was loose. It met specs, but I put a new one in." He stepped closer to me and lowered his voice. "L.T., I got a buddy who works up at Da Nang. He got me a set of radio crystals so your UHF is set up just like the I Corps birds. If anybody asks any questions, you don't know where they came from. We could both loose a stripe. Did the same for the other airplane. The one the major's got." I understood. I knew when a regulation should be bent.

The airframe rigger: "You know I was pissed at you, Lieutenant, when you bashed that aileron on me last April, but this bird will fly sweet. If there's any problem after the test hop, I'll stay around and adjust it." I knew that he finished at 1600 hours, but would work all night if need be, until the flight controls responded to the slightest touch. He knew I disliked slack in the controls.

Engine mechanic: "Sir, I checked each cylinder. Max compression. I put a couple of spare plugs behind the seat just in case they don't have any in Khe Sanh."

And on it went—brakes, tires, fuel system. The extra work they put into that aircraft never showed up in the log book or work orders. They had a foreboding premonition that I was to push that aircraft far beyond its design specs in the next few weeks. A lump formed in my throat and my eyes watered. I turned away from the group. It never occurred to me that I could get killed, but I felt they would be very angry if I didn't bring that aircraft back.

The bird landed. The test pilot gave the thumbs up. The aircraft was perfect. The duty day was over. A cooler, filled with beer, materialized from the CONNEX container. I didn't know where my career was going, but I promised to spend informal time with the enlisted troops whenever I had the opportunity. I'd like to feel I kept that promise.

On Tuesday morning, November 29, the weather finally showed signs of breaking. As I walked out of the Delta Hilton at dawn, I looked at the sky and thought I'd give Khe Sanh a try. I went to the communications hooch. The weather report from Khe Sanh, although not real pure, at least indicated some breaks in the overcast, with two miles of visibility in the fog. I called DASC Alpha on the land line. They confirmed that my aircraft was in commission, the Qui Nhon weather was VFR, and Da Nang was forecast to go VFR in the next few hours. Although Da Nang was only 235 nautical miles up the coast, it would take two and a half hours to get there, and it was another hour to Khe Sanh. The weather trend was for improvement. The O–1 had only an ADF radio for blind navigation. In 1966 the only ADF stations were at Saigon and Da Nang. But I had enough in my favor to at least make Da Nang and take my chances from there.

I had commo send a message to Khe Sanh: AIREDALE TO DEPART NHA TRANG 0900 HRS STOP WILL MAKE BEST EFFORT TO LAND KHE SANH STOP ETA 1230 HRS LOCAL. I asked the sergeant on duty to send the message in code.

After the radio eavesdropping in Tuy Hoa and the mysterious surveillance aircraft in Tay Ninh, I was careful not to disclose my whereabouts. If the weather didn't improve at Khe Sanh, I would have to fly 20 miles up the river valley between the mountains to reach the field. The mountains and valley still belonged to the VC and NVA. I didn't want any welcoming parties armed with 12.7mm machine guns or 57mm recoilless rifles. I'd take my chances against the usual 7.62mm weapons.

I packed my gear and had the duty sergeant drive me to the airfield, going directly to the airplane. The standing water had receded overnight. The maintenance crew was expecting me. The DASC must have alerted them. When they saw me in my tiger suit they knew it was time for me to head north. I started my usual meticulous preflight inspection. The mechanics stowed and tied my gear in the rear seat. I hung my survival vest from the rocket tube while the crew chief followed me around the aircraft.

A young sergeant, carrying a parachute, approached the aircraft. I didn't recognize him. "Sir," he said. "Would you please sign for this?" He extended the chute and a hand-receipt.

"Thanks, Sarge, but I'm not going to bother. At the altitudes I fly, I won't get a chance to use it," I explained. Flying in the mountains of I Corps, I also wanted to reduce all excess weight in the aircraft, including a chute for the backseat observer. A back-seater couldn't get out anyway.

"But sir, they came out with a new regulation which requires all FACs to wear parachutes."

"OK, I'll sign." I would put it over the back of the seat and it would stop any rounds coming up from the rear. I installed the flak vest securely under the seat cushion. I slipped on my new survival vest, chambered a round into my carbine, checked the safety to on, and stowed the weapon. I climbed into the cockpit, adjusted the seat and belt, locked the shoulder harness, and fidgeted around to get comfortable. I had a three-and-a-half hour flight ahead of me, and already I could feel the extra ammo magazines, jutting into the small of my back.

The crew chief was standing at the ready with a fire extinguisher. I gave the start signal, slid the mixture to rich, nudged the throttle, switched the magneto to *Both*, hit the boost, and punched the starter button. The little Continental O–470 eagerly swung through a couple of blades and fired. My hands started to shake as I flicked familiar switches. This would be my last combat operation.

I gave the hand signals to the crew chief: pull the safety pins, wheel chocks out. As I was ready to release the brakes, a young airman, arms laden with smoke grenades, ran under the wing. Approaching the open cockpit window, he shouted over the roar of the engine, "The Sarge says you like yellow smoke. I took these out of the other planes. Get some Charlies for me." I recognized him. His brother, with the 1st Cav, had been seriously wounded and was in the hospital in Nha Trang. He put them in the seat pocket. I grasped his hand briefly, and hit the mic button.

"Nha Trang ground, Airedale zero-one, taxi." The sun broke through the single layer of clouds.

"Roger, Airedale," said a Vietnamese-accented voice. "Taxi runway three-zero, winds three-three-zero at ten, altimeter two-nine-nine-four. Contact tower on two-five-nine-decimal-seven, or one-one-eight-decimal-seven when ready for takeoff."

"Copy." I pulled into the run-up area, advanced the throttle, and checked the mags. Left, both, right, both—minimum RPM drop; checked the carb heat—RPM drop again. Everything was OK. I switched to tower frequency.

"Nha Trang tower, Airedale ready to go."

"Cleared for takeoff," replied the tower as I pushed the throttle full forward and watched the RPM wind up. Gauges were in the green. We picked up speed and I nudged her off the ground. My hands had stopped shaking. I was on my way back to war.

12
Khe Sanh Again

I flew north, following the coastline, dodging the scattered clouds, chugging along at 100 mph, to Da Nang and ultimately Khe Sanh. I had the windows open and would extend my hand into the slipstream, deflecting cool air into the sun-roasted cockpit. At 6,000 feet, I was high enough to maintain radio contact with flight-following, but low enough to watch the landscape and villages unfold beneath me. It was simple to identify control of the territory: movement on the roads and trails, friendly; no movement, VC. I was an old hand now; it was my eleventh month in-country. I could smell the VC.

I overflew many of the places that ten months ago were hostile and unknown. Now, they were known, some were less hostile, and each had left its mark on me. Tuy Hoa, where I had met Skinner Simpson with the Screaming Eagles, deployed with Delta and saved the Mike Force, was now the location of a major fighter base. The tent city of Tiger Town had grown. Qui Nhon harbor was still cluttered with ships. Gabrielle and the seminarian had slipped into the past. I passed the Phu Cat mountains where we had destroyed the VC base complex with helicopter gunships. I used the gunships regularly now. Phu Cat village was next. A nearly completed airbase stood where the B–57s had dropped the delay bombs. I missed the Koreans, the gentle breezes and towering palms, but not the patrols. Bong Son crept under the nose, where I had flown the A–1 mission and Delta was mauled before I joined. Quang Ngai, where I'd flown over ten hours in one day and the unsung crew chiefs had rearmed and refueled me in three minutes, went past the left wing. Next was Chu Lai and the Marines, where Jim Ahmann had taught me how to by-pass the system to ensure fighter support.

The Officers' Club had withstood the raucous games of destruction. I noticed the weather was deteriorating as I continued north.

After two and a half hours of flying, I was approaching Da Nang. I called the I Corps DASC on their discrete frequency.

"Water Pipe, this is Airedale on Uniform."

"Roger Airedale, we've been expecting you. Welcome back to I Corps." Bullshit, I thought. The only reason they want to see me is that we find good targets and they want to increase their sortie count in competition with the Marine DASC.

"What's the weather at Khe Sanh?"

"Latest we had, Airedale, was 600-foot overcast with two miles visibility, intermittant one mile with rain and fog." Double shit, I thought again. The elevation at Khe Sanh was 1,600 feet and the mountain tops were 2,200 to 3,600 feet on the way in. I didn't have a TACAN radio with which I could improvise a let-down into Laos and come in the backdoor, from the west, over the lower terrain. Additionally, I would have only 30 minutes, 45 at the most, of fuel left when I reached Khe Sanh. It was an hour to return to Da Nang, which I knew was open. That wouldn't work. However, Hue/Phu Bai was halfway to Khe Sanh, and if it were open on the way in, I could always recover there with 15 minutes of fuel to spare.

The other alternative was to land at Da Nang, retire to the Officers' Club, and locate my classmate and football teammate, Pete Bobko. Rumor said he was flying F–4s there. I'd find a bunk and wait for the weather to lift. But words lurked in my mind—Duty, Honor, Country. I belonged in Khe Sanh with Delta.

I went by Phu Bai. The weather was okay. I was now committed to Khe Sanh and hoped I wouldn't get nailed as I skimmed, below the clouds, across the coastal marshes, out of range of any guns hidden in the parallel mountains. Ambivalently, I spotted the Quang Tri River, positioned at my one o'clock. I was on course. The river would lead me to Khe Sanh. But I would have to turn west, to fly between the cloud-shrouded mountains, unable to avoid the 20-mile gauntlet of NVA guns.

The weather forecaster had lied again. There was no one-mile visibility. At some points the visibility was so poor that I could only see straight down as I followed the wandering river, occasionally glimpsing the remnants of Highway 9, while gradually climbing to the Khe Sanh plateau. If I couldn't see, neither could the enemy gunners. The weather was in my favor. Charlie didn't expect to find anyone flying in his backyard in such miserable weather. I slipped unscathed into Khe Sanh, 3 hours and 25 minutes after takeoff from Nha Trang. I was lucky. I landed in the first third of the runway and taxied down the mud-slick aluminum to the sand-bagged revetment. I realized I had broken my promise. It was only four days since I had returned from Bangkok, six weeks to go home, and I was still taking chances.

Sgt. Tommy Carpenter, who had recovered Swope's and Glidden's bodies from the O–1, and Major Jim Lindsey walked from the Delta camp to the revetment. They were waiting as I taxied in. I stomped smartly on the right brake pedal, pivoting the aircraft, and swung the nose around, pointing at the runway. The wing tip barely missed the edge of the revetment. I performed a magneto grounding check, killed the radios, and pulled the mixture to cut-off. The engine died. I tossed the rocket safety pins to Major Lindsey. He and Tommy put them in. I climbed out of the cockpit, massaging the small of my back, silently cursing the supply system. I missed my survival equipment bag. As Jim and I shook hands, we exchanged the usual banter about my flight.

"Piece of cake, Jim; the vis dropped a bit as I got closer to Khe Sanh, but I recognized most of the bends in the river." Why do pilots understate the arduousness of a flying mission? We deceive ourselves. We think we are invincible, are always on the critical edge, and then surprised when things go wrong. I recalled the admonition for end-of-tour flying; that carelessness, complacency, and false immortality would take its toll. With a hit in either fuel tank, landing at Khe Sanh wouldn't have been an option, but a necessity. I wouldn't have had enough fuel to return to Hue/Phu Bai.

I filled out the log book, unchambered the round from my carbine, and slung it over my shoulder. Tommy helped me with my gear and we walked to the officers' tent. Jim headed to the operations tent. With Jim out of earshot, Tommy said to me, "FAC, are we glad to see you. The old man's getting pressure from up channel to put some more teams in. Street St. Laurent and his team went in yesterday. So far he's okay. The weather has been so bad that even the helicopters couldn't fly. If we put a team in, we might not get them out. If they got in trouble, we don't know what we would do. Without you here, we didn't know if we could get TAC air, and we are outside the range of the Marine artillery. It would be suicide. The guys are real uncomfortable and Doney wanted me to talk to you." Doney was now the senior recon sergeant.

"Okay, Tommy. Thanks for the insight. Let me get a briefing from intel." As I walked to the tent, I noticed the clouds breaking up. Even a few patches of blue sky appeared. Virtually every trooper that I passed offered a greeting.

"Hi, FAC, welcome back. How's Bangkok?"

"Great, really great," I responded.

"This place still gives me a case of the ass."

The helicopter pilots from the 281st had some typical words for me. "Just like you Air Force weenies; the weather goes to hell and you dee-dee out of here." They were referring to my abrupt departure on November 17 from Khe Sanh for Da Nang and Nha Trang, with the weather at zero-zero.

Norm Doney and Sgt. Herman Adler, the Intel NCO, were waiting for me at the ops tent. They flipped the curtain back from the intelligence map and I briefly examined it. The entire map, from our position north to the DMZ and west to Laos, was covered with the red symbols of enemy units. Big units: battalions, regiments, 325C NVA Division.

"What the hell are we doing here? I could spend weeks putting air strikes in here and we wouldn't even make a dent in that concentration."

"That's part of the problem, FAC," said Adler. "We know they are out there but they keep moving around. We suspect they have a roving base here, in the corner by the Laotian and North Vietnam border," as he pointed to the map. I remembered from the last time when I'd spotted the VC, that those bastards wore khaki uniforms. They were hard-core NVA regulars and they were on top of their supply lines from Laos and North Vietnam. The S–3, Major Lundy, and Major Lindsey entered the back of the tent and joined us up front, by the map.

"Welcome back, John," said Lundy. "The weather's breaking. We've laid on a recce with the choppers and, if the weather holds, the old man wants to put a team in at last light, tomorrow—here, in the corner." He pointed to where Adler had pointed.

I turned to Norm. "Who is it?"

"Bott and Stark and the four Vietnamese. They're a good team." I could hear the turbines whining on the chopper pad. The team leader and the American advisors were to recce the area from the Huey, and select a suitable LZ.

"What time is the briefing tomorrow?" I asked Norm.

"Fourteen-hundred hours."

"Okay, I'll be there." I turned to Adler, "Do you have my map? And get one for Major Lindsey too, please." We would use the usual high detail 1:50,000-scale maps, but with a new coded grid overlay. Delta changed the grid for each operation.

"Yes sir, and commo will be right over with your SOI. Your call sign for this operation will be Snake." As if on cue, a communications sergeant entered and handed me the pocket-sized signal operating instructions.

I turned to Major Lindsey, "Sir, you'll be Snake zero-one, and I'll be Zero-two. But don't use the numbers when communicating with the teams. It will only confuse them. What call sign have you given the DASC in Da Nang for the air request net?"

"Ragged Scooper zero-seven." This was his personal call sign.

"That won't work. Ragged Scooper is a II Corps call sign. If we have to contact Hillsboro, the airborne C–130 command post over Laos, or the TACC in Saigon, for additional or diverted fighter support, they'll wonder what an RS is doing in I Corps. They'll deny the request or ask so many questions they'll screw it up. We'll use my personal Delta call sign, Airedale. I'll tell our ROMAD to change it." I missed having Rudy Bishop with us, but I didn't blame him for requesting safer duty at DASC Alpha headquarters. He'd been in the field a long time. I made a mental note to spend some time with our new ROMAD.

Adler brought the maps in and I went over them with Major Lindsey. Our battle area was unchanged; 100 square miles of jungle and hidden guns. It was much different from the 100 square miles of flat rice paddies in Binh Dinh where I had fought Tiger V with the Koreans. But the bullets were the same. I reviewed the grid overlay and the technique for using it. Jim had been on an operation with Omega and they used the same basic procedures that we did. Skinner had done his usual excellent job of training him.

The choppers lifted off. I suggested to Jim that we fly a recce over the area to familiarize him with the prominent terrain features, and point out the ground fire locations from our previous operation. This time I had a surprise for the Clydes—two airplanes for mutual protection.

We took off with Jim flying a loose formation on my wing. After our recce of the area—which extended from Khe Sanh, 15 miles north to the North Vietnam border, 10 miles west to Laos, and 10 miles east to the beginning of the coastal plain—we swapped leads on the way back to the field. Jim rocked the wings, the signal to move in tight; I tucked my wing behind and slightly below his, and we buzzed the Delta encampment at antenna height, then pulled up over the field, took separation, and landed. We taxied in trail to the revetment. It felt great to fly once again, just for the sheer joy of it.

I spent the rest of the afternoon squaring my equipment away. This was routine now. It was like checking into a hotel. I blew up my air mattress, fastened my mosquito net from the overhead commo wire, and tucked the net under the mattress and blankets to keep the bugs and snakes from crawling in. I was all set. One more thing: I ensured that I could roll from my cot into my same foxhole outside the tent. I carefully checked it for rats and snakes.

I introduced myself to the new ROMAD. He had sandbagged the MRC–108 communications jeep next to the SF commo van. This worked out well since they could hand messages back and forth to each other and share monitoring the radios. He was experienced, had been in-country several months, heard that we were doing some interesting things, and wanted to sign on. DASC Alpha, in making the assignment, was following one of the precepts of Delta: it was all volunteers.

The operational tasks of a ROMAD were usually accomplished under the supervision of an officer who had been schooled in all aspects of tactical air support. With Delta, we didn't have that luxury. We delegated much of the responsibility to our sergeant or airman. He chose the target coordinates, the rendezvous points for the fighters, and selected the available strike frequency. Often, from listening to the battles on the radio, he would request the most appropriate munitions. He would take the line-ups directly from the fighters, and direct the jets to a location close to where we were flying. I kept the critical information in my pocket notebook. I reviewed the technical procedures with the young sergeant: target coordinates, rendezvous point, and contact frequencies.

The remainder of the procedures were personal and war-related. I checked his ammo supply, his first-aid packet, and gave him some hand grenades. I also instructed him that if we were attacked, he was not to leave the radios. If wounded or killed, he should have a backup procedure with the Army. The radiator area of the jeep needed more sandbags. He was ready.

Our Nung camp workers prepared a sumptuous evening meal over the open fire. Someone flew in fresh vegetables and meat from the market in Hue. This was one of the ancillary benefits of being with a joint American-Vietnamese unit—we used whatever supply source worked best. In the evening, the recon sergeants and the medics had a small presentation for me in the medic tent. They knew that I had lost my red flying scarf (they didn't know that it had been found and returned) and presented me with a new one with "Project Delta" embroidered over the Delta logo and "Red Baron" under the logo. A welcome back toast was offered; medicinal 190-proof grain alcohol and GI grape juice. I still have the scarf.

As I walked to my tent, I saw distant flares arc skyward and drift earthward, as the Marine outposts calmed their uneasiness. In the flickering light, I saw our Nung sentries, concealed in their sandbagged posts, guns at the ready, scanning the elephant grass for suspicious movement. We were in the same location as our previous deployment. The Marines had found NVA tunnels dug to the outer defense perimeter; they destroyed them with satchel charges and C-4. I gazed up and saw a few stars. Maybe the weather would finally break. The team was scheduled to go in tomorrow.

Morning broke with the usual fog and mist; marginal weather, but comparatively good for the monsoon season. It would either burn off, leaving a reasonable day, or the clouds and rain would move in. At least when it rained, the fog would disappear and there would be adequate visibility for flying. I walked across the runway to the Marine compound to the Tiger Hound FACs, the Coveys, for an update on antiaircraft fire. They faced it every day.

As I passed by the revetment on the north side of the runway, I noticed there were four O–1s parked and tied down. Two were Delta's, the other two belonged to the Tiger Hound FACs. I recalled that the Coveys had two or four aircraft, depending on the activity along their sector of the trail. They now operated from three or four airstrips in the I and II Corps areas. The Marine guard at the complex looked at me suspiciously. They didn't feel comfortable with Vietnamese, Delta's contingent, on the base, and I was dressed like them. The layout was much the same as last time, except I noted more stored artillery shells, empty shell boxes, and that the garbage pile of discarded C-ration cartons and cans had grown. The beer hall was still intact; it remained as the only above-ground structure of any substance. I found the Tiger Hound bunker. I wasn't quite sure of the Khe Sanh etiquette when entering another's domicile. There was no artillery-shell door chime, and it was tough to knock on a sandbag. I shouted, then started down the slippery, dirt and shell-box steps.

The poor bastards were living like moles, but as they told me previously, it was the only safe place. The bunker was still dank, surfaces were now covered with slime, and with the intensified monsoons, water oozed from the walls, dripped from the ceiling, and collected on the floor. Empty C-ration cases had been ripped open and spread on the floor to provide a walking surface over the mud and water. Entering the bunker proper, head stooped, I looked around. Three pilots, a couple of mechanics, the radios, and an operator were in the bunker.

"Hi, John. Good to see you again." They greeted me. "See you have two airplanes this time. Sorry 'bout your wingman." I didn't see Captain Handlebar. Some questions are not asked. Also, something was different about the bunker.

"I can't say it's nice to be back," I replied.

"Someone finally got their head out of their ass. We should send the sonofabitch to Tchepone," said a flightsuit in the corner. I assumed he meant whoever was responsible for not giving us two airplanes the last time. FACs, regardless of unit or mission, had unequaled esprit de corps, a way with words, and weren't much for command protocol. Strange, he singled out Tchepone for proposed retribution, or maybe it was revenge.

"You guys finally pay your electric bill? You can almost see in here." I realized what was different; it was brighter.

"Nah. The Marines brought in a bigger generator so they upped our juice. Now we get 300 watts instead of 150. Fortunately, the radios have their own generator or they'd probably make us live in the dark," said the NCO behind the equipment. A mechanic warmed to the conversation.

"We have a target pistol now, .22 caliber. We're on even terms with the rats. The .38s made too much noise—hurt your ears, and got the Marines pissed." They continued to endure abysmal living accommodations, battling the prolific rats for co-existence. But their spirits were undaunted; a score board on the wall tallied truck kills on the trail, and rat kills in the bunker.

"Well, we're here," I said. "Same area. Thanks for the help last time. Incidentally, I got to Bangkok. First time out in eleven months. It was like heaven. But after all the screwing around that I did, I don't think I'll ever get to heaven." They laughed. "What's with Tchepone?" I asked. I had flown some F-4 missions there in May. It was in the middle of the trail network. One of the FACs pointed to the map tacked to the end of the wooden bunk bed. Tchepone, in Laos, was 25 miles west of our area. It was marked in red.

"They've moved the big guns in again. Crew served 12.7mm and 37.5mm antiaircraft guns. Shot up some of the F–4s and the rescue helos, the Jolly Greens," he said.

"The place looks like an aircraft scrap yard," added a youngish looking lieutenant. I recognized him. He was a Zoomie. I intended to stay away from Tchepone.

★ ★ ★ ★ ★

In 1989, I was talking with Denny Hague about Tchepone. Denny was in the Air National Guard and, besides running his insurance business, was the adjutant general for Air in the state of Washington. Denny was number two in the ad hoc A–1E three-shipper that suppressed the ground fire when Bernie Fisher landed at A Shau to pick up Jump Myers. Denny was at Tchepone in early 1966 and he admitted to me that, "I was never so scared in all my life. They had shot down a FAC, an F–4, an Army Mohawk, and beat up the A–1s pretty badly. When we dove in on those guns, I really didn't expect to come out of there alive." Denny also told me about a B–57 that had been badly hit. The pilot, Larry Mason, ordered the backseat navigator, Jere Joyner, to bail out. The nav passed him a blood-covered note, saying that he was badly hit in the arm and leg and couldn't get out. They barely recovered at Da Nang. Dave Holmes was the shot-down FAC. Denny sang Irish songs with him in a bar in Destin, Florida during training at Hurlburt. They promised to get together on St. Patrick's Day, March 17. Dave was killed on the sixteenth. Uncommon bravery from common men.

★ ★ ★ ★ ★

The Coveys also told me that there were A–1Es around, call sign Sandy. They were staging out of Nakhon Phanom (NKP, or Naked Fanny) in Thailand. They were covering the trail area and flying combat escort for the rescue helicopters. I could request the Sandys through Hillsboro on VHF frequency 125.0. I would need the Sandys in the future.

The Tiger Hound FACs provided valuable updates which were not contained in any official intelligence summary, on the movement of the NVA troops and the availability of friendly airpower. They shared everything they knew with me, honestly and openly. They unselfishly offered to look after our two airplanes, refueling, rearming, and performing necessary maintenance, even though they were short of mechanics to look after their airplanes. I learned something about management: there is no substitute for "management by wandering around." This was to become a popular management technique in the 1980s; we practiced it in 1966 in order to stay alive.

The weather was marginal all day, but good enough for the C–130s to shuttle in and out of Khe Sanh. They brought supplies and replacements in; they took people out, some of them dead. The Herky birds never stayed on the ground long; this invited a mortar attack. I often wondered what the enemy's reward system might be; two weeks holiday in Hanoi if you hit a C–130, two weeks anywhere if you shot down an F–4, an autographed picture of Ho Chi Minh for a helicopter? What was a FAC worth?

The new FAC for Delta, Captain Al Groth, was one of the passengers on the C–130s. We finally had a permanent replacement FAC assigned to Delta. Major Lindsey had succeeded where Skinner and I had failed. I welcomed him and told him to follow me around and ask questions. He'd learn. Al was my ticket home. I'd take good care of him. I didn't tell him about Charlie Swope's shoot-down and death. I assumed he knew.

The team—Bott, Stark, and the Vietnamese lieutenant—presented their concept of operations and method of execution to the assembled staff at 1400 hours, as scheduled. I listened attentively to their escape-and-evasion plan. If they ran into trouble, they would separate and evade west into Laos and look for friendly help to pick them up. Unfortunately, their route would take them toward Tchepone. I made a note to brief the Tiger Hound FACs if anything should go wrong.

The weather deteriorated through the afternoon and the C–130s ceased their landings at Khe Sanh. The two Covey FACS that were flying landed early, which was highly unusual. I met them when they taxied in, and true to their way with words, they described the weather as "dog shit." It was even bad in Laos, where the terrain elevations were lower and, consequently, the cloud ceilings higher. I didn't like the scenario; there were too many factors against us. I was fearful.

The insertion helicopters took off before last light, in the middle of fog patches, rain showers, and low ceilings. Usually, more than one helicopter would fly an insertion profile, intending to confuse the enemy and screen the primary insertion bird. With the bad weather, it would be fortunate if even the primary helicopter landed on the selected LZ.

The helicopters returned in the early darkness and the pilots entered the operations tent for a debrief. The team was in, but my fears about the weather were well founded. With the rising terrain in the insertion area, the weather was even worse than at Khe Sanh. The pilots skirted the fog and rain, weaved around the mountains, avoided the concealed, multifarious gun positions—all while maintaining course to the LZ in the impending darkness. Under these circumstances, pilots could exercise their prerogative and abort the mission, but they were under intense command pressure to insert the team. From a low altitude, they made a critical navigation error, mistaking a monsoon-swollen stream as a river checkpoint. I was amazed they even reached the general area of operations, let alone inserted the team. The consensus of the helicopter pilots was that they had missed the LZ, and inadvertently put the team someplace in Laos.

There was unusual consternation as to the precise location of the team, apparently due to the potentially embarrassing political implications. From what I could determine, the U.S. government was assiduously avoiding any appearances of U.S. ground troops operating outside of South Vietnam. There were Americans, with indigenous mercenaries, operating in Laos, but they were in deep cover. There were Vietnamese troops operating in North Vietnam, but without Americans. All out-of-country helicopters, except American rescue helos, were Vietnamese. We had inadvertently landed a U.S. Army helicopter in Laos. As a result, the team was instructed to move east and north. An honest operational error, committed under the stress of a high-risk combat environment, was exacerbated by the distorted political scenario. I walked slowly to my tent. I would have to find the team in the morning.

Sheets of rain bombarded the tents and the winds howled throughout the night. The camp laborers had replaced the normal one-foot tent stakes with four-foot sections of steel fence posts. Even some of these were pulled free from the deep mud, allowing the blowing mist to enter the tent and soak our mosquito nets. We rolled up in our ponchos to ward off the wet cold, thankful for our jungle sweaters and insulated poncho liners. We slept fitfully. It was pre-dawn, not yet first light, when I pulled on my fatigues and boots. I had kept them dry by rolling them in the poncho with me. The camp was stirring; the ever-faithful and stoic Nung sentries were still at their posts, peering across the rain-flattened jungle grass. There was fresh coffee brewing in the ops tent. There were no further developments during the night; no contact with the team, not even on the long-wire radio.

Shortly after sunrise, the Army radio-relay aircraft arrived on station and reported that the entire operational area was completely socked in. I could have guessed as much. They made FM radio contact with the team, who wanted to know when the FAC would be up to give them a position fix. Without a known position, they could stumble into the middle of an NVA camp, become trapped against a mountain, or thwarted by a river, with no avenue of escape. During the morning, the team made brief contact with an NVA patrol, which they broke, and continued moving east and north. Now the enemy knew they were there and the search would intensify.

By late morning, the winds had died to 20 knots. I could see the O-1 parked in the revetment. The visibility was one-eighth of a mile, with signs of improving. Clouds and blowing scud were hovering at 200 feet. I huddled with Major Lindsey, Sergeant Doney, and the commander of Delta. Al was there, listening and learning. The commander was anxious to get a fix on the team. I thought that by descending after takeoff, flying north along the river from Khe Sanh, hugging the plateau west around the mountains, then turning north once again, I could approach where we thought the team was. If nothing more, it would be a morale booster for them to hear the sound of the engine and know I was airborne. I might be able to give them a position fix. Even though Al offered to fly my wing, I decided to fly the mission single ship. The weather was so bad that the other aircraft would be unable to keep me in sight, and if we flew close formation to maintain visual contact the same enemy gun could get both of us. The plan was agreed to and Norm sent one of the recon sergeants to fly in the backseat with me. As we walked through the mud and driving rain to the airplane, I briefed the trooper.

"We're goona look for Russ and Willie. No one is sure where they are. From the chopper pilots, I think they're probably a bit farther north and east, maybe into North Vietnam, but we'll start from this point here." I pointed to the map, the LZ circled where they supposedly went in last night. I continued, "The weather is not too pure, and I'll have my hands full, keeping the aircraft right-side-up and from hitting the mountains. You keep a sharp eye out and see if you can spot anything, friendly or otherwise. Keep a look for muzzle flashes or tracers. The local FACs told me that some big guns have been turning up in the area. I doubt if I'll be able to get much higher than 500 feet, and we probably won't stand a chance against much of anything. If something does zero in on us, I'll pull the nose up and we'll disappear into the clouds and hope we don't hit a mountain." He nodded his head; he understood, but I didn't think he knew how hazardous the mission really was. He trusted me. My plan, if we came under heavy fire, was to hide in the clouds, fly east to the coast, and hope the radar at Dong Ha could pick us up with a skin paint and bring us in with a ground-controlled approach, GCA, to their patch.

I checked the fuel and oil and pulled the rocket pins while the sarge strapped into the back seat. I climbed in the front seat and strapped in. The prop rotated as soon as I hit the starter, but the engine took its sweet time firing. It was probably wet like everything else, and after a few more swings of the prop, reluctantly shuddered into life. After the radios warmed up, I called Khe Sanh tower on 135.9. They thought I was crazy, but we took off anyway.

In order to see, I had to look out the side windows which I left open. After takeoff, I descended into the valley and turned north to follow the river. It took us 15 minutes to reach the team's approximate location, but there was no contact from the team. Usually, when they heard the engine they would come up on the radio. I gunned the engine a couple of times, causing a popping sound, which was the signal to establish radio contact. No luck. Their situation could include almost anything: ambush, capture, lost, broken radio, or silent hiding. I started a zigzag search pattern in the vicinity of where I thought the team was. We heard a radio call.

"Snake, this is Viper. We heard your engine but we couldn't see you." It was the team. I looked over my shoulder; the sergeant and I grinned at each other. The team was safe for now.

"Roger, Viper. Can you hear the engine now?"

"Negative." That was the good news. I had been following our ground track on the map; we were over North Vietnam. The bad news was I had never seen so many paths and trails criss-crossing through the elephant grass. Every place I looked, I saw fresh earth from bunkers and gun emplacements. My back-seater called me on the intercom.

"FAC, over there on the right. There's a half-dozen of them on the trail. All of them in khaki uniforms and carrying weapons." He was right; these guys were through digging. They didn't even try to hide and were looking for a fight. Time to head south and find Viper.

The rain was getting worse and I temporarily lost sight of the ground. I broke out of the clouds, in what seemed an eternity, but was only a few seconds. There was a nasty 3,500-foot mountain two miles southwest of me and a towering 5,300-foot mountain two miles southeast of me, both buried in the clouds. I was roaming around, at 500 feet above the ground, between them, within the effective range of small arms fire and lethal range of anything bigger. If I had to execute my evasion plan to escape ground fire, I was sure to hit one of the mountains. The O–1 couldn't climb fast enough.

"Viper, I'm coming back toward you. Listen for my engine and tell me what direction I am from you."

"Snake, this is Viper. We think we hear you. Sounds like you are to the north," replied the team.

"Roger, Viper, stand by." I had two choices: one was for them to transmit a steady signal that I could home in on, but I was concerned that at an altitude of 500 feet, this would disclose their position; the other was to fly on a southwesterly heading and wait until they could hear me. I had drawn a line on my map from my northerly position extending south, and if I could cross it with a line from the west, I would have an approximation of the team's location. I opted for the southwest heading, still following our ground track on the map with my finger, flying with my left hand.

"Snake, we hear you again. Sounds like you are to our west." I let go of the stick, controlling the aircraft with rudders alone, and pulled the throttle back with my left hand, to make the engine pop and backfire. "Snake, we heard ground fire to our west—near where you are." They mistook the engine popping for ground fire.

"Roger, Viper. Just testing your hearing." With a grease pencil, I hastily drew a line on my map from my present position extending to the east. As I glanced down to confirm the topography, I saw more fresh bunkers and gun emplacements. These guys were worse than Con Edison digging up the streets of New York.

"OK, Viper, I have you in the vicinity of block ———— ." I gave them the coded coordinates of where the two lines crossed on my map. They were in Laos. "We spotted recent activity three to four klicks to your north and two klicks to your west. I have to get out of here before the weather closes down all the way."

I sneaked south between the two mountains, but I had to detour to the southwest into Laos; I couldn't get over the foothills of the 5,300-foot mountain. I flew around the backside of the plateau, through Laos, before I could pick up the valley that went east and south to Khe Sanh. On the return I gave Hillsboro a call on Victor, 125.0, and said something clever like, "What's happening?" and they, being an airborne command post, felt they had to exercise their command authority and asked me who authorized my flight in such lousy weather. I thought that I should tell them to take a flying leap. Instead, I inquired about the weather for the next couple of days.

"Roger, Snake. The forecast shows increasing rain over the next few days with continued low clouds and fog. Tops are over 25,000 feet. Winds are forecast to pick up to thirty knots, with gusts to fifty, as the eye of this storm approaches. It should break by Sunday or Monday." Today was Thursday.

"Roger Hillsboro. Thanks for the good news. Anything flying with any ordnance?" I wanted to know if any fighters were available. I took satisfaction knowing they were bouncing around in the middle of the clouds at 17,000 to 21,000 feet.

"Negative. We had some Sandys earlier, but they couldn't get down," replied Hillsboro. If the A–1s couldn't find a way in, through, or around the weather, then it had to be solid all the way from Thailand, across Laos and into Vietnam, a distance of 120 nautical miles.

"Thanks again."

I picked my way down the river at treetop level. I could only see a couple of hundred feet and that was usually straight down. It was a 15-minute return flight to Khe Sanh, but the winds were tossing the O–1 around as if it were a barrel tumbling over Niagara Falls. As I approached Khe Sanh, I thought I would have some fun. The field was on a plateau and I was below it. When I was opposite the extended center line of the runway, I popped up and materialized from below the field—and buzzed the Delta camp. I taxied in and tied the bird down. The Tiger Hound mechanics were there to help. They put a couple of sandbags on the tail and on the wing, to hold the aircraft down and to disturb the airflow. I never thought that the practical application of my aerodynamics courses from the Academy would prevent my aircraft from flying out of its own chocks. We logged one hour. We were happy; the team was safe. For now.

I entered the ops tent and debriefed the S–2 and S–3. Doney was there, on the side. I told them I could not give the team a precise position fix, but that I thought they were four or five klicks northeast of where the plot showed them. They were in Laos, close to the DMZ, and in the center of a suspected NVA Regiment. I also mentioned the signs of recent NVA activity, including the sighting of armed troops. I'm not quite sure they believed me. They didn't change the plot position of the team on the operations map.

I tried to sleep again that night. The wind howled around the tent, and the rain beat on the canvas. One of the adjacent tents broke loose along an entire side and went crashing to the ground. I was bothered by a recurring, ominous question to which I had no answer: Why didn't the NVA shoot at me?

If Thursday's weather was bad, Friday's was horrendous. The weather forecaster had not lied. Clouds were blowing across the entire Khe Sanh complex. I couldn't see across the runway to the Marine complex, a distance of less than a half-mile. The tents were flapping in the wind, which was at least the promised 30 knots, and I had visions of the entire tent complex being blown into Laos. At least the rain was only intermittent. In one of the breaks, I walked to the TOC to see if there were any further developments. I half-filled my canteen cup with hot coffee. The Army radio relay bird, from Da Nang, was flying someplace, at around 10,000 feet, between the cloud layers. They had picked up a garbled transmission from the team in Laos, Viper, that they had made contact with enemy troops and had been in a fire fight. One or more of the team members was wounded, but the information at this time was still very sketchy. We had heard nothing from St. Laurent, the other team. The commander decided to launch the helicopters—two gun ships, a pick-up chopper, the command chopper, and a spare.

The choppers lifted off and I walked to my radio jeep to listen. I barely sipped my coffee, but the cup made a good hand-warmer. The Delta commo van, adjacent to the jeep, was tuned to the operations FM frequency and could receive the transmissions among the command helicopter, radio relay bird, and the operations tent. Because of the distance, terrain, and the line-of-sight propagation of the FM, the team's transmissions could be heard only from an aircraft, and the staff at Khe Sanh could receive only the airborne portion of the conversation. Additionally, I had my ROMAD tune into the VHF net, which was used by the helicopters for their flight control. I didn't like what I heard.

"Roger, Viper, we have lifted off and are headed to your location. What is your status?" inquired the C and C chopper. A pause, while Viper responded, and the C and C bird repeated the message received from Viper, "You have one American wounded and you are unable to move."

By now the choppers were well out of sight and I was monitoring their VHF frequency. They were trying to keep each other in sight as they picked their way north through the clouds and rain showers, following basically the route that I flew yesterday. As an aviator, I empathized with their difficulties in maintaining flight integrity. They had to circle frequently, to find one of their separated formation members, or to orient themselves with the terrain as they lost contact with recognizable landmarks. They had the very worst of conditions in which to fly, including the threat of a potential mid-air collision.

I heard on the FM radio, "Understand, Viper, you are receiving sporadic fire, and have one seriously wounded and two others with lesser wounds. We're on the way to get you." I had commo connect me with the Tiger Hound bunker, and asked them if they would send their crew chief out, untie my airplane, and perform a preflight. They questioned my sanity, but I told them we had a team in trouble and I didn't like the situation at all. They offered assistance and luck, which I appreciated. That up-tight feeling of fear was gradually creeping into my gut.

I asked Al Groth to get my pistol belt and carbine from the officers' tent. I had my map and I didn't want to leave the radios. My radio operator checked in with Water Pipe, the DASC; nothing flying, no fighter support available. The winds were picking up and it was difficult to walk. The rain started again and felt like tiny steel darts hitting my face. As I monitored the radios, my worst fears were realized; the helicopters couldn't find the team. They were probably looking where the team was last plotted, which was at least four klicks from where I thought the team was. The team would occasionally hear the whup-whup of the rotor blades but couldn't identify which of the five helicopters that it was. The radio transmissions on the helicopter net told me that they could barely keep each other in sight, let alone look for the team. And then there were the 3,500- and 5,300-foot mountains with their associated foothills. Norm Doney had walked over and joined us at the radio jeep. He didn't ask any questions, but by his presence I knew what he wanted.

"Norm," I said, "I don't like it at all. They can't find the team and the choppers are running low on fuel. There are no fighters available, and the winds are so bad I'm not even sure I could get the O-1 airborne, let alone get it back on the ground. That's if I don't hit the mountains in the middle of the rain." As I outlined the situation to Norm, that bitter taste of bile crept into my mouth and the tightness in my throat kept me from swallowing. I now realized why they hadn't shot at me yesterday. It was a trap and the team was the bait. I walked behind the commo van and, hoping that no one could see me, threw up what little I had in my stomach. I returned to the jeep.

A plaintive call came over the command net radio, "We can't locate the team. Can you send Snake to help?" I recognized the voice of the commander of the Army helicopter detachment. I looked at Major Lindsey. He didn't say a word. The call was all mine. I placed my canteen cup on the hood of the radio jeep, picked up my carbine and map, put on my red scarf, shrugged, ducked from under the tarp that was stretched over the jeep, and walked into the pouring rain to the airplane. I hadn't gone more than a dozen steps, through the water and mud, when one of the ever-present recon troopers was at my side with his full complement of web gear, extra frag grenades, and M–16 rifle. It was Sergeant Tommy Tucker. I stopped, and turned to him.

"Tommy, I'm going alone on this flight. I don't like this one and I'm not sure that I'm coming back."

He looked up at me and said, "FAC, no matter how bad it's been, no matter what kind of trouble we've gotten in, you have never let us down. If you get shot down, it's my job to take care of you on the ground." I looked out the corner of my eye and saw Doney and the other recon sergeants watching us from the ops tent. That menacing look on their faces told it all. Each and every one of them was with us. OK, they win. I'd rather take on the entire North Vietnamese Army than those guys.

The crew chief had untied the aircraft, and when he saw us coming, he removed the sandbags from the tail and wings. The wind showed no sign of subsiding, and if anything, had intensified. A quick preflight, pulling the rocket pins, cranking the engine, and we were airborne en route to the team. I intended to start looking in the vicinity of where I had located them the previous day. On the way north I called Hillsboro, thinking that maybe some A–1s would be around. No luck. "How about some Jolly Greens?" I asked, realizing that the Air Force rescue helicopters had more armor, greater fuel endurance, and heavier weapons than the Army Hueys. Another negative. I quickly briefed Hillsboro that I had a team in deep trouble and could use some Sandys or Jollys if they turned up. They confirmed that there were no breaks in the weather. I was on my own, as far as the Air Force was concerned.

The weather in the operational area was even worse than the previous day. I backtracked yesterday's flight path, fighting to keep the aircraft under control, as the vicious winds swirled over the mountains and tore through the valley. I was now contending with the forecast 50-knot winds. I was heading north and gradually climbing, to stay above the ascending terrain, and then swung west to slip around the backside of the mountain. I ran into a solid wall of clouds and rain that extended to the ground. I now had radio contact with the choppers, and from what I could tell, they were a couple of miles to the north of me on the other side of the foothills. They reported ragged cloud ceilings of about 300 feet. Okay, here goes nothing. I pulled back on the stick, punched the elapsed time button on the clock, and eased up into the clouds, flying exclusively on instruments. I climbed 500 feet, which, according to my map, was ample to clear the foothills. I flew for two-and-a-half minutes on a westerly heading, taking me past the 5,300-foot mountain, and then I headed north. Now, two minutes north, no, better make it two-and-a-half to compensate for the winds, and I'd start down. Any miscalculation and it would be an ignominious end, as I would splatter Tommy and me against the 3,500-foot mountain. I was trying to thread the needle between the mountains, relying on nothing more than compass headings and time hacks. The good Lord was with us. I broke out 300 feet above the ground, narrowly missing one of the helicopters.

"We've got the FAC, we've got the FAC in sight. He just went past my nose," exclaimed one of the helicopters.

"OK, Lead, rock your rotors," as I tried to get control of the gaggle. "Roger, I've got you. Take your flight two klicks south over the grassland area and set up an orbit." I needed room to maneuver and search for the team, and I didn't need the additional hazard or confusion of dodging helicopters and figuring which one was which. "How much fuel do you have on station?" I asked them. They needed enough to return to Khe Sanh.

"About fifteen minutes, twenty max." When it goes bad, it all goes bad.

"FAC, this is Viper. We heard you. Can you help us?" I heard the incessant background chatter of automatic weapons fire when the team transmitted. They were in deep trouble. I also knew they were in trouble because, after working with these guys for over seven months, the formality of call signs quickly evaporated under the stress of combat or circumstances of extreme danger. After sharing many hours of camaraderie with them, I immediately recognized the unmistakable Massachusetts accent of Sergeant Russ "Pete" Bott.

"Roger, Russ, I read you. What's your status?" All the time, I'm flying a zig-zag pattern trying to locate the team, with Tommy peering out one side of the aircraft, and I the other.

"Stark's hit pretty bad and a couple of Vietnamese must be hit." Pause. "We've been separated." I heard a grenade explosion over the radio. "We're pretty much surrounded and you'll have to take us out of here." But I still didn't know their precise location. I kept searching. Vainly.

Because of the clouds, rain, and low altitude, our field of vision was severely restricted. The ground disappeared as we went into some ragged clouds and I jammed the stick forward, hoping to see the ground before hitting one of the cloud-buried hills. Okay, ground again.

"Russ, I want you to transmit a steady tone on your radio. Just key the mike and hold it. I'm going to locate you electronically." I flipped the FM homing function switch on. The FM homer was aural with no cockpit needles to point to the source. Once the "home" function was selected, there would only be tones, dots, and dashes, over the radio. Any voice transmissions would be blocked by the homing signal. It also didn't solve the ambiguity problem; a series of turns would have to be flown to deter- mine if the flight path was headed toward or away from the source. After 15 seconds, I flipped the homing function switch off.

"Payoff, payoff, payoff," I heard on the radio, which was the codeword for when I passed over the team. The choppers chimed in. "They gave you a 'Payoff'. Did you see them?" No, I didn't, but I had probably missed them in the dense elephant grass. I could imagine the team's disappointment to see me fly overhead and not see the O–1 rack into a steep turn around them, followed by a wing rock, indicating that I had spotted them. The chopper's transmission reminded me they were running low on fuel. My anxiety and frustration were building. We were so close to finding the team. I had the helicopters depart the orbit point on a northerly heading.

"Okay, Russ, I hate to ask you to do this, but I need a smoke. The choppers are on their way." A few seconds later a purple smoke cloud blossomed above the wind-whipped elephant grass. They were located on the crest of a small, undulating knoll.

"I have your smoke." I flew, still at 300 feet, over the team. I could see four people huddled in the grass, no signs of enemy activity. I drew no ground fire. We were running out of time. I cleared in the pick-up helicopter, with the gunships remaining at the ready. Normally, I'd have the gunships make an ID pass over the team before bringing in the pick-up chopper, but everyone knew where the team was. But just as the helicopter approached a hover attitude, all hell broke loose.

"We're taking fire! We're taking fire! It's hot!" the crew frantically transmitted. I could hear the slugs hitting the fuselage, and the door gunners returning fire with their M–60s. I saw the elephant grass part, and from dozens of camouflaged spiderholes and gun emplacements, automatic weapons fire poured at the helicopter. *Oh shit, it's a trap and I got sucked in.* The patient and clever bastards wouldn't shoot at me. They were waiting for the helicopter.

"Get out of there, get out!" I shouted over the radio, as the chopper vainly struggled back into the sky. All the fresh gun emplacements that I'd seen the day before had been covered with elephant grass, and each contained NVA regulars with automatic weapons. I picked out the gun emplacement closest to the team and in one motion, reached up, hit the arm switch over my head, and squeezed off a rocket. The gunships were on the tail of my smoke rocket and poured machine gun and rocket fire into the emplacements. In the meantime, the pick-up chopper had banked around to the left, climbing to 200 to 300 feet, but kept right on banking and rolled over, plunging steeply, nose first, into the elephant grass. It burst into a ball of flame.

"Bring it closer FAC, bring it closer," the team transmitted. The gunships rolled in for a second run. I focused on the gun position that had the best field of fire and dove at the emplacement, trying to draw their fire. No luck. They shot out the fire control system on the lead gunship. I orbited to the north to give the gunships room to maneuver. We were being slaughtered. I switched to the VHF radio and called Hillsboro.

"Hillsboro, this is Snake. I have a Mayday. I have Americans in critical contact, a chopper shot down, and no fire support. I desperately need A–1s with CBUs or napalm."

"Roger, Snake. We have no resources. Nothing's flying and we may be heading home ourselves." While talking to Hillsboro, I heard parts of an FM transmission instructing the team to break up and escape and evade. The helicopters then transmitted on FM that they were at critical fuel and returning to base. The team, overhearing the FM transmission, realized that rescue was slipping from their grasp. Tears came to my eyes and to this day, I don't know if they were tears of anguish or anger.

"FAC, please help us. We're hit bad." The team was back on the radio. This is what war was all about. It's not about political goals, championing the rights of the oppressed, and fighting for one's country or anyone else's. It's about a brave soldier, a sergeant, who was looking for help, faithful to his small unit, trying to get them out alive, and would not abandon his wounded comrade, even when instructed to do so. It was the unparalleled demonstration of personal warrior values.

"Okay, Russ. I'll do my best." Alone, armed only with smoke rockets and smoke grenades, it was all my war now. I was east of the team, trapped under the 300-foot cloud deck. I pushed the stick forward, crammed the throttle full open, and accelerated as fast as I could make that little Cessna go. I told Tommy to look to the left and check out the downed chopper for survivors, while I looked to the right to pick out the team and toss some smoke grenades for distraction. I leveled off at 50 feet above the grass, doing 120 mph, and knifed between the team and the chopper. Unseen bullets snapped past the window. Out with the yellow smokes, thanks to that young airman in Nha Trang.

"Look out FAC! On the left!" screamed Tommy, as I looked up to see a fusillade of tracers converging on us. It was the guns that hit the chopper and they were looking for their second kill. I yanked back on the stick so hard I thought the wings would come off, as we hurtled straight up into the clouds, the tracers falling below us. Now I had a problem. The attitude gyro had tumbled, the airspeed was bleeding off, and I had no visual references with which to control the aircraft. We were going to die in a crash!

Instinctively, I released back pressure, gently fed in right rudder, knowing that should bring the nose down, to gain airspeed before we stalled. Hopefully, we would break out of the clouds before we hit the mountainside. I saw grass. The nose was pointed down, the wings were straight, and as fortune would have it, I was aimed at a gun emplacement. I had done a wingover in the clouds. You bastards, I thought, I bet you're surprised to see me, as I hosed off a rocket at point-blank range and pulled up on the far side of the gun. I looked over my shoulder, expecting to see the emplacement engulfed in smoke and white phosphorus. The sergeant at Nha Trang guaranteed it. Nothing happened. I was so close to the gun that the rocket hadn't traveled far enough for the fuse to arm. No explosion. It was nothing more than a high speed spear. Buddha saved your ass, Nguyen!

I flew to the east, to a clear area that was away from the mountains and out of range of the guns, and listened for anything on the radios. I monitored Guard channel on the UHF in case any of the chopper crew had survived, which was doubtful, and were trying to call. Nothing.

After 10 minutes of all quiet, I told Tommy over the intercom that we were returning to take another look and to keep a sharp watch. I looked over my shoulder to see his reaction, he nodded affirmative, and I noticed he had a lapful of hand grenades and his M–16 poised to fire out the window. If Tommy was ready to continue the fight, so was I.

We initially flew over the team's position. All I could see was trampled grass. There was no sign of them. We then flew over the helicopter. A whisp of smoke emanated from the crumpled, blackened hull and dissipated in the gale. There was no sign of movement. We had completely lost a team, two Americans, four Vietnamese. I was the last person to see or talk to them. We had lost the pick-up helicopter; two pilots, two door gunners, and a Special Forces medic. Seven Americans, four Vietnamese, brave warriors, dead or unaccounted. I knew them all. I was shaking. The tears returned, streaming down my face. I could taste the salt. I was helpless.

The NVA must have been satisfied. They didn't bother to shoot at us, but we were unwilling to press our luck any further. I focused on getting ourselves home to Khe Sanh. The aircraft itself was flawless. The premonition of the mechanics in Nha Trang was realized. I had pushed that aircraft far beyond its design limitations. We were still getting battered by the turbulence, the airframe absorbing one jolt after another. Through the entire episode, Tommy was steadfast, unperturbed, and a comforting presence. We deserved a smoother flight home so I turned west and then south, flying at 1,000 feet, under the clouds, and over the grasslands of Laos. I intended to approach Khe Sanh through the back door.

During the 20-minute flight to Khe Sanh, I had time to reflect on what had transpired. In the seven months that I had been with Delta, this had been the first time that I had lost a team or a helicopter when I was directly involved as the mission FAC. Skinner had lost a chopper in Song Be, Moreau had been ambushed in war zone C, and the Rangers had been shot up in both places, but somehow I had been able to get the teams out and keep the helicopters intact. We had used every bit of wherewithal and cunning that we could muster. Sometimes it was the skillful accuracy of the helicopter gunships. Other times it was the saturation ordnance of the fighters, or we would slip the pick-up chopper in, right under Charlie's nose, before he even knew what happened. Then at night there was Spooky with his Gatling guns that kept the VC at bay. My luck had run out.

Now I had another small challenge: to get the machine on the ground in a 50-knot crosswind without killing us both or cartwheeling down the runway. The Army field manual, from what I recalled at Hurlburt, stated that 90-degree crosswinds above 15 knots were considered dangerous, and that flight with winds exceeding 25 knots was prohibited. As I turned downwind at Khe Sanh, I considered landing into the wind on the Marine helicopter pad. With the strength of the wind, I could stop in about 100 feet. There was only one problem; the pad was covered with CH–46 helos.

As I turned base, I remembered how chagrined I was in March when it took me three tries to land at Tiger Town. I elected to use no flaps. I wanted the smallest wing area possible. I stuck the right wing down, into the wind, to kill the drift, and cross-controlled with left rudder to keep the nose aligned with the runway. I hit on the right wheel, but every time I tried to slow the airplane to put the left wheel and tail wheel on the runway, the plane would be blown to the left edge of the runway. I realized what was happening. The runway was covered with rain and mud, and the wheels were sliding sideways as soon as I touched down. OK, another try, as I pushed the throttle forward and climbed onto the downwind once again. This time I aligned the aircraft with the far right edge of the runway and picked an area that had less mud. Success. One hour and five minutes of flight time; fleeting for us, but eternal for others. Tommy and I were safe; I had cheated death once again.

I walked into the ops tent. The staff's primary concern was the fate of the helicopter and that of the crew. They started to ask me questions. Yes, I saw the chopper go down. No, I didn't think anyone could survive the crash. Yes, I flew over the chopper afterward. No, I didn't see any signs of life. No, I didn't see any NVA near the chopper, except for the bastards that opened up on Tommy and me. No, I didn't see any team member get on the helicopter. Right, the helicopter only approached a hover before it was driven off by ground fire. No, I don't think anyone could jump up 10 feet and get into the helicopter. The questions continued. No, I didn't see anyone jump from the helicopter. No, I didn't see any bodies. The fire was out. The helicopter was only smoking. Why? Had anybody put it out? No. Probably because there was hardly any goddamn fuel left on it, since you all dee-deed out of there due to low fuel. Now I was aggravated. Would you sign a statement, Lieutenant, to what you have just told us? Yes, I would. Thank you, Lieutenant. That will be all.

"But what about the team? Don't you want to know about Russ and Willie?" I asked.

"Thank you, Lieutenant. I said that will be all." I left the tent. Confused. Dejected.

I walked to the radio jeep and thanked my ROMAD for his help in seeking fighter support. My canteen cup was still on the hood. I dumped the coffee into a puddle, now a small lake, and headed to my tent. I was drenched and freezing. I passed the tent where the recon sergeants and the Ranger advisors were staying. They beckoned to me and I entered the dripping tent, welcoming the chance to get out of the rain. Inside, there was a ghostly light, a funereal hush, but that was understandable; they had just lost two of their own. One of the Sergeants spoke to me, quietly, comfortingly. He was older; he'd been around.

"John," it wasn't often they called me by my Christian name, "we know you did all you could. We appreciate it and we're glad you made it back." Tommy had apparently told them the details of what had happened. Walking back from the airplane, Tommy had admitted that the only time he was frightened during the entire mission was when I had to abort the first landing at Khe Sanh. Brave man.

"Well," I said, "just as soon as the weather breaks, I'll look for Russ and Willie. I know their E & E plan, and I didn't see any bodies at their location. Maybe some of them slipped away. That grass was awfully heavy."

"How 'bout a drink?" another one asked. A bottle of Scotch appeared from under a cot. I extended my canteen cup. Some others joined me. The straight whiskey burned my mouth and warmed me inside.

"Thanks," I mumbled to the closely gathered group. "They'll pay for it. Just let the weather break. I'll rain so much shit on their heads, they'll wish they'd never heard of Delta. I'll kill every one of them." After three days in Khe Sanh, Bangkok and civilization were distant memories. I had reverted to a calloused killer, vindictive, my promise of caution gone. I had the power; the troopers knew it. The war was now personal.

I entered the officers' tent, threw my gear on an empty cot, and scrounged around my kit bag until I found a dry tiger suit. The one I had on was not only wet, it stunk. I filled an aluminum basin with water, stripped, gave myself a whore's bath, and put on the clean fatigues. I felt much better. Temporarily. I reached under my cot and took out the Christmas package I had been saving. It contained a couple of wind-up toy animals that my wife had sent to me. It seemed so unreal. Under different circumstances, they would be humorous. Now everything was absurd and immaterial. Except death. That was real. This was the same tent where I had packed Charlie Swope's belongings, less than a month ago.

I tried to stretch out on my cot, to rest, the adrenaline of combat gone. But every time I closed my eyes, I could see nothing but a hail of tracers and hear the echo of Russ's plea, "FAC, Please help us. We're hit bad." So much for rest. Major Lindsey walked in. He shoved my gear aside and sat on the empty cot. He told me that he had been talking to the chopper pilots and to recon. He was recommending me for the Silver Star. Big deal. The team had been hit. I didn't save them. A chopper and crew had been lost. Charlie Swope got a Silver Star. He was dead. The last time I was recommended for the Silver Star, some desk jockey in Nha Trang or Saigon had disapproved it.

We lost the team and helicopter on Friday, December 2, 1966. That date, those events, are indelibly etched in my mind, and haunt me to this day.

Was it because I had failed or made an error in judgment? Had the enemy outsmarted me? Brave men died; and from today's perspective, it wasn't worth it. They died needlessly. Would I feel any differently if we had won? I'll never know that answer.

I created a plan to search for the missing team members. I knew Viper's escape-and-evasion route; their plan was to split up and exfiltrate to the west into Laos. As soon as the weather broke, I'd start a search for them. This is what the survivors, if there were any, either Vietnamese or American, expected. Al Groth needed indoctrination to our operating procedures. This would be a good start. I'd also enlist the help of the Tiger Hound FACs. I'd ask them, on their return flights from Laos, to alter their flight path, and watch for any signaling devices or friendly personnel on the ground. They were flying six sorties a day into Laos, and they offered to help.

Major Lindsey left Khe Sanh that same afternoon on one of the cargo flights that periodically slipped in and out whenever the weather permitted. Before departing, he called Al and me together. Al was to be the boss; as a captain, he outranked me. That was the Air Force way. I was expected to lend all possible advice and assistance, since I was the more experienced, and Al should listen to my advice. Beautiful. No more dangerous missions for me. Now my problem was to convince the Army of this.

The Army message traffic increased during the afternoon and continued into the night, with requests from Saigon and Nha Trang for more information. They wanted confirmation of the location of the downed chopper and the location of the team. I still had a difference of opinion with the Army on the precise coordinates, but we did agree that the chopper was in Laos and so was the team's last location. I realized we had a potentially embarrassing international incident on our hands. Downed U.S. Air Force and Vietnamese Air Force aircraft were scattered throughout Laos, but there were no U.S. Army helicopters in Laos, nor were there any U.S. forces in Laos. The downed helicopter and missing crew would confirm a U.S. ground incursion into Laos, which was not part of the acceptable political scenario.

A politically attuned recovery plan was implemented. A non-Delta "Hatchet Force," comprised of mercenaries and "sterile" Americans, would recover the bodies. They found the five booby-trapped and barbarously mutilated bodies neatly aligned on a trail. The recovery team was forced to flee due to the approach of enemy troops before they could recover the bodies. Subsequent air strikes were called in, followed by the insertion of a second recovery force. They recovered parts of three identifiable bodies. More air strikes were to be directed at the incriminating helicopter. I was consulted. The weather was still miserable. The command bureaucracy decided on a B–52 strike using massive carpet-bombing techniques through the clouds. B–52 targets were now requested from Saigon, with review at

Hawaii and Washington. The bombs missed. I think the "cover-up" coordinates were confused with the correct coordinates.

Another portion of the command-directed political plan was revealed. The day following the loss of the team, I was summoned to the operations tent for a meeting with the Delta commander. The weather was unsuitable for flying. I still had no personal knowledge of the fate of the team, other than what I saw and experienced the previous day. The Army didn't realize that I was no longer the senior-ranking Air Force officer, but it didn't matter much to me. I'd keep Al advised.

"Lieutenant," said the Lt. Colonel, "are you aware of the E & E plan of the missing team?"

"Yes, sir. They plan to exfiltrate west into Laos. Shouldn't be too difficult, since my last plot had them in Laos." I pointed to the map. "They intend to follow either one of these narrow river valleys, until it opens up here, near the village of Ban Nathon, a distance of maybe fifteen or twenty klicks, depending on which route they take. Should take them at least a few days. They're wounded, or at least Stark is. I've already advised the Tiger Hound FACs to keep a sharp eye, and to be particularly careful if they put any air strikes in the area. I'll search the area as soon as the weather breaks. I shouldn't have much trouble spotting them from the air, once they reach the grassland area."

"Lieutenant, you are not to search for the team. You are to remain within our assigned area of responsibility. Do you understand?" I couldn't believe it. The team was to be abandoned. A commander would not abandon his own men. It must have come from Saigon. Maybe higher. Good God, what was happening? The institutional value system had collapsed; the integrity of the commander had been prostituted. It was obvious he was following orders, orders to abandon the search for the team. Maybe there were other avenues of search, but I didn't know about them.

"Well, sir," I responded, "although I'm assigned to Delta, my rules of engagement, as an Air Force pilot, permit me to overfly Laos, and if necessary conduct air strikes by obtaining clearance from the airborne command post, which has a Laotian official on board."

"Just a minute, Lieutenant." He summoned another officer into the tent. Reinforcements. He continued, "I was telling Lieutenant Flanagan that he is forbidden to fly outside the area. He assures me that he has the proper authority to do so. I just want it to be known that if you go down, we're not coming to look for you. You're on your own."

I had been set up. Not only did he have a witness to my proclamation of authority, but now he had a valid disclaimer for any responsibility for my welfare.

"Yes, sir. I understand." I saluted and hurried out of the tent. Shaken. I'd been with Delta almost eight months and served under four Army commanders. The recon teams, the Rangers, and the chopper pilots trusted me implicitly. I firmly believed that to a man, if I went down, everyone would do their utmost to rescue me, just as I would do for them. But now I was cut off. The trust and camaraderie of warriors had been overridden by the command structure. I didn't know what to tell Al or the members of recon. Al was yet to be trained in the techniques and procedures of Delta. Could I lead him into Laos, knowing that immediate rescue was not available? And what about Russ, Willie, and the four Vietnamese who were counting on me to search for them? Where was my honor code now? My values? Do I tell the truth, cover up, or quibble?

I spotted Al. "We have a problem. The Army doesn't want us going into Laos. If we go, we're on our own. If we don't go, the troops will wonder why. They are anxious to fly with us, to look for Viper. If we tell the truth, there's liable to be a mutiny or a serious degradation of morale."

"You're right, John. What do you suggest?" So this is what command and decision making was all about. He bucked it back to me.

"Well, Al, for the first time in three months of flying in I Corps, we have the security and mutual support of two airplanes. We'll fly always in pairs, over Laos only in good weather, and keep Hillsboro advised. If we get into any trouble, they can send one of the Air Force Jolly Greens out of Dong Ha, or NKP or wherever, to pick us up. Screw the Army."

"Fair enough. Let's do it. And don't tell the Army." It was a good decision and avoided confrontations. We would do what we believed was right. But we were taking risks again, and I was definitely antirisk. We would search for Russ and Willie and the Vietnamese.

The weather continued marginal for the next five days. At least we were able to get airborne. Street St. Laurent's team was extracted without incident. We continued our search for the missing team. We picked up two of the Vietnamese members, north of Khe Sanh. From their debriefing, they indicated that they were able to make their escape during the confusion of the battle. My deception had apparently worked. When I threw out the smoke grenades, the enemy fled to their bunkers, thinking that an air strike was coming. They confirmed that Willie Stark was badly wounded, and Russ Bott wouldn't leave his comrade. The rescued Vietnamese thought they were taken prisoner. This correlated with my last pass over the team's position, where I saw nothing but trampled grass. The remaining two Vietnamese were presumed killed.

Delta continued to insert teams throughout the area. We were using new map codes now; the others had been compromised. The teams observed enemy movements along the trails. Processions of NVA troops marched single file through the night, past our hidden teams. From a safe distance, the teams saw small lights, evenly spaced, weaving through the jungle. From these observations, Intelligence extrapolated the volume of enemy traffic. One intrepid team crept within earshot of the jungle trail. They discovered that every fifth enemy soldier was carrying a small lantern or shielded candle. The size of the enemy force had been grossly underestimated. We were observing the early buildup of NVA forces for the inglorious siege of Khe Sanh that was to begin a year later.

I was now more determined to find the NVA forces. They were obviously buttoning up someplace during the day, which meant that sleeping platforms, bunkers, arms caches, and supply points had to be in the area. The problem was to find their precise location in order to hit them with air strikes. I also had a promise to keep. I wanted to even the score for the loss of Russ, Willie, and the helicopter crew.

The Delta commander, with the concurrence of his Vietnamese counterpart, Major Tut, ordered a force reconnaissance by a platoon of Rangers. This tactic had been successful in war zone C, and in Khe Sanh in November, when they had uncovered the supply stations. A suitable landing zone was selected about 15 klicks east of the previous reconnaissance, but located on the opposite side of the north-south mountain range. The presence of converging trails and a readily available water supply indicated the possible location of a major way station. The four choppers, escorted by the gun ships, went into the LZ only to be driven off by intense ground fire. Hillsboro diverted a flight of A–1s loaded with CBUs to help us. We pounded the area with air strikes, but the mountain twilight thwarted the reattempt of the helilift. In spite of the aborted mission, Delta did its job. As a reconnaissance unit, it confirmed the presence of concentrated enemy forces. As a bonus, the gunships and Skyraiders beat up a few Charlies.

The monsoon weather broke temporarily with crystal clear skies and occasional cloudy and showery afternoons. Adler and his boss, the intelligence officer, meticulously debriefed the teams and recorded the sightings on the intel map. A pattern began to emerge. Most enemy activity was spread from the northwest corner of the area, near Laos, where we lost the team, and extended to the east and southeast toward the coast and Khe Sanh. As customary, the recon sergeants would fly with Al and me in the backseat of the O–1s. With their sightings from the jungle as a foundation, we located and plotted the most heavily used trails. We scheduled flights of fighters daily and bombed along the trails, seeking the arms caches and hidden caves. We had taken some large caliber ground fire from a mountainside area. One of our road-runner patrols confirmed the location. The position gave a commanding view of the entire river valley and provided covering fire for the enemy trail complex that snaked along the valley floor. It was a heavy weapon which would fire one or two rounds and then a smoke ring would emerge from the jungle. It was a 57mm recoilless rifle that alternated between firing explosive rounds at the Hueys when they landed, and cannister rounds of buckshot at the O–1s when we overflew the valley. This was the weapon that had shot down Charlie Swope and his observer three weeks prior in the same area. Recently, we had taken some buckshot hits in the tail and aft fuselage of the O–1s.

Al and I evaluated the gun threat with the Delta intelligence staff. In spite of the overcast cloud deck, we decided to take out the gun position before the NVA moved it. The visibility was three miles in the mountains and five miles over the coast, good enough for a tightly controlled air strike. There was a Demon flight of Air Force F–4C Phantoms scheduled for that afternoon. We had to communicate the decision up-channel to increase our chances of success.

Al and I sloshed through the mud from the TOC to the radio jeep. Al was medium height, slight of build, and had blond hair—a contrast to my six foot three, two hundred pounds, and dark hair. We were like Mutt and Jeff. The troopers of Project Delta were initially suspicious of unproven newcomers, but with my tutelage and his tenacity, Al earned the acceptance of the Delta professionals.

"Sarge," I said to our ROMAD, who was quickly learning the subtleties of clandestine operations. "I want you to call Water Pipe on HF and tell them we want Mark 82 snake-eyes on the Demon flight, fourteen hundred hours TOT." It was nine o'clock. That would allow five hours to reconfigure the ordnance, if snakes weren't already loaded. We needed the high drag fins on the 500-pound bombs in order to work under the cloud deck. "Also, tell them the new rendezvous is TACAN Channel 46. The target is a gun emplacement on a mountainside about twenty miles west of the rendezvous. Elevation approximately 1,000 feet." We would bring the fighters to a flat, coastal rendezvous instead of the mountains of Khe Sanh. After flying backseat in the F–4, I knew any additional information helped the fighter jocks plan their mission. They would get their weather briefing before takeoff.

Al and I launched on a visual reconnaissance mission in the two O–1s. We contacted the three teams that were in the jungle. Nothing new had developed since the previous night, but one of the teams wanted a position verification. They were in the western sector of the area. We accomplished that without incident. We headed to the eastern sector where the gun was. Instead of following the safer valley route, we took the shortcut across the saddle that separated our operating area. With the 1500-foot cloud deck, we were 500 feet above the terrain when we crossed the saddle. Some sporadic tracer rounds from a machine gun reached out for us. The gun was well to our south and the rounds were falling short. We flew along the east-west valley where we suspected the recoilless rifle was located. I orbited to the south while Al went looking for the gun. Suddenly, I saw the initial muzzle flash.

"Break right, break right," I shouted over the VHF radio. The gunners fired from Al's blind seven o'clock position. They had waited in ambush until he passed them. They missed. The telltale smoke ring floated above the jungle. Abruptly changing the flight path compounded the tracking problem for the gunners. They only got off one round. I circled the location on my map and punched the mike button.

"Let's get outta here."

"Roger that," Al responded.

Back on the ground at Khe Sanh, Al and I planned how we would get that gun. I had the gun plotted. It was two-thirds up the mountainside, between 1,200 and 1,300 feet, and just below the cloud deck. The top of the mountain chain was buried in the clouds.

"Al, we're going to split up," I said. "You stay in the target area as much out of sight as possible. I'll bring the fighters down, through the overcast, and start them up the proper valley. They'll be doing about seven miles a minute. When they're about thirty seconds out, put a smoke rocket in. Let's hope the damn thing goes off. We only have one chance."

"Will you call me when they start up the valley?" he asked.

"Sure will. Stay on Victor radio. That way the fighters won't get confused on their UHF radio. They'll have difficulty keeping track of each other. The vis is going to hell. I hope we have three miles."

"Lieutenant," shouted our ROMAD over the roar of the jeep engine and cackling radios, "Water Pipe confirmed the fourteen hundred TOT. Two aircraft. Snakes and gun."

"How many bombs?"

"They didn't say, sir." Typical. Operating at remote locations, we were fortunate to get any information. Sometimes the fighters just showed up and we would improvise as we went along.

"Sergeant Doney," I called to the ops tent. "Do you have a couple of flyers for the backseat? We're going after that big rifle or whatever it is."

"Sure do, FAC. A guy from commo and one of the Ranger advisors. They don't get much of a chance to fly." We would have four pairs of eyes on the mission. No sooner were we airborne, when I heard Demon.

"Snake zero-one, this is Demon five-one."

"Rog, Demon. Understand you're a flight of two. Where are you and how many snake-eyes do you have to go with your six-shooters?" The 20mm Gatling gun had six barrels and was carried in a centerline pod.

"How'd you know we have snakes? We have six apiece and we're forty south of Da Nang," replied Lead.

"FACs know all things in order to keep fighter jocks honest. Head for Channel four-six. Are you on top? Any holes?" I asked. I looked over my shoulder. Al, in the other O–1, was flying a loose wing position at my four o'clock. We were flying over the saddle again. No ground fire this time. I did a quick calculation. The fighters were 15 minutes from the rendezvous, Dong Ha, on the coast. So were we, but we would pass the target area on the way. I flipped to VHF.

"Al, we're five minutes from the target. When we reach the entrance to the valley, drop off and orient yourself. I'm going to Dong Ha and pick up Demon."

"Snake, Demon. We're at Flight Level 180, descending through some broken and scattered decks. Looks like a solid undercast. What do you have in mind?" I heard on UHF as I switched back to the UHF transmitter.

"Keep comin', Demon. Get yourself between layers and keep your flight together. Stay east of Channel four-six; that will keep you over the sea. We've got a 1,500-foot overcast with barely three miles visibility in the target area. Some light rain. Looks clearer to the east over the coastal plain and water."

"John, I've got the valley," said Al on VHF. I kicked the rudders in acknowledgement as Al broke off and dove under me heading to the valley. I could now concentrate on the fighters.

"Demon, when you reach Channel four-six, turn east over the water and start your penetration. You should break out at 1,500 feet. Then head back in and pick up the river that extends to the west from four-six. I'll pick you up about fifteen miles west on the 270-degree radial at the base of the mountains. Don't lose the river. It leads to a valley where the target is."

"Rog," Demon Lead acknowledged.

"Copy, Two?" I inquired. He responded with two clicks of the mike. He understood. "We're after a gun emplacement on a mountainside. Elevation is 1,200 feet, the tops of the mountain are in the clouds. There's another FAC up the valley who will mark. I'll lead you up the valley. The FAC should be at your eleven o'clock. The target will be at your two o'clock as you go up the valley. Where are you now?"

"We're just starting down to the east," replied Lead.

I continued, "You get one pass, so set up your trail spacing." I paused while Lead transmitted arming and spacing instructions to his wingman.

"Two, set Ripple, point-zero-six. Take trail spacing when we break out underneath. This one looks tight," instructed Lead. I picked up the transmission again.

"After you pickle, pull straight up until you break out on top. There's five-thousand foot mountains buried in the clouds and I don't want you staying underneath. Break, break. Snake zero-two, are you copying on Uniform?" I wanted Al to hear everything since I would hand the fighters off to him only seconds before the final bomb run.

"Rog. Copy five-by," replied Al.

"We broke out. We're turning inbound," said Demon 51.

"Two, do you have me?" asked Lead.

"Rog," his wingman responded. "I'm taking spacing in the turn."

I had controlled over a thousand fighter sorties in Vietnam, but I could still feel the adrenaline surging through my body. I glanced up the valley, toward the target. I saw Al's silvery O-1 orbiting above the ridgeline. He was exposed. If he got too close to that gun he'd get taken out before we ever had a chance to get on the target. Or the gunners would be waiting for Demon.

"Snake zero-two, stay behind the ridge line," I cautioned. I switched to intercom and asked my Green Beret for help.

"Keep a sharp eye toward the coast. I need to see those fighters as quickly as possible." The camouflaged F–4s were hard to see down low. He gave me a thumbs up. He understood.

"It's the big river, FAC?" queried Lead. I checked my map. They must be at the coast line, doing 400-plus knots.

"That's it, but it gets smaller on the other side of the town," I cautioned.

"We got it. Set 'em up hot, Two. Ripple and check retard," said Lead. Oh Christ, if those fins don't open we'll kill two pilots. Blown up by their own bombs. Like what I thought happened to Terry Griffey near Qui Nhon in May. Please God, I prayed, let those fuses be good. I can't take any more of this.

My back-seater pounded me on the shoulder and pointed excitedly to the eastern horizon. There it was. The unmistakable silhouette of the F–4 Phantom, trailing its plume of black smoke from the twin J–79s. I had Lead. Where's Two? Must be in a rain shower. Come on you ugly monsters. We're going to war!

"Demon, I got a tally on you. I'm at your eleven o'clock low, about three miles. Keep coming on that heading. Two, I've got you now. Looks good." I flipped to VHF.

"Al, they're about a minute out. Get ready." Back to UHF.

"Demon, when you get to me, I want you to take the valley that juts off about thirty degrees to the right. The FAC is two miles up the valley."

"Tally ho, FAC." Lead had me. Back to VHF.

"Lead's thirty seconds out, Al," I transmitted. The F–4 tore by me and racked into a steep bank to the new heading. I saw the O–1 pop over the ridge line, emitting a puff of smoke from under the wing, as Al fired his marking rocket.

"I see the other FAC," said Lead.

"Cleared hot. Hit my smoke," transmitted Al on UHF.

"I've got you and the smoke," confirmed Lead. Two screamed by me barely a hundred feet away. I could see the markings on the pilots' helmets. I bounced in his jetwash. He headed up the valley. I followed him. Lead climbed straight up as I saw the shock wave of his detonating bombs erupt from the mountainside. Six 500-pounders on target. Al gave a correction. He saw something.

"Two, from Lead's hit come down the mountain twenty meters and right ten meters," said Al. Lead's bombs had uncovered the edge of the gun position. Two was in. I was close enough to see the bombs come off the triple ejection racks. The bomb fins opened, slowing their descent, giving the plane sufficient time to escape the lethal shrapnel. A series of booms. *Shack!* Bull's-eye!

The Phantom's tailpipes winked red as the pilot crammed the throttles outboard into full afterburner and chased Lead up through the overcast. Exposure time was no more than ten seconds for each of the fighters. Two secondary explosions boiled up from Two's bombs. I joined on Al in a loose wing formation. We flew over the target. Devastation. The jungle canopy was blown away, logs scattered, the bunker wasted. A lump of human-shaped khaki cloth protruded from the bunker. A small fire still burned, a wisp of smoke floated across the jungle. No ground fire.

Al gave Demon the BDA, the bomb damage assessment—one occupied gun position destroyed. Lead complimented our coordinated tactics. He was on top of the clouds in brilliant sunshine. Two joined him at 20,000 feet. Far below, at a thousand feet, Al and I threaded our way under the clouds, through the mountains and valleys, back to the mud-slick runway and rain-soaked tents of Khe Sanh. We would return tomorrow, weather permitting, to destroy the supply caches along the trail network. This time we knew the gun was gone. But there would be other guns waiting for us. Somewhere.

The weather continued to hold and I used every bit of skill and experience that I had acquired over the last 11 months to inflict the maximum amount of hurt on the NVA. Al was a quick learner. He observed as fighters dropped single bombs to blow down the trees and level the deep elephant grass. I was looking for trails and bunkers. On December 17, I was systematically directing bombers through a grassland, light jungle, and trail complex, two miles east of where I had last seen the missing team. Based on the intel data, the intensity of the ambush, and my intuition, I knew there was a supply base nearby. Oxwood 02–1, a flight of Marine fighters hit the jackpot at 1140 hours at coordinates XD675648. They touched off a secondary explosion that went hundreds of feet into the air and could be seen from Khe Sanh, 15 miles away. It took them ten minutes to rip that complex apart, as I surgically spread the bombs around trying to determine the size of the complex. Al followed with another flight of fighters, Bengal 07 and 09, and he did even better than I did. I knew my war was over. My job was to cover Al. I was a spectator at last.

We uncovered another supply complex at XD758648 and a network of caves at XD784642. We had found the main supply line that extended eight miles east from the Laotian border and only two miles south of North Vietnam. We had the hottest targets in all of I Corps. In spite of the juris-dictional disputes among the Marine DASC at Dong Ha, the Air Force DASC at Da Nang, and the airborne command post, Hillsboro, over Laos, we all worked together for those four days. We didn't have to request fighters. They were sent to us as soon as the various command and control agencies knew we were airborne. The radar site at Dong Ha, Water Boy, was diverting fighters returning from North Vietnam missions that had fuel and ammo. The F–4s, instead of looking for elusive truck parks and underwater bridges in Laos, could not hit targets that gave instantaneous job satisfaction, massive secondary explosions. The sky was clear, all we had to do was instruct the fighters to head for the smoke. From altitude, they could see it from 20 and 30 miles away. We were controlling flights of three and four aircraft each from the Air Force, Marines, Navy, and VNAF, with every ordnance combination imaginable, from 5-inch Zuni rocket pods to 1,000-pound bombs to napalm. We had two and three flights stacked up, waiting to hit the targets. We worked fighters that I'd never seen and call signs I'd never heard before. With the clear weather, we directed some of the administrative and rear-echelon pilots flying their monthly sortie or two. They at least hit close to the target. This was now a battle of bomb tonnage. There were plenty of targets.

The VNAF Skyraiders were the best. They had a scent for the targets and would press the attack, undaunted by the ground fire. There was always light to moderate ground fire so even the rear-echelon types could say they experienced true combat. The NVA were never able to bring any concentration of ground fire to bear because we either maintained constant target coverage, neutralizing the guns, or alternated targets using the element of surprise. The fighters took hits but sustained no serious damage. Some of the Air Force F–4s were disappointing. They showed up with all napalm. They had been diverted from heavily defended targets in the North Vietnam panhandle. They had been instructed to dive-bomb their naplam which, although safer, was not the most accurate delivery. In spite of my exhortations, they insisted on dive-bombing it. Maybe it was command directed. We wasted those sorties. As more replacement pilots were coming into the pipeline, we were noticing a significant degradation of aggressiveness and accuracy. We, the customers, suffered the loss of quality.

On December 19, we peaked in our four-day concentrated bombing spree. We directed over 50 sorties, expending over 100,000 pounds of bombs and napalm, and untold amounts of rockets and CBUs. We didn't bother with strafe unless we caught troops in the open. Virtually every bomb crumpled a bunker and touched off an explosion. The napalm started secondary fires wherever it hit. Even the rockets, 2.75-inch and 5-inch, did damage as they snaked into the hillside caves. Personally, I was taking no chances. I was approaching the end of my tour and I was determined to leave Vietnam alive. I was firing my marking rockets from a half-mile away and from altitudes of 3,000 to 4,000 feet. They hit close enough for government work. There were no ground troops in jeopardy. Al was doing a great job. I wouldn't let him take any chances either. He was still my ticket home.

Our Special Forces troops who flew with us loved the action. Doney's rotation scheduled was working; everyone who wanted to fly had the opportunity. For so long they had prowled through the jungle, always wary of an ambush or firefight, never sure what card fate would deal them next. Now they flew with Al and me in relative safety in good weather, as we destroyed one complex after another and killed every visible NVA soldier. We were getting even for Russ and Willie, for the two Vietnamese team members, for the mutilated helicopter crew, and for Charlie Swope and Sgt. Glidden. But it was time to get out of Khe Sanh. We advised CO-MUSMACV of what we'd found. Our reconnaissance and intelligence gathering was complete. The entire area was honyecombed with supply networks and observation points. Delta did its job and we took our losses. We hit the NVA bad. But the worst was yet to come for the Marines: the infamous siege of Khe Sanh in 1967–68.

The weather closed in at Khe Sanh once again. The monsoons crept in, but our mission was over. No teams were out, the reports were compiled, the messages sent. Christmas was approaching, as incongruous as it seemed. Delta was ready to return to Nha Trang. The airlift had been requested to move us back. My ROMAD had done an excellent job. He wanted action in the field and we didn't disappoint him. On the morning of December 21, 1966, I walked across the field and said good-bye to the Tiger Hound FACs. For ten weeks they had provided physical and moral support. The five crew chiefs of the 20th Tactical Air Support Squadron based at Da Nang took on the additional workload of our aircraft, spending many an hour maintaining, fueling, and arming them. They worked in the worst of the monsoons, with absolutely no cover except the storage containers for their tools and meager spare parts. These were the men who kept us going. I appreciated them as did all the FACs, but I'm not sure anyone else did.

Al and I threw our gear in the respective backseats of the O–1s and taxied out for our last takeoff from Khe Sanh. I took the lead and Al followed me. It was like my previous departure from Khe Sanh in November, drizzle and fog. I could barely see the end of the runway, but we were departing under visual flight rules, nevertheless. We had no other choice. Al tucked his wing behind mine, we pushed up the power, I nodded my head, and we rolled down the runway. We lifted off with our wingtips overlapping and barely five-foot fore-and-aft separation. As soon as we cleared the plateau, I descended into the river valley with Al still tucked under my wing. After two months I knew my way around the mountains and valleys of Khe Sanh. The visibility gradually improved to where we could see the ground from 500 feet and we pressed eastward to the coast and then swung south to Da Nang. I took no chances. I kept us over the water. It was a longer flight but no lucky shot could get me. One hour and twenty minutes later, we shut the engines down on the Da Nang ramp.

I went to the DASC, which was situated close to the airfield. Lt. Col. Parker, the DASC director, and Lt. Col. Brewington, the corps ALO, had their hands full since there was never any definitive command responsibility regarding deployment of TAC Air in I Corps. Wherever the Marines went, so too went their assumed authority for airspace control. Even though the Delta operation area was a no-fire zone to all other agencies, and the DASC maintained that restriction, the Marines still managed to put a radar bombing mission dangerously close to one of our teams in November. Col. Parker apologized profusely. He remembered Rudy Bishop's irate radio transmission. I personally thanked them for their assistance and briefed the intelligence officer on our bombing results and sightings. They had eagerly followed our sustained bombing campaign in the northwest corner of Vietnam. We ran up the sortie count for them. The results of the Marine sorties never got into the Air Force intelligence system unless we forwarded them over the radio. I admitted that we were so busy at times that I'd only process the major results. There was only so much room to write with grease pencil on the window of the aircraft, which was our scorecard.

The weather had improved and we climbed to 8,000 feet for my last trip down the coast to Nha Trang. I remember my lighter had run out of fuel and I opened the Air Force survival packet looking for matches with which to light my pipe. There were no matches in the packet. Typical. For a year, I had waged a war with critical shortages and malfunctions; I had no right to expect anything different. I gnawed on my pipe.

We passed my familiar battlegrounds once again. I felt like Odysseus on the last leg of his epic return from Troy. I had overcome insurmountable obstacles, I had toyed with death, and by the grace of God, I was still alive. I was heading home, yet I felt sad. We left some people behind in the jungle, some dead, some alive, and some unknown—the tragedies of war—and I was the last person to see or talk to them.

Two hours and forty-five minutes after takeoff from Da Nang, I returned 498 to the mechanics at Nha Trang. Al touched down right behind me in 601. We were lucky. Between the two aircraft, we had taken only a half-dozen hits during the operation. Having the second aircraft was the key. The mechanics at Nha Trang were glad to see us back. They were pleased with me. Outside of a few bullet holes, I returned their airplane intact. True to form, the cockpits were littered with grenade pins and spent cartridges, and filthy with the red mud of Khe Sanh. So were we. I thanked them for a good bird. I owed my life to their skill and dedication and I told them so.

I had trained my successor. I had watched the warrior sword of the Delta FACs pass from Ken Kerr, to Jim Ahmann, to myself and Skinner Simpson, and now I passed it to Al Groth. I had watched others unsuccessfully attempt to wield it, and one, Charlie Swope, fell honorably in combat. I had worn it longer than any other Project Delta FAC.

It had been a costly operation for Delta, but we did our job to the very best of our ability. It was four days to Christmas and I had the best Christmas present ever. My war was over.

13

Winding Down:
Re-entry into the World

The atmosphere in the Delta compound had changed in the four weeks that I had been in Khe Sanh. The forward elements, the fighters and flyers, were still in Khe Sanh, awaiting a break in the weather to fly the choppers out and airlift the equipment back to Nha Trang. I didn't recognize many of the faces except for some of our loyal Nung and Vietnamese workers, our hooch maids, handymen, waitresses, and cooks. I occupied my time with beach trips, introducing Al Groth to writing after-action reports, and tending to the details for my transition to the United States.

The troopers returned on the transport planes from Khe Sanh. Once again, the 281st's helicopters were on the alert pad. I caught the usual good-natured ribbing about Al's and my hasty and hazardous departure from the Marine base. The returnees recognized the personnel and attitude changes at the base. The seasoned jungle fighters were now standing formations like raw recruits. I was "spoken to" by a newly assigned Army major about drinking beer on the steps of my hooch, while observing the sunset. It was my ritual to watch the shimmering heat of the day fade into evening mists. Ever superstitious, it was my responsibility to supervise twilight. This kept the VC from setting up mortar and RPG positions outside the perimeter for night attacks.

My stateside assignment had finally been resolved and confirmed. My logical explanation of sending me back to Cape Cod to my family and my old flying unit penetrated the assignment bureaucracy of the Air Force. The Air Force administrative specialist in the 21st Tactical Air Support Squadron in Nha Trang, while reviewing my file, noted that I had never been granted a rest and recreation leave and cordially invited me to take advantage of same. "Why should I bother?" I asked. My interest was to get out of

Vietnam as soon as possible, maybe even two or three weeks prior to my official one-year rotation date. I was through fighting.

"Because, Captain, the regulation says that everyone serving in a combat zone is entitled to an R and R," said the administrative officer. After being a lieutenant for four and a half years, I still hadn't adjusted to being addressed as captain, but I recognized an opportunity to get home.

"Okay. Book me on the next open flight to Hawaii, with orders for continued travel, PCS, to the United States." I would have my wife join me. We could get reacquainted without outside distractions, and then continue home together to our children. She would welcome the escape from the cold, damp New England winter and the inevitable post-holiday depression. Besides, I needed an excuse for the pre-departure suntan that I was determined to acquire on the beaches of Nha Trang.

"We can't do that. Everyone who goes on R and R must return to Vietnam."

"Fine. How about Hong Kong?" I had heard many stories about the sights and shopping opportunities of this cultural and business crossroads of the Orient. "Next available opening, and then please book me on a flight back to the States. My DEROS is twenty-six January." I was determined to make myself as scarce as possible until my official return date. I had become an inveterate coward.

"Yes, sir. We'll send notification to you." He looked at a file. "Are you still with Detachment B–52, 5th Special Forces Group?" he inquired.

"Yes, that's correct. Here, in Nha Trang," I replied. The administrative system had finally found me. I had been addressed as "sir" by a fellow officer. Respect in the military was bestowed rather than earned. My perception of the typewriter warriors was changing; they weren't so bad after all.

Christmas Eve, a Saturday, arrived before I even realized it. We would have the traditional lull in fighting; no combat operations were to be initiated. Cardinal Spellman, the military vicar and archbishop of New York, my home diocese, was to offer Mass in the group compound. Walking from the Delta compound to attend the Mass, I recalled I had once served as his altar boy. I noticed the sentry towers, manned by watchful eyes that peered across the rice paddies, searching the hillside beyond. Machine guns protruded from the sandbagged redoubts. Several hundred worshipers, Americans and Vietnamese, had gathered in the open air for this holy occasion. Few had ever been in the presence of an elevated prelate of the Church, only one step from the pope. God and Catholicism were a common bond.

The Mass began. The cardinal granted us general absolution from our sins. We could now receive the Eucharist, untainted by the stain of sin. In an instant, all my sins had been removed; any transgression that I had committed against God, the moral law, or my fellow man, had been absolved. I thought back to the cathedral in Qui Nhon, the church in Song Be, the Masses in the field. It seemed so absurd. Praying, killing, and now absolution, as if it all hadn't happened. The slate was wiped clean. I wanted Him to bring back the lives of my friends. The list had grown in a year.

I nervously watched the surrounding hillsides, the same places where I had directed numerous air strikes, listening for the ominous WHUMP of a mortar. The VC were Buddhists. We respected the sanctity of the temples scattered about the countryside, but when the VC sought refuge in them, we attacked. There was no reason for the VC to treat us any differently. The Christmas congregation was nothing more than a lucrative target.

I shifted under the hot sun, missing my Aussie hat, which I had surrendered for a green beret. That seemed so long ago; so many missions flown since then. God had been good to me. I was still alive. The war was over for me. I would kill no more. The bells tinkled from the altar, announcing the Communion. This time the host didn't stick to the roof of my mouth.

Major Jim Lindsey came to my hooch the Tuesday afternoon following Christmas. "Get a clean uniform and shine your boots. We're going to Saigon tomorrow." I was in my usual attire of Bermuda shorts (I'd had them made on Duc Lop street) and Ho Chi Minh sandals, soled with automobile tires.

"What for, Jim?" I asked. I had a handball game arranged for the morning and intended to head for the beach in the afternoon.

"We've been invited to the TACC to brief the staff on Project Delta and close air support. We'll take an O–1. Plan to return on Thursday." An O–1 was immediately placed at our disposal. I learned a new lesson: Instead of asking for an airplane for a combat operation, I should have been asking for airplanes to visit generals. It brought more expeditious results.

I didn't like the idea of flying 200 miles to Saigon. I only wanted to see the jungle again from 30,000 feet, bound for the States. Nevertheless, it was an enjoyable flight. Tan Son Nhut was as busy as it had been a year ago when I first arrived in-country. We stayed at the Special Forces villa, Detachment B–55, on Duong Pasteur Street in Saigon. They had real beds, private rooms, and were gracious and appreciative hosts.

We started our briefings, which were a series of conversations with one or two officers from the air staff, gradually working our way up the chain of command. We had to first satisfy several colonels, then a one-star general, with the authenticity of our mission and story. When they were as equally well-informed as their boss, we were ushered into the inner sanctum of the commander of the Seventh Air Force, Lieutenant General William W. Momyer. He was seated behind a desk commensurate with his three-star importance, but not as ostentatious as I had observed in other locales. He was wearing the light tan uniform of the era, short-sleeved shirt, open collar, and low-quarter black shoes. We wore fatigues and jungle boots.

He politely dismissed his hovering lackeys. There would be no spies, wags, or witnesses. Major Lindsey started with an explanation of Delta, its composition and mission, and the expansion of the concept with Omega and Sigma. Its effectiveness and tactics he left to me. I was impressed; General Momyer was genuinely interested. He listened attentively, asking broad, but pertinent questions. He seemed pleased that the tactical airpower entrusted to him was deployed by us sparingly and effectively, only on known targets and close air support. He had heard about "monkey-killer" and "toothpick" missions. After several minutes, he excused himself to attend a scheduled briefing, but instructed us to remain.

Once he was out of the room, Jim turned to me. "John," he said. "You're doing great, but please try not to stutter." Shit, I thought, what does he want? I'm barely out of the jungle where I had been surviving for a year, thrust in front of the big boss of the whole goddamn air war, and expected to speak like a polished orator.

"I'll try, Jim. I'm a bit nervous," I explained. My palms were sweaty, but I was chilled. I was not accustomed to air-conditioning.

"Okay," he responded. "But if he asks you what your next assignment is, mention flying the Connies, but emphasize you are in the pipeline for a faculty position to the Academy." Flying the Connies was not considered a prestigious assignment while an Academy assignment was.

"Will do." The general reentered the room. We started to rise.

"No, please remain seated," said the general. "That briefing was routine. My deputy can handle it. I'm more interested in what you have to say." We continued. He interrupted. "Why can't I put Air Force teams on the ground, to find targets like Delta does?"

I looked at Jim. He was tying his boot. "The risk is too high, sir," I replied. "These guys have been prowling the jungles for years. That's all they do. The Air Force doesn't have that experience." He nodded.

"What do you need? What can I do to help?" That was it. He had asked *the* question. A year's worth of frustrations, needless deaths, and shortages, of command ambivalence and compromised integrity, poured from me. Jim slid down in his chair, but General Momyer leaned forward, listening carefully. I had made an impact. Maybe Charlie Swope and Karl Worst had not died in vain, though it was still a high price. My only disappointment was that the general didn't see me in a filthy and reeking tiger suit, boots caked with mud, and my skin, blotched from the sun and dirt, rubbed raw from the shoulder harness, and with sores on my ass from hours of sitting on a flak vest. I don't think the general expected me to answer his question so pointedly. I sensed he was suffering similar frustrations, but at a higher level, unable to achieve acceptable resolutions.

We left General Momyer's office after exchanging banalities, including my next assignment. We had finally penetrated the five levels of Air Force command structure that existed between the FACs of Delta, the war fighters, and the Air commander in Saigon, the decision-maker. Delta, Omega, and Sigma would get the air support they needed. I had high respect for General Momyer. In later years, as I learned more about the cumbersome command structure and political obstacles of the war, my respect increased. He was a leader, not just a commander.

My euphoria of Saigon was short-lived when we returned to Nha Trang and the Delta compound. A new command philosophy was being implemented. The cruelest blow was that the Delta Hilton was placed off-limits to officers, who were encouraged to use only the newly completed Officers' Club, located in the group headquarters compound adjacent to the Delta compound. SF now reminded me of the straight-leg Army administration that I had experienced in Qui Nhon. I went to the Officers' Club and asked some questions. The club had apparently been built for the use of the Group staffers and visitors, but they were embarrassed by its sumptuousness and underutilization. The solution was to force the officers and warrants, the helicopter pilots, the nurses, and the FACs, from the Hilton. The repercussions were the erosion of camaraderie between the junior officers and the non-commissioned officers, the war-wagers and revelers of Delta; and the loss of unit cohesion, that intangible value which turns a collection of skilled individuals into an effective war-fighting unit.

I still went to the Hilton, but I was careful not to flaunt it and wore only civilian clothes. I took Al with me. I wanted him to know these brave men as well as the preceding FACs had. Al listened as Wiley Gray, one of the top recon sergeants, told about the recon member who had solid gold dog tags made in Bangkok. For religion, he had engraved "FAC—Air" on the tags. Al understood the dependency of recon on air support.

My R and R request was honored; Hong Kong for a week. Of course it didn't matter that I was to be rotated back to the States within a couple of weeks. The war had become a labrynth of statistics, and I was now included in the statistic that every GI who wanted an R and R received it. The command structure could report a 99.9 percent R and R success rate, or some other absurd statistic, along with body counts, kilos of seized rice, tonnage dropped, and sorties flown. But I didn't care, I was on a new adventure—outside of the war.

Hong Kong to me was a potpourri of civilization; spacious hotel rooms with clean sheets, concierges, Dim Sum, night clubs, Kowloon, Star ferry, scenic tours, shopping, Ocean Terminal, cable car, floating restaurants, gold traders, the Peninsula Hotel, open markets, teeming streets, polite people, and pleasures of the flesh for the attention-starved GI.

I met Ngaire, a school teacher, from Winton, Southland, New Zealand. She was on sabbatical, touring the world, spending time in whatever city or country met her fancy, and then traveling to the next city, armed with letters of introduction for her stay. She regaled me with her stories of adventure, education, diverse cultures, universal values, and pervading unity and harmony throughout the world.

I welcomed her conversation and company. I had been separated from the female perspective and refinement. While we were dining at an exclusive Chinese restaurant, I noticed an attractive Chinese woman at an adjacent table. She reminded me of Gabrielle in Qui Nhon. Our eyes met several times. During dinner, I unconsciously picked up my rice bowl and, Oriental fashion, brought the bowl to my mouth. I hesitated, my chop sticks poised over the bowl, reluctant as a Westerner to affect an Oriental mannerism. The Chinese woman, noticing my dilemma, nodded her head in approval. We exchanged smiles, sharing a fleeting intimacy unbeknownst to our respective companions. Afterward, Ngaire took me to the night club show at her hotel, the Miramar. It was my last night in Hong Kong. As I stole back to my hotel in the early hours, I realized that she had taken me from war and jungle, to peace and civilization. I called her from Kai Tak airport and thanked her. I don't think she fully understood what she had done for me.

I returned to Nha Trang. The Air Force had notified me, through Delta, that I was booked on a Pan American commercial flight, departing Saigon on January 15, for the United States. Simultaneously, the commander of Delta asked me once again if I would consider extending my tour. Delta still had only one FAC, Al Groth. I politely declined, mentioning my programmed graduate school assignment. I moved out of my Delta hooch, my usefulness exhausted, and into the Air Force barracks for my last four days in Vietnam. It was the same barracks where I had slept a year prior, where I had met the FAC who had hiked to Cambodia. Now I knew what was behind his eyes, why I couldn't see into them. They were my eyes now and I didn't want anyone to see into them. They wouldn't understand what was there and I couldn't explain it.

The enlisted men of Project Delta hosted a surprise dinner for me in one of the finer restaurants of Nha Trang. Similar to European restaurants, it was multi-floor. We were on the second floor with an open balcony that overlooked the street below. It was quiet and aloof, with yet another balcony above us. The night was clear. I remember the stars, the breezes from the South China Sea, the white tablecloths, the fine china and sparkling stemware. But most of all I remember the men; they were the war fighters from recon, commo, the Rangers, and medics, twenty of them. They presented me with an engraved watch, a Rolex, for which I paid a dollar because, "FAC, Army regulations don't allow us to give gifts to superiors, so you bought it." And they gave me a letter, signed by each of them:

Red Baron

This watch is from the men past and present who think so much of you. This watch is but a small token for the number of us that you have saved thru direct air support.

Delta Project

I still wear the watch and cherish the letter. I have kept in touch with many of the signatories over the years. Tragically, several of them died in combat, others have retired, and some have passed on after leading a life of risk and danger.

The magic day, January 15, was only two days away. Although I was physically present, my head was out of Vietnam. I shed my gear, my weapons, and my fatigues as fast as I could. Nha Trang supply was reluctant to accept my M–16 because it was issued in Saigon, but I finally convinced them that I was a noncombatant and not interested in lugging it around. They annotated my records accordingly.

I barely remember leaving Vietnam other than the interminable hours of waiting in the Tan Son Nhut terminal and the stacks of aluminum coffins at the edge of the tarmac. I heard the story of a returnee who was not allowed to board a flight because he was wearing the improper uniform. I had the wrong uniform. I wondered if they checked the coffins for the proper uniform. I went to the BX and bought the correct uniform, any size. I didn't care. I trashed my fatigues in a barrel in the terminal.

I was determined to get on a plane, any plane that was leaving. Many of my fellow officers were in tailored blue uniforms, resplendent with newly awarded decorations. From appearances, they had spent the last two months arranging ribbons and preparing to go home. I was fortunate to find an odd set of wings to put on my rumpled shirt. I pinned my Vietnamese paratrooper wings over the opposite pocket. I boarded the Pan Am jet and settled into my assigned rear seat. Commercial passengers occupied the front portion of the cabin. We taxied out. Runway congestion. The scene hadn't changed from a year ago. We took off and climbed to 30,000 feet. I didn't look back. It was finally over; or so I thought.

14
The Conflict Continues, the Values Endure

It was a raw January day as I rode the airport bus into San Francisco. By the time we had reached the terminal, a light, wind-driven rain had begun to fall. It was unseasonably cool and I was wearing a light-weight, short-sleeved uniform. The weather reminded me of the monsoon season in the Highlands. I could have used my jungle sweater, but it had ended in the trash barrel with the rest of the fetid uniforms. I claimed my suitcase and walked the four blocks to the Sir Francis Drake.

My wife would arrive the next day. She was flying from New York, leaving our two children with their paternal grandparents. Sleep was impossible. My circadian clock was on Vietnam time, reversing night and day. I thought about our daughters; they were now two and three years old. I had missed collectively 40 percent of their earliest years. I had wondered about my wife. I had not seen or talked to her in a year, 25 percent of our married life. But I was home, and Russ and Willie were someplace in the jungle. I turned on the television newscast. There was Vietnam in living color—red blood and orange napalm—the smell was missing. I quivered as I turned it off.

When I met my wife, I hardly recognized her. She had always been thin, having modeled in her college years, but now she was gaunt, her face drawn and haggard, with circles under her eyes which she had gallantly tried to hide. We embraced. We talked. We felt for each other. The year had been as hard on her as me, even more so. The constant waiting, the uncertainty, looking for my letters, but always fearing that dreaded staff car—the one bearing the chaplain, the administrative officer, and the message, "We regret to inform you that your husband/son/brother has been reported killed/

wounded/missing." But she had been spared; there would be no car, no message.

We flew east together. As we passed over the Rocky Mountains, south of Denver, I strained at the window, hoping to catch a glimpse of the Air Force Academy in the late morning sun. A flash—the sun had caught the marble and glass—it was a team signaling me from the jungle! I recoiled from the window, reminding myself there would be no ground fire.

I now fully understood the role of the Academy. So many times I had heard in the lecture halls as a cadet that we were being trained and educated as the future leaders of the Air Force. Maybe, but what they had created were individuals of inner strength and dedication, the depth of which was never realized until the fledgling Academy's graduates had faced and withstood the trials of combat. The Academy had imbued in us the classic warrior foundation; the motivation and dedication of a military professional, the code of duty, honor, and country, the values of bravery, honesty, and integrity. If we didn't have that spirit, that willingness, that commitment, we wouldn't have graduated. There were other officers who served gallantly, products of ROTC and Officer Candidate School, but theirs had been a tested and proven avenue to the battlefield. The Academy had produced its first echelon of combat veterans.

My wife knew what I was thinking. She had first met me at the Academy and had attended my graduation. She had also attended my Boston College graduation, accepting my diploma in absentia. The audience had applauded when told the reason. We talked, and played with words. She knew about Delta from my letters.

Delta
Tippy, tippy toe; through the jungles we will go.
Lookee, lookee here; Delta's air strike you should fear.
Flying, flying low; FAC brings fighters, drops the blow.
Snake-eyes dropping in; we've struck our blow at Ho Chi Minh.
Target hits we cheer; now come get us out of here.
Choppers swooping down; Delta's going back to town.

We smiled at each other. We were rebuilding the bond. "Ladies and gentlemen, please fasten your seatbelts for our landing at New York's La Guardia Airport. The temperature on the ground is twenty-eight degrees." Frigid compared to the jungle. I buttoned my blue uniform jacket. It was dark. I saw the lights from the Whitestone Bridge. It was rush hour. Our daughters would be waiting. They might recognize me. At least I was with their mother.

We deplaned through a jetway, escaping the full impact of the cold. In 1967 there were neither antihijack X-ray machines nor security guards. Passengers, well-wishers, and greeters thronged the gate area, gradually drifting to the main terminal.

"It's my Daddy! It's my Daddy!" two little voices cried out simultaneously, their squeals of joy rising above the din of the terminal. As if by magic, they were propelled into my arms, one into each, as I hoisted them above the crowd, their heads towering over mine as tiny arms encircled my neck and tears streamed down my face. Bystanders shared in our joy. I was home.

My father stood to the side, beaming with pride and privately recalling his return from military service. He was a World War II veteran. My mother had watched a husband and a son enter wartime service. She hid her tears. She was a proud lady. During the year, I had not been alone. The family had held to its values, functioning as an extended support system for me and for each other.

* * * * *

The Vietnam War for Americans dragged on until 1973. With troop strengths of 300,000 to 400,000, sometimes higher, the military institution had returned over three million men and women to the continental United States. One of my fellow FACs, upon returning from his tour, was to be mustered out. He remained at Travis Air Force Base, in California, while his records and pay were processed. "What I remember most," he told me, "were the endless lectures on how to get off drugs and draw unemployment." He received his honorable discharge papers from a clerk, with not so much as a handshake or thank you from any official.

One day it was jungle, fatigues, buddies, firefights, and work details. The next day it was cities, civies, alone, and unemployed. While the military thoroughly prepared men and women to enter the combat zone, they neglected to prepare them for reentry into society. It was more than a jet ride.

* * * * *

I returned to my former base and to my old flying squadron. Even in winter, Cape Cod was beautiful; wind-swept beaches, singing pines, blowing leaves, a solid crunch of nature underfoot, but mostly the clear air, no miasma, no burning waste, no cordite, no napalm. I flew again with some of the same sergeants; now I shared with them my war stories. Tommy Carpenter, from Delta, and his wife, visited with us. We threw a house party. Some of my officer friends were uncomfortable with my close relationship with an enlisted sergeant. They did not understand that Tommy had flown with me on many missions, and had gone into the enemy-infested jungle to pull a dead officer from his smoking wreckage. I distanced myself from those friends.

Glorious spring emerged on the Cape. Buds and flowers blossomed forth. For the previous year, I had thought of the seasons as monsoon and non-monsoon; mud and dust, hot and cold, and any combination thereof. I was weeding dandelions with a knife. My wife quietly walked up behind me, startling me. I whirled to face her, my body in a combat crouch, the knife poised. It was not over yet.

I watched more people leave the base as their turn inevitably came to serve in Southeast Asia; pilots, mechanics, electronics and weapons specialists, security personnel, clerks, cooks, supply and administration specialists. For most it was their first war, and they accepted their duty and responsibility, even though they were fully aware of the hazards as depicted by the media and recounted by returning veterans. A combat crew training squadron was formed to prepare aircrews for electronic surveillance of the Ho Chi Minh trail. The wizardry of technology—electronic sensors sown on the trail to be monitored from lumbering transports flying high above—was to supplement the jungle-stalking SF teams and intrepid FACs. General Momyer would have electronic teams to command. The fortunate departees would live in the comparative comforts of Thailand or the Philippines, safe from ground attacks and terrorism. The less fortunate would be in Vietnam. All aircrews would face the hazards of combat flying, some more than others. No one would escape the miserable onslaught of the monsoons and the insufferable heat.

I also watched the families, uprooted from their base housing and cast to the winds, forced to find accommodations elsewhere. It was hardest on the younger families who did not have the financial resources to live on the local economy, and were invariably thrust upon relatives, or a willing friend to take them in. Financial strain was inevitable as the result of separation. The military families who had relied on the medical, housing, schooling, social and psychological support systems of the base, were divorced by the institution they served. In the same manner that I was plagued with uncertainty for my reentry, so too would many of the families face similar circumstances. For them the war was a double hardship, but they faced it stoically, without complaint.

★ ★ ★ ★ ★

The widow of the FAC shot down in Tay Ninh in 1969 suffered. As the wife of a West Point graduate, she expected separations and hardships. During his Vietnam tour, she lived with relatives in a mid-western college town and enrolled in courses at the university. Due to her vicarious involvement in the war, she elected to conceal her identity, fearing harassment and ridicule. When notified of her husband's death, and fearing rejection also from the community, she withheld his obituary from the newspaper. In 1966, my wife had received applause at a university; by 1969, a widow feared retaliation. The widow, since remarried, still carries the scars.

★ ★ ★ ★ ★

Every night the evening news had the latest from Vietnam. I didn't recognize the war. The press reported nothing but casualties and the stripping and burning of villages, always with American troops in full view. I never saw footage of the advisory teams running clinics, or a new irrigation pump obtained through AID and installed by Army engineers. No one told about the bags of coffee that were flown out of Khe Sanh's plantations because the roads were ambushed, or about the French plantation owner who was providing work for the people. I heard about the disappearance of U.S. materiel in the Vietnamese supply channels, but I never heard about how they were dying in far greater numbers than any Americans. I watched graphic descriptions of the occasional bomb that hit friendlies, but I heard nothing about the pilots who faced relentless odds braving monsoons, mountains, gunfire, and darkness to relieve besieged units, outposts, and camps. The Koreans, who had committed two Army divisions plus a Marine brigade, were never mentioned; nor were the COIN forces and pilots from Australia. I couldn't find the truth; the entire story was not always revealed. As U.S. sentiment was being turned against the war, more troops were being sent, without popular support or defined purpose. I recalled a statement from one of the senior Vietnamese officers in Delta: "You Americans do not understand. We have been at war for hundreds of years. You will send many Americans and they will die because you cannot wait. We will wait." What I thought was an apocryphal statement was closer to prophetic.

I followed the aviation trade journals. The numbers of fighter sorties were announced weekly, with monthly summaries by service, Air Force, Navy, Marines. From a different perspective, I realized what was happening. A finite number of bombs, with a competitive and expandable number of sorties, yielded light bomb loads. This led credence to the story of the B–57 squadron commander who refused to lead his bombers North with token bomb loads when he could have destroyed the target with fewer airplanes, each carrying more bombs. Institutionally, we had inextricably trapped ourselves in a numerical and competitive web because we had lost sight of the objective. I thought we had one while I was in Vietnam, but now I wondered if we ever did. From the perspective of the secretary of defense there was no bomb shortage: we merely had to fly more sorties to drop the same amount of bombs. But that risked more airplanes, and in the case of the two-seat F–4 and B–57, twice as many lives were risked per sortie. We, as combat FACs, recognized that we needed more sorties to destroy a given target, and therefore requested more, which increased the sortie count. It was madness; I had become a tool of the system, implemented by the institutional hierarchy, needlessly risking my life and the lives of others. I didn't have that right, nor did the institution.

With the assistance of the media, I watched the Washington war strategy vacillate as bombing campaigns were turned on and off, to "communicate a message" and "hasten peace negotiations" with the People's government. I learned about the useless targets and restrictive policies in North Vietnam. I compared them with the lucrative and unrestricted targets that I had experienced in South Vietnam—and I couldn't obtain bombers to hit them!

The recognition and participation of the National Liberation Front became an issue of contention and an obstacle to negotiations. I laughed at this. We had spent months vainly searching for their headquarters in war zone C. Maybe they didn't exist. I would have felt much better if I could have seen their pictures in *Paris Match*, gathered in negotiations.

My family and I anxiously awaited my orders to assign me to graduate school in Boston; we had friends there. This would open new horizons. I could bring a fresh perspective to my graduate studies and, in turn, balance that with my Vietnam experiences for my cadet-students at the Academy. We did many things right in Vietnam; but we should also learn by our mistakes. Eventually, I could expect to return to an operational assignment, or a policy position with a major headquarters.

But it was not to happen. My assignment was canceled, in spite of the Academy's intervention. While I was in Vietnam, a policy had been developed at the Pentagon, curtailing Air Force–sponsored concomitant degrees. This eliminated me, regardless of the fact that I had earned my Master's degree completely on my own. As the letter form the Department of Political Science stated, "It is ironic that you have hindered yourself while trying to advance on your own." Whereas the institutional military could be of no help, the Academy held to its promise and offered me a faculty position in the Department of Economics, providing I could supplement my MBA with economics courses. However, the wartime pilot shortage precluded sufficient free time to complete the required courses.

Something was wrong. There had been an inexplicable collapse of the value system. Vietnam had been one system, where decisions were clouded by expediency, actions prompted by basic survival, and right and wrong had lost their meaning. But the same distorted system had spilled into the measured rationale of the institutionalized politico-military system, or possibly the root cause was within the institution itself. I had seen too much; I had fought too many battles; my short-lived career was over.

But the war wasn't over. It plodded on, killing our youth and our seasoned professionals, polarizing our society, destroying our institutions, and casting dispersions on all that was military, particularly in Vietnam. Our college institutions, which had previously provided the military with educated and trained officers via the ROTC program, were coerced, through political activism, to curtail their programs and, in some cases, to temporarily close their institutions. I often thought about those students who had been attending college with ROTC financial assistance—was it right to deny them an opportunity for educational advancement? Other students voluntarily dropped out of the programs. Consequently, a shortage evolved, particularly during the high demand of the war; and the caliber of junior leadership suffered, resulting in battlefield mismanagement and atrocities that shocked not only the American public, but also combat-hardened veterans.

The military and the government were not the only institutions to suffer a loss of purpose and values. Just prior to Christmas in 1972, unprecedented heavy bombing raids, including B–52s, were unleashed on North Vietnam, resulting in fruitful peace negotiations. The Paris Accords were initialed on Tuesday, January 23, 1973, effective Saturday, January 27. I had followed the progress of the talks and they were a subject of discussion at home, particularly at the dinner table on that Saturday.

"Dad," said Regina, now aged nine, "It's all over now. The war, I mean."

"Yes, it is, Reg. Let's remember to pray at Mass tomorrow for all the children whose daddies didn't come home."

"We'll pray for the daddies, too," said Monica, a year younger. "We're glad you came home. You don't talk about it much, Dad." I loved their simple beauty, their caring. They were now the same age as the little Vietnamese girl who had been my tutor in Tiger Town. They were looking for a response from me.

"There's some people we don't know what happened to. They were friends."

"Is that why you sometimes wear that bracelet? With the name on it," asked Monica. She was referring to my POW/MIA bracelet.

"Yes."

"Who is it?" It was Regina's turn to ask questions. I noticed soft tears in my wife's eyes. She was seated opposite me. The events of December 2, 1966 were still not over for me, nor the year for her. I changed the subject. With the end of the war, a full accounting of POWs was expected.

The next morning we attended our customary nine o'clock Mass at St. Catherine's in Pelham, New York. I prayed. A tremendous burden had been lifted from my shoulders, and maybe the shoulders of the country. I concentrated. I listened with anticipation to the announcements in the early portion of the Mass, expecting a letter from the cardinal to be read, or the dedication of the Mass, in thanksgiving for the end of the war. It had been six years since I had returned, and the war had continued, albeit at lesser levels in the 1970s.

The priest gave the final blessing. The Mass was now offered in the vernacular, with the celebrant facing the people. "May Almighty God bless you. . . . " The Mass was over. The priest exited to the adjacent sacristy. There had been no mention of the war! Some parishioners were starting to leave. I pushed out of my pew.

"Wait! Please," I implored, as I hastened to the front of the church. People stopped, even those in the rear of the church, closest to the doors. "My fellow parishioners," I began. "Today marks the first time that this country has not been engaged in war in over ten years." I could see the people were startled. They had become inured to the war, unaware of its longevity, removed from its consequences, and ignorant of its impact. I continued, "I served in Vietnam in 1966. It was the longest war in the history of this nation. We have lost 58,000 sons, husbands, and some daughters, too; it has polarized our nation, pitting families against each other, causing citizens to flee its borders, and I lost some good friends there. There are others that I only pray to God are among the unknown prisoners. Please join with me in offering an 'Our Father' in thanksgiving." And they did—willingly. My daughters met me at the end of their pew.

"Dad, I knew you were going to do something."

"We're proud of you. Is that one of the names on the bracelet?"

"Yes. It's Russ Bott's."

We filed from the church. Parishioners approached me and shook my hand. They thanked me individually and were glad that I spoke. But there was one particularly unnerving comment.

"I hope you don't get in trouble for what you did." I was unaware that the priest had reentered the sanctuary and had shown disapproval of my unsanctioned act. I was distressed that the Church, either officially from the cardinal, or unofficially by the local priest, had not recognized the end of the war, and a parishioner had felt compelled to offer a warning for my actions. I was further distressed by the fact that the diocesan cardinal, who was also the military vicar, had still not issued a statement to his flock. His predecessor, while holding the same offices, had offered Christmas Mass with the troops in Nha Trang. The institutional Church, to me, had lost its opportunity to comfort the afflicted, and to close the schism.

The war was over, but now the healing had to begin, the personal healing and the institutional healing. The foremost priority was the repatriation of prisoners. As groups were released, more information was gained, and lists of names were revealed. There were prisoners seen but never heard from again; unknown prisoners located and released; and many just simply disappeared, their fate unknown.

My life in the business world took me to the far reaches of the world and broadened my perspectives. I had observed my kindred at the Vietnam Veterans' encampment and antiwar demonstration in Washington. I talked with them during the evening hours, around their tents and campfires—most of them, in combat fatigues; I, in a three-piece business suit. Their protest was not against the war but against their rejection by society and their perceived futility of service.

The Soviets were drawn into Afghanistan, to be swallowed into that morass just as the United States had been in Vietnam. I pitied the Soviets, but envied them, too; they were developing combat experience while ours deteriorated. I was in Paris when I read the headlines extolling the virtues of the French-manufactured Exocet missiles which set aflame and sank British warships in the Falkland Islands. As a shipping executive, I watched in dismay as valuable commercial tonnage went to the bottom of the ocean. In Vietnam, we had been shot at and shelled by every imaginable weapon, most supplied by third parties. It was the Brits' turn now.

The U.S. military was not dormant, undertaking small missions such as troops to the Dominican Republic, a brief skirmish in Grenada, and an ignominious rescue failure in Iran. Units for those missions were led by Vietnam veterans, who continued in the service of their country. I watched from the outside, my service complete.

But my war was still not over. On a cold and blustery night in February 1982, I received a call at my home in Westchester County, close to where I grew up.

"Hello," I answered the phone.

"Are you John Flanagan?"

"Yes."

"Were you in the Air Force? Were you a forward air controller?" I didn't recognize the voice, but it was a mature voice, a woman, with a New England accent, Massachusetts rather than Maine.

"Yes, I was."

"Did you serve with Project Delta in Vietnam?" The Delta Force had received notariety for the Iran hostage rescue mission of 1980. Thoughts raced through my head, everything from accusations of baby killing to an unusual sales pitch.

"Yes, I did."

"I have a copy of a report that you signed about a helicopter crash. The location is blacked out, but I know it was in Laos because I have a map. It says that a helicopter was shot down while trying to rescue a Special Forces team." A government investigator, I thought. It was either CIA or a death benefits investigator. I couldn't believe anyone had survived, although they only found parts of bodies. The Hatchet Force had seen the bodies, as far as I could recall.

"Yeah, I kind of remember it." I didn't know where this lady was coming from. I was intentionally vague. It had been 15 years, but some events are never forgotten. That tragedy and similar events had continually drifted through nightmares and dreams.

"The report says nothing about the team. Do you know what happened to the team? My name is Eleanor Bott Gregory. Do you know what happened to my brother?" Oh my God, the accent! It was the same.

I was shaken. I didn't know how to respond. I had no idea how much she knew and how much I was at liberty to disclose. I feared that I would reveal something that would obfuscate the issue, destroying hope, refuting fact, or fostering unwarranted optimism. Fortunately, she continued, "Norm Doney gave me your name and then I found it on the report.

Norman thought you lived on Cape Cod. I reached your father there and he gave me your number." I had time to think. She had been in touch with Norm. He would tell the truth.

"Mrs. Gregory, I did in fact sign that report. I am not aware of any reports regarding your brother or any members of the team. I do know that they were under heavy fire." I was the last person to talk to them and the last person to overfly their position. But she apparently didn't know that.

"Please call me Eleanor," she said. "Norman says you were the last one to talk to Pete." I was confused. I didn't know any Pete. Russ and Willie, yes. Was this some giant hoax or mistaken identities? "Oh," she continued, as if she had realized my confusion. "The family calls him Pete; you knew him as Russ." She had used the present tense. They still had hope. I had a plan. Even though I had been ordered to abandon the search in 1966, which I ignored, I would reopen the search.

"Eleanor, I assume you're in Massachusetts. Is there an airport nearby?"

"Yes. We're close to Worcester Airport." I knew the airport well. It was on a plateau, like Khe Sanh. I had one more mission to fly.

"Eleanor, will you be around on Saturday, the twentieth? I'm scheduled to fly that morning and I can fit in a stop at Worcester." I was a "weekend warrior" and scheduled for a navigational training mission. A stop to visit the family of an MIA was, to me, a humanitarian gesture.

"Oh, John, that would be wonderful! Just call us. We'll pick you up and bring you to the house for coffee." I didn't know who "we" were, but it was obvious that I had been accepted.

"Good-bye, Eleanor. See you on the twentieth if the weather holds." Khe Sanh and the miserable flying weather were still with me.

My business activities occupied my time. However, thoughts of the approaching Saturday flight were no longer lingering, but loomed greatly in my mind. What documents did Eleanor have? Was the episode classified, buried in the secret archives of the government? No one from the government had been in touch with me. Was it my responsibility to protect the institution? I was still an officer, but not considered a "real" officer since I was in the reserves. What was I to do? I had no one to talk to. Once again the decision was all mine.

The Friday night before I was to fly to Worcester, I went into the attic and opened a trunk that had been untouched for years. As I opened the lid, memories spilled out. I picked up the yellowed photographs. I recognized many of the faces. As I looked at the helicopters, with the teams climbing on board, I could feel the vibration of the rotors and I instinctively squinted my eyes to protect them from the blowing dirt. It was quiet in the house. Regina was now away at college; Monica was in high school, in the party throes of senior year. I found some citations. A Distinguished Flying Cross. I looked some more. Air Medals, one of them with a "V" for Valor, awarded by the Army. I had forgotten for what. Another DFC. Then a Silver Star, December 2, 1966, signed by General Momyer.

I was alone. I fumbled in the bottom of the trunk. I found my green beret. It still had a lieutenant's bar on it. Folded inside, was the object of my search. I gingerly unfurled it; wrinkled, but still intact. It was my red flying scarf—Project Delta, Red Baron, the Delta insignia—emblazoned. I had made my decision; I knew what I would do.

Neil Murphy was the pilot for that Saturday mission. I would log instructor time. He was a lieutenant, as I had been in Vietnam. We reviewed the maps that we would use. I filed a flight plan indicating a stop at Worcester. The weather was cold, with scattered clouds, gusty winds, but good visibility. It had snowed in Worcester and the reports indicated that I could expect ice patches on the runway. At Khe Sanh it was mud; at Worcester, ice.

Ironically, the reserve unit had converted to a FAC mission shortly after I had joined it. The aircraft had improved; it was now a twin-engined Cessna, the O-2, which had succeeded the O-1 in Vietnam. The bird we were to fly that day had flown in 'Nam. I wore my red scarf.

After the mission, as we taxied from the runway at Worcester, sliding over the promised ice patches, I thought about Neil Murphy, in the left seat. He had been an enlisted ROMAD, just like Rudy Bishop who had worked with me in 'Nam; he had applied for and received a commission, and then completed pilot training. He was the complete FAC. I was pleased that young men, and now women too, had these opportunities. The military was changing and so was I. I was 42 years old.

A quick phone call; Eleanor was expecting it. And she was right, she was close. I had barely hung up the phone when she arrived with her husband, Ed. Murphy stayed with the plane and I went to Shrewsbury.

It was an attractive Cape style, but what I remember most was the warmth, not of the house, but of the people who had gathered for my visit. In New England custom, we entered through the side door. Neighbors, friends, and relatives were waiting for us in the kitchen drinking steaming coffee. Eleanor made the introductions.

"This is my brother, and my sister." She named each and then continued with several neighbors, and children—her son Peter, named after her missing brother—and finished with, "This is Pete's Mom." His father had passed away.

"This is what we have." Eleanor handed me a file. A brimful cup of coffee was next handed to me, testing my steadiness. "We've been corresponding with everyone in the government. They won't tell us anything. All we know is that Pete is missing and they've awarded him a medal, the Distinguished Service Cross." It's the nation's second highest honor, ranking just below the Medal of Honor. The Silver Star is third.

I was flipping through the papers. Most of them were from Eleanor and the family to the government, Department of the Army, Defense Intelligence Agency, and members of Congress. There were scanty responses, mostly references to some report or regulation. "We really didn't know where to turn next, until we talked to Norman Doney and Tommy Carpenter," said Eleanor. Anxious faces looked at me, expecting a definitive declaration.

I had none. Instead, I replied, "I knew them well. They were good men. Tommy and his wife visited us on the Cape." I noticed copied portions of reports with security classification and the "Secret" or "Confidential" scratched out, or annotated "Declassified." Major sections were blanked out; I didn't recognize the reports. I recognized the copy of the report I had signed, but sections had been obliterated, apparently with a black felt pen. I found a poor copy of a portion of a map, depicting where the helicopter had crashed. It had coordinates on it, but something didn't look right. "Eleanor, could I go someplace to look at these?" I gestured with the papers.

"Sure John. Here, in the dining room." Her mother refilled my coffee cup. Ed showed me into the dining room. A plate of cranberry muffins followed me.

"Anything else, John?"

"No thanks, Ed." I poured through the papers. Everything relating to the team had been either assiduously purged from the reports or had never been there. Most of the material was innocuous and old. It could have been damaging if it had fallen into the hands of the NVA when it was written, but now it was worthless. I recreated the flight of that fateful day. I was 27 when I flew that mission, but it came back to me clearly, particularly with the aid of the map. The partial map showed a village where the helicopter crashed. There was no village there. I was sure of that, but that was a common cartographic error. I couldn't find the knoll where the team was. I ate a cranberry muffin. I hadn't had any breakfast.

I went through the file again. More letters, most of them handwritten and unofficial, from the men in Delta. I found Doney's letter to Eleanor. "Find the FAC. It was John Flanagan. He knows." Eleanor must have talked to him afterward. I saw nothing but evidence of frustration on the part of the family and vague answers from the government agencies. Either they didn't want to tell something or they didn't know what had happened. I assumed the latter. I sipped some coffee. I was confused, but the message came through; over the entire 15 years, the collected family, led by Eleanor, had not given up hope, and were looking for the truth.

I examined the map more closely. I was searching for the team once again. Except there was no ground fire. A label sticker had been placed on the original map, coordinates of the helicopter had been written on it, and the map had then been copied and sent to the family. The label was where the team had been—in Laos. But no one really knew where the team had been, except me and the helicopter crew, and they were all dead.

There were no subsequent sightings of Russ or Willie indicated in any of the reports. They weren't on any POW lists, compiled from sightings by our released prisoners, or provided by the North Vietnamese government. They were truly MIA. The conversation in the kitchen was animated, uplifting. I wanted to keep it that way. I would hold to my decision. I would tell the truth, without creating false hopes.

"Mrs. Bott, Eleanor, everybody, I think I can give you some information. The best that I know about Russ—Pete." I told it all. That I was the last American to talk to them, that I overflew their position after the helicopter had been driven off by ground fire, and saw nothing but trampled grass. There were no bodies, and two Vietnamese had escaped. I also told them that Stark had been wounded and I thought Pete was OK. I also said that I had personally seen enemy troops and they had all been wearing NVA uniforms. The NVA were considered to be well organized and disciplined soldiers who would recognize the political and military value of capturing American soldiers in Laos. Finally, I showed them on the map where the team was located, the precise location distorted by the label that had been copied onto the map.

I sensed an overwhelming feeling of relief from the gathering. Someone had finally taken away the clouds of uncertainty, the families' efforts had not been fruitless. For them, it was like the burden that had been lifted from my shoulders nine years earlier after the Peace Accord. Some pictures were taken, warm embraces and handshakes exchanged, and I was on my way.

I flew the airplane from Worcester. As we winged back to our base near White Plains, New York, I realized that I had finally flown my last mission. But I would not put my scarf away. My war was not over—not until the Bott family knew what had happened to Russ. I was convinced that he had been taken prisoner.

Over the ensuing years I grew to know and love the Bott family. I knew that Russ's daughter Jennifer, who was born after he went to Vietnam, entered law school. We corresponded. Eleanor and Ed's daughter, Mary Ellen, answers the phone frequently when I call. We chat, then, "Who do you want, Mom or Dad?" Ed had been a POW in Korea. Eleanor's brother, Fred, was killed in Korea. He received the Silver Star posthumously. Another brother, George, retired after 20 years of military service. Mrs. Bott died without knowing what had happened to her son, but that only redoubled the families' efforts. They never waivered, finding strength in their values and in each other. Norm and I supported them, just as we tried to support Russ and Willie in the jungle.

Norm Doney had served four tours in Vietnam. He and I met several times over the next eight years and exchanged information continuously, tracing down rumors, plotting alleged sightings on maps, channeling information to Eleanor, suggesting questions that she should ask, and then evaluating the responses. Norman made a sanctioned tourist trip to Vietnam, which included Hanoi. He had some insightful conversations with tourist guides, several of whom were former NVA. Russ's military identification card suddenly appeared in his government MIA file, disappeared, then reappeared. His case is acknowledged as a bona fide discrepancy case.

I talked to and met many more veterans over the years. A former member of a District Advisory Team is now a CPA with a major firm. He told me about installing the irrigation pump for a Vietnamese village. A banking executive had been at Song Be a year after Project Delta had been there. The village had been overrun by the NVA that we had located. I met a lawyer who had been a commander in an elite armored unit that fought pitched battles in war zone C. They had had a tough fight and he extolled the leadership of the hand-picked junior officers and NCOs. An infantry soldier, 11 Bravo, now in the electrical contracting business, had served under three platoon leaders, officers, as they were rotated through his unit; "I just couldn't get comfortable with the constant change in leadership." A former member of Delta, a sergeant, told me even more about the tragedy at Bong Son with the 1st Cav. When Delta's elite all-U.S. teams had been shot up and needed a reaction force, the Cav hierarchy perceived them as merely a fire team or squad, an expendable unit in the masterplan of battalions and brigades; the Cav's promised assistance had been inadequate and Delta's casualties mounted.

Throughout the Vietnam era, gallant men and women served honorably, frequently without support either at home or in the field, overcoming insurmountable and unforeseen obstacles, and resolving the conflicts between personal and institutional values. Bravery, honesty, integrity. Warrior values—embraced by individuals and espoused by institutions—but compromised, prostituted, and disregarded by men who selected the easier wrong in lieu of the more difficult right, and who placed personal interests above the concerns and needs of those entrusted to their care.

But we who served have learned and gained. We have faced adversity, hardship, death, and, in some cases, ridicule, yet our values have survived and we can face eternity alone with them. We have our commitment, our commitment to each other tempered by the will to survive, something that only we fully understand. It is our values and our commitment that we must impart to our children and our successors. We are not obligated to pass the warrior sword to someone who chooses not to hold it as high as we did.

Epilogue

Skinner Simpson and Jim Ahmann are alive and well, residing in San Antonio. We shared remembrances for an afternoon in 1989, the first time we were together since 1966. After I left Vietnam, Skinner continued to have problems finding acceptable replacements. He fired one FAC upon the recommendation of the recon teams, "he'll get himself or us killed," and recruited Tom Jozwiak, class of 1959 from the Academy, who, like Skinner, was an end on the football team. Skinner is now in the real estate development and management business in Texas and apparently still enjoys taking risks.

After Vietnam, Jim Ahmann returned to the United States and flew the F–101 Voodoo interceptor. He eventually closed out his career teaching young men how to fly jets. He enjoyed teaching so much that after a computer systems stint, he signed on to teach math and science in high school. His students prod him for tales of Vietnam. His values are intact and he has found a new strength in Christ. He still refuses to get on a helicopter.

Tommy Tucker has retired from the Army and maintains a low profile in Florida, just as he did while lurking through the jungle in Vietnam. He says he would still fly with me. I think he's crazy.

Tommy Carpenter has also retired, and is conducting counter-terrorist training courses for a security company someplace in Nevada. He always returns phone calls, but from where is a mystery.

Norm Doney was eventually seriously wounded in Vietnam. He recovered, retired from the Army, and went to work for the highway commission in Oregon. He edits and publishes a nationwide newsletter regarding POW/MIAs from all wars. I have been Norm's guest at the annual Special Forces reunion.

Unfortunately, I've lost track of Rudy Bishop. But he's not forgotten.

The other men are memorialized in Washington, DC. Karl Worst is on panel 5E; Terry Griffey, 7E; Gene Moreau, 10E; Charlie Swope and Art Glidden, 12E; Russ Bott, Willie Stark, and the five men on the helicopter are all on 13E, up near the top of the panel, lines three through seven of the Wall. I visit them often. Their war is over.

I rose through the ranks, serving as a classic weekend warrior, balancing my commitments in a business career, as the head of a family, and as a Reserve military officer. It was a difficult period filled with compromises; I endeavored to honor the values instilled at the Academy and reinforced in Vietnam. Along the way, I strove to repay the debts that I owed to my country and to the men and women who had supported and trusted me. However, my military career came to an abrupt end, when shortly after being promoted to brigadier general, I was advised by the State National Guard institution that I was "not up to being the commander," and was summarily dismissed. My war is still not over.

Glossary

A–1/E/H	prop fighter-bomber, primarily used in CAS; Skyraider, Spad, "Flying Dump Truck," Sandy.
A–4D/E	jet fighter-bomber flown by Navy and Marines; Skyhawk
ADF	automatic direction finding; low-frequency navigational radio
airborne	parachute-qualified infantry unit or a jump-qualified soldier
airmobile	helicopter assault infantry unit; "a leg on a rope"
AGOS	Air-Ground Operations School
AK–47	7.62mm automatic rifle carried by VC and NVA
ALO	air liaison officer; Air Force officer assigned to army unit
AO	area of operations; also TAOR, tactical area of responsibility
ARA	aerial rocket artillery; rocket-laden Huey gunships
ARVN	Army of the Republic of Vietnam, South Vietnamese forces
AWACS	airborne warning and control system
B–17, B–24	four-engine prop bombers, World War II vintage
B–26	two-engine prop bomber, World War II vintage; used in Vietnam
B–29	four-engine prop bomber, World War II and Korean War vintage

B–52	eight-engine heavy jet bomber; Stratofortress, sometimes "BUFF"—big ugly fat f_____
B–57	two-engine light jet bomber, two-man crew; Canberra
BARC	amphibious transport, shuttles between ships and beaches
battalion	Army unit of three or more companies, usually 600 men
BDA	bomb damage assessment
BEMO	base equipment management office; Air Force supply unit
Beret Rouge	French paratroopers: red berets
brigade	Army unit of three or more battalions; sometimes separate from division
BX	base exchange, Air Force shopping center; Army facility is PX
C–4	plastique explosive; used as heat tablet for hot coffee
C–7	two-engine prop, light transport; Caribou
C–47	two-engine prop transport; DC–3, Gooney Bird; World War II vintage
C–123	two-engine prop transport; Provider; also sprayed defoliants
C–130	four-engine turbo-prop transport; Hercules, Herky Bird
C and C	command and control; usually in reference to an aircraft
CH–46	twin-engine, twin-rotor Marine helicopter; Sea Knight
C-rations	individual-portion canned meals, various flavors/colors; C-rats
CAS	close air support
CBU	cluster bomb unit; each bomblet is softball-size
Charlie	from VC, verbal shorthand for Viet Cong forces
CIDG	civilian irregular defense group; local Vietnamese forces
co	"Miss" in Vietnamese
COIN	counter-insurgency, usually warfare
commo	verbal shorthand for communications, usually a unit
company	Army unit of usually 150 combat troops, commanded by a captain
COMUSMACV	Commander, U.S. Forces, Military Assistance Command, Vietnam
I Corps	northernmost military region in South Vietnam, adjacent to North Vietnam; pronounced "eye corps"
II Corps	central highlands military region extending from the South China Sea to the Cambodian and Laotian borders

III Corps	military region in the Saigon area, adjacent to the Cambodian border; included such areas as war zone C and the Iron Triangle
IV Corps	southernmost military region in Vietnam; included the Mekong River delta
COSVN	Communist headquartes in South Vietnam; reputedly in war zone C
CP	command post; Charlie Papa; includes TOC, Commo, FSCC
CRC	combat reporting center; a radar ground site; also CRP, Post
daisy cutter	munition specially fused to detonate aboveground
DASC	direct air support center; allocates fighter support; now ASOC
DAT	district advisory team; U.S. Army military and civic action unit
Delta Force	counterterrorist strike unit; successor to Project Delta
deuce-and-a-half	heavy-duty Army truck, off-road capability, 2 1/2-ton load
division	Army unit of two or more brigades; usually over 10,000 men
DMZ	de-militarized zone; zone separating North and South Vietnam
D.O.	deputy for operations; directs flying operations in an AF unit
E and E	escape and evade
F–4C	two-place, twin-engine heavy jet fighter-bomber; Phantom II
F–5	twin-engine, light jet fighter-bomber; Freedom Fighter, Tiger
F–86	jet fighter, Korean War vintage; Sabrejet
F–100	jet fighter-bomber; Super Sabre, Hun
F–105	heavy jet fighter-bomber; Thunderchief, Thud
FAC	forward air controller; AF pilot who directs air strikes
FiDO	fighter duty officer, usually in the DASC
flare ship	any transport or helicopter that drops illumination flares
flight surgeon	specially trained medical doctor on flying status
FO	forward observer; adjusts artillery fire for Army
FOB	forward operating base
Fox	from Fox Mike, verbal shorthand for FM radio
frag grenade	fragmentation grenade, as opposed to smoke or concussion grenade

frag order	daily flying order distributed from the TACC to fighter units
FSC	fire support coordinator; also FSCC, coordination center
Gatling gun	multi-barrel gun; 7.62mm on helicopters and C–47s, 20mm on F–4C
G-suit	anti-gravity suit; worn on lower extremities, prevents black outs during flight
GIB	guy in backseat; reference to the second pilot in the F–4C
GP	general purpose; used in reference to tents and bombs
Greeks	collective term for Projects Delta, Omega, and Sigma
Hanoi Hilton	POW prison in North Vietnam
HEI	high-explosive incendiary, usually in reference to ammunition
HF net	high-frequency radio net
HF/SSB	high-frequency/single side band radio
HH–3	twin-engine, single-rotor rescue helicopter; Jolly Green Giant
hog	slang for Huey gunship
hooch	semi-permanent structure, sometimes tin-roofed
Hotel	phonetic for the letter H; verbal shorthand for HF radio
IFR	instrument flight rules; usually in reference to poor flying weather
IFFV	First Field Forces Vietnam; collective term for U.S. Army forces
J–79	jet engine in the F–4
JCS	Joint Chiefs of Staff
jerry can	reusable five-gallon can, rectangular; usually for gas or water
KBA	killed by air; killed by artillery
KIA	killed in action
klick/km	kilometer; 1000 meters, equal to .6 mile
knots	nautical miles per hour, equal to 1.15 mph
Kowabunga!	exclamation of Buffalo Bob on "Howdy Doody" TV show in 1950s
L–19	Army designation of O–1, flown by Army FOs; Bird Dog
LARC	amphibious transport, shuttles between ship and beach
leg	conventional infantry soldier; from "straight-leg"
LLDB	South Vietnamese Special Forces

LRRP	long range reconnaissance patrols; pronounced "lurps"
L.T.	abbreviation for lieutenant; pronounced "El Tee"; endemic to VN
LZ	landing zone
M1	semi-automatic rifle, .30–06 caliber; World War II vintage
M2	carbine with fully automatic capability, .30 caliber
M–14	U.S. automatic/semiautomatic rifle, .308 caliber/7.62mm NATO cartridge
M–16	U.S. automatic/semiautomatic rifle, .223 caliber/5.56mm
M–60	belt-fed machine gun, .308 caliber/7.62mm
M–79	40mm grenade launcher, single shot, break action, hand-carried
M–151	standard Army 1/4-ton jeep
MACV	Military Assistance Command, Vietnam; pronounced, "Mac Vee"
MAF	marine amphibious force
Mark 82	500 pound bomb
Mayday	*M'aidez*, "help me" in French; international distress call
medevac	medical evacuation, usually via helicopter, the "Dust-offs"
Merci	"thank you" in French
meter/m	metric unit of linear measurement equal to 39.37 inches
MIA	missing in action
MIG	collective term for Soviet-manufactured/designed jet fighter
mike force	indigenous strike force of usually three companies; SF commanded
mike-mike	spoken term indicating millimeter, usually in reference to guns
Montagnard	mountain tribesmen, smaller in stature than Vietnamese
MPC	military payment currency as substitute for dollars
MRC–108	Air Force radio jeep, M–151 chassis; pronounced "Mark one-oh-eight"
mufti	casual clothes, non-uniform; slang
napalm/nape	jellied gasoline bomb; carried underwing in aerodynamic cans
NCO	non-commissioned officer, a sergeant
Nung	ethnic Chinese assimilated to Vietnamese culture

NVA	North Vietnamese Army
O–1/E/F	single-engine observation aircraft flown by FACs; Bird Dog
P–38	small can opener, came with C-rats
PCS	permanent change of station; permanent duty
PFs	Popular Forces, South Vietnamese
pickle	to drop a bomb; from "pickle switch" on top of control stick
platoon	Army unit of 40 to 50 men; smallest unit commanded by an officer
POL pit	petroleum, oil, lubricants; refueling point
POW	prisoner of war
Project Delta	autonomous US-VN recon unit, countrywide operations
Project Omega	similar to Delta, but usually II Corps operations
Project Sigma	similar to Delta, but usually III Corps operations
puff	from "Puff the Magic Dragon," C–47 gunships with tongues of fire
PX	post exchange; Army shopping center
R and R	rest and rehabilitation; usually out-of-country leave
Rangers	specially trained infantry, usually an elite unit and airborne
recce	reconnaissance, usually an aircraft
recon	reconnaissance, usually a unit
regiment	organizational unit similar to a brigade
REMFs	rear-echelon mother f_____; derogatory term used by combat forces
rendezvous	"a meeting" or "coming together" in French
RFs	Regional Forces, South Vietnamese; "ruff-puffs," RFs and PFs
roadrunner	Project Delta Vietnamese patrol disguised as VC or NVA
ROK	Republic of Korea, South Korea; pronounced "rocks"
ROMAD	radio operator maintenance and driver; enlisted member of TACP
RPG	rocket-propelled grenade; common weapon of VC and NVA
S–2	Army intelligence staff function; also G–2
S–3	Army operations and training staff function; also G–3
SAS	special air service; elite British commando unit

SF	Special Forces; SFer, member of Special Forces, a Green Beret
SHAPE	Supreme Headquarters Allied Powers Europe
SITREP	situation report; Army formal status report
slick	a transport; comparative—as a slick helicopter, or slick jeep
slick bomb	non-retarded bomb; also "slicks," as opposed to "snakes"
smoke grenade	smoke cannister used to identify positions
snake-eyes	retarded bombs; also "snakes"; very accurate, low-level delivery
SOG	studies and observation group; operated cross-border surveillance
SOI	signal operating instructions; radio frequencies and call signs
sortie	one mission flown by one aircraft
Spooky	call sign for Air Force flare/gunships
STOL	short take-off and landing
Systems Command	Air Force Command responsible for research, testing, and acquisition
T–37	twin-jet, two-place trainer; "Hummer"
TACAN	tactical air navigation; radio signal giving bearing and range
TACC	tactical air control center; assigned strike sorties for SVN
TACP	tactical air control party; smallest autonomous AF unit with Army
TASS	tactical air support squadron; parent unit for FACs and ROMADs
TDY	temporary duty
thermite	grenade with intense heat; capable of melting steel
tiger suit	camouflaged pattern fatigues
TOC	tactical operations center; unit level command center
U–10	single engine STOL aircraft; Courier
UH–1B/D	single-rotor helicopter, four-man crew, used as a work-horse; Huey
UHF	ultra high frequency radio
Uniform	phonetic for letter U; verbal shorthand for UHF radio
USO	United Servicemen's Organization; sponsor of entertainment shows
UTM	universal transverse mercator, usually as geographical grid

VC	Viet Cong; Victor Charles; collective term for the enemy
VHF	very high frequency, usually radio
Victor	phonetic for letter V; verbal shorthand for VHF radio
Viet Minh	adversary of French in Vietnam; predecessor to the Viet Cong
VFR	visual flight rules; usually in reference to good flying weather
VNAF	Vietnamese Air Force
VOR	VHF omni range; navigational radio, bearing only
VR	visual reconnaissance
war zone C	an area north of Tay Ninh; Viet Cong's "home turf"
web gear	personal equipment carried on soldiers' harness and belt
WIA	wounded in action
Winchester	slang term for "out of bullets"
WP	Willie Pete, slang abbreviation for white phosphorous marking rockets
Zoomie	Air Force Academy graduate

Bibliography

Anderson, Charles. *Vietnam: The Other War*. Novato, CA: Presidio Press, 1982.

Atkinson, Rick. *The Long Gray Line*. Boston: Houghton Mifflin, 1989.

Beckwith, Charlie A. *Delta Force*. New York: Harcourt Brace Jovanovich, 1983.

Boettcher, Thomas D. *Vietnam: The Valor and the Sorrow*. Boston: Little, Brown, 1985.

Broughton, Jack. *Thud Ridge*. New York: Bantam, 1985.

———. *Going Downtown*. New York: Crown Publishers, 1988.

Chinnery, Philip D. *Life on the Line: Stories of Vietnam Air Combat*. New York: St. Martin's Press, 1988.

Clodfelter, Mark. *The Limits of Air Power: The American Bombing of North Vietnam*. New York: Macmillan, 1989.

Coffee, Gerald. *Beyond Survival*. New York: G. P. Putnam's Sons, 1990.

Davidson, Philip B. *Vietnam at War: The History 1946–1975*. New York: Oxford University Press, 1988.

Egendorf, Arthur. *Healing from the War*. Boston: Shambhala, 1988.

Fall, Bernard B. *Hell in a Very Small Place*. New York: J. P. Lippincott, 1967.

———. *Street without Joy*. Harrison, PA: The Stackpole Company, 1967.

Fitzgerald, Frances. *Fire in the Lake: The Vietnamese and the Americans in Vietnam*. Boston: Little, Brown, 1972.

Gray, J. Glenn. *The Warriors: Reflections on Men in Battle*. New York: Harcourt, Brace and Company, 1959.

Hammel, Eric. *The Assault on Khe Sanh: An Oral History*. New York: Crown Publishers, 1989.

Jensen-Stevenson, Monika, and William Steveson. *Kiss the Boys Goodbye*. New York: Dutton, 1990.

Karnow, Stanley. *Vietnam: A History*. New York: Viking Press, 1983.

LeBoutillier, John. *Vietnam Now*. New York: Praeger Publishers, 1989.

MacPherson, Myra. *Long Time Passing: Vietnam and the Haunted Generation*. Garden City, NY: Doubleday, 1984.

Marshall, S.L.A. *West to Cambodia*. Nashville, TN: The Battery Press, 1968.

Mason, Steve. *Johnny's Song*. Toronto: Bantam Books, 1986.

McDaniel, Eugene B. *Before Honor*. Philadelphia, PA: J. P. Lippincott, 1975.

Moore, Robin. *The Green Berets*. New York: Crown Publishers, 1965.

Prashker, Ivan. *Duty, Honor, Vietnam*. New York: William Morrow, 1988.

Risner, Robinson. *The Passing of the Night: My Seven Years as a Prisoner of the North Vietnamese*. New York: Random House, 1973.

Robbins, Christopher. *The Ravens*. New York: Crown Publishers, 1987.

Schlesinger, Arthur M., Jr. *The Bitter Heritage: Vietnam and American Democracy 1941–1966*. Boston: Houghton Mifflin, 1966.

Schlight, John. *The Years of the Offensive 1965–1968*. Washington, DC: Office of Air Force History, 1988.

Scigliano, Robert. *South Vietnam: Nation Under Stress*. Boston: Houghton Mifflin, 1968.

Severo, Richard, and Lewis Mumford. *The Wages of War: When America's Soldiers Came Home—From Valley Forge to Vietnam*. New York: Simon and Schuster, 1989.

Sheehan, Neil. *A Bright Shining Lie: John Paul Vann and America in Vietnam*. New York: Random House, 1988.

Simpson, Charles M. *Inside the Green Berets*. Novato, CA: Presidio Press, 1983.

Valentine, Douglas. *The Phoenix Program*. New York: William Morrow, 1990.

———. *The Wall*. New York: Collins, 1987.

Wheeler, John. *Touched with Fire: The Future of the Vietnam Generation*. New York: Avon Books, 1984.

Yarborough, Tom. *Da Nang Diary: A Forward Air Controller's Year of Combat over Vietnam*. New York: St. Martin's Press, 1990.

Young, Marilyn B. *The Vietnam Wars: 1945–1990*. New York: HarperCollins, 1991.

Index

ABOUT THE AUTHOR

JOHN F. FLANAGAN was among the first graduates of the United States Air Force Academy and earned an MBA from Boston College. After Vietnam, he worked as an international business executive, a presidential exchange executive, and a college professor and business consultant in New York. He attained the rank of brigadier general in the Air Force Reserve and is now contemplating politics and a second book.